"In this compilation of a lifetime of teaching and research, augmented by discussion questions and beautiful images, Robert Hubbard and Andrew Dearman offer their encyclopedic knowledge of the text of the Old Testament."

— SANDRA RICHTER

Westmont College

"Dearman and Hubbard have together produced a new introduction to the Old Testament with accessible prose, beautiful pictures, charts, tables, and maps that present the data in engaging ways. . . . When it comes to what I look for in an introduction, this one checks all the boxes."

— STEPHEN BRECK REID

Truett Theological Seminary

"With a winning combination of hermeneutical insight, critical awareness, and theological sensitivity, Dearman and Hubbard have produced an outstanding volume that amply fulfills the goal of introducing readers to the Old Testament. Those using this book will find themselves in the hands of skilled teachers who enable them to read the Old Testament more effectively and to appreciate its abiding significance."

— DAVID FIRTH

Trinity College Bristol

INTRODUCING THE
OLD TESTAMENT

Robert L. Hubbard Jr.

J. Andrew Dearman

WILLIAM B. EERDMANS PUBLISHING COMPANY

GRAND RAPIDS, MICHIGAN

Wm. B. Eerdmans Publishing Co.
2140 Oak Industrial Drive NE, Grand Rapids, Michigan 49505
www.eerdmans.com

Published 2018
Printed in the United States of America

27 26 25 24 23 22 21 20 19 18   1 2 3 4 5 6 7 8 9 10

ISBN 978-0-8028-6790-2

Library of Congress Cataloging-in-Publication Data

Names: Hubbard, Robert L., Jr., 1943- author.
Title: Introducing the Old Testament / Robert L. Hubbard, J. Andrew Dearman.
Description: Grand Rapids : Eerdmans Publishing Co., 2018. | Includes bibliographical
    references and index.
Identifiers: LCCN 2017048809 | ISBN 9780802867902 (hardcover : alk. paper)
Subjects: LCSH: Bible. Old Testament—Introductions. | Bible. Old Testament—Textbooks.
Classification: LCC BS1140.3 .H83 2018 | DDC 221.6/1—dc23
    LC record available at https://lccn.loc.gov/2017048809

To all of our students—
past, present, and future

Contents

PART 6: CONCLUSION

List of Illustrations

TABLES

DIAGRAMS

MAPS

TIMELINES

Acknowledgments

This book has been a long time in coming—too long, perhaps. But as the awesome and long-suffering novelist, Snoopy, once glumly observed, "Good writing is hard work!" Amen to that, Snoopy!

But to emerge, a book needs more than just toiling authors who string thoughts into words; it also requires the wisdom, support, and encouragement of other people for it to see the light of day. So, now that this book is finally in the hands of the reading public, a few brief thank-you's are due to those who played crucial roles in its appearance. At the top of the list is Bill Eerdmans, who long ago invited us to write this volume for his publishing house. We thank him for his confidence and hope that the book proves to be the very kind he had in mind. We owe a great deal to Allen Myers, the editor at Eerdmans who in the beginning wisely counseled us on the book's concept, cheered us on through one major crisis, and over time patiently persevered and firmly kept us accountable. Allen, many thanks for all you did. At Allen's retirement, the editorial torch passed to Dr. Andrew Knapp, whose superb editorial help has taken a manuscript and skillfully transformed it into a book. Thank you, Andrew! We are also grateful to the impressive production team at Eerdmans, particularly Leah Luyk, for the beautiful volume design.

This book includes an array of photographs and other images, many of which were provided to us by generous colleagues. In this arena we would especially like to thank Shlomit Bechar, Michael Connor, Jonathan Greer, Anat Harrel, Eilat Mazar, Patrick McInerney, and Julian Reade.

Thanks also go to the seminaries on whose faculties we have each been privileged to serve for their encouragement, generous granting of sabbatical leaves, and institutional support of our efforts. Rev. Markus Nikkanen and Brandon Benziger, assistants to one of us, also deserve recognition for their help with bibliography. Our wives, Pam and Kathy, likewise are to be thanked for their interest in the project and practical help in seeing it to completion. Without them, we couldn't have enjoyed the journey half as much. As co-authors, we'd also like to thank each other for the privilege of working together—for personal companionship on the journey, including high-level intellectual interaction and ongoing, gracious, and trustworthy feedback. Finally, we voice fervent praise to the Lord our God, whose providence generously gifted God's people with the Old Testament and who called the two of us into a unique, satisfying ministry as its teachers. Human words fail adequately to capture our profound gratitude for that honor.

When Snoopy finally produced his novel's opening line, it said simply, "It was a dark and stormy night"—a sentence drawn from the nineteenth century and often parodied since. Behind this book stand some dark and stormy nights, but primarily bright and quiet days of the work we love. We hope that this book will provide a suitable, infectious tool for other teachers, their students, and other readers. May it cultivate love for God's complex, remarkable Word and ignite a passion for living out its truth.

ROBERT L. HUBBARD JR.

J. ANDREW DEARMAN

Abbreviations

General

Akk.	Akkadian
ANE	ancient Near Eastern
Arab.	Arabic
b.	tractate in the Babylonian Talmud
BCE	Before the Common Era (alternative for BC)
ca.	Latin *circa* ("approximately")
CE	Common Era (alternative for AD)
CEB	Common English Bible
cent.	century
ch(s).	chapter(s)
DH or DtH	Deuteronomistic History
DSS	Dead Sea Scrolls
EM	Ezra's Memoirs
ESV	English Standard Version
ET	English translation
Gk.	Greek
HB/OT	Hebrew Bible / Old Testament
Heb.	Hebrew
Hist. eccl.	Eusebius, *Historia ecclesiastica* (*Ecclesiastical History*)
Lat.	Latin
lit.	literally
LXX	Septuagint

MT	Masoretic Text
N.B.	*Nota bene* ("note well")
NIV	New International Version
NM	Nehemiah's Memoirs
NRSV	New Revised Standard Version
NT	New Testament
OT	Old Testament
PostHB	postexilic Historical Books
PreHB	preexilic Historical Books
TNIV	Today's New International Version
v(v).	verses
vol(s).	volume(s)
//	parallels, is parallel to

Reference Works

AB	Anchor Bible
ABD	*Anchor Bible Dictionary.* Edited by David Noel Freedman. 6 vols. New York: Doubleday, 1992
ABRL	Anchor Bible Reference Library
ANET	*Ancient Near Eastern Texts Relating to the Old Testament.* Edited by James B. Pritchard. 3rd ed. Princeton: Princeton University Press, 1969
ApOTC	Apollos Old Testament Commentary
BAR	*Biblical Archaeology Review*
BASOR	*Bulletin of the American Schools of Oriental Research*
BBRSup	Bulletin of Biblical Research: Supplements
BHS	*Biblia Hebraica Stuttgartensia.* Edited by Karl Elliger and Wilhelm Rudolph. Stuttgart: Deutsche Bibelstiftung, 1983
BZAW	Beihefte zur Zeitschrift für die alttestamentliche Wissenschaft
CBQ	*Catholic Biblical Quarterly*
CC	Continental Commentaries
COS	*The Context of Scripture.* Edited by William W. Hallo. 3 vols. Leiden: Brill, 1997–2002
CurBR	*Currents in Biblical Research*
FCB	Feminist Companion to the Bible
FOTL	Forms of the Old Testament Literature

HSM	Harvard Semitic Monographs
IBC	Interpretation: A Bible Commentary for Teaching and Preaching
ICC	International Critical Commentary
IEJ	*Israel Exploration Journal*
ISBL	Indiana Studies in Biblical Literature
JBL	*Journal of Biblical Literature*
JSOT	*Journal for the Study of the Old Testament*
JSOTSup	Journal for the Study of the Old Testament Supplements
KTU	*Die keilalphabetischen Texte aus Ugarit.* Edited by Manfried Dietrich, Oswald Loretz, and Joaquín Sanmartín. Münster: Ugarit-Verlag, 2013
LHBOTS	Library of Hebrew Bible/Old Testament Studies
NAC	New American Commentary
NICOT	New International Commentary on the Old Testament
NIDB	*New Interpreter's Dictionary of the Bible.* Edited by Katharine Doob Sakenfeld. Nashville: Abingdon, 2008
NIVAC	New International Version Application Commentary
OBS	Oxford Bible Series
OTG	Old Testament Guides
OTL	Old Testament Library
PBM	Paternoster Biblical Monographs
SBLDS	Society of Biblical Literature Dissertation Series
StBibLit	Studies in Biblical Literature
TBST	The Bible Speaks Today
TOTC	Tyndale Old Testament Commentaries
TynBul	*Tyndale Bulletin*
UTBC	Understanding the Bible Commentary
VT	*Vetus Testamentum*
VTSup	Supplements to Vetus Testamentum
WBC	Word Biblical Commentary
ZAW	*Zeitschrift für die alttestamentliche Wissenschaft*

Important Periods and Events
for the Study of the Old Testament

ca. 2000–1500: the patriarchs

ca. 1500–1220: the exodus

1220: Israel's settlement in Canaan

ca. 1220–1000: the Heroes

ca. 1050: the priest-Hero-prophet Samuel enters Yahweh's service in Shiloh

CA. 1020–587: THE ISRAELITES ARE SUBJECTS OF MONARCHIES

1010: David becomes Israel's king with the prophets Nathan and Gad as his advisers

970: David's son, Solomon, becomes king

931: Solomon's son, Rehoboam, becomes king

931–722: THE DIVIDED KINGDOM BEGINS UNDER KINGS REHOBOAM (JUDAH) AND JEROBOAM (ISRAEL)

900s: the prophets Ahijah and Jehu are active in the Northern Kingdom

930: the prophet Ahijah of Shiloh condemns Solomon and appoints Jeroboam king of Israel

800s: the prophets Elijah, Micaiah ben Imlah, and Elisha are active in the Northern Kingdom

853: at the battle of Qarqar (NW Syria), Ahab and the Israelite army join the Aramaean forces in opposing Shalmaneser III and his Assyrian army

700s: the prophets Hosea, Amos, and Micah announce the Northern Kingdom's demise, while Isaiah is active in Judah, and Jonah addresses the Assyrians

722: Assyria conquers the Northern Kingdom, exiles the Israelites to Mesopotamia, and resettles foreigners in Israel

722–587: DESCENDANTS OF DAVID RULE THE SURVIVING KINGDOM OF JUDAH

716: Hezekiah succeeds Ahaz as Judah's king

701: the Assyrians under King Sennacherib destroy most cities in Judah and nearly conquer Jerusalem

687: Hezekiah's son, Manasseh, becomes Judah's king

640: Amon's son, Josiah, becomes Judah's king (died 609 BCE)

ca. 630: the prophets Zephaniah and Huldah are active in Jerusalem

627: the prophet Jeremiah is called to serve in Jerusalem

622: the rediscovery of Deuteronomy and the completion of the Deuteronomistic History (DH 1.0) advance the reformation goals of King Josiah

612–605: Babylon defeats Assyria and absorbs its holdings

609: Josiah's son Jehoiakim becomes king

605: at Carchemish, Babylon defeats the Assyrian–Egyptian allied army, subjecting Egypt to Babylonian rule

597: the first deportation of Judahites to Babylon includes King Jehoiachin, national leaders, and Ezekiel

592: the prophet Ezekiel serves the exiles in Babylon

588–587: the Babylonians besiege, conquer, and destroy Jerusalem

587: the second deportation sends more Judahites into exile in Babylon

587–538: THE EXILE OF JUDAH IN BABYLON (OR THE EXILIC PERIOD)

561: King Jehoiachin is released from captivity and welcomed at the Babylonian king's table

ca. 550: the Deuteronomistic History (DH 2.0) appears in Babylon

539: the Medo-Persian army under Cyrus conquers Babylon and absorbs its holdings

538: Cyrus's decree permits exiled Jews to return and to rebuild their temple, but many remain in Babylon, Persia, and Egypt

538–332: PERIOD OF PERSIAN RULE (POSTEXILIC PERIOD)

522: Darius I begins to rule the Persian Empire

520–518: the prophets Haggai and Zechariah inspire Judahite returnees to rebuild the temple

520: temple rebuilding begins in Jerusalem

515: temple dedication and Passover celebration take place in Jerusalem

486: Xerxes I (or Ahasuerus) begins to rule the Persian Empire

465: Artaxerxes I (Longimanus) begins to rule the Persian Empire

458: the priest Ezra arrives to teach the Torah in Judah

445: Nehemiah rebuilds Jerusalem's ruined walls

400–350: Writers in Jerusalem publish a new Israelite history, 1–2 Chronicles

332: Alexander of Macedon conquers the Persian Empire; his empire-wide Hellenization program begins

332–63: PERIOD OF HELLENISTIC RULE

322: Alexander dies; rival generals fight for control of the empire

305: the Ptolemies in Egypt begin to rule Palestine and Syria

198: the Seleucids wrest control of Palestine from the Ptolemies

175: Antiochus Epiphanes IV begins to rule Palestine

160s: Antiochus Epiphanes' ban on Torah-based temple worship sparks a Jewish rebellion

167: the Maccabean (Jewish) revolt against the Seleucids begins

140: Hasmonean family rule in Judea is institutionalized

63: General Pompey of Rome conquers Palestine; Roman rule begins

PART 1
Getting Started

1 INTRODUCTION

SWIMMING LESSONS ARE AN IMPORTANT rite of passage for any young person. In some cases, family members taught us to swim, while the rest of us probably received lessons at school, summer camp, or community swimming pools. The curriculum usually involved two steps. In an initial orientation held in the shallow end of the pool, we were taught how to kick and paddle (and to breathe too!), followed by practice times (for example, short swims to the sidewall; then all the way across the pool). The instructor's watchful eye and guiding voice was our constant companion. The final exam for the course—the goal of the whole process—was to jump into the deep end of the pool, either from the side or from the diving board, and apply our new swimming skills without touching the bottom. This marked a sink-or-swim moment (in some cases, a challenging struggle) of reaching the nearest exit ladder, where congratulations from the instructor and fellow-swimmers greeted us for successfully passing the test.

In a sense, the design of this book is similar to that swimming curriculum. First, each chapter orients readers to the background and contents of the OT book (or books) under consideration. They learn the basics—how the book originated, its historical or cultural background, its literary features and main characters, and its structure. Along the way, we highlight seven *programmatic texts*—key biblical statements that articulate the OT's foundational theological themes—themes that the NT further develops and that form the basis for Christian beliefs. These texts mark theological and thematic threads that knit the OT and NT together to form the Bible. A central section in most chapters is either "the story" (mainly in narrative books) or "the presentation" (in prophetic and poetry books), which further orients readers by means of a survey of sample chapters from each biblical book. Finally, each chapter also concludes with a bibliography suggesting other books that readers may consult to enrich their understanding of what they've read.

But, in our view, the most important section—the goal driving our book's unique design—is the *reading* section. It asks the reader to dive into the deep end—the adventure of actually reading and engaging with the OT itself, every chapter, warts and all. But the deep dive also requires one additional step of engagement after the reading. It provides readers with a list of questions to which they are to formulate their own thoughtful responses. This provides an opportunity for readers to interact in more depth with what they have read. Some questions ask for the reader's general impressions, others foster further reflection, and still others probe personal responses or social implications. Professors who use this volume in their courses may find the questions useful in stimulating class discussions, whether on campus or online. More crafty faculty may even include some of these questions in their examinations! In short, this volume is not a kind of "Masterplots" digest about the OT; its plain goal is to prepare readers to take the plunge into the deep end—the OT itself.

The book is organized in six main parts. "Part 1: Getting Started" is home to this introductory chapter and to a second one that introduces the historical context of the OT, including the intersection of Israel's history with the histories of other nations. Each of the next four parts begins with a scene-setting introduction to, respectively: the Torah (part 2), the Historical Books (part 3), the Prophets (part 4), and the Poetry (part 5). Part 3 includes a chapter on the postexilic Historical Books as a preface to the survey of them, and part 4 specifically includes an introduction to Hebrew poetry, since both the prophets and the poetic books employ poetry as their primary medium of communication. The final section (part 6) has one chapter, and it tells the story of how we got the text of the literature that parts 1–5 have introduced and how Jews and Christians came to consider that text their authoritative canon. A glossary of key terms and indexes bring the book to a close.

Readers will soon notice the high importance that we, the authors, place on the historical context of each biblical book. Speaking broadly, a *context* is any historical moment in which a writer, compiler, or editor produces a piece of literature that wins acceptance as being worthy of preservation, if not as being authoritative, by a community. The surrounding historical situation helps shape the literary piece and, consequently, it is best understood in light of that situation. And there's one more context to mention—in reality, a *series* of historical contexts over time—in which readers or hearers played a key role: that is, in responding to, if not adapting that literature to their contemporary situations. Thus, we advise our readers to consider the historical context of each individual literary piece identifiable within a biblical book (where possible), of the book's original compilation and/or composition, and of its reception and adaptation by later audiences. In the end, it is these three contexts that produced the OT in its final form—the form we have in our Bibles—whose context was the Jewish community of the so-called intertestamental period. In each case, we must ask, what did any given OT piece, section, whole book, or whole canon say to them?

Below are several practical points of clarification useful to readers:

1. In reporting historical dates, we use the now-common abbreviations BCE and CE (= "before the common era" and "the common era").
2. Unless otherwise indicated, all translations of biblical texts are ours (the authors'). The list of abbreviations includes the standard acronyms for various translation versions.
3. Rather than cite sources for quotations in traditional end- or footnotes, this volume cites them in parentheses, identifying the author and page number of the source. Complete source information is available in the bibliography that concludes the section or chapter in which the citation occurs. For example, "Berlin, p. 99" refers the reader to the succeeding bibliography, which contains the entry "Berlin, Adele. *The Dynamics of Biblical Parallelism*. Rev. ed. Grand Rapids: Eerdmans, 2008."

Finally, we wish to stress that, in reading and wrestling with the OT, our readers in reality are joining an ongoing conversation that goes back at least 2,500 years. Imagine the loving care of countless anonymous hands, of individuals whose careful, dogged work produced and passed on the literature that we now—thousands of years later and dispersed in thousands of locales—have in translation in our Bibles. Imagine their devotion to God and to the text, their resistance to oppression and despair, and at times the risk of life that their work demanded. Picture their audiences, eagerly reading or listening to the words of the same texts that grip us today—the stories of our heroes, the beauty of the Psalms, the brave passion of the prophets, and the provocative wisdom of Job and Ecclesiastes. Above all, join them in hearing through the OT the voice of God still today speaking to his beloved people.

2 OLD TESTAMENT HISTORY IN CONTEXT

I T WILL SOON BECOME APPARENT that this book places great importance on the historical context of the Old Testament (OT). Obviously, its contents trace the history of a specific ethnic group within the larger human family, with special attention to its relationship with its God. Geographically, it begins in southern Mesopotamia, moves northwest along the Euphrates River, then southwest into Syria-Palestine and Egypt. Eventually, ancient Canaan along the Mediterranean coast becomes its permanent setting, a stay interrupted (for thousands of people) by five decades spent in Babylon before their return. Along the way, their history of necessity intersects with the histories of other human groups with other gods—for example, the Hittites, Egyptians, Hivites, Amalekites, Canaanites, Midianites, Phoenicians, Philistines, Aramaeans, Assyrians, Babylonians, Persians, and Greeks (see also Gen 14). Some intersections are friendly (see Gen 23 and 34), but most entail power struggles due to the threats of superior powers. In short, that geography and those people groups are the historical and cultural fertile soil (the matrix) from which OT literature itself springs and the historical context in which it is best understood. In this chapter we introduce readers to the basics of ancient history, including basic terms that are commonly used to designate major eras of Israel's history.

Ancient History: The Big Picture

Genesis 10 presents the inhabited world known to the OT writers, a chapter often called the Table of Nations, because it classifies various people groups as descendants of Noah and his three sons. Essentially, the area in view is

7

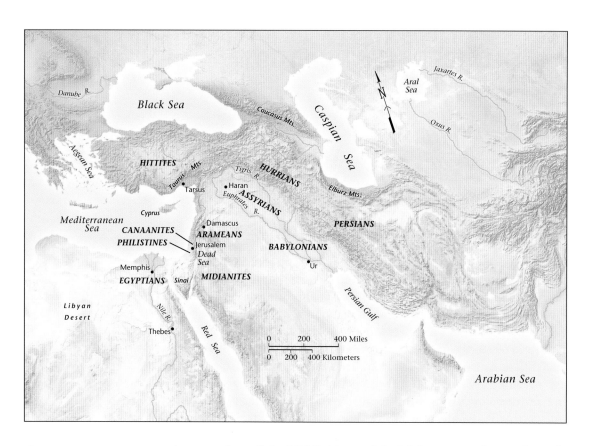

The Ancient Near East

what we today call the Middle East and the Mediterranean basin, the wide region comprising the ancient cultures that formed the matrix for the literature of the OT. In reading it we are inevitably thrust into one aspect or another of an ancient context. Interpreters have various ways to refer to this matrix. A widely used, general term is the *ancient Near East* (ANE)—a term that we will use here as well. For more-specific references to antiquity, however, interpreters must choose between various options, depending on the established terminology that independent disciplines of research have developed over time.

Egyptologists, for example, can refer to the *New Kingdom period*, the *18th Dynasty*, or the *Amarna period* when talking about a matter during the reign of Pharaoh Akhenaten, who ruled from the city of Amarna in the 14th century BCE. Historians referring to that same time in ancient Canaan would likely use the terminology *Late Bronze Age* and perhaps also the *Amarna period*. They can use the latter term because many of the governors or rulers of cities in ancient Canaan were vassals of the Egyptian pharaoh during the 14th century BCE. Historians have known about these vassal relationships for well over a century, since the discovery of a cache of ancient cuneiform tablets in Amarna. These tablets constitute diplomatic letters that offer fascinating details about the relationships between 18th Dynasty pharaohs and their Canaanite vassals in cities such as Jerusalem, Megiddo, and Shechem.

Discoveries of such things as texts or tools can influence the way subsequent historians refer to a historical period. Generally speaking for the ANE, historians and archaeologists use either political terms, such as the *18th Dynasty*, or cultural designations, such as the *Late Bronze Age*, in referring to a specific time and region. We too employ a number of these accepted shorthand terms for historical reference in this volume—most of which are defined briefly in the glossary. The two categories of terms below and their approximate dates illustrate how these terms can overlap.

Over time, interpreters have also generated various categories of reference for the story line in the OT. They are internal to the OT, and they too intersect in various ways with the categories listed above.

There are other categories, also generated by previous interpreters, that provide ease of reference to portions of the story line. These too intersect in various ways with the cultural and political categories listed above. Here are several examples:

Table 2.1. Cultural Periods in the Eastern Mediterranean

Early Bronze Age	ca. 3200–2100 BCE
Middle Bronze Age	ca. 2000–1550 BCE
Late Bronze Age	ca. 1500–1200 BCE
Iron Age I	ca. 1200–950 BCE
Iron Age II	ca. 950–600 BCE

Table 2.2. Political Periods in the Eastern Mediterranean

Neo-Assyrian Period	ca. 745–612 BCE
Neo-Babylonian Period	ca. 605–539 BCE
Persian Period	ca. 538–332 BCE
Hellenistic Period	ca. 332–63 BCE

Table 2.3. Major Periods in Old Testament History

Proto-History	Gen 1–11
Ancestral or Patriarchal Period	Gen 12–50
Israel in Egypt	Exod 1–15
Wilderness and Wandering	Exod 16–Deut 34
Conquest or Occupation of Promised Land	Josh 1–24; Judg 1–2
Period of the Judges	Judg 3–1 Sam 8
United Monarchy	1 Sam 9–1 Kgs 11
Divided Monarchy	1 Kgs 12–2 Kgs 17
State of Judah	2 Kgs 18–25
Babylonian Exile	2 Kgs 25; 2 Chr 36; Daniel
Postexilic Period/Return from Exile	Ezra; Nehemiah

Table 2.4. Political Periods in the Old Testament

Davidic Dynasty	2 Sam 3–2 Kgs 25; 1 Chr 11–2 Chr 36
Omride Dynasty	1 Kgs 16:21–2 Kgs 10:17
Preexilic Period	1 Kgs 12–2 Kgs 25; 2 Chr 10–36
First Temple Period	1 Kgs 6–2 Kgs 25; 2 Chr 2–36
Second Temple Period	Ezra; Nehemiah; Esther

How Do Historians Date Ancient Historical Events?

The list of categories in the OT story line above does not provide dates. We provide a number of them in this volume, including below. Historians basically analyze data from ancient sources and then translate them, when possible, into some form of a modern calendar. The choice of BCE (Before the Common Era) and CE (Common Era), using a form of the Gregorian calendar worked out in medieval times, is very widely used in modern times.

The OT writers, like their ANE counterparts, used various ways of reckoning chronology. One of them was genealogical. Genesis 5, for example, lists the descendants of Adam until the time of Noah's flood, along with the years of their lives. Another chronological marker is that of regional events and tribal history. In the book of Judges, we are told that God repeatedly raised up judges, whom we call Heroes, from different tribes to defeat their enemies and that at the conclusion of their work the land had rest for a specified period of time (e.g., Judg 3:7–11). The books of 1–2 Kings use regnal-year dating in sketching the history of Israel and Judah under their respective monarchs (e.g., 2 Kgs 13:1). The superscription to the prophecies of Amos (1:1) places his work during the reigns of Uzziah in Judah and Jeroboam in Israel, "two years before the earthquake." The latter event obviously had made an impression on Amos's audience! Perhaps there is an analogy for this Amos reference in the ways that some Americans talk about things that are pre- or post-9/11, meaning before or after the terrorist attacks on September 11, 2001, events that changed American travel practices and security precautions.

The OT itself often gives chronological data, so one might think it relatively straightforward to add all the years in a book such as Genesis, Judges, or Kings from a later fixed point and thus provide dates for the events in the biblical story line. James Ussher, a learned clergyman from the 17th century, undertook such a process and concluded that God created the world in 4004 BCE! Of course, we recognize today that matters of historical chronology and of dating the natural world aren't that simple. Years in the Bible, for example, can be reckoned according to lunar or solar calendars, and they can begin in either the spring or the fall! Consult the entries on chronology and calendars in a modern Bible dictionary or encyclopedia to see how intricate this conversation can become.

Genealogies in the ANE served several functions, and in comparing them it is clear that generations can be skipped, as the important thing is to show kinship and continuity. With regard to the genealogy in Gen 5, the long lives attributed to humankind before the flood has a literary parallel with an ancient Sumerian list of kings, but we have no evidence that a human life span ever reached several centuries, much less the thousands of years listed in the Sumerian text. The chronological scheme in these instances is possibly symbolic and certainly part of a premodern worldview. One can, for example, add up all the years that the Judges served and that the land had rest, and the sum is just over 400 years. But should we think of the work of the Heroes as sequential? Did the work of Deborah in northern Israel (Judg 4–5) overlap or occur simultaneously with that of Samson southwest of Jerusalem (Judg 13–16)? In any case, almost all historians have concluded that the period of the Judges was less than 400 years. As for calculating royal reigns, the ANE had multiple ways to do so. Does the system in 1–2 Kings use an accession-year dating method like Assyria's, in which the first year of a new king is reckoned from his first full calendar year, or a nonaccession-year dating system like Egypt's, in which a new pharaoh is accorded a year's rule, even if he begins to reign in the last month of a year? And what about coregencies, in which a king and his successor ruled simultaneously, the presence of variant readings in manuscripts, and the possibility of errors in preserving numbers? If this sounds complicated, it is!

We are fortunate in having a few secure dates in antiquity from which to extrapolate the approximate dates commonly used by historians in their reconstructions of the past. The dates come from descriptions of astronomical phenomena (e.g., a solar eclipse) in ancient texts, which can be plotted backwards by modern scientists to provide fixed points from which to interpret chronological data culled from other ancient sources. Although geology doesn't help us date Amos's earthquake, archaeology might find evidence of it in excavations. These fixed dates from astronomy and other sources are most influential for the first millennium BCE but are not limited to it. A battle at Qarqar in northern Syria, for which an Assyrian record says the Israelite king Ahab participated, is now commonly fixed at 853 BCE (below). A list of officials (Eponyms) from the Neo-Assyrian Empire has provided a fixed point in the year 763 BCE that influences modern chronological reckoning for several states and people groups of the ANE.

To take another example, the *Babylonian Chronicle* of King Nebuchadnezzar describes his taking of the city of Judah (= Jerusalem) on the second day of the month of Adar in his seventh year. This can be fixed as March 15 or 16, 597 BCE. This event corresponds to the account of Jerusalem's surrender to the Babylonians during the reign of Jehoiachin in 2 Kgs 24:10–12. Of course, not all dates in biblical and ANE history are so precisely known, but the margin of error for dates in political history for much of the first millennium is relatively small, as it can be even in the second millennium for some aspects of Egyptian and Mesopotamian history.

Interpreting Old Testament History

All history is interpreted history. This statement is not meant to downgrade the importance of historical thinking to a matter of opinion but to acknowledge a fact of central importance: writers interpret and select data as they report. It is as true of the OT writers as it is, say, of a biographer of Mother Teresa (see the discussion in chap. 10, "What Are the Historical Books?").

The period of the Israelite and Judahite kings presented in Samuel, Kings, and Chronicles is a central part of the OT story line and a good starting point for thinking about how one presents OT history. The monarchs lived during the Iron Age, a term that is so named for the primary metal used in making tools and military hardware at the time and used to describe the historical period of the various polities living in the eastern Mediterranean. We are told, for example, that David and Solomon had contact with King Hiram of Tyre, who assisted them with royal building projects (2 Sam 5:11-12; 1 Kgs 5:1-10) and that Solomon married Ammonite and Moabite women (1 Kgs 11:1-8). Historians have data for the Phoenician city-states and the nation-states of Ammon and Moab with which to compare the biblical accounts and the material culture of Iron Age Judah. Indeed, Hiram's royal name is known in ancient sources as Ahiram. One can, therefore, interpret Israel as a state in an Iron Age context with its king interacting with neighbors such as Tyre or Moab. At the end of this chapter, Table 2.5 lists some references to the kings of Israel and Judah in extrabiblical texts. Table 15.2 on p. 187 gives proposed dates for the kings of Israel and Judah, and other historical data that assist us in the historical interpretation of a central period in the OT story line appears at pertinent places in the volume.

Let's take the account of the Omride dynasty in Israel (1 Kgs 16:21-2 Kgs 10:17) as a further case in point to see how the story line in Kings intersects with ANE history. In doing so, we will see that this approach also puts the characteristics of OT narratives in sharper relief. The narrators present Omri, the founder of a three-generation dynasty, as the builder of a new capital for Israel named Samaria. He is succeeded by his son Ahab, who with his wife, Jezebel, supports the worship of Baal in Israel, and who persecutes Elijah and others in his realm. When he dies fighting against the Aramaeans, Ahab is succeeded by two of his sons, first Ahaziah and then Jehoram. Moab had been a vassal of Ahab, and it rebelled against Israelite hegemony after Ahab died. An Israelite army officer named Jehu initiates a coup and murders the members of the ruling house.

This quick summary follows the story line as basic political history, but it also includes a reference to Ahab and Jezebel's religious policies, which the narrators oppose. In their view, these dangerous policies led Israel away from the Lord and ultimately brought disaster on the nation. The Kings narrative thus includes a number of stories about the prophets of the Lord (Elijah, Micaiah, and Elisha) and their work during a time of religious upheaval. Indeed, in terms of space devoted to the subject, much of the Kings presentation of the Omride dynasty has to do with its religious practices and their consequences for Israel. That likely explains why their report on the reign of Omri, the dynasty's founder, whom modern historians regard as historically important, is summarized in only six verses.

Historical analysis potentially sheds light on any number of details in the Kings narrative about the Omride rulers. They ruled during the early and mid-9th century BCE, a secure setting, even if the dates of their reign might be off a year or two from the scholarly consensus. For example, archaeologists have partially excavated the remains of Samaria and Jezreel, two cities of residence for Ahab. The data from those excavations, along with those from excavations of some other prominent cities in his realm, show that the Omride dynasty was wealthy and strong. In terms of material culture, this was the pinnacle of Israelite development. A likely contributor to this development was Jezebel, Ahab's wife and a Phoenician princess (1 Kgs 16:31). Their marriage was a political arrangement to solidify relations between Israel and Phoenicia. The Phoenician city-states were in a period of general prosperity, and as they expanded commercially, so did the influence of various Canaanite deities they worshiped, several of whom bore the title Baal. These data assist readers with the historical context of the dynasty and with some perspective on the conflict at Mount Carmel between Elijah and the prophets of Baal, and the later murder of the Omride family and worshipers of Baal by Jehu.

Historians also have data to illumine the Iron Age Kingdom of the Moabites. According to 2 Kgs 3:4–27, the Moabite king Mesha rebelled against the hegemony of Israel, and there was war between Moab and Israel under the rule of Jehoram, who was supported also by the king of Judah. In 1868, a Moabite inscription from Mesha was discovered in the Arab village of Dhiban, near the ruins of the Moabite city of Dibon, Mesha's capital. In it, Mesha describes the humiliation that Omri had inflicted on Moab due to the anger of Chemosh, the Moabite deity. He then recounts a series of battles against the Israelites to regain territory, along with some building projects. Comparing the account in 2 Kgs 3 with that of the Mesha Inscription is a fascinating exercise! While the two accounts may render aspects of the same rebellion, they clearly interpret matters with different audiences in mind. Elisha speaks for the Lord in the biblical account, and Mesha interprets the will of Chemosh as active in his bid for independence.

As noted briefly above, Ahab is mentioned once in the annals of Shalmaneser III, the Assyrian ruler who campaigned repeatedly in the eastern Mediterranean area. Ahab is depicted as one of the ringleaders of a regional coalition opposing Shalmaneser during several years of campaigns by the Assyrians. While the coalition leadership and membership may have varied, Shalmaneser claims victory over it. Nothing of this activity, however, is described in the Kings account of Ahab's reign. His role as a regional leader

Moabite Stone, or Mesha Stele. Ca. 840 BCE, King Mesha of Moab (modern Jordan) had this stone inscribed. The stele tells how Moab's god, Chemosh, angry with his people, let Israel conquer them but later helped Moab regain its freedom and recover its lost lands. It parallels 2 Kings 3 and mentions Israel's King Omri and "his son" (i.e., Ahab). The Mesha Stele provides a rare glimpse into the Moabite language. It is presently in the Louvre in Paris. ©*Mbzt 2012 (Wikimedia Commons, GNU 1.2)*

I (am) Mesha, son of Chemosh-[. . .], king of Moab, the Dibonite. . . . As for Omri, king of Israel, he humbled Moab many years, for Chemosh was angry at his land. And his son [Ahab] followed him . . . but I have triumphed over him and over his house, while Israel has perished forever! (Now) Omri had occupied the land of Medeba, and (Israel) had dwelt there in his time and half the time of his son, forty years; but Chemosh dwelt there in my time. . . . Now the men of Gad had always dwelt in the land of Ataroth, and the king of Israel had built Ataroth for them; but I fought against the town and took it and slew all the people of the town as satiation for Chemosh and Moab. . . . And Chemosh said to me, "Go, take Nebo from Israel!" So I went by night and fought against it from the break of dawn until noon, taking it and slaying all, seven thousand men, boys, women, girls and maid-servants, for I had devoted them to destruction for (the god) Ashtar-Chemosh. . . . And the king of Israel had built Jahaz, and he dwelt there while he was fighting against me, but Chemosh drove him out before me.

(ANET, 320)

is consistent both with the archaeological portrait of a prosperous realm and with his connection with wealthy Phoenician traders, who did not have standing armies and needed regional partners to defend common interests. Shalmaneser had his reasons for presenting Ahab as a leader of a coalition that he defeated. Is it possible, for example, that Shalmaneser exaggerated or that during the time of Ahab's participation the coalition held strong? Even if the narrators of Kings knew about this international activity of Ahab (which can't be determined but is likely), it apparently didn't serve their purpose to use the information as part of their national narrative. One might say that they presented a one-sided portrait of Ahab; any successes he may have had in the political realm or in national security were less important to them than exposing his theological failures.

As interpreters, then, we are left with data from various sources regarding Ahab and his family, and sorting them out to present a historical reconstruction requires a critical weighing of options. Written history is interpreted history, with the principle of selectivity already at work in the sources available to the historian and in the ways in which the historian draws upon them to present his or her account. There are value judgments at work in both the sources and their interpreters. The narrators of Kings see the hand of the Lord in judging Ahab and his family, while Mesha claims Chemosh guided Moab's success. Shalmaneser credits the superiority of the Assyrian deities in his defeat of his enemies. However we may interpret the historical fortunes of Ahab and his family, the historical method itself cannot confirm or adjudicate the claims of the sources about divine activity. That is a matter of faith, on the part of both the writers and modern readers.

Putting Old Testament History in Contexts

Given our discussion, Table 2.3 shows our proposal for placing the periods derived from the OT story line in the context of ANE history.

Historians, of course, will differ on the details of our proposals, particularly for the periods before the divided monarchy. Our proposal assumes accurate historical memory for elements of the primary history, where others may not. Readers may wish to consult several studies listed in the bibliography, which go into greater detail on these matters. One can profitably compare, for example, the historical reconstructions offered by Provan, Long, and Longman with those by Knauf and Guillaume. To use current terminology in the discussion, the former scholars qualify as "maximalists" (= those who give more credence to the historical reliability of the Bible) and the latter as "minimalists" (= those who give less or little credence to its historical reliability). Minimalists typically cite some form of the following two reasons for their approach: (1) The final form of the literary traditions in the Pentateuch comes from centuries after the time periods depicted, making them less reliable for historical reconstruction. (2) The persons and events depicted in the stories are conflations by much later writers of memories and traditions from various periods and thus cannot be rooted in a single historical period. In what follows, we provide some short sketches to illustrate ways by which to evaluate the earlier parts of the OT story line. As we noted, all history is interpreted history, so it is important to consider how each of the following reconstructions weighs evidence and chooses among options.

In the Torah the ancestral period appears generations before the time of Moses and the subsequent emergence of Israel in Canaan (Gen 15:13; Exod 12:40). The first extrabiblical reference to a people named Israel appears in an inscription by the Egyptian pharaoh Merenptah in the year 1209 BCE. In a list of campaign victories, the pharaoh claims that a people group (notably not a city or a political state) named Israel has "been laid waste, their seed is not." Israel is mentioned along with Gezer, Ashkelon, and Yanoam. Readers will recognize the bombastic style of claiming victory over Canaanite opponents, whether there were "victories" or not. This marks an important intersection between the internal data of the OT and that surviving from the ANE. Interpreters who give more historical credence to the OT's early traditions (i.e., the maximalists) see this as a reference to the tribal association of Israel not long after its settlement in Canaan during the period of the judges. Put another way, they take the basic identity of Israel presented in the Pentateuch and assume that Merenptah refers to it. The location of Yanoam is unknown, but the mention of Gezer (the lowlands) and Ashkelon (the coastal plain) might suggest that the location of "Israel" is near them. Minimalists caution against reading a biblical identity into Merenptah's reference, and they stress that Israel is a Canaanite entity like the other three entities.

With regard to the OT presentation of Israelites in Egypt and the exodus from Egypt, interpreters generally take one of three positions.

(1) The Israelite slaves escaped Egypt about the year 1445 BCE. One reason for this is the chronological datum given in 1 Kgs 6:1, which lists 480 years between the exodus event and the beginning of temple construction in Jerusalem in Solomon's fourth year. The exodus, then, would have taken place during the long reign of Pharaoh Thutmose III (ca. 1479–1426), the New Kingdom period in Egypt, and the Late Bronze Age in Canaan. Furthermore, a date for the exodus in the mid-15th century BCE would result in a subsequent period of approximately 300 years of tribal life during the period of the judges. Interpreters who take this position give primacy and historical credence to the biblical data. Since there are no direct connections to Abraham or Moses in extrabiblical texts, scholars look for cultural connections in the Middle or Late Bronze Ages to bolster the placement of

the biblical story line in them. For example, interpreters cite the parallels of names such as Abraham and Jacob with similar names in ANE literature of the Middle Bronze Age, or connections between the stories of Joseph and what is known of Semites in Egypt in the second millennium BCE.

(2) The Israelite slaves escaped Israel about the year 1250 BCE, during the long reign of Ramesses II (ca. 1279–1213 BCE). Historians have reconstructed quite a transition period in the ANE at the end of the Late Bronze Age through Iron Age I (ca. 1250–950 BCE; see our introduction to Joshua). The traditional powers in the eastern Mediterranean, the Hittites and Egyptians, suffered stages of decline and, after a couple centuries of transition, a number of states and people groups emerged for the first time in recorded history. Among these are the Aramaean Kingdom centered in Damascus, the Philistines on or near the Mediterranean coast, and the Transjordanian states of Ammon, Moab, and Edom. The Israelites were part of this large transition in the ANE, according to this view. Such a date for the exodus would result in a period of 150–75 years of tribal life before the rise of monarchy. Interpreters also give credence to the basic biblical story line as they look for ways in which to put it in the context of second-millennium history. They find, for example, the reference to the building of the store cities of Pithom and Rameses a primary datum for dating the exodus (Exod 1:11). The name Rameses for a royal building project seems best dated to the time of the 19th Dynasty, which had several pharaohs named Ramesses. They conclude, furthermore, that the departure of a substantial slave population was more probable historically during the 13th century rather than the 15th century.

(3) Although there may have been connections between Egypt and Israel's ancestors, there was no large-scale enslavement of them there. There is nothing in Egyptian literature about Israelite slaves and thus no reason to assume they were there for generations without corroboration. A tribal group called Israel was located in Canaan in Iron Age I, as Merenptah's Inscription indicates. This was their home before the eventual development of an Israelite state. A number of stories and fragmentary memories about their ancestors go back to traditions of individual clans and tribes. These would include stories about Abraham, Isaac, and Jacob, who are composite figures in the final form of Genesis. Stories of a national enslavement and exodus to the promised land in Canaan developed into a foundation myth of the state to show the greatness of Yahweh. Minimalists begin, therefore, with the fact that Israel was a people group and then a state in Canaan. All ANE references to Israel assume a location in southern Canaan. Hebrew is

Merenptah Stele. The last lines of this inscribed stone by the Egyptian king Merenptah (1213–1203 BCE), now in the Egyptian Museum in Cairo, celebrate his victorious campaign in Syro-Palestine. They mark the first extrabiblical reference to "Israel" (a "foreign [nomadic] people") with implications for their location and the state of their settlement in Canaan. ©Alyssa Bivens (Wikimedia Commons, CC-SA 4.0)

Canaan is plundered, Ashkelon is carried off, and Gezer is captured. Yenoam is made into non-existence; Israel is wasted, its seed is not; and Hurru is become a widow because of Egypt.

(COS 2.41)

a Canaanite dialect, and the material culture of early Israel a form of Canaanite culture with nothing particularly Egyptian about it.

We should be careful to say that maximalists are not necessarily uncritical as historians, nor should we conclude that minimalists are excessively skeptical. But they do weigh matters differently—a difference that is not unique to biblical studies. One can, for example, see a range of perspectives on the historical background of the *Iliad*, the foundational epic of Classical Greek culture about struggles between a Greek army and the city of Troy, which is traditionally attributed to a man named Homer. It too is set in what we call the Late Bronze Age, even though the text of the *Iliad* was composed some centuries later (8th/7th centuries BCE). Modern readers will perhaps recognize the term *Trojan War*, which comes from the account, or the movie *Troy* (2004), which starred Brad Pitt as the Greek hero Achilles and Eric Bana as the Trojan prince Hector. Some interpreters find in the account a number of connections between Mycenaean history and that of the Late Bronze Age in western Anatolia. Others doubt that there ever was a man named Homer and find a rousing story in the *Iliad* but very little of a connected history in it. Our approach essentially follows option 2 above, but we include a variety of perspectives in the bibliography below and those included in other chapters.

The Terms *Exile* and *Diaspora*

The phrase *Babylonian exile* or simply *the exile* is commonly used in presenting OT history. We should begin by noting that there is more than one exilic experience presented in the OT. The Neo-Assyrians took multiple groups of Israelites into exile in the last third of the 8th century BCE, culminating with those deported by Sargon II in the year 720 BCE. Over a century later, the Babylonians under King Nebuchadnezzar twice surrounded Jerusalem and took waves of Judahites into exile in 597 and 587 BCE. When someone refers to the exile in the OT or in ancient Israel without further qualification, it is typically the Babylonian exile that is in mind. Some recent interpreters, however, prefer the term *forced migration* to describe the Assyrian and Babylonian practices of removing portions of a captured population and forcing them to resettle elsewhere. Historians and anthropologists use the term cross-culturally, and its employment by biblical interpreters puts this part of ANE history in the larger context of world history.

Diaspora is a term related to exile. It refers to the dispersion of Israelites and Judahites from the promised land to live in other places, irrespective of the impetus for their departure. One could relocate simply as a refugee fleeing war or as a trader expanding a business network. And once in a "foreign land," subsequent generations can put down roots and stay there. Thus, over time Jewish communities developed in Egypt, Syria, Mesopotamia, and Persia. This is important to keep in mind particularly in defining the postexilic period. People and events portrayed in this period of OT history lived in various places in the ANE. Jerusalem and Judah were not completely depopulated by the Babylonian victors, and in the transition to Persian rule, when there were opportunities for Jews to return to their ancestral home, many remained in the diaspora. The recently discovered Al-Yahudu Tablets offer a rare glimpse of nearly ninety years of life in the diaspora, including physical and financial conditions, in a small town of Judahites in Babylon (572–484 BCE). Ezra was a Jewish priest living in Babylon who was sent to Jerusalem in 458 BCE during the reign of Artaxerxes I, decades after initial waves of Jews returned to Jerusalem. There was a significant Jewish community remaining in and near Babylon for centuries after the Persian period. Indeed, a thousand years later, Jews in the area of Babylon compiled the Babylonian Talmud, the cornerstone of rabbinic teaching!

Esther and Mordecai lived in the Persian capital of Susa during the reign of Xerxes I (for his dates, see the appendix). Nehemiah was a highly placed servant in Susa from a slightly later period who went back and forth between it and Jerusalem, beginning in the year 445 BCE. A large group of Jews lived in the Hellenistic city of Alexandria on the Mediterranean coast of Egypt. As with the Jewish community in Babylon, the Jews in Alexandria were well versed in their ancestral traditions as well as participants in the larger economic and cultural life of their Egyptian setting. The diaspora, therefore, is the setting for several changes in terminology and culture. Under the Persians, Judah becomes the province of *Yehud*. Over time Israelites and Judahites in the postexilic period are called *Jews*, a term derived from the name *Yehud*. The term *Jew* applies to them, whether their ancestral home was Samaria or Jerusalem. Jews in the diaspora learn to speak Aramaic and then Greek, for these are the primary languages of the ANE in the postexilic period. Jews in Alexandria provide the initial translation of the Torah from Hebrew to Greek in approximately 250 BCE, a momentous occasion toward the end of OT history.

In short, the context of OT history is in reality the history and culture of the ANE, not just of Canaan proper. Its national birthplace lies in lower Mesopotamia, from which its Mesopotamian parents, Abram and Sarai, migrate to Canaan and sojourn in Egypt. Along the way, they interact with other historic peoples, as do their descendants later, from their home base in Canaan. Written records of those ancient peoples supply a historical context in which we may date and interpret events in Israelite history. The exile and the diaspora that it fostered decisively multiplied the places and opportunities for future intersections between Jewish communities and their neighbors. The historical data now available to illumine the context of OT history constitutes a rich treasury from which we greatly benefit and which also requires the respectful weighing of a variety of interpretations (see Table 2.5).

Table 2.5. Israelite and Judahite Rulers in Extrabiblical Texts

Ruler	Reference	Source(s)
David	"House of David"	*Aramaic*, Tel Dan Inscription
Omri	"Omri, king of Israel"	*Moabite*, Mesha Inscription
	"House of Omri"	*Neo-Assyrian*, Nimrud Annals of Shalmaneser III
Ahab	"Ahab the Israelite"	*Neo-Assyrian*, Monolith Inscription of Shalmaneser III
Jehu	"Jehu, son of Omri"	*Neo-Assyrian*, Black Obelisk of Shalmaneser III
Joash	"Joash from Samaria"	*Neo-Assyrian*, Rimah Stela of Adad-nirari III
Menachem	"Menachem from Samaria"	*Neo-Assyrian*, Iran Stela of Tiglath-pileser III
Ahaz	"Jehoahaz the Judean"	*Neo-Assyrian*, Annals of Tiglath-pileser III
Pekah	"Pekah their king"	*Neo-Assyrian*, Annals of Tiglath-pileser III
Hoshea	"Hoshea, I appointed"	*Neo-Assyrian*, Annals of Tiglath-pileser III
Hezekiah	"Hezekiah, the Judean"	*Neo-Assyrian*, Prism Account of Sennacherib
Manasseh	"Manasseh, king of Judah"	*Neo-Assyrian*, Annals of Esarhaddon
Jehoiachin	"Jehoiachin . . . and 5 sons"	*Neo-Babylonian*, ration tablet of Nebuchadnezzar

For translations of all the texts containing these references, see *COS*.

BIBLIOGRAPHY

Ahn, John J. *Exile as Forced Migrations: A Sociological, Literary, and Theological Approach on the Displacement and Resettlement of the Southern Kingdom of Judah.* Berlin: de Gruyter, 2011.

Ahn, John J., and Jill Middlemas, eds. *By the Irrigation Canals of Babylon: Approaches to the Study of the Exile.* New York: Bloomsbury, 2012.

Arnold, Bill T., and Richard S. Hess, eds. *Ancient Israel's History: An Introduction to Issues and Sources.* Grand Rapids: Baker Academic, 2014.

Cline, Eric H. *1177 B.C.: The Year Civilization Collapsed.* Princeton: Princeton University Press, 2014.

———. *The Trojan War: A Very Short Introduction.* New York: Oxford University Press, 2013.

Faust, Avraham. *Judah in the Neo-Babylonian Period: The Archaeology of Desolation.* Archaeology and Biblical Studies 18. Atlanta: Society of Biblical Literature Press, 2012.

Finkelstein, Israel. *The Forgotten Kingdom: The Archaeology and History of Northern Israel.* Atlanta: Society of Biblical Literature, 2013.

Gerstenberger, Erhard S. *Israel in the Persian Period: The Fifth and Fourth Centuries B.C.E.* Atlanta: Society of Biblical Literature Press, 2011.

Grabbe, Lester L., ed. *Israel in Transition 1: From Late Bronze II to Iron IIA (c. 1250–850 B.C.E.). The Archaeology*. New York: T&T Clark, 2008.

———, ed. *Israel in Transition 2: From Late Bronze II to Iron IIA (c. 1250–850 BCE). The Texts*. New York: T&T Clark, 2010.

Grabbe, Lester L., and Oded Lipschits, eds. *Judah between East and West: The Transition from Persian to Greek Rule (ca. 400–200 BCE)*. New York: T&T Clark, 2011.

Hallo, William W., and K. Lawson Younger, eds. *The Context of Scripture*. 3 vols. Leiden: Brill, 2002.

Kitchen, Kenneth A. *On the Reliability of the Old Testament*. Grand Rapids: Eerdmans, 2004.

Knauf, Axel, and Philippe Guillaume. *A History of Biblical Israel: The Fate of the Tribes and Kingdoms from Merenptah to Bar Kochba*. Equinox, 2015.

Millard, A. R. *The Eponyms of the Assyrian Empire 910–612 BC*. State Archives of Assyria Studies 2. Helsinki: Neo-Assyrian Text Corpus Project, 1994.

Moore, Megan Bishop, and Brad E. Kelle. *Biblical History and Israel's Past: The Changing Study of the Bible and History*. Grand Rapids: Eerdmans, 2011.

Provan, Iain, V. Philips Long, and Tremper Longman III. *A Biblical History of Israel*. 2nd ed. Louisville: Westminster John Knox, 2015.

Schoors, Antoon. *The Kingdoms of Israel and Judah in the Eighth and Seventh Centuries B.C.E.* Atlanta: Society of Biblical Literature, 2013.

Ussher, James. *The Annals of the World*. London: Crook and Bedell, 1658.

Wiseman, Donald J. *Chronicles of Chaldaean Kings, 626–556 B.C.* London: Trustees of the British Museum, 1961.

PART 2
The Torah

3 WHAT IS THE TORAH?

ARLIER, WE POINTED OUT THAT the Torah (or "the Law") marks the first canonical section of both the Hebrew Bible and all translations, including our English translations. It thus sets the stage for the whole story of God and Israel that plays out in the canonical sections that follow, including the NT. Indeed, no OT section casts as long a shadow across the Bible's theological landscape as does the Torah. Its pages lay the theological foundation on which the whole Bible rests.

What Is the Torah?

So, what is the *Torah* and where does that word come from? The simple answer is: the Torah comprises the first five books of the OT—Genesis, Exodus, Leviticus, Numbers, and Deuteronomy. Together they tell a single story that begins with the origin of the universe and the spread of humans over the ancient world. Then they narrate the ups and downs of one particular family line over many centuries. This latter subplot debuts with the family's founder, a man from Mesopotamia named Abram (later, Abraham) and ends with the twelve tribes of his grandson, Jacob, camped east of the Jordan River and listening to speeches by their leader, Moses. The Torah's five books thus develop the story of Israel as follows:

> *Genesis*: God promised Abraham a wonderful land (Canaan) and many descendants, but his twelve great-grandsons and their families ended up living in Egypt instead.

Exodus: Centuries later God sent Moses to lead their descendants from slavery in Egypt to Mount Sinai, where they agreed to a special covenant relationship with their ancestral God.

Leviticus: God explained in detail, through Moses, what God required for that special relationship to continue and thrive.

Numbers: The rebellious older generation died in the desert, and Moses led the younger one to just outside the promised land.

Deuteronomy: Moses prepared the Israelites to possess Canaan by reiterating the requirements of their covenant with God.

Each of the five books has a unique identity, yet each helps develop the larger story:

1. Genesis has two parts. It recounts the origin of the universe as a whole in seven days (1:1–2:4), then follows the long story of human life on earth from Adam and Eve in Eden to Joseph and the Israelites prospering in Egypt (2:4–50:26). Part 1 of that story recounts primeval human history, the eras of Adam and Noah (2:4–11:9); part 2, the lives of the Shemites Abraham, Isaac, Jacob, and Joseph (chs. 12–50).
2. Exodus opens with the Israelites still in Egypt (but now enslaved) and tells how God miraculously freed them through Moses (chs. 1–12). It tracks the Israelites' travels from the Red Sea to Mount Sinai (chs. 13–18), their agreement to obey the Torah, and the construction of the tabernacle (chs. 19–40).
3. Leviticus first instructs the Israelites, still encamped at Sinai, on proper sacrifices and offerings for God (chs. 1–7). Second, it designates who among them may serve as priests and explains the important concepts of *clean* and *unclean* (chs. 8–16). It concludes with the Holiness Code, which comprises detailed instructions concerning *holy* and *unholy* conduct (chs. 17–26).
4. Numbers recounts events at Sinai, during the wilderness transit, and at the plains of Moab on the edge of the promised land. Its first part features Israelite preparations to leave Sinai, including censuses of the men of military age and of the size of priestly clans (1:1–10:10). It then follows Israel's itinerary from Sinai to the edge of the promised land (10:11–21:35). It marks a grumpy trip full of complaining and an

angry controversy over whether or not to turn back for Egypt. The final section reports events during Israel's encampment at the plains of Moab, where the Israelites receive an additional section of laws and conquer Moab (chs. 22–36).

5. Deuteronomy features a series of instructions spoken by Moses to the encamped Israelites. He recounts their history with Yahweh (chs. 1–4) and exhorts them to obey the Torah (chs. 5–11). He reviews in detail Yahweh's statutes and ordinances (chs. 12–26) and pronounces curses and blessings for not keeping or keeping them, respectively (chs. 27–28). The concluding appendix compiles Moses's farewell speeches, his poetry, and the report of his burial (chs. 29–34).

But why is this long story called "Torah"? The word *Torah* is simply the English rendering of the Hebrew word *torah* ("teaching, instruction"), the title Jews have used for the first canonical section of their Bible for more than 2,000 years. Other non-Jewish Bibles describe them as the "Five Books of Moses," recognizing Moses's central role in the last four books and perhaps affirming his hand in the origin of the first one. Christians more commonly call the collection the "Pentateuch" (lit., "five-part book"), a term first coined by the church father Jerome (4th cent. CE). That term, however, simply tells us how many books the collection has but not what they contain or even why we should read them. Finally, most Bible translations render the word *torah* as "Law," so most readers know the five collectively as "the Law." This at least tells us something about what's in the five books, and there are good reasons to support use of that designation:

1. the Torah certainly has plenty of laws;
2. the Greek Bible (or LXX) usually translates *torah* as "law" (Gk. *nomos*);
3. the NT refers to the whole Pentateuch as *nomos*.

Nonetheless, while we may use all the above expressions at one time or another, *Torah* (or "the Instruction") remains our preferred term for the Bible's first five books. In our view, it best sums up their content and purpose.

Look What's Inside!

A quick read of Genesis to Deuteronomy shows that the Torah features two kinds of literature. The first and most prominent type is *story*. As noted above, a central narrative strand threads its way through all five books and weaves the collection together into a literary whole. Geographically, the story begins in Mesopotamia, proceeds to Canaan, Egypt, and Mount Sinai, and ends at the very edge of the land God had promised the Israelites. Table 3.1 provides a summary of the Torah's locales and chronology.

The second type of literature in the Torah is *embedded law*. The larger story incorporates within it three major collections of laws, two associated with Israel's year-long stop at Mount Sinai and one with the people's month on the plains of Moab just east of the Jordan. These three legal collections include (in this order of appearance):

1. The Covenant Code (Exod 21-23);
2. The Holiness Code (Lev 17-27);
3. The Deuteronomic Code (Deut 12-26).

The Torah also includes other legal instructions, notably two smaller collections (Lev 1-7; Num 28-30), and two slightly different versions of the Ten Commandments (or Decalogue) in Exod 20 and 34 (set at Mount Sinai) and in Deut 5 (set in the plains of Moab). The large quantity and narrative prominence of legal instructions in the Torah undoubtedly account for its popular name, "the Law."

But, again, we reiterate our preference for the term *Torah* (or "the Instruction") as the title that, in our view, best describes the nature and purpose of the material. It is instruction, not just law. We affirm that the purpose of much OT law is in fact to mediate God's grace to Israel and her neighbors.

Table 3.1. The Torah: Books, Locales, and Time Lengths

Book	Chapters	Locales	Time Lengths
Genesis	1–11	Mesopotamia, Mediterranean lands	Thousands, if not millions, of years
Genesis	12–50	Mesopotamia, Canaan, Egypt	Several centuries
Exodus	1–18	Egypt	Several decades
Exodus	19–40	Mount Sinai	Eleven months
Leviticus	1–27		
Numbers	1–10		
Numbers	10–36	The desert, the plains of Moab	Thirty-nine years
Deuteronomy	1–34	The plains of Moab	One month

The Torah and the Historical Books

The story the Torah tells, of course, continues for many centuries in Joshua, Judges, Samuel, and Kings. Indeed, one scholar proposes that later editors compiled Genesis-Kings into a single story line that he entitles the *Primary History*. Granted, many separate episodes compose that longer story, much as weekly episodes make up a TV series such as *Law and Order* or *Homeland*. Each weekly show both stands on its own and contributes to the larger impact of the whole series. But despite the solemn dramatic pause that Deut 34 sounds, the Torah's story at that point, in fact, is incomplete. Its main theme—the promise that Abraham's descendants will possess Canaan—actually only reaches fulfillment in Joshua, and even then, only somewhat (see Josh 13). The Torah thus forms part 1 of a longer, two-part story, with the Historical Books as part 2. Apparently, this "somewhat" completion of the promise of land did not trouble those who compiled the Torah and Historical Books. To them, Deut 34 literarily and theologically sets off the Torah from what follows, as a unique, unrepeatable, foundational era of revelation—a unique status that it retains among Jews and Christians to this day.

How Did We Get These Books?

The Torah is in reality an anonymous literary work. The OT nowhere directly names the person(s) responsible for the Torah, or recounts how any of the Torah's five books came to be, or tells the story of their collection. The revered scribe Ezra probably completed the Torah under Persian auspices in connection with his return from exile to Jerusalem in the mid-5th century BCE (Ezra 7:6, 10-26). Traditionally, Jews and Christians have regarded Moses as its author, a view still held by many readers today but one that we wish to nuance (see below). Its primary evidence is the Torah's claims that Moses wrote things down on scrolls—for example, a battle report (Exod 17:14; cf. vv. 8-13) and Israel's desert itinerary (Num 33:2; cf. vv. 1-49) and so on. On the other hand, the third-person formula "and the LORD said to Moses" that dominates Exodus, Leviticus, and Numbers seems to point to writing by people other than Moses (e.g., Exod 24:12; Lev 8:1; Num 11:16). Additionally, would Moses or someone else have described him as "more humble than anyone else on the face of the earth" (Num 12:3)?

makes us different from those nations?" In reply, Gen 12–50 reminds the Israelites of their unique ethnic and covenant identity. They are kinfolk descended from revered ancestors, promised a great destiny, and linked closely to Yahweh. Indeed, Exod 4–11 reminds them that Yahweh refers to Israel as God's firstborn son (Exod 4:22–23)—a poignant metaphor implying family-like ties between God and the Israelites and rights to the family inheritance. At the same time, however, episodes of grumbling in Exodus and Numbers also confront them regarding their well-documented bent toward rebellion and impulsiveness—and their need for national self-discipline.

5. *This land we've been given—can we keep it?* Two disastrous historical events probably drove the Israelites to ask how permanent their ownership of the land that God had given them was—or whether it was slipping from their grasp. The question would have certainly arisen after 722 BCE, when the Assyrians destroyed the Northern Kingdom, shipped the Israelites off to Assyria, and settled non-Israelites in their place. The same question also likely hit home in 587 BCE, when the Babylonians destroyed Jerusalem and exiled thousands of Judahites to Babylon. Would those despairing, rag-tag descendants of the once-glorious empire of David and Solomon ever again form a vibrant, thriving community back home? And, if they were to return home, could they lawfully reclaim their former possessions? Finally, as the years in exile waned, consideration of the question would have intensified as Israelites in far-off Babylon dreamed about going home. In reply, Exod 23 and 33 reaffirm God's ancient promise to give Israel the land; their generous God certainly wants them both to possess it and to profit from it fully. They still have good reason for confidence in the future. Finally, the passionate voice of Moses in Deuteronomy prepares their generation for a successful return—an entry that will not repeat the mistakes that followed the original entry of their ancestors.

6. *Now that we're free, can we do as we like?* This question concerning what boundaries limited their new-found freedom probably surfaced once the Israelites had comfortably settled in Canaan as land-owning, free people. Several subquestions might occur to them. Could they worship both Yahweh and the gods and borrow the alluring practices of their Canaanite neighbors? Against such thinking, however, the Torah flashes warnings again and again: "Don't even think about it!" (e.g., Exod 23:13; Lev 26:1; Deut 17:2–7). What about warfare. Was it forbidden? This was a common experience in the ancient world, especially for people whose towns sat along time-tested invasion routes. Rather than outlaw warfare, however, Deut 20

Important Events for Contextualizing the Old Testament

1220: Israel's entry into Canaan fulfills God's promises in Genesis and implements Moses's commissions in Deuteronomy.

1100s: The instructions in Exod 21–23 and 33–34 possibly reflect Israel's life before the Israelites had a king, although there is little evidence that they actually lived by the Torah at that time.

1000: A monarch now leads the Israelites — a narrative that may provide background to the Genesis narratives that foresee it and favorably feature the tribe of Judah.

1000–722: The Israelites' life becomes more urban and temple centered, possibly the setting for Leviticus.

700s: Prophets such as Hosea protest that worship and community life in the Northern Kingdom (or "Israel") ignore the Torah; Israel rejects such protests, and Assyria destroys Israel.

622: Josiah's reformation rediscovers and elevates Deuteronomy to guide Judah's life again.

587: Prophets such as Jeremiah and Ezekiel urge Judah to stop ignoring the Torah in its worship and life, but Judah ignores them, and Babylon destroys Judah. The exile of most of the Judahites imposes a time for reassessment.

538: Cyrus the Persian, conqueror of Babylon, permits the exiles to return to Judah and rebuild their temple at imperial expense. Many Jews return, but many remain in Babylon, Persia, and Egypt.

458: Ezra comes from Babylon to Jerusalem as a teacher of the Instruction. He and Nehemiah urge the city to base its life on the Torah.

445: Nehemiah comes from Babylon to Jerusalem and begins rebuilding the city walls.

332: Alexander the Great, a Greek, conquers Persia and begins to spread Greek culture throughout his vast empire.

160s: Antiochus Epiphanes bans worship based on the Torah in the temple, so the Jewish community rebels against him and reinstates worship in line with the Torah.

seeks to temper its violence with compassion and common sense, exempting some prospective soldiers (cf. Deut 24:5) and dictating the proper conduct of a city siege. Finally, can the Israelites eat anything they want? "No," the Torah says. All cultures have their lists of acceptable and unacceptable foods, and so do the Israelites, in the food laws in Leviticus and Deuteronomy (e.g., Lev 11; Deut 14:3–21).

7. *What do we do when we fail?* The history of the Israelites is not short on failures: for example, the scandalous golden calf episode (Exod 32) and the controversy over Canaan (Num 13–14). So, the Torah publically airs the Israelites' dirty laundry but also teaches them how to wash their failures away, instruction applicable in every era. Exodus 26–40 establishes the place and personnel for making things right with God, while Lev 1–16 instructs the people on the procedures for doing so. Leviticus 17–26 also urges them to pursue holiness, both corporate and personal—the lifestyle that promises them personal and national success. Some items in Leviticus strike us as trivial: what to eat or not eat, taboos about handling corpses, which bodily fluids or skin problems disqualify someone from attending worship, and so on. But the Israelites understood them as fundamental to daily life lived in relationship to their gracious, generous God (for background, see chap. 7 below on the book of Leviticus).

In sum, speaking broadly, the Torah invokes two grammatical forms to address the Israelites' questions. It speaks to them with *imperative* verbs, commanding them to do what pleases God and to avoid things that made him angry. Exodus 20 and Deut 5 give the Israelites the Ten Commandments, not the Ten Suggestions! Leviticus 18 and 26 and Deut 30–32 also warn Israelites, whether in the land or in exile, and in every era that their possession of the land and avoidance of exile depend on heartfelt, ongoing covenant faithfulness to Yahweh alone. The Torah underscores that the land was still theirs to retain—and, alas, to lose again. Later, Ps 95 would review one such historic episode and challenge later Israelites to get it right this time! The Torah also spoke to them with *indicative* verbs, its stories simply recounting what happened long ago, to display the character of their God. Numbers 10–20 and Deut 1–3 offer memorable cautionary tales of the heavy price tag their ancestors paid for stubborn unfaithfulness. Exodus 1–18 and Num 10–26 teach the Israelites that their rescue from Egypt and arrival near the promised land show how kind, merciful, patient, and powerful their God is. Yahweh is worthy of worship: a reliable guide toward the promised land and powerful enough to conquer it.

The Torah: History or Fiction?

You may have noticed above that we describe the Torah as *narrative* and *story* rather than as *history*. Though ambiguous, we prefer those words because their ambiguity serves an important purpose. We observe that the Bible contains a variety of literary genres, including history—reports of what happened back then (e.g., much of 1–2 Kings, the Gospels)—as well as non-historical forms—for example, the parables of the prophets (e.g., Ezek 17) and of Jesus. In our view, the latter genre dispels the popular notion that God is skittish about speaking through fiction. The prominence of parables also undercuts the assumption that, in the Bible, truth can only be packaged as history—that history connotes "good" and "true," and fiction "bad" and "false." So the possibility that the Torah may comprise both history and fiction remains. Rather than thinking of history and fiction as incompatible opposites, however, we propose that narratives instead fall along this literary spectrum:

Factual  Traditional

Narratives whose content and intent center more on historical facts than traditional storytelling-invention tend toward the "factual" pole—call them "more historical"—while those in which literary artistry dominates ("traditional") tend toward the opposite end—call them "less historical." Our point is that to a greater or lesser degree all narratives, including historical ones, involve some element of literary artistry and creativity. Theologically, we affirm that God can inspire (and has) all sorts of literary types and sovereignly assigned them their place in our Bibles for his voice to be heard. That's why we prefer to speak of narrative and story: it leaves open the door for voices to be heard across the spectrum of biblical genres. At the same time, we believe that some events are too important *not* to be thought factual because, in Goldingay's words (p. 5), "The historical 'having happened-ness' of the story matters." For example, the basic salvation story of Israel told by Exod 1–18 and the resurrection of Jesus forever define Israel's (and Christian) identity and purpose and also make claims about the nature of Israel's God. Were they not historical, there would be no reason to pay the Torah or the gospel any attention and no reason to worship or rely on the God who claims to hear the cries of his people and to act with compassion and power toward them. There would be no firm basis for us to believe that God is present and active in our own histories today.

The Torah and Later Readers

To conclude, let's "roll the Torah forward" as though it were a DVD to highlight its lasting influence on Israelites over the centuries. When we scroll past Malachi into Matthew, we quickly see the fingerprints of Torah-shaping in the community of faith that receives the newborn Jesus. We glimpse them in the pious family circle that welcomes him—Mary, Joseph, Zechariah, and Elizabeth—and in the excitement and celebration of his birth in the wider, devout community—the shepherds, Anna, Simeon, and the Magi. Torah-shaping prepares many later to recognize the rabbi Jesus as the Messiah and devoutly follow him: the twelve, his cousin John the Baptizer, Mary Magdalene, and Nicodemus. Devotion to Torah drives some of them to spread the good news about Jesus around Israel and the Mediterranean (Peter, Philip, James, Paul, and Barnabas) and draws others (Priscilla, Aquila, Apollos, Lydia, the Galatians) gladly to receive their message. And the Torah has likewise shaped us. It's our kindergarten teacher—the first storyteller to introduce us to the Bible's leading character, God the Loving Creator and Rescuer, and to tell us God's story. Through that story we first learn about God's eternal plan through Abraham to rescue both creation and us creatures from our sad, fallen, and painful alienation from God. Torah-shaping has likewise prepared us to welcome the same good news and to worship the Creator-Redeemer and his Son.

BIBLIOGRAPHY

Alexander, T. Desmond. *From Paradise to the Promised Land: An Introduction to the Pentateuch.* 3rd ed. Grand Rapids: Baker Academic, 2012.

Blenkinsopp, Joseph. *The Pentateuch: An Introduction to the First Five Books of the Bible.* ABRL. New York: Doubleday, 1992.

———. *Treasures Old and New: Essays in the Theology of the Pentateuch.* Grand Rapids: Eerdmans, 2004.

Crüsemann, Frank. *The Torah: Theology and Social History of Old Testament Law.* Translated by Allen W. Mahnke. Minneapolis: Fortress, 1996.

Friedman, Richard E. *Who Wrote the Bible?* New York: Summit, 1987.

Goldingay, John. "How Far Do Readers Make Sense? Interpreting Biblical Narratives." *Themelios* 18/2 (1993): 5-10.

Milgrom, Jacob. "The Case for the Pre-exilic and Exilic Provenance of the Books of Exodus, Leviticus and Numbers." Pages 48-57 in *Reading the Law: Studies in*

Honour of Gordon J. Wenham. Edited by J. Gordon McConville and Karl Möller. LHBOTS 461. New York: T&T Clark, 2007.

Schnittjer, Gary E. *The Torah Story: An Apprenticeship on the Pentateuch.* Grand Rapids: Zondervan, 2006.

Wenham, Gordon J. *A Guide to the Pentateuch.* Exploring the Old Testament 1. Downers Grove, IL: InterVarsity Press, 2003.

Wijk-Bos, Johanna W. H. van. *Making Wise the Simple: The Torah in Christian Faith and Practice.* Grand Rapids: Eerdmans, 2005.

4 THE BOOK OF GENESIS 1–11

Important Dates for Genesis 1–11

Dates for stories in the Proto-History are uncertain

THE WORD *GENESIS* MEANS "ORIGIN" or "beginning," and that name fits this first book of the Bible. It relates how the universe itself received its present shape and how all kinds of other things—all familiar to us—first appeared in history. Two prominent literary phenomena in Genesis further underscore the book's theme of beginnings. The *formula* "This is the account of . . ." recurs 10 times as a kind of topical heading for the second creation account (2:4) and the story of each main character:

> Noah and Family (Gen 6:9)
> Noah's Descendants (Gen 10:1)
> The Shemites (Gen 11:10)
> Terah (Gen 11:27)
> Ishmael (Gen 25:12)
> Isaac (Gen 25:19)
> Esau (in Canaan [Gen 36:1]; in Edom [Gen 36:9])
> Jacob (Gen 37:2)

For the formula's other occurrences, see Num 3:1 and Ruth 4:18 (cf. Gen 5:1; 10:32; 25:13; 1 Chr 1:29).

The book's second literary feature is the placement of three *genealogies* at key junctures in it. Their literary purpose is to establish narrative bridges between the main historical periods of the book. The first bridge (Gen 5) is chronological: it traces Adam's descendants over many centuries, thus linking the eras of Adam and Noah. The second (Gen 10) is ethnographic: it tracks Noah's descendants, with an eye on the ethnic groups that they father and the places where they live. The third bridge (11:10–25) is also chronological: it follows the descendants of Noah's son Shem (or the Shemites), thus linking the era of Noah with that of the Israelite patriarchs, whose lives the rest of the book recounts.

Genesis has two parts:

1. Genesis 1–11 relates the *Primeval History*, the early history of the earth and its peoples
2. Genesis 12–50 presents the *Patriarchal History* of Abraham, Isaac, Jacob, and his son Joseph

Notice how, as it plays out, the story of Genesis varies its focus between wide shots and close-ups. Genesis 1:1 introduces the whole vast universe, but v. 2 immediately spotlights its primary interest, the earth and the family line of Adam (Gen 2–5). After the flood, its view widens to survey the geographical dispersion of Noah's three sons and their descendants (Gen 10) before narrowing in on one specific branch, the Shemites (Gen 11). Next, among all humans, the story hones in on one Shemite family line, that of Abraham, and amid that group ends with a close-up on one of his grandsons, Jacob, the ethnic ancestor of the Israelites. The rest of the Torah—indeed, the whole OT—recounts the story of that ethnic group. However, as we noted above, the special focus on the Israelites does not exclude other peoples from the Torah's radar screen. On the contrary, although they play a minor role in the Bible, God's concern for them echoes throughout it.

The Story

Two accounts of creation open the Primeval History, the Bible's report about how the world's story began. Each has its own event-sequence, point of view, and purpose. The first creation report features a seven-day structure of events through which God creates the universe (Gen 1:1–2:3). Its point of view is cosmic, its style formal and stately, its mood majestic and hopeful, and its structure almost poetic. On Christmas Eve of 1968, the orbiting Apollo 8 astronauts captured its grandeur by reading it as they transmitted a

"Firsts" in Genesis

The Sky
Seas
Dry Land
Sun, Moon, Stars
Vegetation
Humans
Animals, Birds, Fish
Gender
Childbirth
Offerings
Murder
Domestication of
    Animals
Musicians & Musical
    Instruments
Cities
Arts and Crafts
Metallurgy

The Garden of Eden, by Erastus Salisbury Field. Ca. 1860.

live television view of sunrise on the moon below them. As we noted earlier, the passage also introduces the God of the Bible, the one whose awesome power brought everything into existence, still sustains it, and remains its cosmic sovereign. It is the same God whose shadow hangs over history and who "loved the world" enough to send Jesus to bring the earth and its creatures the gospel (John 3:16).

The second creation account (Gen 2) introduces a review of early human history, the era of Adam (2:4–5:32). Set in an ancient garden, its focus is more intimate and story-like than stately Gen 1. It details how the humans who debut in Gen 1:26–27 came to be. Alas, their otherwise wonderful introduction ends in catastrophe. They succumb to temptation, gravely injuring the created order, and earning expulsion from the garden (ch. 3). Symptoms of the new disorder soon appear: Cain murders his brother Abel, and Lamech arrogantly boasts of his own greatness (ch. 4). At the same time, human creativity among Adam's descendants shows that something of the creator's good, original design still survives. Cain begins to raise crops and Abel to raise sheep (4:3, 4). The descendants of the murderer Cain figure out how to make musical instruments and music, to live together in tents or towns, to raise livestock, and to produce arts and crafts. Some even develop skills in smelting ore and shaping metals (4:20–22). The narrator reiter-

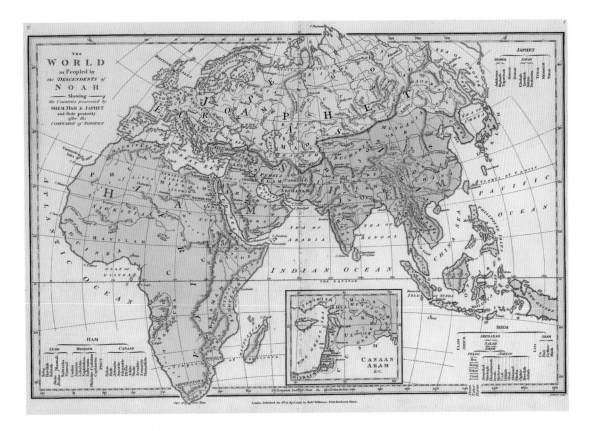

ates that, notwithstanding the garden disaster, humans still show signs of being kin to their divine creator (5:1-2). The genealogy of Adam (vv. 3-32) fast-forwards through his descendants across hundreds, if not thousands of years, ending at Noah.

Noah's era (Gen 6-9) marks a watershed in biblical history (pardon the pun!). Human beings' misbehavior drives God to regret having made them. But rather than wipe them all out and create a second, completely new batch, God sends a deluge to cleanse the earth and permit a new start. God spares Noah and his family (and pairs of all animal life) as a kind of *Adam 2.0*, through whom to repopulate the earth. Noah lives in Mesopotamia, a region bordered by two great rivers that regularly flood. So, the Bible's Great Flood probably remembers the Mother of All Floods (or in California-earthquake terms, "the Big One"). Peoples around the world have stories of a memorable, ancient flood that may go back to the cataclysm behind the biblical story.

Map depicting the Table of Nations from Robert Wilkinson's 1823 *Atlas Classica*. The Table of Nations is the title commonly given to the genealogy in Genesis 10, which describes the dispersal of descendants of Noah throughout the known world. The Table's accuracy in describing human origins is now in serious question, but until the last century it inspired many maps such as this.

The massive, restored pyramid or ziggurat at ancient Ur (near modern Nasiriya, Iraq) built in the Early Bronze Age (21st century BCE) to honor the city's patron deity, the moon god Nanna. Such multistoried temples were common in Mesopotamia, but since the gods were thought to dwell inside, only priests could ascend the side ramps to conduct ceremonies on the summit. The Tower of Babel in Genesis 11 may have been a ziggurat.
©Kaufingdude (Wikimedia Commons, CC-SA 3.0)

A genealogy often called the Table of Nations (Gen 10) brings the No-ahic era to a close just as Adam's genealogy did. But Gen 11:1–9 actually reports the well-known episode of the Tower of Babel (or Babylon), an event that chronologically preceded the spread of Noah's descendants in the table. The enormous tower that has captured the imagination of artists for centuries in reality probably resembled the large, rectangular, stepped structures called *ziggurats* that towered over many Mesopotamian cities in the 3rd millennium BCE, many topped by temples. Only the division of the monolingual crowd into language groups caused them to disperse geographically (cf. Gen 10) and, in so doing, at last to obey God's command to "fill the earth and subdue it" (1:28 TNIV). Finally, as the Primeval History closes, two other genealogies narrow its focus even further: the first elaborates on Shem's descendants, the Shemites (11:10–26), while the second follows one specific Shemite branch, the family line of Terah, father of Abram (11:27–32). This sets the scene for the story of Abram and his descendants, the story that preoccupies the OT and is told among Arabs and Jews even today.

Other Ancient Accounts of the Creation and Flood

Israel is not the only nation with a story about creation and a catastrophic flood. Both Mesopotamia and Egypt have stories that tell how the universe originated. Like the biblical account, they seek to understand the nature and purpose of the world as their readers knew it (see Table 4.1). The best-known account, the Enuma Elish from Babylon, dates to at least 1700 BCE. It is polytheistic, and conspiracies and conflicts between the gods are central to its story. Some main features of the universe originate by a pregnant god's giving them birth. The whole story honors its hero, the god Marduk, who defeats other gods, holds back the waters threatening the earth, and establishes day and night and the annual seasons. He also molds clay into the form of a human, whose purpose is to relieve the gods of all daily dirty work.

Though lesser known, Egyptian creation stories in some ways more closely resemble Gen 1–2 than does the Enuma Elish. They begin with an infinite, lifeless sea out of which emerged a pyramid-shaped mound, symbol of the emergence of life from primeval chaos. One story tells how the sun-god Ra reposed beneath the primeval waters, leaving the surface shrouded in darkness, then emerged from a mound, lighting the landscape with the first-ever sunrise. In another version, a series of births by gods created the physical universe (i.e., the gods of air, moisture, and earth). Humans originate in the tears of joy that Ra sheds when reunited with two of his divine children after a period of separation and estrangement.

Did the Torah borrow its creation account from the Egyptians and/or the Babylonians? In our view, probably not. Granted, as Table 4.1 shows, the stories share some common ideas (i.e., preexistent waters, a hard heav-

Table 4.1. Ancient Creation Accounts Compared

Motif	Enuma Elish	Egyptian Stories	Genesis 1–2
CREATION . . .			
By many gods	Yes	Yes	No
By conflict among gods	Yes	Yes	No
By divine command	No	Yes	Yes
By divine birth	Yes	Yes	No
With preexistent waters	Yes	Yes	Yes
With a hard firmament	Yes	Yes	Yes
To establish days/seasons	Yes		Yes
HUMANITY . . .			
Gods' menial servants	Yes	Yes	No
Made of dirt and breath	No	Yes	Yes

enly firmament, creation by divine commands, etc.). But those shared ideas probably go back to the rich ANE culture on which the various accounts drew and in which they arose. Two motifs set the biblical account apart from its parallels, however: the actions of a single god, not of many gods, create the universe, and no struggles disrupt or complicate God's sovereign actions.

As for the flood, one copy of Tablet XI of the Gilgamesh Epic (Babylon, ca. 700 BCE) resembles the account of Gen 6–9 most closely. It features a god instructing someone to build a huge vessel so that he, his family and friends, and the animals will survive a catastrophic flood. In one Egyptian account, by contrast, the paranoid sun-god Ra commands the goddess Hathor to wipe out humanity. But the slaughter floods the Nile and the ocean with bloody water, and the sight so shocks Ra that he acts to end it, leaving survivors that again start the human race.

READING

Read Gen 1–11 and formulate answers to the following questions:

1. Read Gen 1.
   a. List what you think are its main teachings about creation. One clue: look for words or phrases that are repeated.

b. What is the logic of the sequence of creation events?

c. Comment on what you think the seven-day structure contributes to the chapter's meaning.

d. Who are the main characters, and what role(s) do they play?

2. Read Gen 2–3.

a. What are the differences between this second creation report and that of ch. 1?

b. Describe the development of the plot of these chapters. How does ch. 1 set the scene for chs. 2–3? How do chs. 2–3 follow up ch. 1?

3. Read Gen 6–9.

a. What does the author say are the causes of the flood? What was it intended to accomplish?

b. What is it about Noah that qualifies him to be the flood story's hero? What do you think of him?

c. How (if at all) does God's covenant with Noah (ch. 9) relate to the mandates God issues for humans in Gen 1?

d. Summarize the impression of God's nature and character with which the story leaves you. What challenges or promises do you take away for your own life?

e. Read Isa 54:7–10; Ezek 14:14, 20; Matt 24:37–38; Heb 11:7; 1 Pet 3:18–22; 2 Pet 2:5, 9. List the themes that Noah and/or the flood echo in later biblical writers' works.

4. Read Gen 11.

a. Looking back over Gen 1–11, connect the dots that link them: in your own words, paraphrase the story that those chapters develop.

b. What do you learn about God, the creation, and humanity and its history?

c. What do those chapters say to you?

BIBLIOGRAPHY

Arnold, Bill T. "The Genesis Narratives." Pages 23–45 in *Ancient Israel's History: An Introduction to Issues and Sources*. Edited by Bill T. Arnold and Richard S. Hess. Grand Rapids: Baker Academic, 2014.

Atkinson, David J. *The Message of Genesis 1–11: The Dawn of Creation.* TBST. Leicester: Inter-Varsity Press, 1990.

Blenkinsopp, Joseph. *Creation, Un-creation, Re-creation: A Discursive Commentary on Genesis 1–11.* London: T&T Clark, 2011.

Day, John. *From Creation to Babel: Studies in Genesis 1–11.* LHBOTS 592. London: Bloomsbury, 2013.

Hess, Richard S., and David T. Tsumura, eds. *"I Studied Inscriptions from before the Flood": Ancient Near Eastern, Literary, and Linguistic Approaches to Genesis 1–11.* Sources for Biblical and Theological Study. Winona Lake, IN: Eisenbrauns, 1994.

Hoffmeier, James K., et al., eds. *Genesis: History, Fiction, or Neither? Three Views on the Bible's Earliest Chapters.* Grand Rapids: Zondervan, 2015.

Kikawada, Isaac M. *Before Abraham Was: The Unity of Genesis 1–11.* Nashville: Abingdon, 1985.

Lim, Johnson T. K. *Grace in the Midst of Judgment: A Grappling with Genesis 1–11.* BZAW 314. Berlin: de Gruyter, 2002.

Lowery, Daniel D. "Toward a Poetics of Genesis 1–11: Reading Genesis 4:17–22 in Its Near Eastern Context." BBRSup 7. Winona Lake, IN: Eisenbrauns, 2013.

Mathews, Kenneth A. *Genesis.* NAC 1A–1B. Nashville: Broadman & Holman, 1996–2005.

Rogerson, John W. *Genesis 1–11.* OTG. Sheffield: JSOT Press, 1991.

Walton, John H. *The Lost World of Adam and Eve: Genesis 2–3 and the Human Origins Debate.* Downers Grove, IL: InterVarsity Press, 2015.

5 THE BOOK OF GENESIS 12–50

ca. 2000–1500: the patriarchal period

ca. 1600: Jacob's migration to Egypt

ca. 1600–1500: deaths of Jacob and Joseph

THE FOCUS OF THE GENESIS story now narrows to a specific Shemite family line and its trinity of famous ancestors—Abraham, Isaac, and Jacob. (For the dates of the Patriarchal History, see the next section below.) Abraham and Jacob receive the fullest treatments, probably because of the specific honor the Israelites accorded the pair. Isaac's short account lays a literary bridge between the two longer sections, affirms the ethnic continuity across the generations, and confirms that the patriarchal covenant and its promises remain in effect. On the other hand, two family members, Ishmael (25:12-18) and Esau (or Edom), each found an ethnic offshoot of the Israelites in territory outside the heartland of Canaan. Of the two, only the Edomites, who settled closer to Canaan (south of the Dead Sea), later intersect with Israelite history.

The patriarchal narratives have two major sections:

1. The Lives of the Ancestors (Gen 12-36)—story tracks . . .
   a. How Abram/Abraham migrated from Mesopotamia to Canaan, became rich, and bought his family's first land in Hebron (12:1-25:11)
   b. How Ishmael, though legally Abraham's firstborn, was destined to life as a desert nomad because of Sarah's jealousy toward him and his mother, Hagar (25:12-18)

c. How Isaac fathered rambunctious twin boys (Esau and Jacob) and, in his old age, fell victim to an inheritance scheme of his wife Rebekah and their younger son (25:19–27:46)

d. How her co-conspirator, Jacob, ran away from home to escape Esau's revenge but returned later, the wealthy father of twelve sons and one daughter (chs. 28–35).

e. How Esau settled in the land of Edom and fathered many descendants, including a line of kings (ch. 36)

2. The Story of Joseph (Gen 37–50) reports . . .

a. How Joseph's jealous brothers cruelly sold him into slavery in Egypt

b. How in Egypt Joseph found surprising success and became a nobleman

c. How famine in Canaan reunited Joseph, his father, and his brothers in Egypt

d. How Jacob's descendants remained and prospered in Egypt

What Was Going On Back Then?

When did the ancestors live? The absence of specific chronological data denies us a firm answer, but they probably lived in the first half of the second millennium (2000–1500 BCE). In Mesopotamia, their ancestral homeland, that was a time of political flux and instability. Major cities in Sumer warred with each other for regional supremacy, and two major waves of invasions swept the region. About 2000 BCE, the Amorites, the ethnic group of the later famous ruler Hammurabi, came from the west to conquer and rule the area. About 1600 BCE, Hurrians entered Mesopotamia from the north and conquered northern Mesopotamia. From the human standpoint, one wonders whether such regional instability contributed to Abram's departure from Ur (Gen 11:31).

Meanwhile, in Egypt under the Middle Kingdom dynasty centered at Memphis, political stability prevailed, and prosperity blossomed. The peace and prosperity enabled art and literature to flourish there and may also explain why, when famine hit Canaan, the patriarchs went to Egypt rather than Transjordan or Mesopotamia. As for Canaan and the region of Syria-Palestine, no written records have surfaced yet to tell us what was going on there. The culture was predominantly Canaanite, with population centers primarily along the Mediterranean coast and in the Jordan Valley. Important city-states at the time were Hazor north of the Sea of Galilee,

HITTITES

TAURUS MTS.

Tarsus

Carchemish

Haran

YAMHAD

Alalakh

Aleppo

AMURRU

Ugarit

Ebla

Hamath

Kadesh

Tadmor

Cyprus

Byblos

Mediterranean Sea

SYRIAN
DESERT

Sidon

Damascus

Tyre

▲ Mt. Hermon

Hazor

Megiddo

CANAAN

Jordan R.

Shechem

Jerusalem

Rabbah (Amman)

Gaza

Beersheba

Zoan (Tanis)

Rameses
(Avaris)

EGYPTIANS

Ezion-geber

MIDIANITES

SINAI

Mt. Sinai? ▲

N

| 0 | 50 | 100 Miles |
| 0 | 50 | 100 Kilometers |

Jericho near the Jordan River, and Gezer in the western lowlands. By contrast, Canaan's central mountains were sparsely inhabited, a fact that may explain why the Israelite ancestors primarily settled there (think "Shechem" [Gen 33–34]).

What Kind of Literature Are These Narratives?

Genesis 12–50 features a unique genre that we call *family history*. It doesn't recount the great achievements of fabled kings or the profound teachings of revered priests; it narrates the lives of the ancestors of the original audience of Genesis, the Israelites. We might even describe these chapters as the Israelites' "ancestral memories"—the stories of their ancestors and ancestresses remembered, retold often, and passed down from generation to generation. Several specific literary features typify them. First, they are quite episodic: many of them can stand by themselves, even as they are now set in a larger narrative. Together, this family history comprises a collection of separate episodes involving the same character(s). You may even notice that some episodes involving characters a generation apart feature similar situations, settings, and narrative structures. For example, the betrothals of Isaac to Rebekah and Jacob to Rachel occur through chance meetings at wells (Gen 24; 29; cf. Exod 2). Robert Alter suggests that these similar scenes invoke a well-known literary convention, the betrothal type scene.

These ancestral stories also share a common web of important themes:

1. God's promise of blessing
2. A lifestyle of wandering
3. Occasional, unexpected appearances by God
4. Recurrent childlessness that threatens the promise
5. Departure from the cultural norm of primogeniture

Evocative proper names and symbolic name changes also figure prominently. Revered Ancestor (Abram) becomes Ancestor of Many Nations (Abraham), and Sarai becomes Princess (Sarah), to symbolize their grand, new historical destiny (Gen 17:5–6, 15–16). Laughter (Isaac) recalls how his parents found the notion that postmenopausal, old Sarah would get pregnant just too funny. Jacob (Heel-Grabber) remembers how he hoodwinked his brother and father-in-law, and Israel (perhaps God-Fights) that he survived a wrestling match with God. In short, among later generations the names would evoke memories of that cast of characters familiar from stories passed down over time.

Are They Historical?

It is a fact that Abraham, Isaac, Jacob, and Joseph left behind no written traces of themselves except for what we have in the Bible. An Egyptian record (925 BCE) lists a place called the "Enclosure of Abram" in the Negev of Canaan, an area certainly frequented by both Abraham and Isaac. But that's the only possible ancient extrabiblical mention of any of the four ancestors. There are, thus, many readers who regard them as ancient ideal figures invented by later writers rather than historical persons. On the other hand, we should remember that, as someone has said, the "absence of evidence is not evidence of absence." The lack of evidence only means that ancient sources offer no external confirmation of the Bible's claim that they existed. They are not the only ancient persons or clans whose names survive in only one literary tradition from antiquity.

Several things, however, commend the patriarchs as actual ancient persons and their stories as historical. Their names certainly compare with names typical of the second millennium BCE but not of the following era. The family stories also reflect customs typical of that same period, as do their semi-nomadic lifestyle (i.e., periods of both settlement and movement) and their location primarily in central Canaan. Table 5.1 shows the motifs that the patriarchal stories, for the most part, have in common. Each motif emphasizes a particular theological theme in Genesis. For example, infertility commonly occasions God's direct intervention so that a wife con-

Table 5.1. Shared Motifs in the Patriarchal Stories

Motif	Abram/Abraham Sarai/Sarah	Isaac Rebekah	Jacob/Israel Leah, Rachel
Infertility	Gen 11:30	Gen 25:21	Gen 29:31
Altar Building	Gen 12:7–8; 13:18; 22:9	Gen 26:25	Gen 33:20; 35:7
Famine	Gen 12:10	Gen 26:1	Gen 42:5
Wife-Sister Confusion	Gen 12:10–20; ch. 20	Gen 26:7–11	—
Divine Protection	Gen 12:17; 20:3–7	—	Gen 31:24, 29, 42
Prosperity	Gen 13:2; 24:35	Gen 26:12–13	Gen 30:43; 31:1

ceives, and two divine interventions with the wife-sister confusion result in an increased patriarchal prosperity. Such moments confirm that God is beginning to fulfill the blessings promised. Altar-building at patriarchal stopping places in Canaan constitutes acts of worship that live out the patriarchs' unique, close relationship with God. In two cases, famines drive patriarchs from the promised land to survive in Egypt (12:10; 42:5; cf. 26:1), and that survival further attests God's protection of the patriarchal line. Their sojourns in Egypt also anticipate the historic, memorable events that Abram is told about (15:13–14) and that the book of Exodus narrates.

The Story

Genesis 12:1–25:18: The Abraham and Sarah Stories

In Programmatic Text #1, God sends the Revered Ancestor (Abram) to Canaan and promises him an astounding destiny—a great nation, blessings, and fame (compare Heb 11:8; *programmatic* means that a text guides God's program for humanity throughout the Bible). Genesis 12 and 20 (two wife-sister confusion scenes) sound the theme that Abram and Sarai now enjoy God's special protection and provision of wealth. In Gen 17 Yahweh joins with Abram in a covenant relationship that formalizes the promises (see also Gen 15; see our ch. 6 below on Exodus, concerning covenants and a land promise). New names signal the expanded destinies of Abraham (Father of Many Nations) and Sarah (Princess), and from now on a new ritual (circumcision) initiates newborn males into the covenant, a tradition still practiced today. The story's very elderly protagonists laugh at the theme about a promised son, but God has the last laugh in Gen 21 when, incredibly, the two bring Laughter (Isaac) into the world! Alas, in Gen 22 God demands the slaughter of the young boy Isaac as a test of Abraham's faith, but his radical, unwavering trust in God in that moment elevates him forever as the paradigm of true faith (cf. 15:6; Rom 4; Gal 3; Heb 11:8–12). Finally, Sarah's death in Gen 23 leads Abraham to buy a burial plot for her near Hebron—the first piece of Israelite-owned property in Canaan—where Isaac and Ishmael later bury Abraham himself (Gen 25). The two sons symbolize that God's promise

PROGRAMMATIC TEXT #1

The Lord had said to Abram, "Go from your country, your people and your father's household to the land I will show you. I will make you into a great nation, and I will bless you; I will make your name great, and you will be a blessing. I will bless those who bless you, and whoever curses you I will curse; and all peoples on earth will be blessed through you." (Gen 12:1–3 TNIV) to Abraham comes true, in part: he leaves behind two major ethnic family lines and title to at least a small piece of the promised land.

Genesis 25:19–27:46: The Isaac and Rebekah Stories

Isaac and Rebekah mark a bridge between the longer stories of Abraham-Sarah and Jacob-Leah-Rachel (Gen 12:1-25:11; chs. 28–36). The recurrence of several important motifs strongly links the stories of the first two patriarchs and somewhat links them with the stories of Jacob (see Table 5.1 above).

Partial view of the Iron Age remains of Tel Beersheba, located just outside the modern city of the same name. In the northern Negev, Beersheba plays an important role in the stories of Abraham, Isaac, and Jacob. ©*Daniel Baránek (Wikimedia Commons, CC-SA 2.5)*

Pregnancy eluded Abraham and Sarah for decades, but in Gen 25 God quickly answers Rebekah's plea for fertility, leaving rambunctious twins jostling in her womb and a prophecy that the second-born (Jacob) would rule his brother (Esau). In Gen 27, parental favoritism and fraternal competition between the grownup brothers make the Isaac-Rebekah story the tale of a very dysfunctional family—an ancient version of *Mad Men* or *Ashamed*. Ultimately, the dysfunction comes to a head when Rebekah and Jacob cleverly dupe old, blind Isaac into bestowing on Jacob the traditional patriarchal blessing—the rights and duties of a firstborn heir. To escape Esau's fury, Rebekah packs Jacob off to her brother Laban in Mesopotamia under the cover story that "back home" (subtext: where Rebekah originally came from) Jacob might find a nice wife rather than marry a local Hittite, as Esau did.

Genesis 28–36: The Jacob, Leah, and Rachel Stories

We call the third and final patriarch the ethnic ancestor of the Israelites. In a sense, Jacob's life brackets the rest of Genesis: he's clearly the star of Gen 28-36, cedes center stage to his son Joseph (Gen 37-46), and then reappears in Gen 47-50 to bless the next generation before he dies.

Rachel Hiding the Idols from Her Father Laban (Gen 31), by Giovanni Battista Tiepolo. 1724–29.

Appearances to Jacob by Yahweh at a town called Bethel frame Jacob's story (chs. 28, 35). In between, chs. 29–30 tell a soap-opera-like scenario in Mesopotamia between Jacob and his wily Uncle Laban. Jacob acquires two wives, Leah and Rachel (his real love), who along with their maidservants bear him twelve sons, and twice the Heel-Grabber (what "Jacob" means) even outwits his conniving uncle. Genesis 32 remembers a life-changing event en route to Canaan—an eerie, mysterious wrestling match with "a man" (actually, an angel) that Jacob wins. He thus earns a new name, Israel (i.e., "God Fights"), and status as the ethnic ancestor of "the Israelites." In Gen 35, back at Bethel, God reaffirms his promise and officially recognizes the new name, but later, en route south to Hebron, Rachel dies while birthing son number twelve, Benjamin. Fittingly, Gen 35–36 summarizes God's blessing on Jacob in Mesopotamia, shows his reconciliation with Esau as they bury Isaac at Hebron, and recounts Esau's family history, including a list of Edomite kings as further evidence that the Abrahamic promises are being fulfilled (see Gen 17:6, 16; 35:11). Interestingly, the designation of a single successor among his thirteen children is now unnecessary. All Jacob's children belong to the chosen people, so the new question for the Torah is: who will emerge as their leaders?

"Household Gods"

The "household gods" that Rachel secretly steals from her father and carries to Canaan (Gen 31) may be small images of ancestors thought to be good-luck charms. They probably are among the items that Jacob later buries at Shechem (Gen 35:4).

Genesis 37–50: Joseph's Story

With the life of Joseph, the long family saga of Genesis ends. His story marks the longest section within Gen 12–50 and for the first time features a patriarch's son who is not his father's heir-designate. Literarily, the story spotlights the tribes of Judah and Joseph's son Ephraim (Gen 38; 43–44; 46:28; 48) and moves back and forth between Canaan and Egypt. Theologically, it reflects the influence of the cause-and-effect principle of wisdom literature and uniquely presents God as, for the most part, working unobserved behind the scenes.

Fraternal jealousy drives the brothers to sell Joseph into slavery in Egypt. Genesis 39 highlights an important theme: Joseph's impressive success in Egypt as a slave and even as a prisoner incarcerated unjustly. Chapters 41–43 headline additional success two years later: his interpretation of Pharaoh's dreams wins him a royal appointment as Vice-Pharaoh, and his wise administration of Egypt's unstable food supply saves Egypt and also his own family. When his brothers come to buy food, they don't recognize him, so during each visit he sternly trifles with them to detect any sign of remorse regarding the way they had mistreated him. In Gen 44–45 Joseph finally identifies himself, reassuring his brothers with the Joseph story's key theme: God's providential turning of their "evil" deed into a "good" outcome, his family's survival (see also Gen 50). Chapter 46 recounts how Jacob and his sons, at Joseph's urging and with Pharaoh's help, emigrate to Egypt and settle in the lush grasslands of Goshen. Finally, like a prophet, in ch. 49 Jacob pronounces the future destiny of each of his twelve sons—some positive, some negative—and then dies. Chapter 50 describes the solemn, state-sponsored funeral pilgrimage that honors Jacob's wish to be buried in the family gravesite in Canaan (see ch. 23). Later, the Israelites honor Joseph's similar desire by embalming and storing (but not burying) his body for later transport and burial in Canaan (see Exod 13:19; Josh 24:32; cf. Gen 33:19).

READING

Read Gen 12–50 and supply answers to the following questions:

1. Which character (male or female) did you find yourself relating to (or perhaps reacting against) most? Explain why you think that character so affected you and what you learned from that person.

2. List the things that these stories have taught you about God and the ways he relates to people. In what way (if any) has this affected your own relationship with God?

3. What do you observe about the women in the stories? Describe how you see God connecting with them. What questions or concerns do their stories raise for you? What do you learn from their stories about what it means to be a woman today?

4. What picture of family life do you think the stories portray? What problems do you observe, and what can the stories teach us about family life today? In what ways might you even consider them to be exemplary? Describe God's relationship to the families and what our family life can learn from them.

5. What's your impression of the way the stories treat ethnic groups outside the so-called "chosen people"? How do they portray God's relationship to them? What attitudes toward other peoples do the stories seek to cultivate in readers? With what concerns do they leave you?

6. Looking back, how (if at all) do you think Gen 1–11 prepared you to read the stories of Gen 12–50? What do you think these main sections of Genesis have in common? In what way(s) do you think they differ?

7. Read Acts 7:2–16, Rom 4:3–22, and Heb 6:13–20. List the memories of the patriarchs that these passages include. What lesson(s) do the passages underscore that speak to later readers, including yourself?

8. What do the stories in Gen 12–50 contribute to your understanding of God's mission in the world today?

BIBLIOGRAPHY

Alter, Robert. *The Art of Biblical Narrative*. New York: Basic Books, 1983.
Baldwin, Joyce G. *The Message of Genesis 12–50: From Abraham to Joseph*. TBST. Leicester: Inter-Varsity Press, 1986.
Blenkinsopp, Joseph. *Treasures Old and New: Essays in the Theology of the Pentateuch*. Grand Rapids: Eerdmans, 2004.

Brueggemann, Walter. *Genesis*. IBC. Louisville: Westminster John Knox, 1982.

Cohn, Robert L. "Narrative Structure and Canonical Perspective in Genesis." *JSOT* 25 (1983): 3-16.

Evans, Craig A., Joel N. Lohr, and David L. Petersen, eds. *The Book of Genesis: Composition, Reception, and Interpretation*. VTSup 152. Leiden: Brill, 2012.

Fisher, Loren R. *Genesis, a Royal Epic: Introduction, Translation, and Notes*. Eugene, OR: Cascade, 2011.

Friedman, Richard E. *Commentary on the Torah*. San Francisco: HarperSanFrancisco, 2001.

Hamilton, Victor P. *The Book of Genesis*. 2 vols. NICOT. Grand Rapids: Eerdmans, 1990, 1995.

Hess, Richard S., Gordon J. Wenham, and Philip E. Satterthwaite, eds. *He Swore an Oath: Biblical Themes from Genesis 12-50*. Carlisle: Paternoster; Grand Rapids: Baker Books, 1994.

Kitchen, Kenneth A. "Founding Fathers or Fleeting Phantoms: The Patriarch." Pages 313-72 in *On the Reliability of the Old Testament*. Grand Rapids: Eerdmans, 2003.

Mann, Thomas W. *The Book of the Torah: The Narrative Integrity of the Pentateuch*. Atlanta: John Knox, 1988.

Martin, Oren R. *Bound for the Promised Land: The Land Promise in God's Redemptive Plan*. New Studies in Biblical Theology 34. Nottingham: Inter-Varsity Press, 2015.

Mathews, Kenneth A. *Genesis*. NAC 1A-1B. Nashville: Broadman & Holman, 1996, 2005.

Moberly, R. W. L. *Genesis 12-50*. OTG. Sheffield: JSOT Press, 1992.

———. *The Theology of the Book of Genesis*. Old Testament Theology. Cambridge: Cambridge University Press, 2009.

Wenham, Gordon J. *Genesis 16-50*. WBC 2. Dallas: Word, 1994.

Westermann, Claus. *Genesis: A Commentary*. Translated by John J. Scullion. CC. Minneapolis: Augsburg, 1984-1986.

———. *Genesis: An Introduction*. Translated by John J. Scullion. Minneapolis: Fortress, 1992.

6 THE BOOK OF EXODUS

Important Dates for Exodus

1500–1069: New Kingdom pharaohs (18th and 19th dynasties) rule Egypt

ca. 1280: the exodus

THE NAME *EXODUS* IN OUR Bibles retains the title first given to the book in the Greek Bible (*exodus*, meaning a "going out, departure"), which is a reference to the book's main event (see below). In Exodus, the intimate family history of Genesis gives way to the national epic of the Israelites—the series of events that determine their identity and purpose as a people. Cosmic conflicts between competing gods and between an ancient and an emerging nation drive a story plot unbelievably dramatic and gigantic in scale. This book is home to some of the Bible's best-known stories and best-known words. In Exodus we meet the first section of law embedded in the narrative, a unique feature of the Torah noted earlier.

Exodus narrates what we commonly call *the exodus*—Israel's dramatic salvation experience, including liberation from Egyptian slavery and marriage to Yahweh as his own people at Sinai. The exodus figures prominently in Israelite Credos, short summaries of their formative history (see Table 6.1), and echoes in the teaching of psalmists and the preaching of prophets (e.g., Ps 78:12-16; Hos 11:1-4). Indeed, in the prophets a reverse exodus (i.e., a return to Egypt) becomes a metaphor for the worst divine judgment imaginable (e.g., Hos 9:3; 11:5) while a second exodus (i.e., a return from exile to the promised land) inspires hope (Isa 40:3-5; 55:12-13; Ezek 20:33-44). Most important, however, the book of Exodus marks the debut of Moses, the historic leader who guides the march from Egypt through

Table 6.1. Echoes of the Exodus in Credos

Deuteronomy 26	Joshua 24
My father was a wandering Aramaean, and he went down into Egypt with a few people and lived there and became a great nation, powerful and numerous. But the Egyptians mistreated us and made us suffer, subjecting us to harsh labor. Then we cried out to the LORD, the God of our ancestors, and the LORD heard our voice and saw our misery, toil and oppression. So the LORD brought us out of Egypt with a mighty hand and an outstretched arm, with great terror and with signs and wonders. (vv. 5–8 TNIV)	. . . but Jacob and his family went down to Egypt. Then I sent Moses and Aaron, and I afflicted the Egyptians by what I did there, and I brought you out. When I brought your people out of Egypt, you came to the sea, and the Egyptians pursued them with chariots and horsemen as far as the Red Sea. But they cried to the LORD for help, and he put darkness between you and the Egyptians; he brought the sea over them and covered them. You saw with your own eyes what I did to the Egyptians. Then you lived in the wilderness for a long time. (vv. 4–7 TNIV)

Sinai to the Jordan River. Fittingly, the Torah bears his name ("the Torah of Moses") and ends with an editor's eulogy extolling his unparalleled greatness (Deut 34). Of all the famous OT figures, only he and Elijah the prophet appear with Jesus on the Mount of Transfiguration (Matt 17; Mark 9), and the Hall of Faith in Heb 11 rightly accords his faithful life in-depth treatment (vv. 24–28).

In short, the exodus forever defines the Israelites' unique identity and shapes their national ethos: they are a unique ethnic group (the Israelites) with a unique story (a free people of former slaves) and a unique religious community exclusively bound to Yahweh (the covenant). The Instruction of Moses (or Torah) that debuts in Exodus cultivates the same loyal promise-keeping and passion for justice and mercy that produced the people's own liberation. Carol Meyers writes (p. xv) that Exodus is arguably the most important book in the Bible; we would certainly rank it as one of the Bible's most important books.

What Was Going On Back Then?

Like Genesis, Exodus lacks specific chronological data and even omits the pharaoh's name, but Moses and the Israelites probably lived in Egypt in ca. 1500–1200 BCE. At that time Egypt remained the preeminent political and

The Seventh Plague of Egypt, by John Martin. 1823.

cultural center it had become after 2,500 years of history. In approximately 400 BCE, the Greek historian Herodotus, a onetime visitor to Egypt, applauded Egypt's greatness:

> It has more wonders in it than any country in the world and more works that are beyond description than anywhere else. (Herodotus, *The Histories*, 2.35)

Chronologically, events in Exodus probably play out during the New Kingdom period (1550–1069 BCE), the time of political stability and economic prosperity that followed two centuries of chaos and economic stagnation.

Ironically, this healthy transition (from an Egyptian perspective) may account for how the generous treatment under Joseph's pharaoh turned horribly sour under a later one. About 1650 BCE, a line of foreign rulers called the Hyksos (pronounced "HICK-sauce")—Semites like the Israelites—began to rule Northern Egypt from their capital in the Nile Delta. Their rule seemed very "Egyptian" (it incorporated many existing governmental and cultural practices), but the Hyksos also enriched Egypt by introducing new crops and advances in military and metallurgical technology (the horse and chariot, for example). These advances enabled New Kingdom pharaohs to establish the ancient world's first great empire stretching from Nubia (southern Egypt) to the Euphrates River in North Syria and including hegemony over nearby Canaan. Eventually, native Egyptians who ruled Southern Egypt from their capital at Thebes successfully drove out the Hyksos and reunited Egypt in ca. 1570 BCE. Granted, neither Genesis nor Exodus betrays any awareness of this history, but it may be the backstory behind the positive welcome of one (Semitic) pharaoh based near Goshen and the strong antipathy of the xenophobic, oppressive pharaoh(s) that Moses confronts.

Interestingly, one controversial pharaoh, Amenhotep IV (ca. 1379–1362), launched a religious revolution that compelled Egyptians, who had previously worshiped various gods, to worship only the sun-god Aten. The king renamed himself Akhenaten (pronounced "a-KEN-a-tin" or "servant of the Aten"), the name he also assigned his new capital in central Egypt (later called Amarna). When he died, however, his successor strongly repudiated Akhenaten's revolution, returned the capital to Thebes, and reestablished traditional Egyptian polytheism. It is pure speculation to suggest that this Egyptian monotheism-like impulse in any way influenced Moses or the Torah's theme of the exclusive worship of Yahweh, but it is at least an intriguing coincidence. (See below for the specific dating and location of the exodus event itself.)

Carved sculpture of Moses in St. George's Collegiate Church, Tübingen, Germany. The "horns" reflect the Vulgate's mistranslation of the verb "to shine" in Exodus 34:29 – the translator states that "Moses did not know his face was horned after conversation with the LORD."
©LepoRello (Wikimedia Commons, CC-SA 3.0)

The Story

Exodus has two main parts:

1. The Great Escape (Exod 1–15) relates . . .
   a. How Pharaoh cruelly oppresses the Israelites and how Yahweh calls Moses to liberate them (1–6)
   b. How Yahweh trounces Pharaoh in the Ten Awesome Blows contest so he'll free the enslaved Israelites (7–12)
   c. How Moses miraculously leads the Israelites to freedom across the Red Sea (13–15)

2. The Great Sinai Transactions, Part 1 (Exod 16–40), tell . . .
   a. How Yahweh and Moses bring the Israelites from Egypt to Mount Sinai (16–19)
   b. How Yahweh and the Israelites enter into a covenant relationship (20–24)
   c. How the Israelites follow Yahweh's blueprint to construct a portable sanctuary to lead them to the promised land (25–40)

Exodus 1–15: The Great Escape

Exodus 1 opens several generations after Gen 50 with a pharaoh who knows nothing about Joseph and reads the Israelites' high birth rate—the dawn of the "great nation" promised to Abraham (Gen 12:2; 15:5)—as a serious threat to his regime. (If memory of the foreign Hyksos rulers lies in the background, the pharaonic xenophobia makes sense.) Ironically, however, to curb the birth-rate threat, the pharaoh imposes a series of ruthless measures on the Israelites but then adopts their future deliverer, Moses, into his palace family. (Moses is probably an Egyptian name that puns on the Hebrew verb "to draw out [of water].") Theologically, the divine providence that places Moses there in Egypt also later places him in the Sinai wilderness, where God calls him to return to Egypt, liberate Israel, and lead them to Sinai. That's the Great Escape.

Exodus 3–4 finds Moses tending his father-in-law's flock in Midian (northeast Saudi Arabia). Flaming bushes are a common desert phenomenon, but this strange one that burns without turning to ashes draws the curious shepherd into conversation with Yahweh himself. Strikingly, the catalyst for Moses's call is what Yahweh has himself seen (the extreme Egyptian cruelty) and heard (anguished Israelite cries), but Moses parries Yahweh's call and each follow-up promise with an excuse. Given Moses's extreme reluctance here (and

Table 6.2. Jacob and Moses: Parallel Motifs

Motif	Jacob	Moses
Crisis	Theft	Murder
Enemy	Esau	Pharaoh
Exile	Haran	Midian
Theophany	Dream at Bethel	Burning bush
Love at a well	Rebekah	Zipporah

the subsequent stiff resistance from Pharaoh and the Israelites in chs. 5–6), the supreme stature he later achieves is astonishing. Two key themes surface in these events. First, henceforth, God's name among the Israelites will be *Yahweh* (Exod 6:3; 9:16; compare its linguistic kin, "I Am," in 3:14–15) instead of *God Almighty*, as with the patriarchs. Scholars read the name change as a clue to possible literary sources that underlie the Torah. Second, God intends to stiffen Pharaoh's resistance to freeing the Israelites so that, once God's mighty power hits Pharaoh, the king himself will drive them from Egypt.

Chapters 7–12 recount Yahweh's "hits," the Ten Awesome Blows against Egypt (Table 6.3). Their twofold purpose is to show the Egyptians Yahweh's power (see 7:5, 17; 10:1–2) and to boost the Israelites' faith in their God. Blows 1–9 emphatically display Yahweh's absolute rule over creation and expose the semidivine Pharaoh as both powerless and foolish. (We call them "Blows" rather than "Plagues" because the latter term today specifically

Table 6.3. Yahweh's Ten Awesome Blows (or Plagues) against Egypt (Exodus 7–12)

Text	The Blow	Comment	Pharaoh's Response
7:15–25	1. Water to blood	Egyptian duplication	"No"
8:1–15	2. Frogs	Egyptian duplication Moses's prayer for relief	"Yes," then (after relief) "No"
8:16–19	3. Dust to gnats	No Egyptian duplication	"No"
8:20–32	4. Flies	Goshen exemption Moses's prayer for relief	"Yes, but . . . ," then (after relief) "No"
9:1–7	5. Diseased livestock	Goshen exemption	"No"
9:8–12	6. Soot to boils	Magician no-shows	"No"
9:13–35	7. Thunder, hail	Yahweh's merciful warning Goshen exemption Moses's prayer for relief	"I've sinned . . . ," then (after relief) "No"
10:1–20	8. Locusts	Yahweh's merciful warning Pharaoh: Only male attendees Moses's prayer for relief	"I've sinned . . . ," then (after relief) "No"
10:21–29	9. Darkness	Pharaoh: No flocks or herds to attend	"No." And banishment of Moses
chs. 11–12	10. Death of firstborn	Yahweh passes over obedient Israelites	Sorrowful Pharaoh releases the Israelites

Do the Blows Have Cultural Background?

Some scholars have proposed that the Blows have specific cultural background. For example, taking their cue from Exod 12:12 ("I will bring judgment on all the gods of Egypt" [TNIV]), some scholars believe that each of the Blows specifically targets (and aims to embarrass) an Egyptian god known to be associated with water, frogs, flies, and so forth. In our view, however, this seems unlikely. First, in context the "cue" text relates specifically to Blow 10, not to Blows 1-9, so to read that comment backward into the latter seems to us improper. Second, Exod 7–12 gives no explicit evidence to support our making those connections. In fact, to read into the Ten Blows a critique of various Egyptian gods may cause us to miss what the text intends to tell us.

Alternatively, for some scholars Blows 1–9 represent God's sovereign use of known natural phenomena in ancient Egypt, albeit in a miraculous way. For example, sometimes an increase in red silt from Ethiopia gives the Nile a reddish, blood-like color, and that phenomenon may explain how the river might look as though blood rather than water filled it. But the Blow would still retain traits of something miraculous: its *intensity* would far exceed the ordinary red color of the Nile phenomenon suggested; its *duration* would last longer than it would typically; Moses (not nature) would dictate the *timing* of its starting and stopping; and its *selectivity* — its targeting of Egyptians but not Israelites — would be a final trait of a miracle in this case. This approach is certainly possible, but in our view it seems simpler to accept what Exod 7 claims — that God did amazing wonders.

describes diseases [cf. Exod 15:26].) The sad, dramatic Blow 10 displays Yahweh's sovereign control over life and death and finally brings Pharaoh to his knees. Yahweh's decisive victory over Pharaoh finally liberates the Israelites from Pharaoh's cruel grip—a victory that Passover, the Feast of Unleavened Bread, and the consecration of firstborn males celebrate to this day.

Finally, chs. 13–15 narrate the exodus itself—its route, the fate of Joseph's bones, and the two clouds that visually symbolize Yahweh's guiding presence 24/7. One final, fatal hardening of Pharaoh's heart suckers him into chasing the Israelites, only to drown with his army in the Red Sea after a successful Israelite crossing. The event marks an unforgettable divine victory by Yahweh the Warrior—one momentous enough to inspire both prose and poetic accounts (see Judg 4–5). It boosts the Israelites' fear of Yahweh and confidence in Moses—a defining moment still celebrated by Jews today. The Great Escape, indeed!

The Exodus: Its Route and Date

Was the exodus historical? Testing when and where the exodus occurred results in a possible "positive" for its historicity. Here, certainty again eludes us because the locations that the Bible lists on the Israelites' itinerary are uncertain. Map 6.1 suggests four possible crossing points, but Exod 13:17 immediately eliminates the heavily traveled northern route because of its large Egyptian military presence. The middle routes would take the Israelites across one of two ancient freshwater lakes, the southern route across the northern tip of today's Gulf of Suez, which presumably in ancient times extended farther north. The latter view enjoys one terminological advantage over the other possibilities: the Bible consistently reckons the waters of both the east and west gulfs around the Sinai Peninsula as the "Red Sea."

When did the exodus probably occur? The evidence points to dates either in the 15th or the 13th century BCE (see Table 6.4), each date under a different pharaoh. The earlier date (1447 BCE) is based on 1 Kgs 6:1, which says that Solomon's fourth year (967 BCE), the year he began to build the temple, marked 480 years since the exodus. Proponents of this view argue that an early date fits best with archaeological evidence for the conquest under Joshua. Those who hold the later date (ca. 1275 BCE) cite the city name *Rameses* (Exod 1:11; 12:37) as evidence that the pharaoh of the exodus was Ramesses II (13th cent. BCE). They argue that the number in 1 Kgs 6:1 is not a chronological summary figure (i.e., twelve 40-year generations). Certainly, at the latest the exodus must precede ca. 1210 BCE, the date of the Merenptah Stela which, along with the defeated city-states in Canaan, lists a "foreign people" (not a city) called *Israel*. The context recognizes Israel as a sizable threat requiring suppression, but the hieroglyphic terminology implies a location between cities (an encampment or camps?) and a sense of foreignness. Currently, scholars for both dates invoke the inscription to support their preference.

Qetef Hinnom amulet. A tiny silver scroll amulet (ca. 600 BCE), one of two from a burial cave near Jerusalem. Written in ancient Hebrew script, they bear the oldest copy of a biblical text, the Priestly Benediction (Num 6:22–24), still used in Jewish and Christian worship today. It is now in the Israel Museum in Jerusalem. ©*Tamar Hayardeni (Wikimedia Commons)*

Exodus 16–40: The Great Sinai Transactions (Part 1)

The Exodus story's second part (but part 1 of the Great Sinai Transactions) chronicles the journey of the Israelites through the desert to Sinai (chs. 16–18), their agreement to be Yahweh's covenant people (chs. 19–24), and the

Table 6.4. The Exodus: Early versus Late Dates

	Date	Pharaoh	Dynasty
Early date	1447 BCE	Thutmose III (1479–1425)	New Kingdom 18th Dynasty
Late date	ca. 1275 BCE	Ramesses II (1279–1213)	New Kingdom 19th Dynasty

preparation of the tabernacle—the portable shrine to Yahweh that will lead them to Canaan (chs. 25–40). This part is also home to two Programmatic Texts (19:4–6; 34:5–7) and closes with Yahweh's descent from Mount Sinai (near his people) to reside in the holy tent (among them)—that is, much closer to the Israelites and for a much longer stay (ch. 40).

Sadly, as if warning later readers, the section debuts twin themes that thread their way through the Torah: the Israelites' incessant grumbling against Moses and Aaron and the hardships of desert life (chs. 16–18; cf. Deut 33:8; Ps 95:8), and Moses's mediation with Yahweh that averts disaster (cf. Num 14–17; 20; Table 8.2 in ch. 8 on Numbers below lists all such episodes). More positively, Exod 20 presents the Ten Commandments (or Decalogue; see Table 6.5), the familiar, easy-to-remember, ten-item preface to the Covenant Book (chs. 21–23; cf. Deut 5). Words 1–4 concern Israel's relationship with Yahweh, while Words 5–10 concern social relationships among Israelites. Exodus 25–27 introduces Yahweh's verbal blueprint of the tabernacle—both the central tent and its surrounding courtyard (see Diagram 6.1). It marks the site where the Israelites worship Yahweh and perform rituals that Leviticus teaches, to keep the covenant in good order.

Chapters 33–34 narrate the ultimate example of disorder—the long-remembered golden calf incident (Deut 9:16–21; Neh 9:18; Ps 106:19–20; Acts 7:41)—and another intervention by Moses with an angry Yahweh (compare with the scene's later echo in 1 Kgs 12:28). In a dramatic appearance, Yahweh movingly proclaims what the name *Yahweh* means (Programmatic Text #3), whose truth echoes elsewhere (Ps 145:8; Joel 2:13; Jonah 4:2), and announces a new covenant with Moses and the Israelites. When Moses returns to camp, he brings not only the new tablets but also, more strikingly, a face so radiant that he must wear a veil to address the Israelites (see also 2 Cor 3:13–18).

Finally, chs. 35–40 explain how Israel builds the tabernacle, per Yahweh's blueprint. A bleary-eyed Homer Simpson might yawn and dismiss the

PROGRAMMATIC TEXT #2

"You yourselves have seen what I did to the Egyptians, and how I carried you on eagles' wings and brought you to myself. So now, if you faithfully obey my voice and keep my covenant, you will be to me a precious treasured possession out of all the peoples, for the whole earth belongs to me. In your case, you will be for me a kingdom of priests and a holy nation." These are the words you are to speak to the Israelites. (Exod 19:4–6)

PROGRAMMATIC TEXT #3

Then Yahweh . . . proclaimed his name, Yahweh. . . . "Yahweh, Yahweh, a compassionate and merciful God, slow to anger and brim-full of loyalty and faithfulness, keeping his loyalty available to thousands, forgiving every kind of sin and rebellion, but holding the guilty fully accountable by punishing children and grandchildren for their parents' sins to the third and fourth generations." (Exod 34:5–7 authors' translation) endless details as "boring!" but the story includes all of it. And on New Year's Day of the second postexodus year, Yahweh dramatically moves, setting the scene for the instructions concerning proper worship at the tabernacle that the Torah's next book, Leviticus, records.

Table 6.5. The Decalogue: Exodus 20:1–17

Prologue (v. 2): Who's Speaking

verse	grammar	teaching	
3	Prohibition	1. Other Gods	
4–6	Prohibition	2. Images	Vertical
7	Prohibition	3. Abuse of God's Name	Relationships
8–11	Command	4. Sabbath	
12	Command	5. Parents	
13	Prohibition	6. Murder	
14	Prohibition	7. Adultery	Horizontal
15	Prohibition	8. Theft	Relationships
16	Prohibition	9. Perjury	
17	Prohibition	10. Envy	

Diagram 6.1. The Tabernacle (Exodus 25–27)

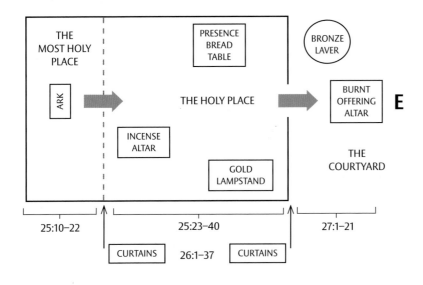

Where Is Mount Sinai?

Locating Mount Sinai requires one to arrange several puzzle pieces into a coherent picture. The primary pieces are: (1) biblical data that touch on Sinai's larger region and (2) Deut 1:2, which states, "[It] takes eleven days to go from Horeb to Kadesh Barnea by the Mount Seir road" (TNIV). This would require each potential site to: (a) fall within an eleven-day journey to Kadesh, (b) have plenty of water and pasturelands, and (c) offer enough open space for the Israelite camp. Concerning (1), Moses first visited Mount Sinai during his exile in Midian (northwest Saudi Arabia), and other biblical data associate the name *Sinai* geographically with Edom and Seir (southeast of the Dead Sea and just north of Midian). Certainly, ancient roads connected Egypt with the Edom-Midian region, so many scholars have proposed a site in northwestern Arabia as a possibility (Jebel al-Lawz, marked "Mt. Sinai [proposed]" on the map on p. 71). At twenty miles per day, however, the trip there would take about fifteen days, the farthest site from Egypt—perhaps too long a distance for serious consideration.

One site (Jebel Karkom) between Kadesh Barnea and Elath, on the east side of the Sinai Peninsula, has also been suggested. Archaeological evidence confirms its occupation at the time of the exodus, and it has the minimum amenities listed. But it is located too close to Kadesh Barnea, which means that the time for the Israelites to travel there (see the comment in [2] above) would be shorter than eleven days; furthermore, it may be located too far from Egypt. In the western Sinai another site (Jebel Sin Bisher) meets the minimum requirements above. Its name may also echo the name *Sinai*, and the distance to Kadesh is acceptable. But its location seems too close to Egypt. Finally, Jebel Musa in the southern Sinai peninsula is the traditional site that scores of visitors climb each year. Its distances from both Egypt and Kadesh are acceptable, but it shows no archaeological traces of occupation at the time of the exodus. It also lacks the minimum amenities noted above unless one assumes (with some scholars) that the Israelites camped some distance away. Since all these sample sites have plusses and minuses, we conclude that the location of Mount Sinai is currently unknown—and will probably remain so forever.

Going out
National epic
Ten Awesome blows

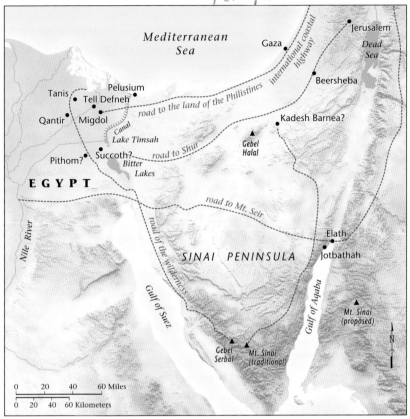

Excursus: What's This Thing Called a *Covenant*?

A *covenant* is a solemn, formal agreement to which at least two parties bind themselves in good faith by swearing an oath. Each accepts the responsibility of keeping the covenant's promises and of satisfying its stipulations. The viability of a covenant hangs on the integrity of the parties — their honesty, sincerity, good will, and the value they place on maintaining a friendly relationship with each other. A *parity covenant* unites two private parties of relatively equal status who voluntarily enter the pact: for example, the compact between David and his lifelong friend, Jonathan (1 Sam 18). At times, a covenant unites parties of *unequal social status*: for example, a king or wealthy landowner with one of his exemplary, loyal servants. At times, a militarily weak nation may form an alliance with a militarily strong nation to relieve a threat (1 Kgs 15:19). In some covenants, the oath simply voices the parties' wishes for certain consequences (good or bad) to occur if the parties keep or violate the agreement, while other covenants specifically appeal to God to enforce the parties' compliance.

Two types of covenants unite Yahweh and humans in an ongoing relationship (i.e., parties of unequal status), and each enlists a widespread ancient practice as a theological metaphor for the transaction. In the *land-grant* custom, ancient kings or wealthy landowners would reward exemplary, faithful servants with gifts of land from their properties. In Genesis, the land-grant custom seems to underlie the Abrahamic covenant — Yahweh's grant of the land of Canaan to Abraham and his descendants. Theologically, the covenant assumes Yahweh's ownership of the land being granted (perhaps his kingship as well) and honors Abraham's faithful conduct. The second covenant type is a political one, the *suzerain-vassal treaty,* which joins a politically dominant power (and its ruler, the suzerain) and its subordinate (whose ruler is a vassal). The suzerain promises (among other things) to protect the vassal from invasions by other nations in exchange for the vassal's promise not to conspire with enemies against him and periodically to pay him *tribute* (i.e., specified amounts of money and materials). The treaties initiated by the Hittites (14th–13th cent. BCE) and the Neo-Assyrians (8th–7th cent. BCE) exemplify this type of political agreement. (A translation of one Hittite treaty is available at http://ccat.sas.upenn.edu/~humm/Topics/Contracts/treat01.html. See also the sidebar here.)

Scholars believe that the suzerain-vassal treaty influenced the Israelites' concept of the covenant. If so, the Mosaic covenant assumes that Israelites are the vassals of King Yahweh, albeit a suzerain infinitely more powerful and benevolent than any Hittite or Neo-Assyrian monarch. Like the treaty prologue, biblical references to the covenants typically recount select aspects of Yahweh's history with Israel, and the Torah's legal instructions constitute the stipulations. Prophets who announce disaster or restoration trace that destiny to the Israelites' disobedience or obedience of the covenant, respectively. The disasters or triumphs that the prophets decree are thought to impose the covenant curses or blessings, respectively, corresponding to the Israelites' level of covenant compliance. The influence of ancient treaties on the Torah is most evident in the structure and content of the book of Deuteronomy, a point to which we will return below.

Basic Elements of Hittite Treaties

1. Preamble
2. Prologue (i.e., the history of the two nations' past relationship)
3. Stipulations (the "Dos" and "Don'ts")
4. Master Copy and Periodic Public Readings
5. List of Treaty Witnesses
6. Blessings and Curses

READING

Read Exod 1–40 and formulate answers to the following questions:

1. Which section or episode in the Book of Exodus particularly sticks in your mind? Explain why you think it particularly caught your attention. If it spoke to something in your own life, summarize what you heard it say.

2. Please summarize your impressions of the character of Moses in Exodus. From your perspective, evaluate his strengths and weaknesses both as a person and as a leader. What can you take away from his example?

3. List the things that Exodus has taught you about God. In what way (if any) have they affected your own relationship with God? How do they compare to what you learned in Genesis?

4. What (if anything) do you observe about the women in Exodus? Describe how you see God connecting with them. What questions or concerns do their stories raise for you? What do you learn from their stories about what it means to be a woman today?

5. What picture of family life does Exodus portray? What problems do you observe, and what can that picture teach us about family life today? Describe how God relates to God's family and what our family life, including our larger communities, can learn from that relationship.

6. What's your impression of the way Exodus treats non-Israelite ethnic groups? How does it portray God's relationship to them, and what might it teach the Israelites (and us) about how to treat other peoples? What concerns does Exodus raise for you on this topic?

7. How does Exodus contribute to the theme of God's mission in the world?

8. Read Acts 7:17–44 and Heb 11:24–29. What memories of the Israelites

and Moses do these texts recall? What implications for later readers, including yourself, do they draw?

9. Read Isa 61:6; 1 Pet 2:5, 9; and Rev 1:6. Compare their understanding of Israel's programmatic destiny with what Exodus portrays.

BIBLIOGRAPHY

Blackburn, W. Ross. *The God Who Makes Himself Known: The Missionary Heart of the Book of Exodus*. New Studies in Biblical Theology 28. Nottingham: Apollos; Downers Grove, IL: InterVarsity Press, 2012.

Bruckner, James K. *Exodus*. UTBC. Grand Rapids: Baker Books, 2008.

Childs, Brevard S. *The Book of Exodus: A Critical, Theological Commentary*. OTL. Philadelphia: Westminster, 1974.

Dozeman, Thomas B., Craig A. Evans, and Joel N. Lohr, eds. *The Book of Exodus: Composition, Reception, and Interpretation*. VTSup 164. Leiden: Brill, 2014.

Fretheim, Terence E. *Exodus*. Louisville: Westminster John Knox, 1991.

Greengus, G. "Covenant and Treaty in the Hebrew Bible and in the Ancient Near East." Pages 91–126 in *Ancient Israel's History: An Introduction to Issues and Sources*. Edited by Bill T. Arnold and Richard S. Hess. Grand Rapids: Baker Academic, 2014.

Hoffmeier, James K. *Ancient Israel in Sinai: The Evidence for the Authenticity of the Wilderness Tradition*. New York: Oxford University Press, 2005.

———. "The Exodus and Wilderness Narratives." Pages 46–90 in *Ancient Israel's History: An Introduction to Issues and Sources*. Edited by Bill T. Arnold and Richard S. Hess. Grand Rapids: Baker Academic, 2014.

———. *Israel in Egypt: The Evidence for the Authenticity of the Exodus Tradition*. New York: Oxford University Press, 1997.

———. "'These Things Happened': Why a Historical Exodus Is Essential for Theology." Pages 99–134 in *Do Historical Matters Matter to Faith? A Critical Appraisal of Modern and Postmodern Approaches to Scripture*. Edited by James K. Hoffmeier and Dennis R. Magary. Wheaton, IL: Crossway, 2012.

Kürle, S. *The Appeal of Exodus: The Characters God, Moses and Israel in the Rhetoric of the Book of Exodus*. PBM. Milton Keynes: Paternoster, 2013.

Meyers, Carol. *Exodus*. New Cambridge Bible Commentary. Cambridge: Cambridge University Press, 2005.

Miller, Patrick D. *The Ten Commandments*. Interpretation: Resources for the Use of Scripture in the Church. Louisville: Westminster John Knox, 2009.

Moberly, R. W. L. *At the Mountain of God: Story and Theology in Exodus 32–34.* JSOTSup 22. Sheffield: JSOT Press, 1983.

Sprinkle, Joe M. *The Book of the Covenant: A Literary Approach.* JSOTSup 174. Sheffield: JSOT Press, 1994.

Wood, Bryant G. "The Rise and Fall of the 13th Century Exodus-Conquest Theory." *Journal of the Evangelical Theological Society* 48 (2005): 475–89.

7 THE BOOK OF LEVITICUS

Important Dates for Leviticus

ca. 1280–1278: the law given at Mount Sinai

LEVITICUS'S TITLE DROPS THE FIRST clue about its contents and purpose. *Leviticus* is the Latin form of its title in the Greek Bible (Gk. *leuitikon*) and means "Levitical scroll"—in other words, its contents concern priests and other religious functionaries from the tribe of Levi. The rabbis nicknamed it "instruction for priests," but both that nickname and the Greek Bible's title are slightly misleading. Granted, interpreters often refer to the book's editors as "P" for their connection to priestly concerns but, in reality, Leviticus primarily concerns the religious life of ordinary Israelites. Its instructions on sacrifices, festivals, and practical ethics comprise a "Maintenance Manual" to guide the people about how to maintain their covenant relationship with Yahweh. It teaches them "best practices" for covenant faithfulness—what the covenant expects of them and how to keep the relationship in good working order. It also instructs them on "troubleshooting"—how to repair the relationship when their failure to follow those best practices causes a breakdown. Literarily, it is an anthology organized topically rather than chronologically to promote the book's main theme, holiness.

The Story: The Great Sinai Transactions (Part 2)

Leviticus follows Exodus with the Great Sinai Transactions (Part 2) in five main structural parts:

76

1. Instructions about sacrifices and offerings for God (Lev 1–7)
2. Report: the ordination of Aaron and his family as priests (8–10)
3. Instructions on "clean" and "unclean" things (11–15)
4. Instruction for Aaron on the Day of Atonement (16)
5. The detailed, comprehensive Holiness Code (17–27; and see Table 7.1 below)

The logic underlying this structure is this: the book's "troubleshooting" section (Lev 1–16) comes first because it explains how, so to speak, to restore the default settings of the Israelites' relationship with Yahweh (Lev 1–7, 11–15, 16) and designates those responsible for doing so (8–10). Of course, the Day of Atonement (16) effects the annual "master reset" for the whole nation. The final section, often described as a Holiness Code (17–27), presents the book's "best practices" section, fine-tuning the instruction of 1–16, laying out comprehensive ethical instruction, and teaching about Israel's other basic worship practices.

> **PROGRAMMATIC TEXT #4**
> I am the LORD, who brought you up out of Egypt to be your God; therefore *be holy, because I am holy.* (Lev 11:45 NIV, italics ours)

Chapters 1–6 review the five standard Israelite sacrifices and offerings, four of which require the slaughter of an animal. The term *sacrifice* is well chosen: those who offer gifts to God surrender ownership of them and their potential profits, thus "sacrificing" something of value to honor God. Here are the five types:

1. The *burnt offering* or *'olah* (ch. 1) literally means "something ascending," that is, the rising smoke and the scent of cooking meat (a modern backyard barbecue scene comes to mind). With this offering, the altar fire consumes the whole sacrifice, and its pleasing scent wins Yahweh's favor and acceptance—that is, it atones for the offerer's sins.
2. With the *grain offering* or *minhah* (ch. 2), the offerer gives God the fruit of human labor. Some of the grain goes to the priests for their personal use, and the rest is burned up as a gift to Yahweh. It always accompanies other offerings, as if to enhance the acceptability of its companion sacrifice.
3. Unique to the *shelamim* or *well-being offering* (ch. 3) are its festive, celebratory mood and its purpose: for human consumption. It is often paired with the burnt offering, as if the latter "nourished" God (theologically) and the former nourished the Israelites, who (literally)

consumed the sacrificial leftovers. It expresses thanks or pays off a vow (7:11–18).

4. The *purification offering* (*hattat*) seeks to purify an individual or the community from an unintentional sin or ritual uncleanness (ch. 4). Its ritual features the pouring of blood on the altar's sides, the burning of the animal's fat, and special disposal of the remains.

5. The *restitution offering* or *'asham* (ch. 5) is the most difficult of the five to define and to distinguish from the purification offering. The restitution offering deals with forms of impurity while the latter imposes monetary penalties for profane usage of sacred objects.

The instructions in Lev 11–15 concerning clean and unclean things mark the reader's first encounter with the book's central theme of holiness applied to common aspects of daily life (e.g., menstruation, seminal emissions): (1) Foods permitted and forbidden (ch. 11; cf. Deut 14:1–21);

Table 7.1. The Holiness Code (Leviticus 17–27)

Ch.	Audience	Topic(s)
17	Priests	Proper blood sacrifices
18	Israelites	Sexual conduct
19	Israelites	Community ethics
20	Israelites	Penalties for holiness violations
21	Priests	Violations of holiness (1–15)
	Aaron	Priestly defects (16–24)
22	Priests	"Clean" and "unclean" (1–16)
	Israelites, Priests	Acceptable offerings (17–25)
	Israelites	Proper animal sacrifices (26–33)
23	Israelites	Passover, Unleavened Bread (1–8)
		Firstfruits offering (9–22)
		Annual rest day (23–25)
		Day of Atonement (26–32)
		Feast of Tabernacles (33–44)
24	Israelites, Aaron	Lamp oil, Presence Bread (1–9)
	Israelites	Penalty for blasphemy (10–23)
25	Israelites	The Jubilee Year, other redemptions
26	Israelites	Results of obedience/disobedience
27	Israelites	Votive offerings

(2) postpartum purification (ch. 12); (3) skin diseases and household molds (ch. 13-14); (4) male and female bodily fluids (ch. 15).

Some readers may wonder why ordinary bodily functions require atonement and why people with skin diseases should become social outcasts. Concern about hygiene among the Israelites may explain some provisions (e.g., cases of contagious skin diseases), but several factors are probably in play. Anthropologist Mary Douglas proposes helpfully that purity in Israel equates to normalcy and wholeness as defined by Israel's cultural standards. The sacrificial "diet" that Israel "feeds" Yahweh (cattle, sheep, goats, birds) closely parallels the "pure" Israelite diet of the food laws, so to follow the latter is to follow Yahweh's example and to distinguish the Israelites from their neighbor nations. Both G. Wenham and J. Milgrom trace the laws to a popular association of impurities with death and purities with life. So, one may not touch a carcass or eat carnivorous birds, and normal human conditions that involve the loss of life-giving liquids (e.g., menstruation, childbirth) or the handling of blood (source of life and vitality) require legislation. In their view, these unique practices act out Israel's submission to God's sovereignty over both life and death.

Chapter 16 brings the book's troubleshooting section to a dramatic close, detailing the year's most solemn day, the Day of Atonement, held in early fall. Theologically, this annual "master reset" of the Yahweh-Israel connection effects total "atonement," a word invented in the Middle Ages by translator William Tyndale to denote the end of estrangement and the return

Holiness 101

Theologically, the Israelites' concept of holiness underlies what Lev 10–27 presents and requires a brief introduction. God is the only person or thing that is holy in and of itself; all other persons and things (reality as we know it) are by nature unholy. This is due to the wide effects of sin and to human failure ritually to cultivate or maintain purity. For example, both adultery (a sin) and touching a corpse (a cause of impurity but not a sin) leave a person ritually unclean. Holiness and sinfulness/impurity are like invisible magnetic force fields of opposite polarities affecting the world (and people) near them. Dangerous fireworks erupt when the two fields are too close, with holiness destroying its opposite. Additionally, simple contagion may spread uncleanness from one party or thing to another until ritual actions regain the lost cleanness. Typically, God shows his presence by withdrawal or separation to avoid a force-field collision, while humans head off the danger by following the Torah's teachings on how to maintain ritual purity and ritually to restore it when compromised. Finally, we should mention that a holiness gradient governs who can access tabernacle areas (for details, see ch. 6 above on Exodus). Only the high priest, who maintains the highest level of holiness, may enter its holiest place, but only annually. Other priests may safely access the holy place and the open courtyard around the tent, but ordinary Israelites may approach the courtyard and proceed no further.

to perfect unity. One striking feature of the ritual is the role played by two goats. The one designated for Yahweh is slaughtered as a sin offering (i.e., to obtain forgiveness), while the symbolic "scapegoat"—the one over whom the high priest confesses Israel's sins—survives to bear the sins outside the camp, thus ending the threat of punishment. For Christians, the scene anticipates the full atonement that the NT says Jesus Christ achieved for the whole world, and the image of the sin-bearing goat echoes in the NT theme of Jesus the sin-bearer on the cross (1 Pet 2:24; cf. Isa 53:4, 12).

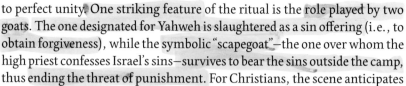

Sculpture of the high priest Aaron, now in the Metropolitan Museum of Art in New York City. France, twelfth century CE.

Chapters 17–27 present the Holiness Code, the best practices for maintaining Israel's covenant relationship with Yahweh in good order. Table 7.1 shows the wide-ranging scope of its instructions and its several addressees.

New themes that the Holiness Code (Lev 17–27) sounds include passionate condemnation of sexual violations that defile the land and potentially provoke Yahweh to throw the Israelites out (chs. 18 and 20). These chapters also presume a positive view of marriage as the proper context for sanctioned sexual intimacies. The dangers that idolatry and its related practices (e.g., divination, omen-interpretation, etc.) pose to the Israelites receive similarly harsh treatment (17:7; 19:4, 26, 31; 20:6; 26:1, 30). Behind the passionate Levitical voice runs a concern that the Israelites maintain their own unique identity and ritual purity, not succumb to the alluring, defiling legacy of the Canaanites (18:24; cf. 18:22, 26, 29, 30; 20:23). The same concern drives the broad sweep of community ethics—both civil and cultic laws—in ch. 19. We tend to equate holiness with morality, particularly sexual morality, but the chapter lists a surprising range of behaviors that cultivate holiness—for example, Sabbath observance (19:3), leaving crops for the poor to harvest (vv. 9–10), impartial justice (v. 15), frank rebukes (v. 17), respect for the elderly and foreigners (v. 32), and

Table 7.2. Annual Festival Calendar: Leviticus 23

Order	Month and Day	Modern Month	Festivals	Duration	Reference
1st	Nisan[a] 14	March/April	Passover	1 day	v. 5
	Nisan[a] 15		Unleavened Bread	7 days	vv. 6–8
	Nisan[a] 15		Wave Offering of Firstfruits	1 day	vv. 9–14
2nd	Iyar	April/May			
3rd	Sivan	May/June	Weeks	1 day	vv. 15–21
4th	Tammuz	June/July			
5th	Av	July/August			
6th	Elul	August/September			
7th	Tishri 1	September/October	Trumpets	1 day	vv. 24–25
	Tishri 10		Day of Atonement	1 day	vv. 26–32
	Tishri 15		Tabernacles	8 days	vv. 33–43
8th	Heshvan	October/November			
9th	Kislev	November/December			
10th	Tevet	December/January			
11th	Shevat	January/February			
12th	Adar	February/March			

a. The first month, Nisan, is called Aviv elsewhere in the Old Testament. See, for example, Exod 23:15 and Deut 16:1 (Table 9.2 on p. 98).

so on. Jesus ranked one provision ("love your neighbor as yourself" [v. 18]) among the two best commandments ever (Matt 22:39; Luke 10:27). Finally, ch. 23 supplies the Israelites with a religious calendar listing the important annual festivals (see Table 7.2).

In short, it is the passion for holiness that drives the strange landscape that is Leviticus Land.

READING

Read Lev 1–27 and formulate answers to the following questions:

1. What symbolism do you detect in the various sacrifices in Lev 1–7? What meaning(s) do you think each seeks to convey?

2. In your view, what is God like in Leviticus? In what way(s) does Leviticus enrich, expand, or challenge your understanding of God?

3. Describe how you see the view of women in Leviticus. In what way(s) does it enrich, expand, or challenge your understanding of God's relationship with them?

4. Discuss how (if at all) the instructions in Leviticus advance or impede God's mission in the world. Explain the reasons for your opinion.

5. Which of Moses's instructions or Israel's religious practices particularly stick in your mind? Why? In what way(s) do they cause you to reevaluate your own way of life, worship, or religious practices?

6. Read Lev 11. Which common foods does this instruction omit? Why do you think they might have been omitted?

7. Read Lev 16 and ponder the symbolic actions the high priest performs. What theological truths do they act out, and in what way(s) do they anticipate the atonement of Jesus?

8. Read Rom 3:25; Heb 9–10; and 13:11–12. Discuss what "take" (or "takes") the NT has about the Day of Atonement. What has Israel's ancient practice contributed to Christian theology and the life of faith today?

9. Read the Holiness Code (Lev 17–27). Summarize the concept of holiness you find there. In what way(s) does it change your view of holiness and challenge you to be more genuinely "holy"?

10. List the three most important things that this study of Leviticus has taught you.

BIBLIOGRAPHY

Anderson, Gary A. "Sacrifice and Sacrificial Offerings: Old Testament." Pages 870–86 in vol. 5 of *ABD*.

Douglas, Mary. *Purity and Danger: An Analysis of the Concepts of Pollution and Taboo.* London: Routledge, 2001.

Harrington, Hannah K. "Clean and Unclean." Pages 681–89 in vol. 1 of *NIDB*.

Jenson, Philip P. *Graded Holiness: A Key to the Priestly Conception of the World*. JSOTSup 106. Sheffield: JSOT Press, 1992.

Milgrom, Jacob. *Leviticus*. 3 vols. AB 3. New York: Doubleday, 1991–2001.

Redditt, Paul L. "Leviticus." Pages 52–58 in *Theological Interpretation of the Old Testament: A Book-by-Book Survey*. Edited by Kevin J. Vanhoozer. Grand Rapids: Baker Academic, 2008.

Sklar, Jay. *Leviticus: An Introduction and Commentary*. TOTC. Downers Grove, IL: InterVarsity Press, 2014.

Wenham, Gordon J. *The Book of Leviticus*. NICOT. Grand Rapids: Eerdmans, 1979.

———. "The Theology of Unclean Food." *Evangelical Quarterly* 53 (1981): 6–15.

Wright, David P. "Holiness, Holy: Old Testament." Pages 237–48 in vol. 3 of *ABD*.

———. "Unclean and Clean: Old Testament." Pages 729–41 in vol. 6 of *ABD*.

Wright, David P., and R. N. Jones. "Discharge." Pages 206–7 in vol. 2 of *ABD*.

8 THE BOOK OF NUMBERS

Important Dates for Numbers
ca. 1278–1220: the wilderness period
the deaths of Aaron and Miriam
Israel's arrival at the Jordan's east bank

NO, THE BOOK OF NUMBERS is not an ancient Israelite math book! The book's English name translates its titles in the Greek and Latin Bibles and probably goes back to the head counting of four censuses that the book reports (chs. 1; 3; 4; 26). In Numbers, storytelling resumes, moving the Torah's larger story forward again from Mount Sinai, across the wilderness to the oasis at Kadesh Barnea, and finally to the plains of Moab at the edge of the promised land. At last, the Israelites will see the long-dreamed-of land across the Jordan River! Appropriately, the book's main theme is preparation for life in the new land. It requires the Israelites to make major transitions—for example, new campsites on the journey and a generational change of leadership, too. Two and a half tribes even receive their ancestral inheritance east of the Jordan, but a sense of tragedy also haunts the book, given the sad fates that the exodus generation (for this term, see Table 8.1) and even Moses suffer. In sum, Numbers offers a cautionary tale of rebellious conduct that the wilderness generations and their descendants (including us) must not repeat lest promised blessings be squandered. God faithfully, patiently sticks with the grumpy Israelites, prepares them for the new land, and leads them there, giving the book a hopeful ending.

Table 8.1. Numbers: Some Basic Definitions

Term	Definition	Text
The exodus	The Red Sea crossing led by Moses	Exod 14
The exodus generation	Israelites born in Egypt and exodus participants	
The wilderness period	Between the exodus and the Jordan River crossing under Joshua, when the Israelites lived mainly in the desert	Exod 15–Deut 34
The wilderness generation	Israelites born in the wilderness period	
The conquest period	Between the Jordan River crossing and the land distribution	Josh 1–12
The land distribution period	Division of land in Canaan among the tribes	Josh 13–24

The Story

Numbers tells its story in four main parts, explaining:

1. How the Israelites begin preparations to depart from Sinai and head towards Canaan (Num 1-10)
2. How the Israelites grumble their way across the desert and how Yahweh angrily condemns the exodus generation to die in the desert (Num 10-21)
3. How the prophecies of the non-Israelite Balaam reaffirm that God's blessing rests on them and frustrates the king of Moab's plans to curse them (22-24)
4. How on the plains of Moab Yahweh and Moses ready the Israelites to conquer and settle in Canaan and even allot two-and-a-half tribes their inheritance east of the Jordan (25-36)

Two censuses in Num 1-4 initiate the preparations for Israel's departure from Sinai toward the promised land. The first counts the prospective soldiers available for battles that lie ahead (see chs. 21 and 31), while the other tallies the members of the clans of Levi available for tabernacle duties. The clerical inventory marks the first time that the Torah distinguishes between the priests and the Levites, the ministry assistants who figure prominently in Numbers and in postexiic Historical Books (see our ch. 10 on the Historical Books). "Momentous" certainly describes Num 13-14, the angry-crowd scene where the spies' report about Canaan and the Canaanites ignites panic and leads Yahweh to condemn the exodus generation to die in the wilderness rather than see the promised land. Thematically, the chapters underscore that the land belongs to those who fully trust Yahweh (Joshua, Caleb); the faith-less clamoring of the crowd disqualifies them from settling there. Yet again, Moses proves the consummate mediator, his bold appeal to Yahweh's international reputation sparing the wilderness generation the fate of their unfortunate ancestors. The surprising background to Num 20 is that desert rocks actually store fresh water accessible to travelers by breaking the rock's surface. But Moses's approach shows impatience and a lack of faith, denying Yahweh the chance to reassure the Israelites by a display of his power (20:12; for the telltale place-name, see Table 8.2).

Table 8.2. Desert Names Commemorating Memorable Events

Name	Meaning	Cause	Outcome(s)
Marah (Exod 15:22–26; cf. Num 33:8–9)	"Bitter"	Lack of water	1. Piece of wood removes bitterness 2. Lesson: Obedience spares Israel the Egyptian diseases (vv. 25–26)
Wilderness of Zin (Exod 16)	n/a	Lack of meat	Morning: manna Evening: quail
Massah and *Meribah* (Exod 17:1–7; cf. Num 11:3; 20:1–13, 24; 27:14; Deut 9:22; 32:51; 33:8; Ps 81:7; 95:8)	"Testing and Quarreling"	Lack of water	Moses strikes a rock
Taberah (Num 11:1–3; cf. Deut 9:22)	"Burning"	Desert hardships	Fire strikes the camp's outskirts
Kibroth Hattaavah (Num 11:34–35; cf. Deut 9:22)	"Graves of Desire"	Lack of meat	Divine plague strikes the Israelites
Waters of Meribah or *Meribah Kadesh* (Num 20:1–13; 27:14; Deut 32:51; Ps 106:32	"Quarreling"	Lack of water	Moses strikes (not: speaks to) a rock Moses not to enter Canaan
Near *Mount Hor* (Num 21:4–9)	n/a	Lack of bread, water, good food	Poisonous snakes Antidote: glimpse of Moses's bronze snake

Numbers 22–24 abruptly shifts the scene from the Israelite camp on the Jordan's east bank to a bluff high above it, the setting of the oracles of the non-Israelite prophet Balaam. An ink wall inscription from Deir ʿAlla in Jordan (ca. 840–760 BCE) records a vision seen by a Balaam, suggesting that the latter and the biblical character may go back to the same person. In the ancient world, a spoken curse was thought to inflict calamity on an enemy, provided, of course, that a deity permitted it. Thematically, after two momentous divine judgments on the Israelites, Balaam the non-Israelite testifies that they still enjoy Yahweh's irrevocable blessing and destiny; indeed, his climactic final vision of a "star" (24:17) points to David and, ultimately, to Jesus the Messiah (Matt 3; for Balaam's apostasy and death, see Num 31:8, 16; cf. ch. 25). Numbers 27 and 36 extend one such blessing, the inheritance of ancestral property,

> **Numbers in Numbers**
>
> The first census of the Israelite young men of the exodus generation concludes that Israel has 603,550 potential soldiers (Num 1:46). Assuming that each young man has living parents and at least one sibling, the Israelites would number more than two million — on the face of it, an improbable number, as most everyone agrees. Recent studies of ancient agricultural methods estimate that food produced in Canaan could probably feed a million people at best, that is, a terribly inadequate food supply for two million people. Further, the sheer numbers of such a sizable Israelite army would make the conquest very easy, whereas Yahweh twice remarks how small Israel's population is (Exod 23:29-30; Deut 7:7). One possible solution is that the present text may cite data from a later period — for example, the era of David or Solomon — as figures for the wilderness period. Or the word "thousand" (*ʾeleph*) may actually mean "clan" or "family" (its original sense) and, hence, designate simply a "large group," without specifying numerical size. If so, 603 *ʾeleph*s would yield a significantly smaller total: roughly, 5,500–72,000, depending on the clan size used in the calculation. Finally, the large numbers may simply be symbolic or even emotive, exaggerated figures that intend to verify the fulfillment of Yahweh's promise to Abraham that his descendants would be as impossible to count as the dust and the stars (Gen 13:16; 15:5).

to daughters of families with no sons to inherit it. The two rulings anticipate Israel's imminent settlement in Canaan and mark an important forward step in social importance for Israelite women. Finally, in Num 32–33 another momentous Mosaic decision permits two and a half tribes to settle in conquered land in Transjordan—the first actual settlement of Israelites in land promised to Abraham (cf. Josh 1:12-18). That ruling also concludes the book of Numbers and sets the scene for Moses's passionate farewell speeches in the Torah's final book.

READING

Read Num 1–36 and formulate answers to the following questions:

1. Who for you is the most memorable character (e.g., person, small group, tribe, etc.) in the book? Why do you think s/he so captures your attention?

2. Which chapter, episode, or passage in the book especially left its impression on you? Discuss why you think that happened.

3. List and briefly discuss what you think the main themes are in the book of Numbers. Which one(s) interest you the most? Why?

4. Theologically, what does the book portray about God? What implications do you draw for your own relationship with God from that portrait?

5. What role(s) do women portray in the story? How do you think God relates to them? In what way(s) does the book's portrait enrich your understanding of women's roles in God's work in his people?

6. With what impression do the people of Israel in Numbers leave you? What is their relationship with God like? What implications do you draw from watching them for your own Christian life or for church life today?

7. Which of Moses's instructions or Israel's religious practices particularly stick in your mind? Why? In what way(s) do they cause you to reevaluate your own way of life, worship, or religious practices?

8. Read Num 22–24.
   a. In light of Israelites before and after these chapters, what purpose(s) do you think the Balaam section serves in the book? What portrait of God does it display?
   b. Read later mentions of Balaam in Deut 23:3–5; Josh 24:9–10; 2 Pet 2:15–16; and Rev 2:14. What aspect(s) of his life do they remember, and how do they apply those memories to the lives of their readers?

BIBLIOGRAPHY

Ashley, Timothy. *The Book of Numbers*. NICOT. Grand Rapids: Eerdmans, 1993.

Brown, Raymond. *The Message of Numbers: Journey to the Promised Land*. TBST. Downers Grove, IL: InterVarsity Press, 2002.

Budd, Philip J. *Numbers*. WBC 5. Waco, TX: Word, 1984.

Camp, Claudia V. "Gender and Identity in the Book of Numbers." Pages 105–21 in *Imagining the Other and Constructing Israelite Identity in the Early Second Temple Period*. Edited by Ehud Ben Zvi and Diana V. Edelman. LHBOTS 456. London: Bloomsbury; New York: T&T Clark, 2014.

Douglas, Mary. *In the Wilderness: The Doctrine of Defilement in the Book of Numbers*. JSOTSup 158. Oxford: Oxford University Press, 2004.

Leveen, Adriane. *Memory and Tradition in the Book of Numbers*. New York: Cambridge University Press, 2008.

McCarter, P. Kyle, Jr. "The Balaam Texts from Deir 'Alla: The First Combination." *BASOR* 237 (1980): 49–60.

Sparks, Kenton L. "Numbers." Pages 59–66 in *Theological Interpretation of the Old Testament: A Book-by-Book Survey*. Edited by Kevin J. Vanhoozer. Grand Rapids: Baker Academic, 2008.

Wenham, Gordon J. *Numbers: An Introduction and Commentary*. TOTC. Leicester: Inter-Varsity Press, 1981.

9 THE BOOK OF DEUTERONOMY

<table>
<tr><td colspan="2">**Important Dates for Deuteronomy**</td></tr>
<tr><td>**ca. 1220:** death of Moses</td></tr>
<tr><td>**705–701:** reforms of Hezekiah</td></tr>
<tr><td>**640–609:** reign of Josiah</td></tr>
<tr><td>**622:** discovery of the book of the Torah in Jerusalem (also DH 1.0)</td></tr>
<tr><td>**550:** Babylonian exile (also DH 2.0)</td></tr>
</table>

THE FIFTH AND FINAL BOOK of the Torah continues the narrative setting provided at the end of the book of Numbers, with Israel camped on the east side of the Jordan River valley and poised to enter the promised land. The name *Deuteronomy* (= "Second Law") comes from the Greek translation of Deut 17:18, where the king is to keep a copy of the Deuteronomic law nearby for instruction. A scene-setting introduction and a retrospective, postmortem comment on Moses's unparalleled greatness bracket the book. In between, Moses is presented as giving a series of farewell speeches—final exhortations and instructions to the second generation after the exodus from Egypt—before his death is briefly noted in the final chapter. He acts as a prophet, covenant-renewal mediator, and teacher of statutes and ordinances.

A Capstone to the Torah

Deuteronomy is inadequately described as the final book of the Pentateuch (Torah). It is certainly that, but as it elaborates on several elements now presented in Genesis through Numbers in sermonic mode, it does so in order to instruct Israel about corporate life as God moves the people forward. In some ways, therefore, it serves not only as the conclusion to the Torah but as a capstone to it, distilling and expanding on earlier materials once more before Moses dies. In doing so, Deuteronomy also points forward and foreshadows what will happen after Moses dies and the tribes enter the land promised to their ancestors. Deuteronomy assumes they will face grave challenges to their status as God's people. The larger story presented by the Torah has pointed to this part of Israel's history since the ancestral accounts in Gen 12–50, which indicated that the descendants of Abraham and Sarah would become a great nation in Canaan. That part of the story is still to come as Moses offers something like a rhetorical last will and testament on the plains of Moab, and so there is a sense in which the capstone that is Deuteronomy also consists of corporate instructions for Israel's subsequent life in Canaan.

Covenant Renewal and the Origin of Deuteronomy

The theme of *covenant renewal* is central to Deuteronomy. What God instituted at Horeb is foundational to Israel's identity and must be appropriated by future generations. This conviction may also be a clue to the origin of the book and its particular shape. According to 2 Kgs 22–23, a scroll of the Torah was discovered during temple repairs in the eighteenth year of King Josiah, ca. 622 BCE (see discussion of 2 Kings, pp. 198–99 below). Upon reading the document, Josiah tore his clothes, signifying distress at its content and what it portended for Judah. He then embarked on a national covenant-renewal ceremony, followed by a purge of syncretistic worship practices at the temple in Jerusalem. Many interpreters have identified this Torah scroll (also called the "book of the covenant," 2 Kgs 23:2) with Deuteronomy or an earlier form thereof. Intriguing questions remain. Does this mean that some anonymous authors compiled a Torah document in Josiah's day; or that an older document of Mosaic instructions had fallen into disuse, only to be rediscovered and subsequently updated; or that the writer(s) of 1–2 Kings wanted later readers to associate Deuteronomy with the tradition of reforming measures undertaken by Josiah?

The answer to this last question is almost certainly "yes," however one answers the question of the book's literary origins. A plausible case can be made that Deuteronomy originated with reform-minded circles during the monarchic period, who drew upon Mosaic tradition (using his voice)

A section of an Assyrian palace wall relief from Nineveh that pictures King Sennacherib accepting the surrender of the Judahite city of Lachish in 701 BCE. It offers historical background to 2 Kings 18–19 and an ancient artist's rendering of what Judahites looked like. It is now in the British Museum in London. *©Osama Shukir Mohammed Amin FRCP(Glasg) (Wikimedia Commons, CC-SA 4.0)*

in charting a course for national renewal in the context of severe political pressure from Assyria, and that Josiah's reform measures were influenced by it. Decades before Josiah, King Hezekiah carried out reform measures in Judah (2 Kgs 18:1–8; 2 Chr 29–31), and he too may have drawn on the covenantal wisdom and identity presented in Deuteronomy.

Historians often point out that Hezekiah and Josiah sought to free Judah from vassalage to the Assyrian Empire and that this impacted some of the biblical writers. More particularly for understanding Deuteronomy, Assyrian emperors established vassal treaties with their subjects, following conventional treaty forms inherited from the Hittite Empire of the Late Bronze Age. As we noted in the introduction to the Torah, Deuteronomy has a number of literary and thematic characteristics that are similar to this centuries-long literary tradition. This does not make Deuteronomy a copy of an international treaty any more than the code of statutes in chs. 12–26 makes Deuteronomy a law code, following another great literary tradition of the ANE (see pp. 97–100).

Deuteronomy certainly adopts and adapts recognized modes of expression in its presentation of Yahweh as the cosmic Lord who calls for loyalty to his revealed will from his people. It is likely, however, that the circumstances of Judah's vassalage to Assyria during the eighth and seventh centuries BCE influenced the shaping of covenant renewal in Deuteronomy, even as the book drew upon traditions reaching back to the founding of the nation.

Deuteronomy and Deuteronomic Tradition

As noted above, some interpreters identify several literary sources or strands of tradition in the completed Torah. In the classical form of the Documentary Hypothesis, earlier national traditions that had a preference for either Yahweh (the J writer) or Elohim (the E writer) were supplemented with the traditions from Deuteronomic (the D writer) circles in late monarchic times, and finally with those from Priestly sources (the P writer) in the postexilic period, when the Torah reaches its final form. We should think of biblical writers first as those who passed along and shaped materials that they inherited. In any case, many interpreters use the adjective *Deuteronomic* or *Deuteronomistic* to describe the distinctive vocabulary of Deuteronomy and echoes of it in other books of the Primary History (see p. 32).

Second, for decades modern interpreters have referred to a segment of the Primary History as the Deuteronomistic History (DH), by which is meant the books of Deuteronomy, Joshua, Judges, 1–2 Samuel, and 1–2 Kings. More details about this term can be found in the resources of the bibliography and in the discussion of the Historical Books (see part 3 below). The theory is that Deuteronomy sets the stage for the rest of the Primary History that follows, which presents Israel's entry to and life in the promised land, and that there are common vocabulary and themes in these books. Readers should compare Josh 24 (where Joshua provides a last will and testament similar to Moses's), 1 Sam 12 (Samuel's last will and testament), and 1 Kgs 8:14–61 (Solomon's words at the temple dedication) for examples of Deuteronomic vocabulary and themes at work.

Look What's Inside!

We noted above that the Torah is broadly composed of story and embedded law. That description certainly fits Deuteronomy and the characteristics just described. The book also supplements narrative and law with such things as lists of blessings and curses (chs. 27-28), a prophetic song (ch. 32), and tribal blessings (ch. 33). At Mount Sinai (called Horeb in Deuteronomy), Moses mediated God's instructions to the generation that escaped Egypt, and enacted a covenant with them. In Deuteronomy Moses rehearses the story line that brought the second generation through the wilderness and to the plains of Moab. He reminds them that they are heirs of promises and responsibilities, both of which he enumerates in some detail, and he calls for covenant renewal and commitment on the part of the second generation as they are preparing to cross the Jordan River. He is prophetic in presentation, projecting a future for the people that will include monarchy and worship at a central sanctuary, and he warns the people of the consequences of failure. The last chapter notes his death.

The Story

The book of Deuteronomy has four main parts: (1) remembering the story (Deut 1-4); (2) a long address to Israel (Deut 5-28); (3) choosing life and covenant renewal (Deut 29-30); and (4) appendixes: who and what follow Moses (Deut 31-34). The book's longest section (2) breaks down into three subparts: (a) an exhortation to Israel (Deut 5-11); (b) Covenant Code of instructions (Deut 12-26); and (c) blessings and curses (Deut 27-28).

Deuteronomy 1:1–4:43: Remembering the Story

A brief introduction (1:1-5) sets the context for reporting Moses's words to an assembled Israel. Geography and chronology (fortieth year since the exodus from Egypt) are noted. The first three chapters rehearse details from the time that Israel departed Horeb until its arrival in the land of Moab to the east of the southern Jordan Valley, and ch. 4 contains a brief sermon. Much of the detail in the historical summary is connected to the wilderness-wandering presentation in Num 10:11-21:35. Moses urges the people to respect the leaders who will shape the future life of the nation (1:9-18; cf. Exod 18:13-27) and then reminds them of their earlier failure to enter Canaan when they disobeyed divine instruction (1:19-45; cf. Num 13-14). This resulted in decades of additional wilderness wandering and the death of the adult generation that escaped Egypt.

Kadesh had been a resting place in the wilderness (Num 13:26; 20:1). Eventually the Israelite tribes traveled east toward the Red Sea and the port city of Akabah, before turning north. Along the way they encountered a variety of peoples, some of whom are obscure, as well as the descendants of Esau, that is, the Edomites, and the Moabites and Ammonites, both of whom were descendants of Lot (2:1-25). The latter three peoples connect the Israelite tribes with ancestral traditions in the book of Genesis (cf. Gen 19:30-38; 36:1-19). Moses reminds the Israelites that God had also granted these relatives their land and that they were not to take it from them.

The book of Numbers contains accounts of fighting with other rulers in the area east of the Jordan River (Num 21, 31), and some of those memories are rehearsed in Deut 2:26-3:29. The historical résumé in the first three chapters of Deuteronomy is prelude to a short sermon in 4:1-40, where Moses reminds the people that the proper response to God's leading them to the land of promise is their obedience to his revealed instructions first given at Horeb.

Deuteronomy 4:44–28:68: This Is the Torah — A Long Address to Israel

In the center of the book is a longer sermon or hortatory address (5:1-11:32) with a code of instructions (12:1-26:19) and appended blessings and curses (27:1-28:68). The sermon, like the shorter address in 4:1-40, contains several of the distinctive themes for which Deuteronomy is noted. The code elaborates on a number of instructions also found in Exodus, thereby illustrating the book's profile as a recapitulation of and updated commentary on earlier material.

The Ten Commandments (Decalogue)

Deuteronomy identifies the Decalogue as the essential charter of the covenant between the Lord and Israel (4:13): "God spoke his covenant to you and charged you to observe it, that is, the ten words" (= commandments). Moses, furthermore, begins his second address in ch. 5 with a reminder that at Horeb God had spoken out of the fire when presenting his covenant. The form and content of the Decalogue in Deut 5:6-21 are similar to those of the Decalogue in Exod 20:2-17, but there are minor differences as well. A comparison of the two texts offers a good example of the reiteration and elaboration that is characteristic of Deuteronomy in particular and the Torah more broadly when it comes to instructional materials. First, note the summary nature of the Sinai setting in Deut 5:2–5, which comes before the Decalogue proper. It stresses the application of the Horeb revelation for a new generation. Second, the motivation attached to the Sabbath commandment in Deut 5:15 is different from that provided in Exod 20:11. In the Exodus account, rest on the seventh day of the week is predicated on God's actions in creating the world; the motivation given in Deut 5:15 is remembering the exodus event and liberation from slavery.

Some interpreters conclude that the Decalogue is strategically placed in Deut 5 as a kind of guiding preface to the instructional code that follows in Deut 12–26, and second that the order of the instructions in the code can be related to the order of the Decalogue. This second proposal is difficult to establish. The Decalogue in Exod 20 also comes before the collection of instructions known as the Covenant Code in Exod 21–23, but clearly there is no correspondence between the Decalogue and the order of instructions there. Nevertheless, the primacy of the Decalogue in defining covenant identity seems clear from its placement in both Exodus and Deuteronomy.

The Shema: "Hear, O Israel!"

Deuteronomy 6:4 is one of the best-known texts in the OT. It is often referred to as the *Shema*, which is a reference to the Hebrew verb "hear," the initial word in the verse. The primary difference between the two modern renderings above is the translation of the concluding Hebrew word. Literally, it is the term "one" (*'ehad*). The NRSV translation reflects a possible translation of the term as "singular" or "alone," while some scholars render it "one"—meaning "one" in contrast to the "many" local Baals in antiquity. However best translated and interpreted, the terse sentence eventually became a common, daily recital for observant Jews. Judaism is not typically thought of as a creedal religion, but Deut 6:4 comes close to being a unifying confession for practicing Jews. In fact, the daily practices of Judaism have several links to Deut 6. Modern Jews may bind a small wooden box with Scripture texts called a *phylactery* on their left arm and one on their forehead in response to 6:8. A somewhat different emblem, a mezuzah, may be affixed to the doorposts of their homes, in accord with 6:9. And the practice of prayer at set times of the day is influenced by 6:7.

PROGRAMMATIC TEXT #6

Hear, O Israel: The LORD our God, the LORD is one. (Deut 6:4 ESV)

Hear, O Israel: The LORD is our God, the LORD alone. (Deut 6:4 NRSV)

Listen up, Israel! Yahweh is our God; there's only one Yahweh. (Deut 6:4 authors' translation)

Deuteronomy 7 presents its audience with two related claims. One is that God took the initiative in choosing Israel as his particular people (7:7-8). This is not because they were more numerous or more virtuous; God's free choice lies deep in the mystery of God's greater purposes, even as it is linked to promises made earlier to Israel's ancestors. In context it is not clear whether the ancestors in mind are just the previous generation—those rescued from Egypt—or more broadly the previous generations, including those presented in Gen 12-50. The latter is more likely in our view. A second claim is that God's choice of them means that they should distinguish themselves by keeping God's distinctive commandments (cf. 4:8) and separating themselves from the corruptions of the Canaanite population in the land. This compares with a prominent theme in the Holiness Code of Lev 17-27, namely, the importance of separating from corrupting influences and engaging in practices that bring the people into conformity with God's will.

Chapters 8-11 continue the broad theme of remaining humbly on the path marked out by God's instructions and God's warning of the consequence of straying from it. Moses offers a fateful choice to the people in 11:26-28 that captures the tone of these chapters and sounds a theme that recurs later in the book (30:15-20). Israel is urged to seek the blessing of a faithful life in the promised land and to reject the curse that will fall on them for disobedience.

Deuteronomy 12–26: A Covenant Code for Life in Canaan

As noted above, there are codes or collections of instructions embedded in the books of Exodus (chs. 21-23), Leviticus (chs. 1-7, 17-27), and Numbers (chs. 28-29). Deuteronomy's core is yet another code, a collection that elaborates on and supplements the briefer Covenant Code in Exod 21-23. A comparison of the slave laws and the details of the sacred calendar illustrates the connection between these two codes (see Table 9.1). The basic circumstances under consideration are the same in both passages—namely, a slave who has served for six years shall be granted freedom in the seventh year. Deuteronomy clarifies in the initial verse that what applies to a male slave (so Exodus) also applies to a female slave. Moreover, the Deuteronomic passage offers motives for slave release (Israel had been slaves in Egypt) and exhorts liberality of support when slaves are released.

In another comparison, two sets of instructions are presented concerning three annual festivals in which Israelites are called to present themselves corporately before the Lord (see Table 9.2). Again, the Deuteronomic

A silver mezuzah, a small case containing a parchment inscribed with the Shema (Deut 6:4), which Jews attach to the doorposts of their homes to affirm their faith as taught by Deuteronomy 6:4–9 and 11:13–21. ©*Sebastian Wallroth (Wikimedia Commons, CC-SA 3.0)*

Table 9.1. Comparison of Slave Laws in the Covenant Code and Deuteronomic Code

Exodus 21: [2]When you buy a male Hebrew slave, he shall serve six years, but in the seventh he shall go out a free person, without debt. [3]If he comes in single, he shall go out single; if he comes in married, then his wife shall go out with him. [4]If his master gives him a wife and she bears him sons or daughters, the wife and her children shall be her master's and he shall go out alone. [5]But if the slave declares, "I love my master, my wife, and my children; I will not go out a free person," [6]then his master shall bring him before God. He shall be brought to the door or the doorpost; and his master shall pierce his ear with an awl; and he shall serve him for life. (NRSV)

Deuteronomy 15: [12]If a member of your community, whether a Hebrew man or a Hebrew woman, is sold to you and works for you six years, in the seventh year you shall set that person free. [13]And when you send a male slave out from you a free person, you shall not send him out empty-handed. [14]Provide liberally out of your flock, your threshing floor, and your wine press, thus giving to him some of the bounty with which the LORD your God has blessed you. [15]Remember that you were a slave in the land of Egypt, and the LORD your God redeemed you; for this reason I lay this command upon you today. [16]But if he says to you, "I will not go out from you," because he loves you and your household, since he is well off with you, [17]then you shall take an awl and thrust it through his earlobe into the door, and he shall be your slave forever. You shall do the same with regard to your female slave. [18]Do not consider it a hardship when you send them out from you free persons, because for six years they have given you services worth the wages of hired laborers; and the LORD your God will bless you in all that you do. (NRSV)

Table 9.2. Comparison of Festival Calendars in the Covenant Code and Deuteronomic Code

Exodus 23: [14]Three times in the year you shall hold a festival for me. [15]You shall observe the festival of unleavened bread; as I commanded you, you shall eat unleavened bread for seven days at the appointed time in the month of [Aviv], for in it you came out of Egypt. No one shall appear before me empty-handed. [16]You shall observe the festival of harvest, of the firstfruits of your labor, of what you sow in the field. You shall observe the festival of ingathering at the end of the year, when you gather in from the field the fruit of your labor. [17]Three times in the year all your males shall appear before the Lord GOD. (NRSV)

Deuteronomy 16: [1]Observe the month of [Aviv] by keeping the passover for the LORD your God, for in the month of [Aviv] the LORD your God brought you out of Egypt by night. [2]You shall offer the passover sacrifice for the LORD your God, from the flock and the herd, at the place that the LORD will choose as a dwelling for his name. [3]You must not eat with it anything leavened. For seven days you shall eat unleavened bread with it — the bread of affliction — because you came out of the land of Egypt in great haste, so that all the days of your life you may remember the day of your departure from the land of Egypt. [4]No leaven shall be seen with you in all your territory for seven days; and none of the meat of what you slaughter on the evening of the first day shall remain until morning. [5]You are not permitted to offer the passover sacrifice within any of your towns that the LORD your God is giving you. [6]But at the place that the LORD your God will choose as a dwelling for his name, only there shall you offer the passover sacrifice, in the evening at sunset, the time of day when you departed from Egypt. [7]You shall cook it and eat it at the place that the LORD your God will choose; the next morning you may go back to your tents. [8]For six days you shall continue to eat unleavened bread, and on the seventh day there shall be a solemn assembly for the LORD your God, when you shall do no work. [9]You shall count seven weeks; begin to count the seven weeks from the time the sickle is first put to the standing grain. [10]Then you shall keep the festival of weeks for the LORD your God, contributing a freewill offering in proportion to the blessing that you have received from the LORD your God. [11]Rejoice before the LORD your God — you and your sons and your daughters, your male and female slaves, the Levites resident in your towns, as well as the strangers, the orphans, and the widows who are among you — at the place that the LORD your God will choose as a dwelling for his name. [12]Remember that you were a slave in Egypt, and diligently observe these statutes. [13]You shall keep the festival of booths for seven days, when you have gathered in the produce from your threshing floor and your wine press. [14]Rejoice during your festival, you and your sons and your daughters, your male and female slaves, as well as the Levites, the strangers, the orphans, and the widows resident in your towns. [15]Seven days you shall keep the festival for the LORD your God at the place that the LORD will choose; for the LORD your God will bless you in all your produce and in all your undertakings, and you shall surely celebrate. [16]Three times a year all your males shall appear before the LORD your God at the place that he will choose: at the festival of unleavened bread, at the festival of weeks, and at the festival of booths. They shall not appear before the LORD empty-handed; [17]all shall give as they are able, according to the blessing of the LORD your God that he has given you. (NRSV)

formulations are longer. In the first festival named, the Passover sacrifice and a week of eating unleavened bread are explicit in Deut 16:1-8, whereas the short description in Exod 23:14-15 mentions only the eating of unleavened bread. The second festival is named somewhat differently in the two listings. The Deuteronomic formulations give chronological specificity along with exhortations to rejoice and to remember Egyptian slavery in the past. Something similar occurs with the third festival. They are named differently and the longer formulation in Deut 16:13-15 has chronological details and exhortations for joy in participation.

It is worth a reminder here that, not only are slave and worship instructions treated in common in Exodus and Deuteronomy, but Leviticus also contains instructions on these two topics (Lev 23, 25). A glance at the these two chapters in Leviticus demonstrates that they provide considerably more detail on Israel's sacred calendar as well as distinctions between Israelites as hired laborers and foreigners who can be enslaved (Lev 25:39–46; note also Table 7.2 on the "Annual Festival Calendar" in ch. 7 above).

Worship at the Place the Lord Will Choose

The Deuteronomic Code begins with instructions for worship. They include practices and people to be avoided and some new practices to be instituted in the promised land. In Canaan the Lord will choose a place from among the tribes to "put his name there," a place for "his name to dwell" (Deut 12:5, 11, 21). These related phrases indicate divine ownership and presence. Various acts of public worship by the tribes will be centralized there. The place is not otherwise named in Deuteronomy. According to Jer 7:12–15 there was an early shrine in Shiloh where the Israelite tribes gathered before the advent of the monarchy (see 1 Sam 1–4). Jerusalem eventually becomes the place of the central shrine with the building of the temple by Solomon (cf. 1 Kgs 8). The Samaritans of the postexilic period believed that Mount Gerizim near Shechem is the place of centralized worship. The difference between Jews and Samaritans on this point is presupposed in the discussion between Jesus and an unnamed woman at a well near Shechem (John 4:1–24). Interpreters differ on whether the Deuteronomic centralizing formula assumes that sacrificial worship can only take place at the central shrine in Canaan or that its primacy is designed for unity and purity's sake. The instructions regarding altars in Exod 20:22–26 assume that sacrifice at an earthen altar can be offered in various locations. Note the discussion of sacrificial practice at an altar across the Jordan in Josh 22:10–34.

Deuteronomy gives attention to the work of judges and the responsibilities of a future king (Deut 16:18–17:20). The central place of worship will have a judge who, along with Levitical priests serving there, can assist with difficult cases that come from different tribes. Surprisingly, the brief description of the monarch's role is all that the Torah contains regarding Israelite kingship. This is one reason why some interpreters conclude that

Deuteronomy preserves old traditions about Israel's public life that took root before the rise of an institutional monarchy. A later document, written after centuries of monarchic rule, might have had more extensive statutes for a king.

If someone puts together all the instructions in the Torah, they would only cover portions of the common life and institutions of Israel. This is well illustrated not only by the brief description of royal responsibilities but also by the case law regarding divorce and remarriage in Deut 24:1-4. The case law concerns a circumstance related to remarriage, but it is the only text in the Pentateuch that provides any procedures for divorce. Marriage is also the subject of the case law in 25:5-10. In this instance, the circumstance in question has to do with family inheritance when a married man dies without an heir and whether a brother-in-law takes the widow as wife in order to produce an heir for the deceased. These two case laws illustrate some fascinating aspects of marriage and family customary law in ancient Semitic society but do not constitute a complete treatment of the subject.

Deuteronomy is concerned with the roles of prophets among the people, offering some evaluative criteria in chs. 13 and 18. Elsewhere in the Torah, Moses engages in prophetic activity (Num 11-12), as does his sister Miriam (Exod 15:20). Moses is the paradigm of a prophet in Deut 18:14-22, and the work of later prophets should be measured by it. It is not clear whether readers should think of this description of Moses's work as something of a prophetic office to be emulated or whether the implication is more broadly that the prophets are to be interpreters of the covenant and the responsibilities that it places on the people. Dreams and visions would not be able to violate or override Torah (see the discussion of how to define a prophet on pp. 264-66 in chapter 21).

Blessings and Curses

In Deut 11:26-28, Moses briefly sets forth future blessings or curses as the result of Israel's choices. Blessings and curses associated with covenant fidelity (or infidelity) are presented in expanded form in 27:11-28:68. Note that the curses are more extensive than the blessings. Yet another listing of blessings and curses comes near the end of the book of Leviticus (ch. 26). The curses in Deut 28 have close parallels to curses listed in treaty texts given to vassals of Esarhaddon, who ruled Assyria 681-669

BCE. Interpreters continue to debate whether these parallels help date the origins of the book of Deuteronomy or whether the Hebrew and Assyrian documents alike draw on traditional formulas for loyalty between overlords and sovereigns (see ch. 6 above for definition of and discussion about covenants).

Deuteronomy 29–30: Choosing Life and Covenant Renewal

In a third address Moses invites those assembled on the plains of Moab to commit to covenant renewal with the Lord. This is a call for the people to choose life (and blessing) over death (and curse). He indicates prophetically that the curse for disobedience will come upon their descendants and that they will be scattered for a time among nations (30:1–5; cf. 4:29–31). For some interpreters, this portion of the book is an indication that Deuteronomy did not reach its final form until after the destruction of Jerusalem in 587 BCE and the subsequent exiling of portions of the population to southern Mesopotamia. However one sorts out this reference to exile—a punishment inflicted on the Northern Kingdom of Israel by the Assyrians in the 8th century BCE and on Judah by the Babylonians early in the 6th century BCE—the tenor of Deut 30 is confidence that God will renew Israel's relationship with God in spite of the people's failures. Note particularly the claim that God will "circumcise" Israel's heart and again take delight in them (Deut 30:6–10; compare Jer 4:4).

Deuteronomy 31–34: Appendixes – Who and What Follow Moses

Joshua is recognized as Moses's successor, who will lead the people to claim their inheritance in Canaan. Every seven years Deuteronomy is to be read publically during the Festival of Booths in the fall, when those who do not live near the central sanctuary come there to worship. The scroll is to be kept near the ark of the covenant.

Moses offers a prophetic song in ch. 32 that rehearses in poetry the essential claims of his addresses elsewhere in Deuteronomy. Israel is the elect of the Lord; it will fail to maintain covenant standards, and it will be judged for its failures. The song is described as a "witness" to the people (32:46; cf. Josh 22:27–34; 24:27). Perhaps the term refers to the impact that a public performance of the song would engender. Moses also offers a final blessing on the individual tribes in Deut 33:1–29, similar to the final blessing of Jacob/Israel on his sons in Gen 49:1–28. And as with Jacob, Moses then dies.

Deuteronomy concludes with a notice that no prophet has arisen in Israel since Moses who knew the Lord face-to-face (compare Exod. 33:11; Num 12:8) and who performed the sorts of signs and wonders he did in Egypt. Such a retrospective comment comes at some distance from Moses's own day and assumes that Moses was the prophet *par excellence*, setting a standard for other prophetic figures who will emerge (see Deut 18:15).

An Ending to the Torah

Deuteronomy's distinctive style of looking back to the Lord's work with the people and forward to life in the land of promise brings the Torah to a conclusion. In the introduction to the book, we called it a capstone to the Torah, bringing a formative period to an end in an authoritative summation, even as the larger story in which it is set continues on under Joshua's leadership. Deuteronomy's already/not-yet dynamic casts an influential shadow over the subsequent books in the Primary History, anticipating an exile from the promised land and through God's mercy a restoration to it. Moses's own life is also an influential paradigm for the dynamics of a faithful relationship with the Lord. He could, for example, look back on the ways in which the Lord had preserved him to this, his life's end, even as he could look over the Jordan valley to a land of promise, a place that he would never enter but that tangibly represented God's faithfulness to bring earlier promises to a blessed conclusion. What is left of Moses is not a recognized grave site but words by which God's people live.

The Zincirli Stele. In 671 BCE, the Assyrian King Esarhaddon defeated Pharaoh Taharqa in northern Egypt and commissioned a stele to commemorate his triumphant return. The original is in the Pergamon Museum, Berlin; this copy is in the Harvard Semitic Museum (Cambridge, MA).

READING

Read Deut 1–34 and prepare answers to the following questions:

1. What do you find interesting regarding the people chosen to assist Moses in governing the Israelite tribes in Deut 1:9–18? Are there important characteristics that you think are missing?

2. There are cities of refuge described in Deut 4:41–43 and 19:1–13. How do you think they functioned and why may they have been important in ancient Israel's society? What else would you like to know about them?

3. Deuteronomy 7:1–6 and 12:2–8 have some hard things to say about the corrupting influences of the Canaanites and about ways that the Israelites should distinguish themselves from the previous inhabitants of the land. How do you respond to these descriptions and instructions? What relevance might these instructions have in contemporary society, or should they be relegated to their ancient context? What other, different instructions or models have you encountered in the OT regarding relations between Israel and Canaanites?

4. Read Deut 15:1–11. How does the passage understand the place of indebtedness and poverty in Israelite society? What does it have to say on the topic of indebtedness, if anything, to contemporary society?

5. Deuteronomy 17:14–20 provides brief instructions for an Israelite king. Which part do you find the most interesting and why? Does the limitation on horse trading remind you of the description of any Israelite kings? Hint: look at the description of Solomon in 1 Kgs 10–11.

6. Inheritance rights for the firstborn son are provided in Deut 21:15–17. What do you learn about Israelite society from this brief passage? What more would you like to know about it in order to understand family structure in Israel better?

7. Deuteronomy 30:6 refers to circumcision of the heart. What do you think is meant by this metaphor? What (if any) meaning does this expression hold for you?

8. What impression does Deuteronomy make on you about Moses as a person and as a leader? Any takeaways for you from that impression?

9. What impression(s) does Deuteronomy make on you about God? How does its portrait of God enrich, expand, complicate, or challenge your view of God?

BIBLIOGRAPHY

Block, Daniel I. *The Gospel according to Moses: Theological and Ethical Reflections on the Book of Deuteronomy*. Eugene, OR: Cascade, 2012.

———. *How I Love Your Torah, O LORD! Studies in the Book of Deuteronomy*. Eugene, OR: Cascade, 2012.

Cook, Stephen L. *Reading Deuteronomy: A Literary and Theological Commentary*. Macon, GA: Smyth & Helwys, 2015.

Firth, David G., and Philip S. Johnston, eds. *Interpreting Deuteronomy: Issues and Approaches*. Downers Grove, IL: InterVarsity Press, 2012.

Lundbom, Jack R. *Deuteronomy: A Commentary*. Grand Rapids: Eerdmans, 2013.

MacDonald, Nathan. *Deuteronomy and the Meaning of "Monotheism."* Tübingen: Mohr Siebeck, 2012.

Miller, Patrick D. "Constitution or Instruction? The Purpose of Deuteronomy." Pages 125–41 in *Constituting the Community: Studies on the Polity of Ancient Israel in Honor of S. Dean McBride, Jr.* Edited by John T. Strong and Steven S. Tuell. Winona Lake, IN: Eisenbrauns, 2005.

Richter, Sandra L. "The Place of the Name in Deuteronomy." *VT* 57 (2007): 342–66.

Rofé, Alexander. *Deuteronomy: Issues and Interpretation*. New York: T&T Clark, 2002.

PART 3

The Historical Books

10 WHAT ARE THE HISTORICAL BOOKS?

WHEN THE TORAH ENDS, THE passionate voice of the aged Moses falls silent, and the editor of Deuteronomy narrates the great man's burial and praises his unparalleled historical stature. As we noted above, however, the Torah only has "somewhat" of an ending. It is complete insofar as it ends with the Israelites camped just across the Jordan River from the country God promised them. But they can only survey it from a distance; their actual possession of it is the central story of the first historical book, Joshua, and that book also has "somewhat" of an ending. When Israel crosses and controls much of it, noticeable pockets of Canaanites still remain to pose the serious problems evident in Joshua and Judges. In later Historical Books, however, the new nation of Israel occupies center stage alone, although awareness of unsettling Canaanite influences in Israel persist.

A Few Unusual Wrinkles with the Historical Books

The OT has twelve Historical Books (only nine if one counts Samuel, Kings, and Chronicles as single works) that track God's history with Israel over the next 800 years—from the death of Moses (ca. 1250 BCE) to the era of Ezra and Nehemiah (ca. 450 BCE; the story of Esther, the last Historical Book in our Bibles, actually precedes the latter by several decades). The Historical Books narrate the grand successes and horrible failures of Israel's subsequent tumultuous history. In addition, the last OT Historical Books—Esther in the Christian canon and Chronicles in the Jewish canon—reflect even later historical situations (ca. 400-350 BCE or possibly later).

Before proceeding however, you'll need to understand three wrinkles in the above scenario. First, Joshua, Judges, Samuel, and Kings tell a continuous story with a clear ending, but the four Historical Books that follow do not. Thus, what we call the *Historical Books* actually comprise two series of books:

1. The preexilic Historical Books (Joshua, Judges, Ruth, 1-2 Samuel, and 1-2 Kings)
2. The postexilic Historical Books (1-2 Chronicles, Ezra, Nehemiah, and Esther)

Obviously, the reason for the discontinuity between the two series—the reason why 2 Kings ends one story, and Ezra, Nehemiah, and Esther begin a slightly later one—is the Babylonian exile (for where Chronicles fits in, see below). This was the period of six decades that Judah spent in far-off Babylon after the Babylonians destroyed Jerusalem and exiled many leading Judahites. Second Kings concludes with the release of Judah's king from prison in Babylon about halfway through the exile (561 BCE), while Ezra, Nehemiah, and Esther focus on Judah's return home and other subsequent events (ca. 450 BCE). Clearly, the beginning and end of the exile mark major turning points for Israelite historians. The postexilic period gives way to the Hellenistic period when Alexander the Great wrests control of Syria and Palestine from Persian rule (332 BCE), an event that is unreported in the OT. These three watershed moments—the exile, the return, and the resettlement—permit us to speak of three distinct periods of Israel's history during which parts of the OT were written:

1. The preexilic period (roughly 1200-587 BCE)
2. The exile (587-538 BCE)
3. The postexilic period (538-332 BCE)

(Some scholars think that a few OT books originated in the Hellenistic period.)

So, let's summarize the story that together these two series of books tell:

1. The PreHB (preexilic Historical Books) pick up the story line with Moses's protégé, Joshua, and carry it down to the release of Judah's king Jehoiachin from prison in Babylon (ca. 1200-561 BCE)

2. The PostHB (postexilic Historical Books) begin with the return from exile (538 BCE) and end with the story of Jews under Persian rule (486–465 BCE)

3. Chronologically, only twenty-five years separate the end of 2 Kings and the return from exile (561–538 BCE) that Ezra 1–6 recounts

4. Literarily, however, the writing of the two historical series involves a larger gap—from ca. 550 BCE (preexilic) to ca. 300 BCE (postexilic)

Thus, each series (and, yes, each book within it) reads and reports the history through the lens of its distinct historical setting. That is one reason these Historical Books so fascinate us—and why we'll need to grasp their specific settings in order to understand them.

Now, the leftover question about where Chronicles fits is the second wrinkle we need to explain. In our Bibles, Chronicles follows Kings, implying that 1 Chr 1 picks up where Kings leaves off. For the most part, however, it offers an updated version of Samuel and Kings that ends with a brief mention of the exile and Cyrus's decree (538 BCE), the catalyst for the return, rather than Jehoiachin's release (cf. Jer 52:31–34). On closer inspection, the viewpoint of Chronicles radically departs from that of Samuel and Kings; it does so to address the concerns of its early-4th-century audience (for details, see our discussion of 1–2 Chronicles on p. 214).

The third wrinkle has to do with the location of the book of Ruth. Christian Bibles place Ruth between Judges and 1–2 Samuel because they follow the book order of the Greek OT (abbreviation: LXX), the preferred Bible of the early church. That order stands to reason: Ruth's lovely story dates to the same era as Judges and also mentions David, whose story 1–2 Samuel features. The Hebrew Bible, however, locates Ruth in its third main section, the Writings, which is mainly a collection of poetic books (e.g., Job, Psalms, Proverbs, etc.) but also is home to Daniel and all of the PostHB. That order also stands to reason: Ruth follows Proverbs because both Proverbs and Ruth praise a "worthy woman" with the same Hebrew phrase (Prov 12:4; 31:10; Ruth 3:11), and that canonical location also puts Ruth near the Psalms, the book associated with David, whose ancestry Ruth narrates. This background explains why we omit Ruth when we treat the PreHB.

Finally, Daniel and the PostHB constitute the final books of the Hebrew Bible, with Chronicles actually coming last. Their placement in the Writings probably derives from their postexilic origin and the canon compilers' desire to end the Hebrew Bible with Historical Books that address

The royal seal (or bulla) of King Hezekiah of Judah. Excavators found it in the Ophel just south of the Temple Mount in 2016. The seal's ancient Hebrew reads "Belonging to Hezekiah [son of] Ahaz king of Judah." The tiny object (0.5 inches wide) features a two-winged sun flanked by two ankh symbols representing life. Given the king's piety, these traditional Egyptian symbols probably refer to the protection of Israel's God, Yahweh. Such clay seals were an ancient signature, vouching for a document's authenticity and securing the strings that kept it rolled up. This example marks the first Hezekiah seal discovered in place, possibly in a royal administrative building, rather than on the antiquities open market. The find confirms that Jerusalem under Hezekiah was a major Judahite administrative center (see 2 Kgs 18–20). ©Eilat Mazar. Photo by Ouria Tadmor. Used with permission.

the unique concerns of a postexilic audience, much as the PreHB did for its exilic audience. Again, below we'll return to expand on this topic (for further discussion, see 37 on the canon and text).

What Is a "Historical Book"?

A *historical book* is a narrative book that intends to recount accurately the people and events from a specific time and place in the past. Its writers are people who love to talk about history and who think that events in the past still have something to teach people living in the present. We say that their writings are "referential": they want us to accept that what they recount closely approximates what actually happened "back then." But, as it turns out, history is a far more complex phenomenon than we may realize. We may assume (as do many people) that writers of "history" and writers of "other literature" are doing radically different, if not irreconcilable things. Perhaps it is better, however, to remember what someone once said: "We do not have history; we only have historians." In other words, history does not exist as an entity in itself; we only know about it when historians report it. Further, as it turns out, in writing their reports historians typically use some of the same literary devices as other writers. That, in part, explains why we earlier stated our preference for speaking of OT histories simply as *narrative* or *story*. Rather than juxtapose history and fiction as opposites, we recommend that you think of them more as history in narrative form—and in some narratives, the literary shaping predominates; in others, the factual content does.

Let's expand on this idea:

1. The historian writes a narrative, not just a bunch of "brute facts" from history. Historians dab their authorial brush in the same palette of narrative literary devices as all authors, including those writing fiction. They pen captivating descriptions; they invoke compelling metaphors; their characterizations often draw on common stereotypes; they indulge in good storytelling; they weave together a plot; sometimes they even aim to entertain; and so on. In other words, they use the same techniques as writers of fiction. By the same token, the latter sometimes borrow literary features more typical of narrative history: their literary strategy may include chronology, cause-and-effect connections, and well-known historical characters.

2. The historian arbitrarily operates as a literary gatekeeper. Ultimately, he or she alone decides which of all the items or data relevant to a topic to include or exclude from the end product. Such choices reflect the same judgment-call that *any* author—including the authors of the book you're reading right now—makes in preparing something in writing. You'll soon see this principle at work in the two longest biblical examples of history writing, Kings and Chronicles, both of which treat the same subject (the Israelite monarchy) but very differently.

3. The historian also arbitrarily decides when the principle of cause and effect links events together. In some cases this connection is quite obvious: it's no stretch to accept that the Jew Mordecai's dishonoring of Haman drove the latter to seek annihilation of all Jews (Esth 3). But the idea that divine providence lurks behind Samson's desire to marry a Philistine woman (Judg 14:4) is less clear; it is the author who asserts this theological connection in a parenthetical comment.

In short, we'll do well to keep this understanding of history and historians in mind when exploring the Historical Books. Be aware that we will return to this topic below in our treatment of the book of Esther (see also our comments on the historicity of the Torah in ch. 3 above).

The Magnificent Seven: The Preexilic Historical Books

As we noted, the seven Historical Books (counting Samuel and Kings as two books each) cover Israel's history from the death of Moses (Josh 1:1) to the middle of the exile in Babylon (2 Kgs 25:30). The sweep of this history—the breadth and detail of its knowledge—is magnificent. During this period, the Neo-Assyrian Empire rose and fell, replaced by the Neo-Babylonian Empire, which dominated the ancient Near East at the conclusion of the events of 2 Kings (see Tables 10.1 and 10.2). Of course, we might wish for more details in some places, but through these books we successfully ride the historical ups and downs, the successes and failures of Israel.

The seven books can be outlined as follows:

Joshua: How God gave Israel the land of Canaan as its homeland for generations

Judges: How God fended off serious threats to Israel and showed it needed a king

> *Ruth*: How God brought a foreigner to Israel who became King David's great-grandmother
>
> *1 Samuel*: How Samuel and Saul led Israel's transition from a tribal federation to a monarchy
>
> *2 Samuel*: How David ruled a single, united kingdom of Israel and founded a royal dynasty
>
> *1 Kings*: How that kingdom split into two countries, both struggling to survive invasions and the lure of idolatry
>
> *2 Kings*: How idolatry, some of it royal sponsored, ended Israel's stay in Canaan

Each of the seven books has its own unique identity, yet each helps develop the larger story:

1. Joshua treats two distinct stages in Israel's transition from migratory life in tents to settled life in cities and towns. Joshua 1–12 recounts the conquest—how God took back his land from the Canaanites to give it to Israel; Josh 13–24 narrates the settlement—how the tribes of Israel divided up Yahweh's land-gift among them. The latter subplot ends dramatically with Joshua's farewell speech (Josh 23) and a solemn, Joshua-led covenant ceremony (Josh 24).

2. Judges follows Joshua with an honest look at what Israel's life in Canaan was like. Judges 1–16 features the exploits of "the judges," famous military heroes who saved the fledgling nation from local and regional foreign threats. Its concluding epilogue (Judg 17–21) presents two unflattering stories of Israel falling apart in idolatry and a violent tribal feud, and falling away from their promised loyalty to Yahweh. In short, it argues that Israel desperately needs a king to restore order.

3. Though contemporary to Judges, Ruth combines the intriguing story of a crisis that hit one family in Bethlehem (Ruth 1:1–4:17) and its genealogy (Ruth 4:18–22). It introduces us to Ruth, a remarkable young Moabite widow; but watch out—the book has a surprise ending!

4. First Samuel brings down the curtain on the judges' era only to raise it on the monarchy. First Samuel 1–7 introduces the last judge, Samuel, who anoints the first king, Saul. First Samuel 8–31 narrates how Saul's reign quickly fails, leaving the paranoid king obsessed with killing his royal rival, David.

5. Second Samuel narrates the rule of David, Saul's successor. Second Samuel 1–10 traces how David overcame the remaining supporters of

Saul, united Israel, and enjoyed success. Second Samuel 11–21 traces the fallout from the Bathsheba episode in palace rivalries and popular discontent with his rule. An epilogue (2 Sam 22–24) evaluates David's reign through his own words and two memorable episodes.

6. First Kings continues Israel's history under David's successors. First Kings 1–11 details the economic empire built by Solomon and explains his ultimate failure. First Kings 12–22 follows the split of the united kingdom into two rival kingdoms, Israel and Judah, and evaluates their kings. In Israel, the prophet Elijah opposes royal sponsorship of Baal worship.

7. Second Kings narrates how Israel's life under the monarchy came to an end. Second Kings 1–17 follows the prophet Elisha's dealings with Northern kings and explains why the Northern Kingdom, Israel, ended in destruction and exile; 2 Kgs 18–25 tells how Judah survived but, notwithstanding two major religious reforms, ended up the same way.

The Six "Early Prophets"

We classify these six books as Historical Books, but the canon of the Hebrew Bible puts them (minus Ruth) among the Prophets, the section between the Torah and the Writings. In fact, it subdivides the Prophets into two sections: the Early Prophets (Joshua–2 Kings) and the Later Prophets (Isaiah–Malachi). This fact, unfamiliar to most Christians, helps us savor the unique flavor that the Historical Books offer. Clearly, the terminology regards these historical books as an early form of what later plays out in the Later Prophets (Isaiah, Jeremiah, Ezekiel, etc.). Whether this assumes (as some suggest) that the Historical Books were written by prophets is unclear. At least it alerts us to the crucial role that the prophets also play in the Early Prophets. In ancient Israel, priests studied and taught the Torah (i.e., the *written* words of God), while prophets spoke an *immediate* word from God (i.e., what God wanted to say right now). In Israel, only appointment by a prophet legitimized a king's authority as divinely sanctioned and worthy of obedience—for example, David (and his dynasty) by Nathan, Jeroboam I by Ahijah, and Jehu by Elisha (cf. Hos 8:4). Since kings ruled on behalf of God, God also called erring monarchs to account through prophets—for example, Elijah's confrontations with King Ahab (1 Kgs 18:15–46; 21:17–27). Indeed, the prominence of prophets in Samuel and Kings is a measure of how spiritually dismal royal leadership and popular religious life were in those days.

How Did We Get All These Long Books?

As noted above, Joshua through 2 Kings constitute the Historical Books that cover 700 years of Israelite history from the death of Moses (Josh 1:1) to the middle of the Babylonian exile (2 Kgs 25:27-30).

Possibly Joshua, Judges, Samuel, and Kings never circulated as individual books. Rather, they and their earlier materials were incorporated into a larger historical work that modern interpreters call the Deuteronomistic History (DH). Sometime around 620 BCE, during the reign of King Josiah, a group of scribes produced DH 1.0, with Josiah's reign as its climax and a passionate warning that growing apostasy threatened Judah with the same disaster that had doomed Israel in 722 BCE. The word *Deuteronomic* (or *Deuteronomistic*) in the title captures the strong influence on Joshua to 2 Kings of the book of Deuteronomy and of Moses's theology on how Israelite conduct affects Israel's history. About 550 BCE, scribes in exile in Babylon produced DH 2.0, an update of the first edition that extended the history from Josiah into the exile (2 Kgs 24-25).

How Were the Historical Books Used?

When people heard the Historical Books being read, what would the text have done for them? First, the Historical Books tell Israel how their ancestors settled in the promised land—and how they later lost it. The books extend the Torah's history, narrating the next six centuries and explaining why the Israelites end up back in Mesopotamia (i.e., Babylon) again. Their history addresses some questions that the exilic and postexilic generations might ask:

1. How did we come to own this wonderful land—and will we ever own it again?
2. When we return, what kind of leaders will assure our success?
3. What kind of people are we, and what kind of God is ours?
4. Are we free to do as we like?
5. What mistakes did our ancestors make, and how can we avoid them?

To answer the first question, the PreHB open with Joshua and the tribes' conquest and settlement of the promised land, followed by a close-up of the settlement's problematic early decades in the book of Judges. Interestingly, the very retelling of the story aims to reassure exiled Israelites that the exile negates neither the identity of their homeland nor their rights to ancestral inheritances there. As for the second question, the PreHB are more concerned with explaining how past mistakes (see below) led to the present reality of exile than with the possibility of return. It is the prophets who announce the future return; the task of the historians is to prepare the people to make it a success. As for future leadership, the PreHB commend leaders who show exemplary, exclusive loyalty to Yahweh—Joshua, Deborah, Samuel, David, Hezekiah—rather than Samson, Saul, Solomon, Manasseh, all kings of Israel (especially Ahab), and most of the kings of Judah. Exemplary priests are those who faithfully follow and teach the Torah—for example, Aaron's son Eleazar (Josh 14:1; 17:4; 19:51), brave Ahimelek (1 Sam 21), Zadok (1 Kgs 2), Jehoiada (2 Kgs 11–12), and Hilkiah (2 Kgs 22). Eli and his sons disqualify themselves (1 Sam 1–4), and understandably the PreHB deny priestly legitimacy or a clerical future to all priests who served the idolatrous shrines at Dan and Bethel—the infamous "sin of Jeroboam" (1 Kgs 12:26–33; 15:34; 2 Kgs 23:15).

Image from a 14th-century volume of Rudolf von Ems's *Weltchronik*. The miniature depicts Ahijah ready to tear his garment into twelve pieces before Jeroboam, showing how God will divide the kingdom after the death of Solomon (1 Kgs 11:26–40).

Among prophets faithful to Yahweh, Nathan, Ahijah, Elijah, Elisha, and Isaiah clearly stand out, and the PreHB remind their audience that what doomed both Israel and Judah was the people's failure to listen to the prophets (2 Kgs 17:23; 21:10–15; 24:2; see also our introduction to the prophets in ch. 21). As for the kings, the case histories of Samuel, Saul, and David (1 Sam 10–16) show that God sovereignly appoints leaders and replaces those who displease him (see also Hannah's Song, 1 Sam 2). Against the unstable leadership that typifies Israel, the Davidic covenant and Yahweh's commitment to it provide Judah with long-term dynastic stability, as the PreHB affirm (2 Sam 7). Interestingly, in the PreHB disastrously unfaithful kings such as Solomon, Jehoram, Ahaz, and Manasseh do not suspend or cancel the Davidic covenant; instead, God's gracious actions toward Judah, including the defense of Jerusalem, continue "for the sake of my [or his] servant David." Also, it is striking that the PreHB conclude with Babylon's kind treatment of exiled King Jehoiachin of Judah (2 Kgs 25:27–30)—a reminder to all who lived after the fall of Judah of Yahweh's long-term commitment to the descendants of David and, by implication, to the nation of Judah as a whole. In passing, we mention that the PostHB give the monarchy theme a completely different twist.

In answering the third question, the PreHB echo themes from the Torah, but they are nuanced in light of the exile and the Second Temple period. The division of the promised land among the tribes (Josh 13-19) fulfills the promise to Abraham and confirms the identity of his descendants as beneficiaries of the promised blessings. It also highlights God's identity as a faithful promise-keeper. The temple (1 Kgs 5-9) affirms the continuing validity of the Mosaic covenant (Israel remains God's special people) and that God still wants to live among them and bless them. The PreHB also report God's stunning routs of Moab and Assyria (2 Kgs 3 and 19), further testimony to the powerful, sovereign God on whom the people may rely, even after witnessing the destruction of Jerusalem. But from their national history of spiritual inconstancy (see Judg 2), Judges warns that idolatry risks disasters akin to the events of 722 and 587 BCE (see 2 Kgs 17). Indeed, the PreHB are painfully aware that the "Israel" they address is basically Judah plus some refugees of other tribes. At the same time, the PreHB also paint God as surprisingly tender and compassionate (see 2 Sam 24)—even welcoming to Israel the Moabite widow Ruth, whose devotion to Yahweh and to family personifies the ideal of Israel at its best.

To the fourth question, the PreHB voice a resounding "No! We are *not* free to do as we like—only free to do what Yahweh likes." The deuteronomistic logic is pretty simple: if you do what pleases Yahweh (and, thereby, avoid what does not), Yahweh's promised blessings will flow. That is what Joshua, Samuel, and David exemplify, and such faithfulness is the only protection against the never-ending cycle of Judges or the sad incompetence of King Saul (1 Sam 13-15). As 1-2 Kings demonstrates, unfaithfulness to Yahweh shrunk once-great Israel to a remnant of Judah. That partly answers the final "mistake" question. For DH, the biggest mistake is that Israel broke the covenant, disobeying the Torah and abandoning Yahweh to worship other gods. Tone-deafness toward prophetic preaching and hard-heartedness toward repentance were also disastrous. To avoid such mistakes, the PreHB call their audience to emulate the positive examples mentioned above. Restored Judah features one country, temple, capital city, priestly family, and Mosaic Torah demanding unwavering loyal devotion to one God, Yahweh.

The Contexts of the Historical Books

Israelites understood how they were to use the Historical Books because they heard them in their original historical contexts. We, too, do well to join them in hearing those books within those same contexts. The timeline on p. 120 shows the key moments and transitions in Israel's history that shaped the development of those books and in light of which Israel listened to them.

Table 10.1. Neo-Assyrian Kings

Name	Dates	Years of Reign
Adad-nirari II	911–891	20
Tukulti-Ninurta II	890–884	6
Ashurnasirpal II	883–859	24
Shalmaneser III	858–824	34
Shamshi-Adad V	823–811	12
Shamiram	811–806	5
Adad-nirari III	806–783	23
Shalmaneser IV	782–773	9
Ashur-dan III	772–755	17
Ashur-nirari V	754–745	9
Tiglath-pileser III	745–727	17
Shalmaneser V	726–722	4
Sargon II	721–705	16
Sennacherib	704–681	23
Esarhaddon	680–669	11
Ashurbanipal	668–627	41
Ashur-etel-ilani	627–624	3
Sin-shar-ishkun	623–612	11
Ashur-uballit II	612	

Table 10.2. Neo-Babylonian Kings

Name	Dates of Reign
Nabopolassar	625–605
Nebuchadnezzar	604–562
Amel-Marduk	562–560
Neriglissar	560–556
Labashi-Marduk	556
Nabonidus	556–539
Belshazzar (son of Nabonidus and appointed regent)	553–539

722: Ephraim falls to Assyria, a catastrophe close-by that compels Judahites to wonder about their own future fate.

622: Josiah's reformation, the moment when Deuteronomy again becomes a living force in Judah's life and DH 1.0 comes out; the former provides Judah fresh theological guidance, while the latter commends Josiah's reformation goals.

587: Judah falls to Babylon after ignoring the warnings of imminent disaster by prophets such as Jeremiah and Ezekiel. The exile begins and with it an opportunity to rethink the past from a healthy distance.

561: The new Babylonian king, Amel-Marduk, releases Judah's King Jehoiachin from prison; more food-for-thought for the exiles, who wonder what their future holds.

ca. 550: DH 2.0 appears in Babylon, its retrospective review of the monarchic period giving Judah clues about why it's in exile and hope for a return home.

539: Babylon falls to Persia, further raising the exiles' hopes that their situation might soon change.

538: The decree of the Persian king Cyrus authorizes and funds the rebuilding of the temple in Jerusalem; many Israelites now return to resettle and rebuild Judah.

520–518: Through the prophets Haggai and Zechariah, God promises renewed greatness for Judah, inspiring the returnees to rebuild the temple.

515: The finished temple in Jerusalem (the "Second Temple") is dedicated with appropriate ceremonies.

486–465: King Xerxes (or Ahasuerus) rules the Persian Empire; taking bold risks, Mordecai and Esther spare Jews empire-wide from annihilation by their enemies.

458: The priest Ezra comes from Babylon to teach Torah-obedience as the sole basis for the success of Judah's new life.

445: Nehemiah comes from Babylon to Jerusalem and spearheads the rebuilding of Jerusalem's ruined walls.

ca. 400–350: Writers in Jerusalem publish a new Israelite history, 1-2 Chronicles, to address the struggling community in postexilic Yehud (i.e., the Babylonian and Persian provincial name for Judah).

332: Alexander the Great defeats the Persians and takes over their empire, including Yehud. Jews everywhere must now reckon with yet another foreign imperial overlord.

BIBLIOGRAPHY

Arnold, Bill T., and H. G. M. Williamson, eds. *Dictionary of the Old Testament: Historical Books*. Downers Grove, IL: InterVarsity Press, 2005.

Chapman, Stephen B. "Ethics of Deuteronomistic History." Pages 61–66 in *The Old Testament and Ethics: A Book-by-Book Survey*. Edited by Joel B. Green and Jacqueline E. Lapsley. Grand Rapids: Baker Academic, 2013.

Chisholm, Robert B., Jr. *Interpreting the Historical Books: An Exegetical Handbook*. Handbooks for Old Testament Exegesis. Grand Rapids: Kregel, 2006.

Endres, John C., William R. Millar, and John Barclay, eds. *Chronicles and Its Synoptic Parallels in Samuel, Kings, and Related Biblical Texts*. Collegeville, MN: Liturgical Press, 1998.

Hood, Jason B., and Matthew Y. Emerson. "Summaries of Israel's Story: Reviewing a Compositional Category." *CurBR* 11 (2013): 328–48.

Knoppers, Gary N., and J. Gordon McConville, eds. *Reconsidering Israel and Judah: Recent Studies on the Deuteronomistic History*. Sources for Biblical and Theological Study 8. Winona Lake, IN: Eisenbrauns, 2000.

McKenzie, Steven L. *Introduction to the Historical Books: Strategies for Reading*. Grand Rapids: Eerdmans, 2010.

Provan, Iain. "Hearing the Historical Books." Pages 254–76 in *Hearing the Old Testament: Listening for God's Address*. Edited by Craig G. Bartholomew and David J. H. Beldman. Grand Rapids: Eerdmans, 2012.

Satterthwaite, Philip, and J. Gordon McConville. *A Guide to the Historical Books*. Vol. 2 of *Exploring the Old Testament*. 4 vols. Downers Grove, IL: InterVarsity Press, 2007.

11 THE BOOK OF JOSHUA

Important Dates for Joshua
ca. 1220–1210: Israel's conquest and settlement of Canaan
ca. 1200: Joshua's death and burial

NAMED FOR ITS HERO, THE book of Joshua tells how Joshua leads the Israelites to conquer and settle in Canaan, the land of promise. It marks the first of several Historical Books that bear the name of their main characters (cf. Judges, Ruth, Samuel, Ezra, Nehemiah, and Esther). The book opens with the Israelites camped east of the Jordan and ends with the burials in Canaan of Joshua, Joseph, and the priest Eleazar (Josh 24:29-33). Two important speeches—Yahweh's to Joshua (1:1-9) and Joshua's farewell to Israel (ch. 23)—bracket the book thematically, and the repeated phrase "to this day" (5:9; 9:27) casts the narrative as a retrospective, backward look at the history. A member of the tribe of Ephraim, Joshua debuts in the Torah as commander of the Israelites who successfully repel an attack by Amalekites as Israel journeys toward Mount Sinai (Exod 17:8-16). He reappears later as Moses's young aide (Exod 24:13), is one of two spies to favor continuing toward Canaan (Num 14), receives divine appointment as Moses's successor (Deut 31), and assumes the mantle of leadership upon Moses's death (Josh 1:1-2). After Israel enters the land, on two occasions he leads the Israelites to renew their covenant with Yahweh (Josh 8:30-35; 24:1-28; cf. Deut 29), and the OT twice praises his exemplary spiritual leadership (Josh 24:31; Judg 2:7). The book of Joshua also credits him with completing the conquest of the whole land (11:16-23). To this day, pilgrims still visit the traditional site of his tomb near Shiloh in the modern West Bank. Oddly enough, he lacks a direct successor, unless we are to accord that role to the Torah and/or to the covenant.

What Was Going On Back Then?

The period ca. 1500-1100 brings some momentous transitions for Canaan, so the situation that the arriving Israelites will face there depends on the date one assumes for their entry. An entry in ca. 1400 BCE (the early date) would encounter a Canaan that was part of a vast Egyptian Empire, visible locally in foreign military garrisons and Egyptian governmental authorities. The hill country would be relatively unpopulated, but sizable, wealthy, Canaanite city-states ruled by local kings would lie along the coast, on the Sharon plain, and in the Jordan and Jezreel valleys. The Amarna letters (14th cent. BCE) also mention threatening encroachments by outsiders (e.g., Hittites, Habiru) and disputes between more- and less-powerful Canaanite kings. An Israelite entry a few decades before 1200 BCE (the late date) would face a similar geopolitical landscape, but notably the Egyptians would be withdrawing or completely gone. Further, the once-stable, prosperous eastern Mediterranean would be in a political and economic "dark age" that would last for two centuries. The Canaanite city-states and their material culture would be in decline, with regional interethnic (not international) connections driving the economy. Large ethnic migrations would have brought new peoples to Canaan, notably the Philistines along the Palestinian coast. In the central hill country, Bethel has become a major city, and an entrenched enclave of Amorites holds the Aijalon valley (Judg 1:34). In sum, the entire region would be in the process of redefining itself—an unsettled time of great transition but fraught with great possibilities for the arriving Israelites.

The Story

Structurally, the book of Joshua proceeds through three main sections of reports concerning (1) the conquest of Canaan (chs. 1–12), (2) Joshua's distribution of tribal inheritances (chs. 13–21), and (3) the early years of the settlement (chs. 22–24).

Joshua 1–12: The Conquest of Canaan

Chapter 1 opens appropriately, with Yahweh's dramatic, formal installation of Joshua as Israel's leader and God's command for him to lead Israel across the Jordan into Canaan. Of course, this action comes as no surprise since Yahweh has already designated Joshua, Moses's longtime aide, as his successor (Num 27:18-23; 32:28; Deut 31:3). Nor is it a surprise that the center of the opening scene is a speech by Yahweh to Joshua (Josh 1:2-9), for speeches, especially speeches in which leaders bid the Israelites farewell or instruct their successors, are a common feature of DH (see the speeches by Joshua that conclude the book [chs. 23-24]). On the other hand, this marks the only speech that Yahweh gives in the book, and it is an important one: Yahweh's personal address here establishes his personal relationship with Joshua and confirms that God has put him in charge now. Verses 6-9 mark the chapter's highpoint and repeat the central demand of Yahweh three times: "Be brave and strong" (vv. 6, 7, 9). The key to retaining that bravery and strength is: "Carefully obey all of the Instruction that Moses . . . commanded you" (v. 7) and "recite it day and night" (v. 8 CEB). With those commands Joshua also receives the promise that "the LORD your God is with you wherever you go" (v. 9). That's why Joshua has nothing whatsoever to fear. In short, the opening scene marks the debut of two prominent themes: (1) God's promise to be as close to Joshua as he was to Moses, and (2) the irrevocable demand that Joshua never let fear or intimidation weaken his confidence in Yahweh's power to bring him success (1:6-9; compare with Deut 31:6-9).

Chapter 2 presents a spy story that is probably well known to readers since it introduces an intriguing character, the prostitute Rahab in Jericho. Like typical spy stories, it features intrigue, danger, secrecy, and even anonymity (the spies are simply "two men"; compare Num 13; Josh 7:2-5; Judg 18). Interpreters have also noted how ambiguous and general Joshua's commission is ("View the land, especially Jericho"; Josh 2:1) and how absent and silent Yahweh seems in the reported events. Two things, however, are particularly striking: Rahab's passionate affirmation of Yahweh's sovereignty and her description of Canaanite morale (2:9):

> I know that the LORD has given you this land and that a great fear
> of you has fallen on us, so that all who live in this country are
> melting in fear because of you. (TNIV)

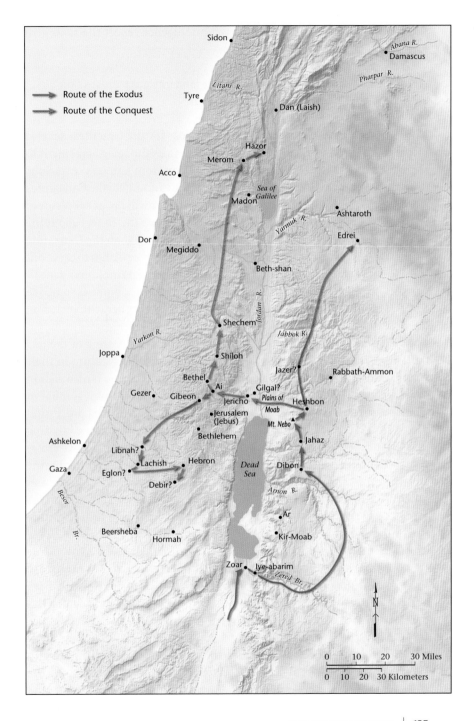

Route of the Exodus

Route of the Conquest

Sidon

Abana R.

Damascus

Pharpar R.

Litani R.

Tyre

Dan (Laish)

Hazor

Merom

Acco

Sea of Galilee

Madon

Ashtaroth

Yarmuk R.

Edrei

Dor

Megiddo

Beth-shan

Jordan R.

Shechem

Jabbok R.

Yarkon R.

Shiloh

Joppa

Jazer?

Rabbath-Ammon

Bethel

Gilgal?

Ai

Plains of Moab

Gezer

Jericho

Heshbon

Gibeon

Jerusalem (Jebus)

Mt. Nebo

Ashkelon

Bethlehem

Jahaz

Libnah?

Hebron

Dibon

Lachish

Dead Sea

Gaza

Eglon?

Debir?

Arnon R.

Ar

Besor Br.

Beersheba

Kir-Moab

Hormah

Zoar

Iye-abarim

Zered Br.

N

0   10   20   30 Miles

0   10   20   30 Kilometers

THE BOOK OF JOSHUA | 125

Readers, thus, are not surprised at the intelligence report the spies give Joshua upon their return (v. 24 TNIV):

> The LORD has surely given the whole land into our hands; all the people are melting in fear because of us.

Notwithstanding this optimistic morale boost for the Israelites, several important questions hang over the narrative: Does the spies' agreement to spare Rahab's life in exchange for her protection from Jericho's suspicious king violate Yahweh's unconditional mandate to annihilate the Canaanites (Deut 20:16–18)? Will the bargain please Joshua, or will he, as successor to Moses, feel obligated to overrule it? And how does Yahweh feel about the deal? Will Yahweh himself disallow it and exclude Rahab the Canaanite from Israel? Or does she represent a niche that the book wishes to carve out for select foreigners in Israelite ranks? One thing is certain: Jesus's genealogy lists her as Boaz's mother (Matt 1:5); for James she exemplifies someone justified by works (Jas 2:25); and the Hall of Faith honors her with inclusion (Heb 11:31).

Chapters 3–4 portray the Israelites' triumphant crossing of the Jordan, an event that Yahweh orchestrates to raise Joshua's stature in their eyes (see Josh 3:7; cf. 6:27). The incredibly dramatic scene is also rich in symbolism: the ark of the covenant—Yahweh's royal throne, symbol of God's powerful presence—leads what amounts to a ceremonial procession across from Transjordan to Canaan proper. The motif of Israel's "crossing on dry land" echoes the exodus event (Exod 14) and connects the two crossings as Yahweh's twin interconnected, spectacular triumphs that enable the Israelites to escape slavery and open the door to their settlement in Canaan (cf. Ps 114). Another powerful symbol is the twelve stones carried from the Jordan's dry riverbed by specially selected Israelites, which Joshua configures into a monument at Gilgal, Israel's first home base on the west bank. The stone pile's function, Joshua says, is to cause their children over time (possibly on ritual pilgrimages) to ask, "What do these stones mean?" so their parents may remind them of both "dry-land" crossings, the Red Sea and the Jordan (4:22–23). Ultimately, such retellings serve to keep earth's peoples aware of Yahweh's great power and to keep the Israelites' reverence for Yahweh strong (v. 24).

Chapter 5 features two traditional religious ceremonies, the circumcision of male Israelites and the celebration of Passover—the first to ensure the ritual fitness of the arriving Israelites to occupy the "holy" land, and the second to obey what the Torah commanded for that specific date (Nisan 14th). How appropriate that the Israelites observed the Passover, which remembers their liberation from Egyptian slavery, on their first day in the promised land! The storyteller also remarks about another first: the very next day the Israelites begin to depend on Canaan's food instead of their desert staple, manna (vv. 11-12). Chapters 6-8 narrate the first three battles of the actual conquest of Canaan, and each highlights an important theological truth. In ch. 6, Jericho is the target, but the story prefaces

Rahab and the Emissaries, by an unknown artist. Ca. 1630.

that event with a brief, mysterious encounter in ch. 5—Joshua's unexpected encounter with "a man" carrying a sword (5:13-15). The mystery intensifies because the man (1) says he's neither for nor against the parties to the coming battle, (2) identifies himself as "the commander of the LORD's army" (v. 14), and (3) commands Joshua to "take off your sandals, for the place where you are standing is holy" (v. 15 TNIV). This obvious echo of the angel of the LORD's appearance to Moses at the burning bush (Exod 3:5) aims to reassure Joshua that victory is certain because Yahweh is now present "on the ground," so to speak, and that the coming battle is Yahweh's to fight, not Israel's (compare Josh 10:42; 23:10). The theological theme of God's invisible, invincible army fighting beside God's people and guaranteeing victory will recur later in the OT (see 2 Kgs 6:16). Indeed, Josh 6 recounts not a typical, violent battle scene but a second stately, ark-led ceremony, the seven-day ritual conquest of Jericho and the sparing of the prostitute Rahab.

Alas, the attack against the next target, the city of Ai in the central mountains (ch. 7), fails miserably because an Israelite named Achan has disobeyed Yahweh by secretly keeping plunder from Jericho. The theological theme here affirms that God regards his people not as a collection of individuals but as a single, collective entity; that is why Yahweh holds all the Israelites accountable for the secret sin of a single Israelite. This corporate view of reality is recognizable in both Old and New Testaments (cf. Adam and Christ in 1 Cor 15:22) and requires us, whose worldview is strongly in-

Did the Sun Really Stop Moving?

Joshua 10:12–14 is certainly one of the book's best-known (and most-discussed) parts. To begin, notice that literarily the verses quote a line from an ancient poem (vv. 12–13a) and add an authorial comment interpreting it (vv. 13b–14). The two key verbs in the poem (Heb. *dom* = "stand still," vv. 12–13; *'amad* = "come to a stop," v. 13) suggest that Joshua calls for a cessation (or, at least, a significant slowing) of the two luminaries midcourse over Gibeon and the Aijalon valley. Some interpreters read the text scientifically, accepting that the earth actually stopped rotating, but there are no scientific traces of such a cosmic event. Other interpreters explain the poem in light of natural phenomena: (1) that the text reports a refraction of light that prolonged the daylight hours; (2) that the sun "ceased shining" (not "ceased moving"), either from a solar eclipse or a cloud cover (note the hailstorm, v. 11); (3) that, consistent with ANE beliefs, Joshua seeks an omen — for example, the sun and moon in the same sky — that Israel would read as favorable or the Amorites as unfavorable. But nothing in the text points to such phenomena, so we aver that the text is best read as a poetic depiction of the military conflict in progress on a cosmic scale (cf. Judg 5:20). Its cosmic terms rhetorically magnify the majestic power of God that won this great victory. The Sun and Moon function as personifications of God's sovereignty over the cosmos (see also Ps 121:6; Hab 3:11), the cosmic sovereignty of Yahweh, for whose intervention Joshua appeals.

dividualistic, to align our thinking with the Bible's more corporate view—for example, to understand "humanity" and "the church" collectively. The fate of Achan himself is another case in point: a formal series of lot-castings publically expose him as the guilty person, but he, his family, and even his property collectively suffer the harsh penalty. Chapter 8 opens with Yahweh's assurance of victory, and Joshua uses a ruse to draw out Ai's defenders and successfully capture the city. It solemnly ends (vv. 30–35) at Shechem with a dramatic covenant-renewal ceremony—in effect, the installation of Moses's Instruction as the law of the land (cf. ch. 24).

In chs. 9–10, however, the Israelites themselves fall victim to a ruse. In ch. 9, people from Gibeon, a major Canaanite city located a short distance from Ai, appear at the Israelite camp pretending to be non-Canaanites on a long journey from their distant homeland. Wearing soiled, tattered clothes and bearing moldy bread and worn wineskins, they paint a bedraggled—and false—picture! After careful scrutiny—but not, the narrator underscores, consultation with Yahweh (v. 14)—Joshua makes a treaty of peace with them, the other leaders ratifying it with an oath. Later, when confronted by Joshua, the Gibeonites explain their deception: they had heard of Moses's command that the Israelites conquer the land and annihilate its inhabitants, and resorted to a ruse to escape that horrible fate (v. 24). Since the oath prohibited their execution, Joshua appointed them as woodcutters and water carriers for the Israelites and for Israel's later central sanctuary. As with Rahab, readers again wonder whether or not Yahweh approves of a second exception to the annihilation policy. The bad news, however, is that in ch. 10 a large Canaanite army besieges Gibeon, and the treaty obligates the Israelites to defend the Gibeonites. But the good news comes when Yahweh reassures Joshua of victory (10:8), amazingly implying divine approval of their treatment of the Gibeonites and perhaps of Rahab. The really good news, however, is that Yahweh subjects the besiegers to "confusion" and pelts those fleeing with "large hailstones" (vv. 10–11). Most important, Israelite pursuit of the chaotically retreating armies unexpectedly results in Joshua's conquest of cities and their kings through all of southern Canaan (vv. 16–43). Chapter 11 follows with Joshua's sweeping conquest of northern Canaan, including the major city-state of Hazor, thus subjecting all of Canaan to his leadership.

Excursus: What Do Historians Say about Jericho, Ai, and Hazor?

Three cities figure prominently in the narrative of Joshua and require special comment. Historians regard Jericho (or Tell es-Sultân) as one of the world's oldest towns (founded ca. 8000 BCE) and, despite its small size (about ten acres), the main eastern border city of Canaan. The difficulty for historians, however, is that the archaeological record shows no evidence of fortification walls or inhabitants about the time the Bible says Joshua and the Israelites arrived (but see the reassessment of the evidence by Bryant G. Wood). Possibly, however, earlier fortifications were reused to fortify Joshua's Jericho (a common ancient practice) and then were washed away over time by the erosion that everyone concedes has affected the site. If so, as Kitchen suggests (p. 187), remains of Joshua's Jericho may lie under the modern road and farmland along the site's eastern side. A similar lack of occupation in Joshua's day haunts the historians' view of Ai (lit., "the Ruin"), the huge site at et-Tell (27.5 acres) near the modern Palestinian village of Deir Dibwan. Some suggest that Josh 7–8 has confused Ai and nearby Bethel, reporting the latter's conquest (definitely inhabited) as the former's. But the topographical details of the Joshua account fit et-Tell better than Bethel. In our view, some biblical data suggest that the ruins of Ai may actually have served as an ad hoc defensive outpost for Bethel (e.g., 7:3; 8:17, 25) or even temporarily housed summer workers tending Ai's farmland (see Josh 8:1–2). Both uses would require only temporary shelters rather than permanent stone homes that typically leave archaeological traces. Two millennia of erosion may also have washed away evidence of occupations at Ai.

The archaeological picture of Hazor is clearer. It confirms that attackers violently destroyed the prestigious Canaanite city in the 13th century BCE and also that non-Canaanite settlers occupied a small portion of the ruined site for a short time in the 11th century. The new arrivals apparently lived in tents and temporary structures — an encampment of transients rather than long-term residents — and vacated the site voluntarily. Tentatively, Ben-Ami identifies them as Israelites (or proto-Israelites) and, citing other prominent "camps" evident in Joshua and Judges (e.g., Gilgal [Josh 4–10], Shiloh [Josh 18:1–10; Judg 21:12], Dan [Judg 13:25; 18:12]), speculates that they represent a pattern of Israelite settlement: encampments prior to permanent settlement. In short, the archaeological picture of Hazor comprises three phases: the Canaanite city that ended violently, two centuries without occupation, a short-term Israelite encampment, and a permanent Israelite city (10th–8th cent. BCE). Though Ben-Ami hesitates to identify Hazor's destroyers as Israelites, he concedes the possibility.

In ch. 12, narrative gives way to a formal list of all the kings defeated by Joshua. Diagram 11.1 is a visual representation of the text, showing that in Hebrew a blank space follows the name of each king, after which comes the word "one."

The chapter reads like a tally sheet of some sort, and were it read publicly, one can imagine the dramatic drumbeat of victory after victory produced. It is an unusual but effective way of concluding the lengthy conquest

Diagram 11.1. How Joshua 12:7–24 Looks in Hebrew: An Excerpt

[7]These are the kings of the land that Joshua and the Israelites conquered on the west side of the Jordan . . . :

[9]the king of Jericho	one	the king of Ai (near Bethel)	one
[10]the king of Jerusalem	one	the king of Hebron	one
[11]the king of Jarmuth	one	the king of Lachish	one
[12]the king of Eglon	one	the king of Gezer	one
. . .			
[19]the king of Madon	one	the king of Hazor	one
. . .			
[24]the king of Tirzah	one		thirty-one kings in all.

section. One question remains: what does Yahweh think about the sparing of Rahab and the Gibeonites? We propose that the narrative contrast between them (humble non-Israelites who acknowledged God's sovereignty) and Achan (an Israelite who ignored Yahweh's express command) reflects a counter theme in the book of Joshua. The contrast seems aimed at justifying these exceptions to the annihilation mandate as honoring Yahweh.

Joshua 13–21: Joshua's Distribution of Tribal Inheritances

Some readers skip Josh 13–19, with its detailed tribal boundary descriptions and lists of towns, as boring and irrelevant. Many interpreters think that the data reported probably incorporate official royal records maintained in Jerusalem during the early monarchy. In our view, however, these chapters mark the most important materials in Joshua because they confirm one of the book's main themes—the fulfillment (finally!) of the Abrahamic promise of land (see 21:43–45). Interestingly, the location of the majority of the cities and towns listed is unknown, so readers may wonder why they are included at all. We suggest that their inclusion theologically celebrates the ideal of an "all Israel" and its unity. It is this ideal that underlies the incorporation of all the tribes and towns, both well known and unknown, in the distribution; all have their proper place. But the section also surfaces something ominous: the tribes' inability to dislodge the Canaanites from their inheritances (15:63; 16:10; 17:12–18), a stalemate that keeps alive the fatal lure of idolatry that ensnares the Israelites in Judges.

The procedure for the distribution of land merits brief comment. First, the casting of lots plays a prominent role, as it did in the trial of Achan (Josh 7), as if theologically, Yahweh was presumed to speak through the results—in this case, who gets what (e.g., 14:2; 18:11; 19:1). Second, chs. 14–19 comprise two subsections that correspond with the overall two-step process. First, two and a half

The six-chambered city gate structure (center of the photograph) and adjoining casemate wall at Hazor built either by Solomon or Ahab. Canaanite Hazor dominated the region north of the Sea of Galilee, including Phoenicia, for centuries. Joshua 11:1–15 reports its conquest by Joshua — fittingly, his final reported victory. ©The Selz Foundation Hazor Excavations in Memory of Yigael Yadin. Photo by Skyview. Used with permission.

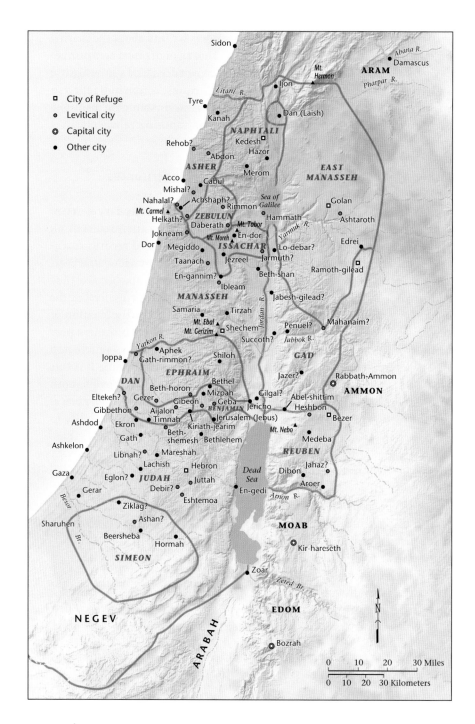

The Settlement of
the Twelve Tribes

□ City of Refuge
○ Levitical city
◎ Capital city
● Other city

Sidon

Abana R.
Damascus

Mt.
Hermon ▲

ARAM

Litani R.
Ijon

Pharpar R.

Tyre
Kanah
Dan (Laish)

NAPHTALI
Kedesh □
Rehob?
Abdon
Hazor

ASHER
Acco
Cabul
Merom

**EAST
MANASSEH**

Mishal?
Nahalal?
Achshaph?
Rimmon
*Sea of
Galilee*
Golan □
Mt. Carmel ▲
Helkath?
ZEBULUN
Daberath ◎
Mt. Tabor
Hammath
Ashtaroth
Jokneam
Mt. Moreh
En-dor
Yarmuk R.
Dor
Megiddo
ISSACHAR
Lo-debar?
Edrei
Taanach
Jezreel
Jarmuth?
En-gannim?
Beth-shan
Ramoth-gilead □
Ibleam
Jabesh-gilead?

MANASSEH
Samaria
Tirzah
Jordan R.
Penuel?
Mahanaim?
Mt. Ebal ▲
Shechem
Mt. Gerizim □
Succoth?
Jabbok R.

Yarkon R.
Aphek
Shiloh
GAD
Joppa
Gath-rimmon?
Jazer?
Rabbath-Ammon ◎
EPHRAIM
Bethel
DAN
Beth-horon
Mizpah
Gilgal?
AMMON
Eltekeh?
Gezer
Gibeon
Geba
Abel-shittim
Gibbethon
Aijalon
BENJAMIN
Jericho
Heshbon
Ashdod
Ekron
Timnah
Jerusalem (Jebus)
Bezer □
Beth-
shemesh
Kiriath-jearim
Mt. Nebo ▲
Ashkelon
Gath
Bethlehem
Medeba
Libnah?
Mareshah
REUBEN
Gaza
Lachish
Hebron □
*Dead
Sea*
Dibon
Jahaz?
Eglon?
JUDAH
Juttah
En-gedi
Aroer
Gerar
Debir?
Eshtemoa
Arnon R.
Ziklag?
Sharuhen
Ashan?
MOAB
Besor Br.
Beersheba
Hormah
Kir hareseth ◎
SIMEON
Zoar
Zered Br.

NEGEV

EDOM

↑N

Bozrah ◎

ARABAH

0   10   20   30 Miles
0 10 20 30 Kilometers

tribes—Judah, Ephraim, and West Manasseh (the latter two descended from Joseph)—receive their allotments from Eleazer the high priest and Joshua, perhaps at Gilgal (Josh 14–17). The narrative offers a sketchy glimpse of the circumstances behind this first allocation but no explanation about what entitles those tribes to get first choice at selecting their land. Presumably, their priority has something to do with their population size and accepted social prominence. Second, a full narrative with dialogues reports how the other seven came into land at an all-Israelite assembly in Shiloh (Josh 18–19). After a delegation surveys the land still available, lot-casting at the assembly distributes it. Interestingly, in an aside the narrative reports that the tribe of Dan's inability to possess its inheritance west of Jerusalem forced it to settle way up north (19:47)—in essence, a tribal relocation necessitated by the presence of non-Israelites in the west. In the end, the distribution of land marks a drawn-out, complex process rather than a simple outcome of a single event (see map 11.2).

Joshua 20–21 reports two final distributions mandated by Moses—cities of refuge (ch. 20; compare Num 35:6–15) and cities with surrounding pasturelands for the Levites (ch. 21; compare Num 35:1–5). The former protect accused murderers from revenge by grieving relatives until a proper trial can take place, while the latter both provide the Levites with places to live and to maintain their herds, and spread their priestly influence throughout the land.

Joshua 22–24: The Early Years of the Settlement

Chapter 22 features a controversial episode centered on an alleged "altar" built on the Jordan's west bank by two and a half east-bank tribes after an honorable dismissal by Joshua. They are headed home, having fulfilled their promise to help west-bank tribes conquer Canaan and settle there (see Josh 1:12–18). The west-bank tribes declare war, thinking it a heretical altar, whereas the east-bank tribes intend it as a "witness" to their genuine devotion. Their fear is that in the future, west-bank descendants may deny their east-bank counterparts access to Israel's central shrine. The controversy ends amicably, but the incident epitomizes the gaping east-bank / west-bank geographical divide—the "outland" versus the "homeland"—that potentially threatens the tribal unity (see the incident in Judg 12). Finally, like Moses, an elderly Joshua exits the scene in chs. 23 and 24 with speeches designed to prepare the Israelites for their future. In ch. 23 he warns them (1) to "be very strong"—never to waver in their obedience to Moses's Instruction (vv. 6, 8); (2) to keep their distance from idolatrous neighbors (v. 7); and (3) to refuse them alliances or intermarriage (v. 12). Not to do so, he warns, will stir up Yahweh's anger and cost them "all the good things" God has showered on them (vv. 15-16).

In ch. 24 at a separate assembly at Shechem (cf. 8:30-35), Joshua speaks in the first person as if Yahweh were the speaker ("I did this, I did that . . ."), reviewing the Israelites' history with Yahweh from Abram to the present. He (as Yahweh) points out the vestiges of idolatry still strong among them, and then (as Joshua) calls them faithfully to worship only Yahweh. Dramatically, he takes his own stand: "as for me and my household, we will serve the LORD" (v. 15 TNIV). The crowd responds positively, and Joshua leads them to renew the covenant one final time (vv. 16-28), even erecting a stone as a "witness" attesting their commitment. The book closes with three burial reports—for Joshua, Joseph, and Eleazar (vv. 29-33)—the end of the Egyptian-Canaanite era for the Israelites.

READING

Read Josh 1-24 and formulate answers to the questions that follow:

1. What specific character, statement, or scene particularly caught your attention? Why did it attract you? And what do you think it might be saying to you?

2. What role does God play in Joshua, and what does the book teach you theologically about God, on the one hand, and the people of God, on the other?

3. Trace Joshua's "career" in the book. What (if any) growth do you detect in him? What does he illustrate about good or bad leadership and how it grows or declines? What does he teach you about a healthy relationship with God?

4. Compare and contrast the characters Rahab and Achan (chs. 2, 6-7). Which do you find more appealing—and why? What sense do you make of the ultimate fate of each character?

5. Deuteronomy 7 and 20 order the Israelites to exterminate the peoples living in Canaan. Discuss how strongly you think the book of Joshua promotes the implementation of that policy. What are your thoughts about what Deuteronomy commanded and how Joshua implemented it?

6. Read Josh 13–19. (Yes, really!) List the kinds of literary genres that appear in these chapters. What do you observe about the treatment that each tribe receives in the allotting of inheritances (e.g., fair, unfair, equal, unequal, etc.)? What view of Israel as a people do these chapters reflect, and what might they teach the Christian community today?

7. What things do you take away personally from your reading of Joshua? What do you think the book contributes to the biblical theme of God's mission in the world?

BIBLIOGRAPHY

Ben-Ami, Doron. "The Iron Age I at Hazor in Light of the Renewed Excavations." *IEJ* 51 (2001): 148–70.

Billings, Rachel M. *"Israel Served the Lord": The Book of Joshua as Paradoxical Portrait of Faithful Israel*. Notre Dame, IN: University of Notre Dame Press, 2013.

Butler, Trent C. *Joshua 1–12*. 2nd ed. WBC 7a. Grand Rapids: Zondervan, 2014.

———. *Joshua 13–24*. 2nd ed. WBC 7b. Grand Rapids: Zondervan, 2014.

Dallaire, Hélène M. "Taking the Land by Force: Divine Violence in Joshua." Pages 51–73 in *Wrestling with the Violence of God: Soundings in the Old Testament*. Edited by M. Daniel Carroll R. and J. Blair Wilgus. Winona Lake, IN: Eisenbrauns, 2015.

Earl, Douglas S. *The Joshua Delusion? Rethinking Genocide in the Bible*. Eugene, OR: Cascade, 2010.

Greenspoon, Leonard. "The Book of Joshua—Part 1: Texts and Versions." *CurBR* 3 (2005): 229–61.

Hawk, L. Daniel. *Joshua*. Berit Olam. Collegeville, MN: Liturgical Press, 2000.

Hess, Richard S. *Joshua*. TOTC. Downers Grove, IL: InterVarsity, 1996.

Hubbard, Robert L., Jr. *Joshua*. NIVAC. Grand Rapids: Zondervan, 2009.

Kallai, Zecharia. *Historical Geography of the Bible: The Tribal Territories of Israel*. Jerusalem: Magnes; Leiden: Brill, 1986.

Kitchen, Kenneth A. *On the Reliability of the Old Testament*. Grand Rapids: Eerdmans, 2003.

Pitkänen, Pekka M. A. *Joshua*. ApOTC 6. Nottingham: Apollos; Downers Grove, IL: InterVarsity Press, 2010.

Stone, Lawson G. "Early Israel and Its Appearance in Canaan." Pages 127–64 in *Ancient Israel's History: An Introduction to Issues and Sources*. Edited by Bill T. Arnold and Richard S. Hess. Grand Rapids: Baker Academic, 2014.

Wood, Bryant G. "Did the Israelites Conquer Jericho? A New Look at the Archaeological Evidence." *BAR* 16/2 (1990): 49.

Younger, K. Lawson, Jr. *Ancient Conquest Accounts: A Study in Ancient Near Eastern and Biblical History Writing*. JSOTSup 98. Sheffield: Sheffield Academic Press, 1990.

12 THE BOOK OF JUDGES

Important Dates for Judges

ca. 1200–1010: the heroic era

THE BOOK OF JUDGES PICKS up the story line where Joshua leaves off, recounting the Israelites' settled life post-Joshua, especially the fate of the covenant made in Josh 24. If Joshua celebrates the "big picture" of conquest and settlement, Judges shows us a candid, on-the-ground glimpse of daily life in the latter period, including ongoing conflicts with remaining Canaanites. The book's theological prologue (ch. 2) also supplies a Deuteronomic yardstick by which the book measures the spiritual status of the people of Israel and their leaders in all the stories that follow (chs. 3–21).

As for leadership, Joshua designated no successor, so it is the "judges" who lead Israel during the Judges period (ca. 1200–1050 BCE), the 200 years between the death of Joshua and the accession of Israel's first king. The leaders are called *judges* because their title (*shofet*) comes from the Hebrew root "to judge, rule" (*shafat*). Some judges did actually settle legal matters (see, e.g., Judg 12:8–15; compare 4:4–5), but most were Spirit-empowered military Heroes who delivered Israel from foreign oppressors. The book of Judges compiles their stories to remember them as important national figures, although their exploits clearly played out only in their home regions (see Table 12.1); sometimes their lifetimes apparently overlapped or coincided. So, as we noted earlier, there is no point in simply totaling up figures that the book provides to decide how long the Judges period lasted.

From her base in central Israel, Deborah defeats the Canaanites way up north, whereas Gideon opposes invading Midianites in the north, Jephthah faces Ammonites east of the Jordan, and Samson battles Philistines in the lowlands southwest of Jerusalem. In our view, the term *judges* fails to convey their unique military exploits, so we refer to them as "the Heroes."

What Was Going On Back Then?

The picture of Israel's situation that Judges paints is dark and dangerous. Politically, loose and locally based organization holds the tribes together rather than a single leader in the mold of Moses or Joshua. The lack of central leadership leaves the nation especially vulnerable to foreign invasions, and several plague it across Israel's northern, eastern, and southwestern boundaries. As noted, regional Heroes successfully drive the invaders out, but none fills the leadership gap left by Moses and Joshua. Along the coast, entrenched Philistines repel attempts by the tribe of Dan to dislodge them from the inheritance allotted the Danites by Joshua. They are forced to carve out territory on the nation's far northern frontier, a great distance from the Israelite heartland but perilously near threats from neighboring city-states such as Hazor and Damascus as well as roving marauders. Two episodes of civil war between tribes—Abimelech versus Gideon (Judg 9:4-5) and a tribal coalition versus the Benjaminites (chs. 19-21)—put a potentially catastrophic strain on the fabric of national unity. Finally, as the compilers of Judges underscore, Canaanite-inspired apostasy has become endemic across the land since death robbed the Israelites of Joshua's steadying influence. The Israelites have forgotten the God whom Moses urged them to "remember," the one who gave them the land that they now inhabit, and instead they have chosen to worship other gods (Deut 8:11). The need for central leadership to counteract these and other threats seems evident.

Table 12.1. The Heroes and Their Regions

Hero	Region	Enemy	Scripture
Ehud	Transjordan	Moabites	Judges 3
Deborah	Center	Canaanites	Judges 4–5
Gideon	North	Midianites	Judges 6–8
Jephthah	Transjordan	Ammonites	Judges 11–12
Samson	West	Philistines	Judges 13–16

The Story

The book of Judges has two parts: (1) the stories of the Heroes (chs. 1–16) and (2) an epilogue of stories featuring non-Heroes (chs. 17–21). A phrase repeated four times in the latter part sounds the theme toward which the entire book points (see below).

Judges 1–16: The Stories of the Heroes

The curtain rises in Judg 1 with a question the tribes pose to Yahweh about which tribe should strike the first blow against the Canaanites (v. 1; cf. 10:18). The answer is "Judah" (v. 2), perhaps because of that tribe's size (and, thus, superior resources) or social prominence, as we noted in connection with land distribution (Josh 14–19). Certainly, Judah shows a profile of leadership since its debut in the Joseph story, and with Simeonite help reels off a series of victories in all directions: the capture of an apparently famous, ruthless Canaanite king, Adoni-Bezek, and the cities of Jerusalem and Hebron. But the lack of chariotry denies Judah success in areas with flat terrain (e.g., the coastal plain; v. 19). The Joseph tribes (Ephraim and Manasseh) also successfully take Bethel, but for the most part the Canaanites stymie efforts by other tribes to dislodge or expel them, only occasionally submitting to forced labor.

Interpreters have long noticed the stark contrast between the overwhelmingly victorious picture of the conquest in Joshua and the struggles, both internal and external, that dominate Judges. Some trace the contrast back to different literary sources that offer competing or contradictory interpretations of the period in question. In our view, however, Joshua and Judges offer complementary pictures—the former a "big-picture" perspective and the later a more "on-the-ground," intimate view. Chapters 2–3 offer a deuteronomistic theological evaluation of this historical period in retrospect, the backward-facing critique preparing readers for what follows. It views the period as a sad, unstable era dominated by repeating cycles of Israelite disobedience, punishment through slavery to invading nations, divine rescue through the Heroes, and interims of peace and (temporary) obedience (see Diagram 12.1). It even argues that Yahweh has intentionally left the nations in place to test the Israelites' devotion to Yahweh (Judg 3:4). Each turn of the cycle pushes another Hero to the fore, the four primary Heroes being Deborah, Gideon, Jephthah, and Samson.

Diagram 12.1. The Cycle of Judges

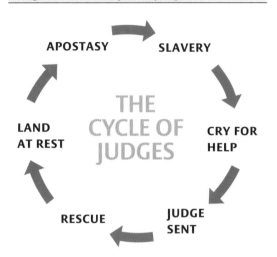

APOSTASY

SLAVERY

LAND
AT REST

THE
CYCLE OF
JUDGES

CRY FOR
HELP

RESCUE

JUDGE
SENT

Chapters 4–5 narrate Deborah's remarkable rescue of northern Israel from the Canaanite king of Hazor, a major, ancient, wealthy, and politically influential city-state north of the Sea of Galilee. The compilers of Judges thought her victory memorable enough to merit telling it in both prose (a historical report) and poetry (a song)—a literary accolade only elsewhere accorded the momentous exodus itself (Exod 14–15). But the story also has a satisfying irony that makes the victory even sweeter: the weapon through which God strikes the decisive blow is an obscure, non-Israelite woman named Jael, not the male Israelite commander on duty, Barak. This point goes along with a subtheme that weaves its way through the Heroes section: the Israelites' hope of achieving national security by their own devices rather than by trusting God is futile.

Chapter 6 introduces Gideon, a Hero whom an angel of the Lord seeks to recruit but whose life experience has made him skeptical of claims that "God is with you" (how does that jibe with our poverty and hunger?) and of the command "Go, save Israel from Midian" (me? I'm from such a small tribe). He is bold enough to ask twice for proof that his recruiter comes from God and brave enough to dismantle his father's idolatrous altar to fashion an altar for Yahweh—a highly unpopular act in the town. But the Spirit of Yahweh comes on him, and he rallies Manasseh to defeat the Midianites. In ch. 7, with Gideon and his troops camped at the spring of Harod just south of the Midianite camp, Yahweh voices the subtheme mentioned above:

> You have too many men. I cannot deliver Midian into their hands,
> or Israel would boast against me, "My own strength has saved me."
> (Judg 7:2 TNIV)

Gideon trustingly carries out Yahweh's water-lapping test to find the right 300 men for his mission and that night obediently reconnoiters the enemy camp, overhearing a soldier recounting a dream that his buddy interprets to say that Gideon will defeat Midian. Immediately, Gideon deploys his troops to frighten the sleeping Midianites and rallies four nearby tribes to cut off their retreat across the Jordan. In ch. 8 he completes his victory by capturing and killing two fleeing kings of Midian east of the Jordan, a victory that leads the Israelites to offer to make him their king. Instead, he requests some gold rings from their plunder to make into an ephod, which people in his hometown come to worship. Sadly, despite witnessing God's defeat of Midian, he lapses into idolatry at the end of his life.

The theme of kingship arises again in ch. 9, when one of Gideon's sons, Abimelech, massacres several dozen of his relatives and lobbies the city of Shechem to appoint him as their king. But the youngest brother, Jotham, escapes, later ascends Mount Gerizim above Shechem just as its citizens are about to crown Abimelech, and recites a now-famous political fable about trees who once anointed as their king a worthless bramble because the more productive trees demurred (vv. 7–15). Some interpreters read the fable as an ironic critique of the monarchy as an institution, while others interpret it as simply a warning of the dangers of entrusting royal power into the wrong hands. Jotham's follow-up commentary (vv. 16–19a) accuses the Shechemites of complicity in the murder of Gideon's family and of plain ingratitude toward his father, who risked his life to rescue them. Jotham ends his oration with a curse (vv. 19b–20), which Abimelech's eventual downfall—death from a millstone dropped on him from above by a woman—fulfills (v. 57). The motif here of the special shame for a man to be killed by a woman echoes the case of Sisera and Jael in chs. 4–5. That Abimelech pays for his violence and arrogance also accords with the idea of the act-consequence connection that is so favored by the compilers of DH.

In ch. 10–12, the cycle of sin turns again, and this time the Ammonites from Transjordan are Yahweh's oppressors of choice, wreaking havoc among Israelites in Gilead to their north and across the Jordan in Judah, Benjamin, and Ephraim. The leaders of Gilead enlist Jephthah, an able warrior but an outcast from his family, to command their forces against the new menace in exchange for their promise to appoint him as their leader if he succeeds. His case suggests that a popular yearning to fill the current lack of leadership may have been abroad in this era.

In ch. 11, the storyteller treats the sad episode that introduced Jephthah

Twentieth-century CE mosaic in the Dormition Abbey in Jerusalem, by Radbod Commandeur. The mosaic depicts Jael, the Israelite heroine who slew the Canaanite commander Sisera with a tent peg (Judg 4–5). ©*Deror avi (Wikimedia Commons, CC-SA 3.0)*

and his unnamed daughter into popular lore. After the Hero's diplomatic message to the Ammonite king fails (vv. 14-28), the Spirit of the LORD seizes Jephthah, and the Hero heads for Ammon, making what will prove to be a fateful vow:

> If you will decisively hand over the Ammonites to me, then *whatever comes out the doors of my house to meet me when I return victorious from the Ammonites will be given over to the LORD. I will sacrifice it as an entirely burned offering.* (Judg 11:30-31 CEB, italics ours)

If we consider Jephthah sane rather than captive to blind enthusiasm, he probably expects the curiosity of one of his animals to greet his return and suffer the slaughter. But, alas, when the victorious Hero arrives, it is his daughter (and only child) who emerges to welcome him (11:34). After the young woman and her friends wander the hills for two months, mourning that she will never marry, Jephthah "did to her as he had vowed" (11:39 TNIV), a sorrow that spawns a four-day annual custom during which Israelite young women commemorate the daughter's story. Interpretations of this unusual episode abound. Some interpreters say that, because the Israelites prohibited child sacrifice, the narrator includes Jephthah's act simply to illustrate further the corruption rampant in those days. Since Jephthah addresses his vow to Yahweh, others fault Jephthah for, in essence, including the fateful stipulation as a kind of bribe to influence Yahweh into granting him victory. Still others observe Yahweh's unusual and very personal role in the story: on the one hand, Yahweh grants our Hero victory (emotionally, God can't tolerate his people's misery) but, on the other hand, does not intervene to spare the daughter's life (God can't completely tolerate their corrupt lifestyle). Finally, some find in the story's stress on the daughter's virginity (v. 39) a clue that Jephthah's act did not take her life but consigned her to life-long virginity, denying her a marriage and children (and denying himself grandchildren)—as his penalty. The variety of interpretations attests the fascinating levels of engagement that the tragic story offers readers (for Jephthah's mention in the Hall of Faith, see Heb 11:32-34).

Chapters 13-16 conclude Judges' Hero section with the exploits of the incredibly muscular, shaggy-haired ne'er-do-well Samson. A new theme also emerges. To be sure, it's an extension of Yahweh's previous ad hoc rescues, but it's a plan permanently to end a more serious, long-term threat. In ch. 13, as the cycle returns to rampant sin and its punitive oppression (the Philistines, this time), an angel of the LORD masquerading as a "man of God" (or prophet; compare 13:6, 8) visits the Danite town of Zorah in the lowlands west of Jerusalem. There he informs a barren, childless woman that she will bear a son who will be a Nazirite (see the sidebar) with the mission "to begin to deliver Israel from the hands of the Philistines" (13:5). Subsequent visits and conversations with the woman and her husband, Manoah, reiterate the prenatal regimen required of women bearing a Nazirite (vv. 13-14; compare vv. 6-7). Finally, as Manoah sacrifices to the LORD, the "man" suddenly vanishes in the ascending flame, terrifying the pair and confirming his identity as an angel (compare with Gideon's experience in 6:21), and in due time the woman bears Samson. The storyteller describes him as someone whom "the LORD blessed" and in whom "the Spirit of the LORD began to stir" (vv. 24, 25)—clear signs that he is a Hero. But in ch. 14 the grown-up Samson disconcerts his parents by falling in love with—God forbid!—a Philistine woman. What the parents don't know, the storyteller interjects, is "that the LORD was behind this. He was looking for an opening with the Philistines, because they were ruling over Israel at that time" (14:4 CEB). In other words, strange as it seems, the LORD's campaign has begun, and for twenty years Samson wreaks havoc with (and gets no little revenge from) the Philistines and their shabby, conniving attempts to control him.

Three times in chs. 14 and 15, the Spirit of the LORD empowers him to a series of near-miraculous feats (14:6, 19; 15:14; compare previous examples in 3:10; 6:34; 11:29; and 13:25), until in ch. 16 his second wife, the crafty, persistent prostitute Delilah, finally learns his secret and passes it on, enabling the Philistines finally to subdue and blind him (16:21). But in captivity, Samson's hair begins to grow back (v. 22), perhaps a symbolic return to his Nazirite status, and while enduring excruciating humiliation, amusing a Philistine crowd of people who are partying in their pillared, pagan temple, Samson quietly

What Is a Nazirite?

The term *Nazirite* designates an Israelite who is "consecrated" or "separated" (Heb. *nazir*) to the service of God under vows to abstain from alcohol, let the hair grow, and avoid defilement by contact with corpses (Num 6). The tenure of the consecration was for shorter or longer periods or for a lifetime. Two familiar OT examples of lifetime service are Samson (Judg 13:5) and Samuel (1 Sam 1:11), both of whom were born to previously barren mothers and became Nazirites prenatally (i.e., involuntarily). In Samson's case, an angel informed his parents of their son's Nazirite destiny and required his mother to abstain from alcohol and avoid defilement while pregnant; but with Samuel, his mother's prenatal oath bound him to serve God. Designation as Nazirites required Samson and Samuel to live devout lives and in return granted them extraordinary gifts such as enormous physical strength (Samson) and prophecy (Samuel). Of the two, only Samson seems to have broken his Nazirite vows and lost his gift as a result (e.g., Judg 14:8–10; 16:15–19). The Nazirite practice apparently persisted because centuries later the prophet Amos castigated the Israelites for disrespecting the Nazirite vow and also for ignoring the prophets (Amos 2:11–12).

prays to the LORD for his strength to return and God assents. In the end, Samson literally "brings down the house," pushing the pillars to collapse the building and killing himself and the revelers—one final exploit in Yahweh's campaign against an enemy that is destined to threaten until its final defeat under David (2 Sam 8:1).

Judges 17–21: The Epilogue of Non-Heroes

The five-chapter epilogue gives Judges a very unhappy ending, but its unhappiness is symptomatic of the depths of the corruption that grips the Israelites and cries out to be fixed. The epilogue comprises two reports: the first concerning an explicitly idolatrous shrine and priesthood centered up north at Dan (chs. 17–18), and the second concerning a scandalous murder that ignites a bloody civil war between the tribes with near-catastrophic consequences for the Benjaminites (chs. 19–21).

The first story features an Ephraimite named Micah who, at his mother's request and with her funding, installs an idolatrous shrine in his home complete with a silver idol, an ephod, other household gods, and his son (not a Levite) as its priest (17:5). One day, however, a Levite from Judah happens by in search of a new life and finds it in Micah's home, where he agrees to become Micah's honorary father and the priest of Micah's personal shrine. Micah thinks that having a Levite priest assures him that "the LORD will be good to me" (17:13 TNIV). In ch. 18, a delegation of Danites also happens by in search of a new location in which the tribe might settle permanently (for background, see above). Surprisingly, they know the Levite personally, learn about his present situation, and request him to "inquire of God [note: not the LORD] to learn whether our journey will be successful." The Levite's immediate response (there's no actual "inquiry" in prayer reported) reassures them: "Go in peace. Your journey has the LORD's approval" (Judg 18:5–6 TNIV). But the Danite search succeeds in finding Laish, a suitable, isolated city up north, which the tribe later conquers and resettles. En route there, however, they lure away Micah's Levite, who brings Micah's idolatrous paraphernalia with him and, despite Micah's later angry attempt to retrieve it, they proceed not only to settle in Laish (renamed *Dan* after their tribal ancestor) but also to establish worship of Micah's idol—later, with a direct descendant of Moses as priest. The narrator notes that worship at Dan persisted and, perhaps, competed with the more legitimate sanctuary at Shiloh (see also 1 Sam 1–3). Theologically, of course, the deuteronomistic compilers know, as do we presumably, that even with a Levite or descendant of Moses presiding, idolatrous worship and feigned inquiry of God in fact greatly displease Yahweh and make its participants, Levitical or otherwise, liable to divine judgment.

In ch. 19, the second report tells about the estranged concubine of a Levite in Ephraim, who has returned to her birth family's hometown, Bethlehem. For a Levite to acquire a concubine seems to violate typical expectations of Levites, and this may be another symptom of the nation's corrupt spiritual state. Four months later, the Levite persuades his concubine to return home with him, and en route, they pass up lodging at Jebus (later Jerusalem but currently non-Israelite) in favor of the Benjaminite city of Gibeah, where ironically they receive no hospitality until an elderly man finally welcomes them to his house. But an angry crowd soon surrounds it, demanding that the visiting man be given to them for sexual purposes. To pacify the mob, their host eventually gives them the concubine, whom they rape and abuse, and whom the Levite finds dead outside the house the next morning. After carrying her home to Ephraim with him on his donkey, he cuts up her body into twelve parts and sends one part to every tribe—a gesture that leaves all of them stunned and bewildered.

Chapter 20 finds an assembly of tribal leaders (all except Benjamin's) gathered at Mizpah to deal with this strange episode. The Levite's lengthy testimony persuades them to mobilize an army against Benjamin, but first they send messengers asking the Benjaminites to identify and punish the perpetrators—"to purge the evil from Israel" (20:13 TNIV)—lest Yahweh avenge the crime by punishing all Israel. The Benjaminites muster a large force to defend themselves, and the two armies violently clash at Gibeah for several days. Twice the attackers seek Yahweh's advice, and twice he approves an attack (vv. 23, 28), eventually turning the tide against the Benjaminites (v. 35). Violent mayhem and ugly death ravage the Benjaminite cities and nearly annihilate the tribe.

In ch. 21, the other tribes meet at Bethel to resolve a sorrowful dilemma: an oath prohibits them from permitting marriages to Benjaminites, yet they grieve at the loss of that tribe and want to provide wives for the Benjamites who survived. A raid on Jabesh-gilead, a city that did not participate in the war, yields several hundred virgin women, but the supply is not up to the current demand. Finally, they agree to permit Benjaminites to carry off as wives virgins who are dancing at "the annual festival of the LORD in Shiloh" (21:19 TNIV). Problem solved—but at what cost! Something needs fixing!

Now, an obvious, repeated refrain literally weaves the two stories together and hints at the solution—the main theme of Judges (17:6; 18:1; 19:1; 21:25):

> In those days there was no king in Israel; each person did what they thought to be right. (Judg 17:6 CEB)

In short, the compilers of Judges aver that Israel needs a king to clean up the mess: to expel invaders, stand against idolatry, and control violent tribal feuds. The example of the bramble-bush Abimelech, however, shows that not just any would-be king will do. The right king must be found. The scene is now set for 1–2 Samuel.

READING

Read Judg 1–21 and formulate answers to the questions that follow:

1. Compare the picture of the conquest/settlement process in Joshua and Judges. Taken together, with what picture of the process do they leave you? What (if any) parallels to issues of contemporary life in the church strike you from that process, and what possible responses to them does that picture suggest to you?

2. In what ways (if any) does the concept of *cycles* in Judges shed light on your own experience of life with God? Theologically, what avenue to escape them does it suggest to you?

3. What role(s) does God play in Judges? In what ways (if any) does Judges enrich or reshape your view of God and your relationship with God? What about God's role in Judges most troubles you?

4. With which Hero or non-Hero do you feel you most resonate? Why? If none grabs you, how might you explain that disconnect?

5. Please list what you think to be the three or four main themes of Judges. Given the book's audience, why would you say the book's compilers gave these themes special stress?

6. What implications for the mission of God and for Christian life today does Judges suggest to you?

7. Comment on how Judges both follows up Joshua and anticipates 1–2 Samuel.

BIBLIOGRAPHY

Ackerman, Susan. *Warrior, Dancer, Seductress, Queen: Women in Judges and Biblical Israel*. ABRL. New York: Doubleday, 1998.

Block, Daniel I. *Judges, Ruth*. NAC 6. Nashville: Broadman & Holman, 1999.

Brettler, Mark. "The Book of Judges: Literature as Politics." *JBL* 108 (1989): 395–418.

Butler, Trent C. *Judges*. WBC 8. Grand Rapids: Zondervan, 2009.

Craig, Kenneth M., Jr. "Judges in Recent Research." *CurBR* 1 (2003): 159–85.

Frolov, Serge. "Sleeping with the Enemy: Recent Scholarship on Sexuality in the Book of Judges." *CurRB* 11 (2013): 308–27.

Groves, J. Alan. "Judges." Pages 92–101 in *Theological Interpretation of the Old Testament: A Book-by-Book Survey*. Edited by Kevin J. Vanhoozer. Grand Rapids: Baker Academic, 2008.

Miller, Robert D., II. "The Judges and the Early Iron Age." Pages 165–89 in *Ancient Israel's History: An Introduction to Issues and Sources*. Edited by Bill T. Arnold and Richard S. Hess. Grand Rapids: Baker Academic, 2014.

Sasson, Jack M. *Judges 1–12: A New Translation with Introduction and Commentary*. AB 6D. New Haven: Yale University Press, 2014.

Webb, Barry G. *The Book of Judges*. NICOT. Grand Rapids: Eerdmans, 2012.

Yee, Gale A. *Judges and Method: New Approaches in Biblical Studies*. 2nd ed. Minneapolis: Fortress, 2007.

13 THE BOOK OF RUTH

Important Dates for Ruth

ca. 1200–1050: the story's setting

ca. 900–450: the book's composition date

THE BOOK OF RUTH REPORTS a peaceful interlude amid the noisy chaos and upheaval in the era of the Heroes. Its story takes place primarily in Bethlehem of Judah, but with a long but briefly told, life-changing interlude in the country of Moab, east of the Dead Sea. It traces how a mysterious series of misfortunes devastate one specific family—Dad, Mom, two sons, and their foreign wives—and how God providentially uses one of the latter to keep the family line alive and eventually to give King David to Israel. The book bears the name of the special, heroic Moabite woman whose remarkable devotion and initiative prove crucial to the outcome. Dialogues and speeches dominate the story, the theme of reversals of fortunes drives its plot, and the story has a surprise ending (see 4:17b). The repetition of key words—for example, Heb. *reqam* rendered "empty" (= "without family") in 1:21 and "empty-handed" (= "without food") in 3:17—serves to knit the book's themes together (for its structure, see Diagram 13.1).

The Story

The book of Ruth has two parts: (1) the story of King David's ancestors (1:1–4:17) and (2) the king's genealogy (4:18-22). Part (1) opens with a short prologue (1:1-6) that leads into the main story proper (1:7-4:17). The book's structure is chiastic, organized around dialogues and locales.

The prologue of ch. 1 sets the scene for the story by reeling off the tragedies that strike a family of four in Bethlehem: a famine that drives them to seek food as resident aliens in nearby Moab; the unexpected deaths there of both the husband (Elimelech) and his two sons that leave their mother (Naomi) and their Moabite wives as widows; no children have been born to either daughter-in-law after ten years of marriage. Some interpreters read the deaths as divine judgment for abandoning the promised land (Elimelech) and taking foreign wives (his sons), but we note that the storyteller says nothing to that effect. In fact, given the book's subsequent, admiring portrait of one Moabite widow (Ruth), the marriages may represent the early signs of divine providence at work. Finally, the prologue's conclusion turns the story in a positive direction (and back toward Bethlehem, too): in Moab Naomi receives news that God has ended the famine in Judah (1:6b), thus paving the way for Naomi to return home. Indeed, the chapter uses *return* multiple times to spotlight it as the key thematic word. The resumption of fertility is said to result from God's having "paid attention to his people" (CEB), a Hebrew verb (*paqad*) that connotes a kind of divine-inspection visit to evaluate whether present conditions merit further hardship or (in this case) gracious relief. Interestingly, this marks the first of only two reports of direct divine intervention in the whole story (cf. 4:13).

The rest of ch. 1 features two dramatic, starkly different speeches by Ruth and Naomi—the former spoken somewhere on the journey toward Bethlehem, and the latter upon their arrival at Bethlehem's front gate. The words read with a nice, almost poetic rhythm:

Ruth (to Naomi):	Stop pressuring me to abandon you and to end my journey with you. Wherever you go, I'll go; wherever you stay, I'll stay. Your people will be my people, and your God my God. Wherever you die, I'll die, and there I will be buried. (A solemn oath follows.)
Naomi (to local women):	Don't call me "Naomi" [= my Darling Girl]! Call me "Mara" instead [= Bitter] because the Almighty has treated me bitterly. I left here full, but the LORD has brought me back empty. Why call me Naomi? The LORD has mistreated me; the Almighty has heaped misfortune on me!

Ruth's statement (vv. 16–17) is a stunning declaration of exclusive devotion to Naomi, Judah, and Yahweh and implies a decisive renunciation of her Moabite ties. The concluding oath in Yahweh's name verifies how seriously she embraces her new commitments, and "there I will be buried" even shuts the door to any return to Moab ever. By contrast, Naomi's angry, bitter lament—a powerful, pained outcry worthy of the psalmists and of David himself (cf. 2 Sam 1)—blames Yahweh for her losses ("full" to "empty") and voices abject despair (vv. 19–21). Theologically, the divine restoration of food raises the questions: Has Yahweh also had anything to do with the tragedies? Is Naomi's accusation in fact true, and if so, for what purpose? And what fate awaits Ruth, the Moabitess, in Judah?

The answer to the latter question appears in chs. 2 and 3, whose three-part structures constitute parallel scenes: brief dialogues between Ruth and Naomi at home (2:2, 19–22; 3:1–5, 16–18) bracket main scenes—crucial dialogues between Ruth and Boaz, one in public (2:8–16) and the other in secret (3:9–15). In the first dialogue (2:2), Ruth proposes to provide them with food by gleaning grain in the community fields, a practice sanctioned by Mosaic law (Lev 19:9–10; 23:22), and voices hope for kind treatment by some as-yet-unknown farmer. Of course, unlike Ruth, readers already suspect that this farmer is Boaz, the wealthy and highly respected relative of Elimelech whom the author introduces in 2:1. As luck would have it (or is it providence, perhaps?), Ruth accidentally lands in one of his fields—and shortly before Boaz himself arrives. Though they had never met before, Boaz immediately shows Ruth the kind treatment for which Ruth had hoped—indeed, probably unusual generosity for a landowner protective of his harvest. Few would probably order reapers to leave extra grain around for Ruth. He explains his kindness as a response to what he has already heard about her—her remarkable devotion to Naomi and, more amazing, her voluntary migration to a foreign country. Then he pronounces a blessing on her for that devotion (2:12):

> May the LORD fully repay you for the good you've done;
> may your wages be paid in full by the LORD . . . under whose wings
> you've recently found refuge.

His words invoke the metaphor of labor and wages, petitioning Yahweh to pay Ruth in full for the work she has already done, especially since she has recently committed herself to God ("found refuge"). Some interpreters suggest that those words also may alert the reader to the possibility that, through subsequent events, Yahweh will repay the Moabitess.

Chapter 2 includes a second important statement toward the end. Naomi's debrief of Ruth about the day's surprising events in the field has identified Boaz as her generous benefactor. Naomi comments, "That man is our close relative; he is one of our guardian-redeemers" (v. 20 NIV). According to many interpreters her comment, first, explains why Boaz treated Ruth so generously and, second, raises the possibility of further assistance, perhaps (as we shall see) even marriage (note the sidebar concerning guardian-redeemers). The immigration of Ruth from Moab to Judah might be instructive for recent contemporary discussions concerning immigration and the treatment of resident aliens. It is helpful, first, to remember that ANE laws provided for and protected that status, if for no other reason perhaps than that ancient cultures realized their own fragile vulnerability to the fickle vicissitudes of nature and history. Certainly, the chance for survival and apparent welcome that Moab offered Elimelech and Naomi illustrates what a blessing life as resident aliens was to them, especially after death reduced Naomi and her two Moabite daughters-in-law to widowhood. Second, the story highlights that ethnic intermarriage establishes family bonds, even if the marriage took place on foreign soil. Further, Boaz acknowledges that Ruth's radical choice—her complete cutting of ties with everything Moabite and embracing of all things Judahite—counted for something important, a reality worthy of recognition by Naomi's family and

What Is a Guardian-Redeemer?

Guardian-redeemer is a technical term in Israelite family law (Heb. *go'el*) for someone in the small circle of close relatives (e.g., an uncle, cousin, other near kin) whose closeness obligates them to assist family members in difficulty (Ruth 2:20; cf. 1 Kgs 16:11). Difficulties may include mortaged ancestral land, houses sold of necessity, or debt-slavery (see Lev 25). The guardian-redeemer's goal is to redeem them—to pay off the debt or buy back the house in order to repair the family wholeness that has been broken by the trouble. The difficulty in Ruth, however, concerns a postmenopausal, childless widow (Naomi) in need of practical care in old age and an heir to continue the family line on the family property. Normally, sons would fulfill those responsibilities, and under the custom known as levirate marriage (Lat. *levir* "brother-in-law"), a brother would marry the childless widow of his late brother so that the latter would have heirs (Gen 38; Deut 25:5–10). But Naomi has neither husband nor sons, much less the capacity to produce offspring, and the Torah nowhere addresses her case. Apparently the Israelites presume that the redemption duties of a guardian-redeemer—in this case, Boaz—include marrying such a childless widow to provide her with care and to produce an heir to continue the family line. He acts as a substitute husband for Naomi's late husband (and also probably for her two deceased sons). Since Naomi is postmenopausal, however, the redemption model apparently also allows a close female relative (her presumably fertile daughter-in-law Ruth) to marry Boaz as a substitute wife in place of Naomi.

the town of Bethelehem. Finally, the case of Ruth shows that resident aliens, especially those with family connections in their new country of residence, may in fact fit so well there that their presence measurably enriches the latter in tangible ways.

As Diagram 13.1 signals (F, F'), ch. 3 marks the story's critical turning point. Many interpreters observe that a new, rejuvenated, assertive Naomi now replaces the broken, pained widow of ch. 1. She recognizes that the harvest has forged an obvious "connection" between Boaz the guardian-redeemer and Ruth the Moabitess, but the end of both barley and wheat harvests also ends their daily contacts. More important, Naomi sees a golden opportunity this very night for the pair to rendezvous at the threshing floor—an isolated spot away from town—and hatches a plan to seize the moment and to arrange for them to marry. Ruth carries out the plan to perfection, although some interpreters observe that Naomi's commission ("find you a permanent home," v. 1) omits the "guardian-redeemer" duty that Ruth's proposal cites ("Marry me for you are a guardian-redeemer," v. 9). So, a marriage specifically in line with that family duty is either implicit in Naomi's words or represents an ad hoc innovation in the proposal by Ruth to maximize the marriage's benefit to Naomi. But Boaz introduces a complication—the existence of a closer relative with a prior right as guardian-redeemer to marry Ruth—and interpreters ponder whether or why Naomi did not know that. Some read Naomi's silence on the matter as evidence of either ignorance or incompetence on her part, but it is also possible that she did know about the

Diagram 13.1. Chiastic Structure of the Book of Ruth

A Prologue (1:1–6)
   B Enroute: Naomi-Ruth Dialogue (1:7–18)
      C Bethlehem Gate: Naomi's Lament (1:19–22)
         D Naomi's Home: Ruth-Naomi Prebrief (2:12)
            E Boaz's Field: Boaz-Ruth Dialogue (2:3–17)
               F Naomi's Home: Naomi-Ruth Debrief (2:18–23)
               F' Naomi's Home: Naomi-Ruth Prebrief (3:1–5)
            E' Threshing Floor: Ruth-Boaz Dialogue (3:6–15)
         D' Naomi's Home: Naomi-Ruth Debrief (3:16–18)
      C' Bethlehem Gate: Legal Process (4:1–12)
   B' Private Home: Naomi-Women Dialogue (4:13–17)
A' Epilogue: Genealogy (4:18–22)

other and presumed that Boaz could circumvent it.

Whatever the case, ch. 4 relates that, as Ruth and Naomi await the outcome elsewhere, Boaz convenes a spontaneous hearing at the city gate, a locale in ancient cities that sometimes functioned as a public courtroom, to settle the legal matter of marriage rights. When Boaz reveals that Naomi has put her land up for sale, the other guardian-redeemer quickly agrees to buy it; he probably understands that the benefits of owning additional land far outweigh the expense of caring for aged Naomi until she dies. But, when Boaz stipulates that the purchase requires the man to marry Ruth, the cost-benefit equation apparently loses its attraction, and he

View looking toward the Iron Age city gate at Tel Dan, built around the ninth century BCE. Although not as celebrated as the contemporary six-chambered gates at Gezer, Megiddo, and Hazor (see the aerial view on p. 131), it is likely that the events of Ruth 4 would have taken place in such a structure. *Photo by Jonathan Greer. Used with permission.*

formally cedes the guardian-redeemer right to Boaz. Interpreters have pondered his explanation that the marriage to Ruth might "endanger my own estate" (v. 6 TNIV). Some think that the man is worried that, under Israelite inheritance laws, (1) the first child born to him and Ruth would inherit Naomi's land, thus denying him the long-term benefits of the land to offset his costs for supporting Naomi; and (2) other children born to the couple would rightly claim a piece of his own estate, thus reducing the size of each parcel for all of his heirs. Other interpreters, however, think the man simply didn't want to be bothered by the duty. In any case, Boaz formally exercises his newly acquired right to both land and Ruth (vv. 9-10), welcomes her to his home, and consummates their marriage. And for the second time, Yahweh directly intervenes: he (lit.) "gives her pregnancy"—that is, "enables her to conceive" (v. 13)—and in the book's closing scene, Naomi and her lady friends welcome newborn Obed (= "servant") with these words,

> May the LORD be blessed, who today hasn't left you without a
> redeemer. . . . He will restore your life and sustain you in your
> old age. (4:14-15 CEB)

Interestingly, the actions that drive the plot of the book are, with two exceptions (1:6; 4:13), performed by its human characters, but in the end the women give all the credit to Yahweh. Theologically, the book teaches that God primarily works through human actions (hidden providence) and sometimes through direct intervention. The women's celebratory cry "Naomi has a son!" (v. 17a) reckons Obed as the heir that will continue the family line of Elimelech and his son. Oh, by the way, the narrator quickly adds, he also turns out to be King David's grandfather (v. 17b)! In short, the story ends with positive, life-changing reversals for Naomi, Ruth, Boaz, and even the nation of Israel—all apparently orchestrated by divine providence. Verses 18–22 probably are David's official, ten-member royal genealogy, formally tracing the course of that providence from Judah's son Perez to David.

READING

Read Ruth 1–4 and formulate answers to the questions that follow:

1. Argue for or against this proposition: the story's prologue (1:1–6) clearly implies that God punished Naomi for things that she, her husband, and their sons did.

2. Summarize the mental picture that the story leaves you of Naomi, Ruth, Boaz, and the other relative. In what ways do you hear their lives relating to parts of your own personal story? What do you take away from them for your story?

3. Observe, on the one hand, statements within the book where the characters refer to or invoke God and, on the other hand, statements that report things that God actually did. Reflect on the book's view of God—that is, when and how he intervenes, when and how he remains aloof. And why?

4. How might the book of Ruth illumine your understanding of how God works in our world today?

5. Trace the development of Ruth's relationship with Naomi's family and with Judah through the book. What attitudes toward foreigners does it seem to promote?

6. Evaluate whether or not, in your view, the closing genealogy provides the story with a good ending.

BIBLIOGRAPHY

Block, Daniel I. *Ruth: A Discourse Analysis of the Hebrew Bible*. Zondervan Exegetical Commentary on the Old Testament. Grand Rapids: Zondervan, 2015.

Brenner, Athalya. *A Feminist Companion to Ruth*. FCB 1st series. Sheffield: Sheffield Academic Press, 1993.

Carroll R., M. Daniel. "Once a Stranger, Always a Stranger? Immigration, Assimilation, and the Book of Ruth." *International Bulletin of Missionary Research* 39/4 (2015): 185–88.

Eskenazi, Tamara Cohn, and Tikva Frymer-Kensky. *Ruth*. Jewish Publication Society Bible Commentary. Philadelphia: Jewish Publication Society, 2011.

Havea, Jione, and Peter H. W. Lau, eds. *Reading Ruth in Asia*. International Voices in Biblical Studies 7. Atlanta: SBL Press, 2015.

Hawk, L. Daniel. *Ruth*. ApOTC 7B. Nottingham: Apollos; Downers Grove, IL: InterVarsity Press, 2015.

Hubbard, Robert L., Jr. *The Book of Ruth*. NICOT. Grand Rapids: Eerdmans, 1988.

———. "The *go'el* in Ancient Israel: The Theology of an Israelite Institution." *BBR* 1 (1991): 3–19.

———. "Kinsman-Redeemer and Levirate." Pages 378–83 in *Dictionary of the Old Testament: Wisdom, Poetry, and Writings*. Edited by Tremper Longman III and Peter Enns. Downers Grove, IL: InterVarsity Press, 2008.

———. "Redemption." Pages 716–20 in *New International Dictionary of Biblical Theology*. Edited by T. Desmond Alexander and Brian S. Rosner. Leicester: InterVarsity Press, 2000.

Jones, Edward Allen, III. *Reading Ruth in the Restoration Period: A Call for Inclusion*. LHBOTS 604. New York: Bloomsbury T&T Clark, 2016.

Nielsen, Kirsten. *Ruth: A Commentary*. OTL. Louisville: Westminster John Knox, 1997.

Schipper, Jeremy. *Ruth: A New Translation with Introduction and Commentary*. AB 7D. New Haven: Yale University Press, 2016.

Weisberg, D. E. "The Widow of Our Discontent: Levirate Marriage in the Bible and Ancient Israel." *JSOT* 28 (2004): 403–29.

14 THE BOOKS OF 1–2 SAMUEL

THE BOOKS OF 1–2 SAMUEL HAVE been named for the story's central character, Samuel, who anoints Israel's first two kings, Saul and David. Samuel is Israel's final Hero and, hence, lays the leadership bridge between the era of the Heroes and the period of the kings. In the Primary History, he stands third in the prestigious line of early Israelite leaders—Moses, Joshua, Samuel, and David—and also occasionally shows traits of a prophet (see 1 Sam 9:6-9). The story of 1–2 Samuel tracks the complex saga of David's rise to power and lengthy royal rule as successor to Saul, Israel's first king. Two poetic pieces—the Song of Hannah (1 Sam 2:1-10) and the Last Words of David (2 Sam 23:1-7)—bracket the books around their central theme, God's sovereign appointment of righteous leaders and judgment on wicked ones. The lives of the story's three main characters—Samuel, Saul, and David—flesh out that truth. Indeed, you may notice that 1 Samuel features three relational pairs: Samuel and Eli, Samuel and Saul, Saul and David—while David alone dominates 2 Samuel. Some scholars suggest that 1-2 Samuel incorporate into its story two prior documents, an Ark Narrative (1 Sam 4-6 + 2 Sam 6) and a Court History of David (2 Sam 6-20).

The Story

The books of Samuel can be outlined in the following five main parts:

1. Samuel, Eli, and Saul (1 Sam 1-15)—narrates the call of Samuel by Yahweh to lead the Israelites and reveals how Saul, anointed king by Samuel, enjoyed initial success but lost his kingship through disobedience
2. Saul and David (1 Sam 16-31)—follows Saul's battles with the Philistines and Saul's attempts to kill David, whom Samuel had anointed to be the next king
3. The Rise of David (2 Sam 1-5)—recounts the complex story about how David actually became king after Saul died
4. The Court History of David (2 Sam 6-20)—reports the tumultuous reign of David as King of Israel
5. Epilogue: David Remembered (2 Sam 21-24)—collects miscellaneous but significant stories, poems, and records to round out the picture of David

The Book of 1 Samuel

1 Samuel 1–15: Samuel, Eli, and Saul

The compilers of 1-2 Samuel open their story against the background of three threats. Set at Israel's central shrine at Shiloh, chs. 1-3 introduce an internal threat: an Israelite priesthood so corrupt and self-centered (1 Sam 2:12 calls the priests "scoundrels") that Yahweh can no longer communicate through them. Chapters 4-6 reflect an ongoing external threat: the increasing encroachment inland of the coastal Philistines (for background, see ch. 12 above on Judges). The second internal threat is inconsistent Israelite loyalty to Yahweh, a threat personified by their questionable demand for a king in chs. 8-11 and by the ultimate fate of King Saul for disloyal rebellion in chs. 13-15.

Samuel: His Early Years (Chapters 1-7). The story of Samuel begins with Hannah's grief over being unable to bear a child in ch. 1. During one family pilgrimage to Shiloh, she tearfully pleads with God for a son, promising to give him up to serve Yahweh as a Nazirite all his life (for the meaning of *Nazirite*, see ch. 12 on Judges). God grants her Samuel, and a few years later she entrusts the young boy into the care of the old priest Eli at Shiloh. In ch. 2, her poetic prayer lifts a victory song that celebrates God's incomparability: no other god has Yahweh's omniscient grasp of the universe (vv. 2-3) and absolute sovereignty over human destinies. Hannah revels in its contrasting results: God disempowers the powerful and strengthens the weak (v. 4); the overfed end up empty, the underfed full (v. 5a); barren women bear many children, those with many children suffer grief (v. 5b); and God elevates the helpless poor to positions of power (vv. 7-8). Hannah's closing affirmation of confidence (vv. 9-10) exults in Yahweh's inevitable victory: his protection of the faithful, especially his anointed king (see below), and his destruction of the wicked. Her song sets the scene for the contrasting fates of Eli, Samuel, Saul, and David that play out in 1-2 Samuel. It also anticipates David's own similar victory song (2 Sam 22), with which it brackets the book thematically. Alas, ch. 3 details the symptoms of the spiritual malaise (vv. 1, 8-10): oracles and visions from God are rare, and even Eli is slow to recognize that the voice calling, "Samuel," is Yahweh's, and slow to teach the boy the formula for receiving divine communications (v. 10). Not unexpectedly, it falls to Samuel to confirm an earlier prophetic message announcing the judgment soon to befall Eli's family (vv. 15-18), but he soon gains national recognition as a prophet through whom Yahweh now regularly communicates with the Israelites (vv. 19-21).

In the story, Samuel personifies a radical turning point in the nation's history and presages the emergence of new leadership. In ch. 4 the prophecy comes true: a Philistine victory over Israel costs Eli and his sons their lives; the enemy carries off as a prize Israel's most sacred object, the ark of the covenant. Remarkably, chs. 4-6 (Ark Narrative 1; compare with 2 Sam 6) follow the ark's short but eventful stay in Philistine hands—a story told almost tongue-in-cheek. A guest in the temple of the Philistine god Dagon, the ark (i.e., Yahweh) wreaks such disrespectful havoc with its divine host that Dagon's frightened devotees send the ark back by oxcart to a joyous welcome by the Israelites. This episode demonstrates that God is also sovereign over other deities—sadly, a lesson the Israelites never quite get—and the sudden deaths of seventy Israelites for simply peeking into the ark (clearly, a no-no in the Torah) leads the Israelites to abandon it for two decades. In biblical terms, to treat it casually was to treat Israel's sovereign God as a servant rather than a master. In ch. 7, at Mizpah, Samuel leads the Israelites to repent and renounce all other gods, an event interrupted by a Philistine attack that Yahweh's thunderous, panic-inducing voice turns into an Israelite victory. To memorialize the victory, Samuel erects a stone near Mizpah, naming it *Ebenezer* (lit., "a stone of help") in honor of the help Yahweh provided Israel that day. Verse 2 of the Christian hymn "Come Thou Fount of Every Blessing" alludes to this event. The narrator's concluding summary (vv. 13–17) recounts how, under Samuel (and with Yahweh's help), Israel has been able to roll back recent Philistine territorial gains decisively; it portrays Samuel as the ideal righteous leader—a Hero, prophet-priest, and judge.

This embroidered linen canvas from 17th-century Britain, now in the Metropolitan Museum of Art in New York City, depicts the background of the prophet Samuel, as narrated in 1 Samuel 1. The central scene depicts Samuel's mother, Hannah, with her husband Elkanah and his other wife, Peninnah. The background scenes show Hannah praying for a son (on the left) and her presenting the child Samuel to the priest Eli.

Samuel and Saul (Chapters 8–12). In ch. 8, the compilers report that Samuel's sons are too wicked to succeed their aging father, so Israel's leaders petition Samuel for a king (Heb. *melek*) as other nations have. Initially, neither Samuel nor (apparently) Yahweh likes the idea, reading it as rejection of their leadership. Nevertheless, Yahweh orders Samuel to do this but also to warn the people that a royal lifestyle carries an expensive price tag that they'll need to pay. (If they'd only seen Solomon's later expense account!) With God's permission, Samuel anoints the Benjaminite Saul from Gibeah as Israel's "leader" (*nagid*), the one to deliver them from all their enemies. Some scholars think that the differing terminology—the people seek a *melek* ("king"), but Samuel anoints a *nagid* ("ruler")—reflects conflicting Israelite opinions on the wisdom of having a king. Whatever the case, Saul overcomes his initial reluctance and, in chs. 9–10, shows commendable leadership traits (wealth, good looks, tall stature) and the Spirit-empowerment of a Hero. He routs the Ammonites in Transjordan (ch. 11). At Gilgal, Samuel seems to inaugurate him officially as "king" (*melek*) in addition to his status as "leader." In ch. 12, like Moses and Joshua, the aged Samuel gives a telling farewell speech, warning the people that things will go well with them and their king only if they serve and obey the LORD and that rebellion will turn Yahweh against them. In one sense, through the speech the compilers provide us the interpretive standard by which to evaluate both Saul's two unfortunate, subsequent actions and the mistakes that plagued Israel in future centuries.

Saul: His Rise and Demise (Chapters 13–15). The compilers of 1–2 Samuel next seek to explain how a promising leader such as Saul in the end loses his kingship. The context of Saul's first act in ch. 13 is his failed attack on an isolated Philistine outpost and his fear of a follow-up rout by advancing enemy reinforcements. Bivouaced at Gilgal near the Jordan, Saul and his remaining troops await Samuel's scheduled arrival to perform two prebattle sacrifices. But when Samuel fails to show, Saul impatiently performs them which, sadly, is something the Torah authorizes only a priest (not a king) to do. When Samuel finally arrives, he tells Saul that his action has ended his chance to found a dynasty; instead, Yahweh has rejected him as king in favor of someone else whose heart aligns closely with God's (vv. 13–14). In ch. 15, Saul's second action adds outright disobedience to his earlier impropriety: rather than completely annihilate the Amalekites and all their possessions as God commanded (cf. Exod. 17), Saul spares the Amalekite king Agag and all the very best sheep and cattle. Because of Saul's disobedience, Yahweh tells Samuel that he regrets having made Saul king, an announcement that leaves the prophet angry and crying out to Yahweh all night. The next morning, Samuel tracks down Saul at Gilgal, and an intense, painful dialogue between the two historic figures ensues. Saul desperately defends his actions as motivated by sacrificial interests, but in the end Samuel reiterates Yahweh's decision to reject Saul as king because Saul rejected God's word. In memorable words, Samuel comments:

> Does the LORD delight in burnt offerings and sacrifices as much as in obeying the LORD? To obey is better than sacrifice, and to heed is better than the fat of rams. For rebellion is like the sin of divination, and arrogance like the evil of idolatry. Because you have rejected the word of the LORD, he has rejected you as king. (1 Sam 15:22–23 TNIV)

In God's eyes, obedience to God's word far outranks sacrifices in God's honor, while "rebellion" and "arrogance" are tantamount to the abominable sins of "divination" and "idolatry," respectively. Humans may prefer to "do (external) things" to win God's favor, but God prefers simple obedience to what God says. Samuel formally executes the Amalekite king, an action that probably fuels the later hatred against Jews by Haman, a descendant of Agag, in the book of Esther. To conclude, the historians remark sadly that Samuel and Saul now part company, never to see each other again, although Samuel does mourn Saul's fate.

1 Samuel 16–31: Saul and David

Saul and David, by
Rembrandt. 1650–70.

With Saul's fate sealed, ch. 16 marks the debut of David, the story's leading
figure from here on. The subtly humorous episode occurs at the home of his father Jesse in Bethlehem, where Samuel seeks Saul's replacement among seven
of Jesse's sons—all of whom are impressive and well qualified in Samuel's eyes.
But Samuel soon learns that God wants more than good looks: Yahweh passes
over the seven to choose David, whom the family thought was too young to
be considered as the king-designate. Against the backdrop of Saul's failure,
Yahweh's rationale for the choice is thematically significant for readers: God
prefers someone with a heart like God's (e.g., David), not just someone with
a beautiful body (e.g., David's brothers, Saul), a truth that is still applicable

The LORD's Anointed

You may notice that the term "the LORD's [or 'his'] anointed" (Heb. *mashiakh*, pronounced "mah-SHE-akh") recurs several times in 1 Sam 24 and 26. In both contexts, David invokes that term — which is, in reality, a special title implying special election by Yahweh — to explain why, despite Saul's rejection by Yahweh and the king's unjustified quest to take David's life, David refuses to kill him. This title is apparently unique to Israel, since no analogies to it have yet been found in the ancient Near East, but Egyptian influence may have shaped the anointing ritual itself. In this title we catch a brief glimpse of the ceremony of royal accession that sums up Israel's understanding of kingship. Literally, to "anoint" (Heb. *mashakh*) means to "wet, rub, or smear (oil)" on someone who is about to become king; both the verb and the noun are technical terms associated with royals. Biblical texts are quite clear that it is Yahweh, not the people of Israel, who "anoints" a king, albeit through authorized representatives such as Samuel (1 Sam 16). Anointing bestows on the king a unique, exclusive relationship with Yahweh and a special, divinely given, indelible status that guarantees the king immunity from everything but divine accountability. As David himself notes, a king's status as "anointed" changes only when God himself strikes him down or when he dies in combat or of natural causes (1 Sam 26:10). Anyone who "lays a hand on the LORD's anointed" (another recurring technical term) without divine authorization incurs guilt and risks suffering its consequences. That is why David passes over two opportunities to kill Saul. It's worth noting that Hebrew *mashiach* becomes *christos* ("anointed") in Greek, a term well known in the NT ("Christ"), and "Messiah" in English. The messianic theme originates in Gen 17:6, finds articulation in 2 Sam 7:11–16, and spawns prophecies about a future David (Amos 9:11; Isa 11:1–9) that Jesus Christ fulfills (Matt 1:1; Acts 13:22–23).

today. Structurally, this section of the story has two parts: (1) David with Saul (1 Sam 17–20); and (2) Saul against David (1 Sam 21–31). To begin the section, ch. 16 clarifies that David is the person to whom Samuel alluded earlier, and the section ends with the sad scene of Saul's death in ch. 31. In short, 1 Sam 16–31 marks the final years of King Saul, during which time the king-designate, David, works to stay alive, bides his time, and awaits his turn.

Chapters 17–20 track a cat-and-mouse game between David and Saul: David, an outlaw on the run, moves from place to place, hunted by a paranoid Saul whenever the king gets wind of the young man's whereabouts. The compilers supply various episodes that confirm whose heart is truly God-like: David is Spirit-empowered, Saul possessed by a divinely sent "evil spirit" (i.e., "foul mood," "depression"); David defeats the arrogant Philistine giant Goliath and forges a lifelong friendship with Saul's son Jonathan; Saul is bitterly jealous of David's success and obsessed with killing him. In ch. 22 Saul kills the priests at the sanctuary at Nob (Judah) simply for hosting the fugitive David. In ch. 23, overruling the fears of his guerrilla band, David risks discovery by Saul by leading a rout of the Philistines at Keilah in the western lowlands. Eventually, after locals in the desert southeast of Hebron betray him to Saul, David and his troops hide in the safe, protective terrain at 'Ein-Gedi near the Dead Sea.

Occasionally, David deploys them to protect farmers and herdsmen from marauders, thus winning the favor of some of those spared. Chapter 25, the story of Nabal ("Fool"), his wife Abigail, and David, provides an illuminating glimpse into David's complex character. When the wealthy stockman Nabal denies David proper payment for the protection that his troops had provided, a hotheaded David angrily vows to avenge the man's contempt— until, in a daring visit to David's camp, Abigail persuades him not to saddle his otherwise bright future with needless bloodguilt (but compare ch. 30, where David avenges a cruel Amalekite raid). Abigail's courage and striking advice earn David's genuine praise, and when Nabal later dies, David and Abigail marry. The compilers also include two similar episodes (chs. 24 and 26) that portray David as honoring Saul's sacred status as "God's anointed." Twice, David bypasses golden opportunities to kill Saul, notwithstanding the latter's relentless, violent pursuit—a threat that drives David, for his own safety, to lodge his band for a time with the Philistines (chs. 27 and 29). The contrast between a merciless Saul and a merciful David is telling, as is the fact that David always seeks and receives military advice from Yahweh, while Saul asks but never receives an answer. The compilers ensure that it is obvious to the reader which of the two is the "man after God's own heart."

In the end, the increasing Philistine threat up north finally pushes Saul's paranoia over the edge. In ch. 28, after receiving no word from Yahweh through normal means, the desperate king seeks to contact the long-dead Samuel through a local witch at Endor. This episode raises questions among some readers, since it seems to imply that the living may communicate with the dead, a practice that the Torah prohibits (Lev 19:31; 20:6; Deut 18:10-11). Saul had apparently enforced this law himself right after Samuel's death (1 Sam 28:3, 9). In *Antiquities of the Jews* 6, 14 (1st cent. CE), Josephus seems to accept the story as credible, but medieval Christian intepreters suggested that the witch conjures up a demon masquerading as Samuel, not his actual ghost (Luther labeled it "the Devil's ghost"). The problem is that demons are virtually absent in the Old Testament, which is the reason perhaps that the Septuagint (2nd cent. BCE) describes Saul's medium as a "ventriloquist," a term probably implying fakery. Three telling features of the story merit mention, however. First, the witch at Endor describes what she sees as an 'elohim, "a god" or "divine being" (28:13), not the typical ancestral spirit or ghost with which she usually dealt. The striking term may reveal this case to be something unexpected, something guided by a power outside the woman's control—perhaps God himself. Second, her picture of Samuel as "an old man wearing a robe" apparently confirms for Saul that it is Samuel. Finally, Samuel's message here, especially the torn robe as a symbol of Saul's removal as king (28:17b echoes 15:28), both reiterates and amplifies Samuel's original message and further points to Samuel as the person speaking. In short, while one is tempted to attribute this report to the narrative imagination of the compilers, the fact that it recounts something extraordinary and unprecedented is no reason to discount it as unhistorical. It certainly comports with the Samuel we meet earlier, and the God of the Bible is well known for acting in unusual and unexpected ways. But we advise readers not to try Saul's method at home!

Saul leaves Endor to meet his fate, a frightened, tormented man. Chapter 31 presents his tragic end on Mount Gilboa, surrounded by Philistines who kill his three sons and seriously wound him. He chooses suicide rather than captivity, thus fulfilling what Samuel had forecast (28:16–19) and echoing the book's theme of Yahweh's sovereignty over the appointment or dethronement of kings. The victorious Philistines put Saul's armor on display in a Philistine temple and hang his and his sons' bodies publicly at Beit Shean; but, grateful for an earlier rescue by Saul (see 1 Sam 11), people from Jabesh-gilead retrieve the bodies and bury them properly at Jabesh. This kindness rings the curtain down on King Saul and opens the door for King-Designate David to reign—but not without some Davidic patience.

READING

Read 1 Sam 1–31 and formulate answers to the questions that follow:

1. What character and/or event in 1 Samuel most catches your attention or causes you admiration or disgust? Why do you think it does (or they do) so? What growth or decline do you detect in that character, or what importance does your selected event play in the story?

2. How are women portrayed in 1 Samuel? What does their portrayal contribute to your view of women in God's kingdom today?

3. What role(s) do you observe God playing in the story of 1 Sam 1–31? In what way(s) does God still play that role today? In what (if any) way(s) do you think God's role has changed?

4. Compare Saul and David as leaders. What positive and negative traits does each display? In what ways do their stories enrich or challenge your understanding of Christian leadership today?

5. Compare Hannah's Song (1 Sam 2:1–10) and Mary's Song (Luke 1:46–55). What themes or theology do they share, and how do they differ? What does each contribute to the literary development of the story in its respective context?

BIBLIOGRAPHY

Bodi, Daniel. "The Story of Samuel, Saul, and David." Pages 190–226 in *Ancient Israel's History: An Introduction to Issues and Sources.* Edited by Bill T. Arnold and Richard S. Hess. Grand Rapids: Baker Academic, 2014.

Bodner, Keith. "Ark-Eology: Shifting Emphases in 'Ark Narrative' Scholarship." *CurBR* 4 (2006): 169–97.

Fokkelman, Jan P. *Narrative Art and Poetry in the Books of Samuel: A Full Interpretation Based on Stylistic and Structural Analyses.* 4 vols. Assen: Van Gorcum, 1981–1993.

Gilmour, Rachelle. *Representing the Past: A Literary Analysis of Narrative Historiography in the Book of Samuel.* VTSup 143. Leiden: Brill, 2011.

Kelly, Brian E. "Samuel." Pages 111–18 in *Theological Interpretation of the Bible: A Book-by-Book Survey.* Edited by Kevin J. Vanhoozer. Grand Rapids: Baker Academic, 2008.

Klein, Ralph W. *1 Samuel.* 2nd ed. WBC 10. Grand Rapids: Zondervan, 2014.

McCarter, P. Kyle, Jr. *I Samuel: A New Translation with Introduction and Commentary.* AB 8. New York: Doubleday, 1980.

Polzin, Robert. *Samuel and the Deuteronomist: A Literary Study of the Deuteronomic History—1 Samuel.* San Francisco: Harper & Row, 1989.

Tsumura, David T. *The First Book of Samuel.* NICOT. Grand Rapids: Eerdmans, 2007.

The Book of 2 Samuel

The book of 2 Samuel marks the closing, climactic section of the long story about David that 1 Samuel began. It has three parts: (1) the rise of David (2 Sam 1–5); (2) the court history of David (2 Sam 6–20); and (3) an epilogue (2 Sam 21–24). The court history of David is commonly thought to be a preexisting source document that the compilers of 1–2 Samuel incorporated within 2 Samuel.

2 Samuel 1–5: The Rise of David

As 1 Sam 1 began the momentous era of Samuel with the bitter sadness of Hannah's infertility, so the groundbreaking era of King David dawns in 2 Sam 1 with news of Saul and Jonathan's deaths reaching David. The messenger is a bedraggled Amalekite who flees to David after surviving Saul's fatal battle on Mount Gilboa. The man wrongly assumes that the news will please David, so he appears to boast about having killed Saul, albeit as an act of mercy. David has the man executed, however, for daring to kill the LORD's anointed (see the sidebar "The Lord's Anointed" above). Rather than rejoice, David cries out in bitter lamentation over Saul and David, bequeathing to readers a classic example of a Hebrew lament and a poignant glimpse of his deep grief:

> Daughters of Israel, weep for Saul, who clothed you in scarlet and
>   finery,
>   who adorned your garments with ornaments of gold.
> How the mighty have fallen in battle!
>   Jonathan lies slain on your heights.
> I grieve for you, Jonathan my brother; you were very dear to me.
>   Your love for me was wonderful, more wonderful than that of
>   women.
> How the mighty have fallen! The weapons of war have perished!
>   (2 Sam 1:24–27 TNIV; cf. 18:33; 19:4)

You might expect Saul's death to open the way for King-Designate David to ascend the vacant throne, but the story, post-Saul, proves to be more complex. In ch. 2, after seeking Yahweh's guidance, David settles his entourage at Hebron, where Judah's leaders soon anoint him king of Judah. Meanwhile, east of the Jordan, Abner, commander of Saul's army, leads Benjaminites loyal to Saul to appoint the late king's son, Ish-Bosheth, king of Israel; thus, for the first time Israel has two reigning kings—and conflict soon follows. In ch. 2, the battle of Gibeon inaugurates a long, violent civil war between troops loyal to David and to Saul. In ch. 3, a falling-out with Ish-Bosheth drives Abner to defect to David, but the defector soon dies at the hands of Joab, Judah's military commander, avenging Abner's killing of his brother at Gibeon. In ch. 4, Abner's death leads two of Ish-Bosheth's military commanders to assassinate him, but David regards their actions as unwarranted vengeance and orders them to suffer the same fate as the bragging Amalekite. Finally, in ch. 5 a formal assembly of all Israel's tribes at Hebron officially enacts the personal covenant brokered by Abner between the northern tribes and David. Sociologically, the two-step accession process of David assumes that, at the time (and for whatever reason), the northern and southern tribes constituted two preexisting, independent political power centers. David and Solomon will preside over the *united kingdom*, but eventually the two centers will split into two countries, Israel and Judah—the *divided kingdom*—when the northern tribes refuse to renew their covenant with David's dynasty (1 Kgs 12). For the present, the compilers immediately recount two historic post-accession steps by David: his capture of the impregnable fortress of Zion (later, "the City of David"), and his expulsion of the Philistines from Judah. Those events—and the births of eleven more children to David in Zion—attest that God is, indeed, with David.

2 Samuel 6–20: The Court History of David

The court history recounts King David's reign over the united kingdom. It thus offers the most comprehensive resource for understanding the compilers' view of it. By way of overview, the following parts comprise the court history:

1. The dramatic arrival of the ark to Jerusalem establishes Jerusalem as Israel's religious capital city (2 Sam 6)
2. Yahweh's announcement of a covenant with David promises that his family dynasty will rule Israel forever (2 Sam 7)
3. David's military victories and other actions picture his reign positively—a stark contrast to the tumultuous period to follow (2 Sam 8–10)
4. David's illicit liaison with Bathsheba causes him painful humiliation and great personal losses (2 Sam 11–19)
5. Discontent with David's reign surfaces in the character of the Benjaminite Sheba (2 Sam 20)

The story of David's reign opens appropriately in ch. 6 with Ark Narrative 2, his successful installation of the ark of the covenant in Jerusalem (for Ark Narrative 1, see 1 Sam 4–6). For two decades, the ark had been stored at Kiriath-jearim in the western lowlands, and its retrieval by David was not uneventful. Initially, an enthusiastic David personally led the large, raucous procession that accompanied the oxcart-borne ark toward Jerusalem. But the sudden death of a man who touched the ark to prevent its falling—an act branded by Yahweh as "irreverent" (2 Sam 6:7)—so scared David that he canceled the procession and left the ark with Obed-edom along the route. Three months later, however, news that the ark's presence had blessed its custodian reignited David's enthusiasm. He personally leads the singing and dancing to greet its final arrival, much to the disgust, however, of his wife, Michal (Saul's daughter), who thinks his processional behavior shameful and over the top. David explains that Yahweh is worthy of such joyous display and, sadly, the writer notes, Michal lives out the rest of her life never having any children.

We designate ch. 7 a programmatic text because of its importance for David, his descendants, and our understanding of Jesus as well (see above). A play on various meanings of the Hebrew word *bayit* ("house") weaves the narrative together and drives home its main point. Events in chs. 1-6 have settled David peacefully and comfortably in his own royal "house" (Heb. *bayit*, "palace"), and they also stir him to express gratitude to Yahweh for generously bringing him to this point. Thus begins Jerusalem's increasing importance as the center of the kingdom, eventually to become central to the OT as well. Now that the ark of the covenant has arrived in Jerusalem and David has built his palace, the city of Jerusalem will become the political and religious center for the tribes, with the future temple to be built by Solomon.

David in fact proposes building Yahweh a "house" (Heb. *bayit*, "temple") himself, but through the prophet Nathan, Yahweh informs David that Yahweh, who's never had or needed such a house, has other plans: God promises to build David and his descendants into a "house" (*bayit*, "royal dynasty"). Yahweh and the Davidic line will share a father-son relationship (a typical ancient metaphor for god-king relationships), and as "father" God will punish any errant "son" of David, though never withdraw his "love" from David's line as he did with Saul. The lone condition is that David's descendants must continue to worship Yahweh alone (see 2 Sam 23:5; Ps 89:3). Theologically, this makes each Davidic king the earthly, personal representative of King Yahweh and, hence, accountable to God for loyal obedience and implementation of God's wishes. As for the *bayit* David had in mind, David's royal successor will build it, an episode you'll soon read in 1 Kgs 5-6. Thus, the story of David introduces what we now call the "Davidic covenant."

PROGRAMMATIC TEXT #7

And the LORD declares to you that the LORD will make a dynasty for you. When the time comes for you to die and you lie down with your ancestors, I will raise up your descendant – one of your very own children – to succeed you, and I will establish his kingdom. He will build a temple for my name, and I will establish his royal throne forever. . . . Your dynasty and your kingdom will be secured forever before me. Your throne will be established forever. (2 Sam 7:11b–16 CEB)

Legend:
- Jebusite city (captured by David's men)
- Solomon's addition
- Modern walls (built in 16th century by Suleiman the Magnificent)
- Hasmonean addition

NORTHEASTERN HILL

CENTRAL VALLEY

KIDRON VALLEY

NORTHWESTERN HILL

TEMPLE

Temple □ ■ Altar

Royal Palace

HILL

MISHNEH

Tomb of Pharaoh's Daughter □

Ophel

SOUTHWESTERN HILL

MAKTESH

Millo

CENTRAL VALLEY

SOUTHEASTERN HILL (ZION)

Gihon Spring

Siloam Channel

Siloam Pool ◇

Lower Pool ◇

MOUNT OF OFFENSE

HINNOM VALLEY

N

En-rogel Spring ○

0	1/8	1/4 mile
0	200	400 meters

Chapters 8-10 track David's wars—a series of royal military successes that reiterate that God indeed supports David (compare the similar pattern of early successes with Saul and Solomon; 1 Sam 10-11; 1 Kgs 3-4, 9-10). Chapter 8 lists the amazing array of neighbor nations that David defeated and subjected to paying him regular monetary tribute (see Table 14.1). Second Samuel 8:15 remarks that "David reigned over all Israel, doing what was just and right for all his people" (TNIV), and 8:16-18 also lists David's royal officials, notably Joab (army chief), Jehoshaphat (royal historian), Zadok and Ahimelech (priests), and Seraiah (secretary). A moving scene in ch. 9 describes how, to honor his dear friend Jonathan, David brings Jonathan's crippled son Mephibosheth (Saul's only heir) to live in the palace and orders Saul's former servant Ziba to farm Saul's land to assist in Mephibosheth's support (for Ziba's later kindness to David and Mephibosheth's vengeful ingratitude, see 2 Sam 16). The incident fleshes out David's literary portrait, adding thoughtful kindness to his other fine qualities. On the other hand, when a new Ammonite king misinterprets David's kindness as veiled espionage, humiliating David's emissaries, 2 Sam 10 portrays the angry side of David that is reminiscent of his proposed vengeance against stingy Nabal (1 Sam 25), except that, in 2 Sam 10, no lovely Abigail intervenes. Furious, David sends Israel's army under Joab to avenge the spurned royal kindness, and the army soundly routs the Ammonites and their Aramaean mercenary allies. That victory further rounds out King David's emerging role as the region's new big dog, notwithstanding the Ammonites' continuing intransigence, which sets the context for what happens next.

It is 2 Sam 11-12 that recounts the now well-known series of events—the Bathsheba incident—which the compilers believe decisively determines the fate of the rest of David's reign. The story is a simple one: strolling leisurely around his palace rooftop rather than leading his troops into battle,

Table 14.1. David's Empire (2 Samuel 8)

Nation	Location
Philistines (v. 1)	Mediterranean Coast
Moabites (v. 2)	Transjordan (Dead Sea)
Aramaeans (vv. 3–8)	Eastern Lebanon, Syria
Edomites (v. 12)	Southern Transjordan
Ammonites (v. 12)	Central Transjordan
Amalekites (v. 12)	Southern Negev (nomadic)

Tel Dan Stele. Discovered during excavations at Tel Dan in 1993–94, the Tel Dan Stele contains part of a victory inscription in Aramaic left by an unnamed king, most probably the important regional figure Hazael of Aram-Damascus (late 9th century BCE). Hazael boasts of victories over the king of Israel, and his ally the ruler of "the House of David" (*bytdwd*). This marks the earliest extrabiblical reference to the name David as the founder of a Judahite dynasty and the fourth inscription to mention the name Israel.
©*yoav dothan (Wikimedia Commons, GNU 1.2)*

My father went up [against him when] he fought at. . . . And my father lay down, he went to his [ancestors]. And the king of Israel entered previously in my father's land. [And] Hadad made me king. And Hadad went in front of me, [and] I departed from [the] seven . . . of my kingdom, and I slew [seventy kings], who harnessed [thousands of chariots] and thousands of horsemen. [I killed Jehoram] son of [Ahab] king of Israel, and I killed [Ahaz]iahu son of [Jehoram king] of the house of David. And I set [their towns into ruins and turned] their land into [desolation].

(Bill T. Arnold and Bryan E. Beyer, *Readings from the Ancient Near East* [Grand Rapids: Baker, 2002], 165) the king sees a beautiful young woman bathing, is told that she's the wife of a mercenary named Uriah, has her brought to the palace for sex (alas, ancient kings thought they owned everything!), and gets her pregnant. Worse, to cover up this evidence of his adultery, David has Uriah returned for a brief leave, but Uriah denies himself sexual intimacy with Bathsheba out of loyalty to his army buddies at the front. So, David sends him back, secretly ordering Joab to deploy Uriah, in essence, where he's most likely to fall in battle—which he does. Thus, the compilers picture David as guilty of both adultery and murder—inexcusable abuses of royal prerogatives and an un-Yahweh-like example to all Israelites. Yahweh holds David accountable in ch. 12 through Nathan, who invokes a legal parable about a rich stockman who helps himself to a poor man's beloved ewe lamb, not from his own stock, to feed a visiting guest. As expected, David angrily condemns the outrage ("That man will die!"), thus unknowingly condemning himself. "You are the man!" Nathan replies and then announces Yahweh's judgment with a wordplay: David secretly murdered Uriah with an Ammonite "sword" (Heb. *herev*) so, fittingly, the "sword" (i.e., murderous violence) will publicly ravage David's family. David genuinely confesses his sin, but the newborn fruit of his adultery dies, just as Nathan said he would.

In remarkable detail, the compilers have assembled chs. 13–19 to narrate how the sword-in-David's-family prophecy plays out. Clearly, they regard these events as an extended cautionary tale to remind the Israelites, including David's successors, how seriously Yahweh takes the Israelites' covenant obligations. To begin, Prince Amnon forcibly rapes his half-sister, Tamar, an outrage that her brother, Prince Absalom, avenges by having Amnon killed two years later (ch. 13). David grieves for Amnon but also greatly misses Absalom, who takes refuge for three years with an Aramaean king east of the Sea of Galilee. General Joab cleverly engineers Absalom's return to Jerusalem, but the narrator notes that two more years pass before prince and king reconcile (ch. 14). Alas, sometime later, Absalom unsheathes another "sword": at Hebron he finally launches a surprising coup attempt against David that has been four years in the making. Sensing grave danger, David leads his loyalists to leave Jerusalem, and in chs. 15–18 the narrator details events and names conspirators in both camps: intimate dialogues and increases in intensity and intrigue dominate. Keeping the large number of characters straight may remind some readers of tracking the characters and creatures in *The Lord of the Rings*! As David exits Jerusalem, one is struck by the warm respect with which David's many friends and advisers, several of them non-Israelites, greet him (chs. 15–16). Strategically, David has his confidant Hushai and the priests Zadok and Abiathar join Absalom as David's moles to keep him posted on his son's actions—which they and their sons do effectively, at great personal risk (see 17:15–29). The coup's decisive turning point comes in ch. 17 when Absalom—at Yahweh's invisible prompting, the compilers interject (17:14; cf. 15:31)—adopts the advice of Hushai (consolidate forces, then attack) over that of the revered Ahithophel (attack now!). The decision proves catastrophic for Absalom: it allows a bedraggled, exhausted David to regain his strength and redeploy his forces to defeat and kill Absalom (ch. 18).

The account of victory, however, maintains a narrative realism, including scenes in which the prophetic "sword" still retains its edge. Certainly, one such is the skillfully told, emotional scene of David's terrible grief after learning of his son's death (2 Sam 18:24–33; see also ch. 19), as is the bitter cursing of the fleeing David by Shimei, a relative of Saul who labels the king a murderer and usurper (16:5–12). But, true to his character, David acknowledges that, given Absalom's rebellion, Yahweh may be speaking through Shimei but that his ultimate hope still lies in divine mercy and its restoration of covenant blessings (16:11–12). Additionally, though unsuccessful, the rebellion of northern tribes against David led by another Benjaminite, Sheba, and the ambivalent welcome-home accorded David even by Judah (ch. 20) reflect a shaken united kingdom and anticipate its eventual end (see the repeated political slogan in 20:1 and 1 Kgs 12:16). Nevertheless, David manifests a heart like Yahweh's in graciously pardoning Shimei (2 Sam 19:16–23), accepting Mephibosheth's explanation for not joining David's flight (19:24–30), and honoring his own loyal friend Barzillai (19:31–40; cf. 17:27–29).

2 Samuel 21–24: The Epilogue

The closing epilogue (chs. 21–24) comprises a kind of scrapbook of miscellaneous mementos that supplement the larger portrait of David's life:

1. Old "newspaper clippings": how David avenges Saul's violent treatment of the Gibeonites and has the bones of Saul and Jonathan properly buried (21:1–14); and further battles with the Philistines (vv. 15–22)
2. Two of David's poems: a long, personal thanksgiving song for Yahweh (also appears as Ps 18) and his so-called Last Words (chs. 22:1–23:7)
3. The honor roll of David's most highly decorated soldiers (23:8–39)
4. The census, plague, divine mercy, and David's purchase of the threshing floor of Araunah (ch. 24)

As noted earlier, ch. 22 quotes David's autobiographical gratitude to Yahweh for rescuing him from his enemies and from Saul (v. 1). To begin, David strings together metaphors symbolic of inviolable protection and salvation from deadly danger to extol God's praiseworthiness:

> The LORD is my rock, my fortress and my deliverer;
>   my God is my rock, in whom I take refuge,
> my shield and the horn of my salvation.
>   He is my stronghold, my refuge and my savior—
> from violent people you save me.
>   (2 Sam 22:2-3 TNIV)

He goes on to recount his own personal experiences of God the Protector and Rescuer who never fails to answer David's cries for help (vv. 2-20), in vv. 11-17 describing Yahweh's intervention as if it were a theophany. In vv. 21-25 David affirms his history of consistent loyalty to Yahweh as the reason why God responds to his cries (vv. 21-25), followed by further autobiography that credits Yahweh with victories and reports about God's refusal to answer his enemies' cries (vv. 38-46). Finally, David owns that his praise is the appropriate response to all these experiences:

> Therefore I will praise you, LORD, among the nations; I will sing the
>   praises of your name.
> He gives his king great victories; he shows unfailing kindness to his
>   anointed, to David and his descendants forever. (2 Sam 22:50-51
>   TNIV)

In the end, David's experiences symbolize the unfailing divine kindness (Heb. *hesed*) promised toward the Davidic dynasty ("David and his descendants"). David's psalm also models the truth that drives all faithful believers—that God's kindness, whatever its form, is occasion to praise the Lord our Protector and Savior. Finally, as noted earlier, ch. 22 forms a thematic inclusio with Hannah's song (1 Sam 2), affirming God's sovereignty over the appointment and removal of rulers—the main theme of 1-2 Samuel. The same theme rings through ch. 23, David's poetic farewell speech packaged as a prophetic oracle (23:1-3a), the inspiration for composer Randall Thompson's anthem "The Last Words of David." David quotes Yahweh's advice to him:

When one rules over people in righteousness, when he rules in the
    fear of God,
he is like the light of morning at sunrise on a cloudless morning,
    like the brightness after rain that brings grass from the earth.
    (2 Sam 23:3-4 TNIV)

What stunning metaphors for a righteous, God-fearing royal reign: like
the expectancy of a glorious cloudless sunrise, like the sparkling, hopeful
freshness after a rainstorm. And what a fitting prelude to God's dealings
with David's dynasty in 1–2 Kings.

Chapter 24 marks the climactic closing of both David's court history
and all of 1–2 Samuel. It begins strangely: for some reason, Yahweh is
angry with Israel (no surprise there!), so God "incites" David (say, what?)
to carry out a census of Israelite males (as punishment for the unnamed
outrage?) to estimate the potential size of Israel's army. Notably, God
neither reiterates nor waives the Torah's requirement—on penalty of
a national plague, no less—that each person counted pay Yahweh compensation (Exod 30:12). But ten months later, the counting done and no
compensation payment reported, through Gad the prophet, Yahweh asks
David which of three penalties he prefers: three years of national famine,
three months of pursuit by David's enemies, or three days of a nationwide plague. David's decision (2 Sam 24:14): "I am in deep distress. Let us
fall into the hands of the LORD, for his mercy is great; but do not let me
fall into human hands" (TNIV). David chooses three days of dealing with
Yahweh rather than humans because, unlike the latter, God is known for
showing great mercy. The next three days see the plague claim thousands
of Israelite lives, but when the destroying angel reaches Jerusalem and the
Lord hears David's confession of sin and his tender, pained plea to spare his
people, God dramatically stops the avenger just as it passes the threshing
floor of Araunah the Jebusite. David obeys God's subsequent command to
build an altar and offer sacrifices there, and later he buys the site—thus,
finally ending the plague. The chapter associates sacrificing, repentant
prayers, and the receipt of God's mercy with that place, but 2 Chr 3:1 supplies the final missing piece: Solomon's temple was built there to grant
all Israel (and foreigners too) access to that same mercy. In retrospect,
David casts a long shadow over Israel through his own foundational reign;
through the centuries of descendants who succeed him; through the prophetic hope of a new future David; and finally, through the NT theme of
Jesus as that new David.

READING

Read 2 Sam 1–24 and formulate answers to the questions that follow:

1. What character and/or event in 2 Samuel most catches your attention or causes you admiration or disgust? Why do you think it (or they) do so? What growth or decline do you detect in that character, or what importance does your selected event play in the story?

2. With which character other than David do you identify the most? Why? Does that character suggest how your life might be different than it is now?

3. How are women portrayed in 2 Samuel? What does their portrayal contribute to your view of women in God's kingdom today?

4. What role(s) do you observe God playing in the story of 2 Samuel? In what way(s) does God still play similar roles today? In what (if any) way(s) do you think his role has changed?

5. Evaluate David as a king and as a parent. In what ways (if any) does David seem destined to be a better king and father than Saul? In what ways (if any) is David *not* a better king and parent than Saul?

6. What do 1–2 Samuel contribute to your understanding of God's ongoing mission in the world today?

BIBLIOGRAPHY

Anderson, A. A. *2 Samuel*. WBC 11. Dallas: Word, 1989.

Athas, George. *The Tel Dan Inscription: A Reappraisal and a New Interpretation*. JSOTSup 360. Copenhagen International Seminar 12. Sheffield: Sheffield Academic Press, 2003.

Baldwin, Joyce G. *I and II Samuel: An Introduction and Commentary*. TOTC 8. Downers Grove, IL: InterVarsity Press, 1988.

Evans, Mary J. *The Message of Samuel: Personalities, Potential, Politics and Power*. TBST. Leicester: Inter-Varsity Press, 2004.

Firth, David G. *1 and 2 Samuel*. ApOTC 8. Leicester: Inter-Varsity Press, 2009.

Halpern, Baruch. *David's Secret Demons: Messiah, Murderer, Traitor, King*. Grand Rapids: Eerdmans, 2001.

Knoppers, Gary N. "The Historical Study of the Monarchy: Developments and Detours." Pages 207–35 in *The Face of Old Testament Studies: A Survey of Contemporary Studies*. Edited by David W. Baker and Bill T. Arnold. Grand Rapids: Baker Books, 1999.

McCarter, P. Kyle, Jr. *II Samuel: A New Translation with Introduction and Commentary*. AB 9. New York: Doubleday, 1984.

Morrison, Craig E. *2 Samuel*. Berit Olam. Collegeville, MN: Liturgical Press, 2013.

Ortiz, Steven M. "United Monarchy: Archaeology and Literary Sources." Pages 227–61 in *Ancient Israel's History: An Introduction to Issues and Sources*. Edited by Bill T. Arnold and Richard S. Hess. Grand Rapids: Baker Academic, 2014.

Polzin, Robert. *David and the Deuteronomist: 2 Samuel*. ISBL. Bloomington: Indiana University Press, 1993.

15 THE BOOKS OF 1–2 KINGS

THE LIFE OF ISRAEL UNDER the monarchy is the focus of 1–2 Kings and accounts for its name. It follows up 1–2 Samuel by tracking and evaluating the performance over more than four centuries of the royal dynasty that, per God's promise, succeeds David's reign. After Solomon, the Israel of Moses, Joshua, David, and Solomon (i.e., the united monarchy) now exists as two separate kingdoms, Israel and Judah (i.e., the divided monarchy), each ruled by its own king. Thus, the story pursues parallel tracks, alternating between the story in both the Northern and Southern Kingdoms (Israel and Judah, respectively) until the Northern Kingdom's demise in 722 BCE. The compilers apparently draw much of its contents from royal annals from both kingdoms, which they often cite as though giving bibliography. It is clear, however, that they view the history theologically through the same Deuteronomistic lens that we first meet in Joshua and Judges.

The Story

The books of 1–2 Kings have three main parts: (1) the story of the united kingdom under Solomon (1 Kgs 1–11); (2) the story of the divided kingdom (1 Kgs 12–2 Kgs 17); and (3) the story of the Kingdom of Judah (2 Kgs 18–25). A chiastic structure may underlie the book (see Diagram 15.1).

The book's center (line D in the diagram)—the orientation point for all of its contents—is the struggle between Yahweh and Baal over the religious loyalty of Israel. Interestingly, this middle section pits the prophets Elijah and Elisha as principal combatants for Yahweh in the battle against

Important Dates for 1 Kings

970: Solomon succeeds David

931: Rehoboam succeeds Solomon

930–722: the divided kingdom period

900s: the prophets Ahijah and Jehu active in the Northern Kingdom

800s: the prophets Elijah, Micaiah ben Imlah, and Elisha active in the Northern Kingdom

ca. 875–841: the era of Ahab and Jezebel

853: the battle of Qarqar (NW Syria): Ahab and allies versus Assyria

ca. 850: Ahab's death in battle

Important Dates for 2 Kings

ca. 850–827: Elisha succeeds Elijah

ca. 841: Jehu's violent purge of Ahab's family

700s: the prophets Hosea, Amos, and Micah (Northern Kingdom), Isaiah (Judah), and Jonah (in Assyria)

722: Assyria destroys the Northern Kingdom; foreigners resettle Israel

716: Hezekiah, Judah's reformer

701: disaster for Judah

600s: the prophets Zephaniah, Jeremiah, Huldah, Nahum, and Habakkuk (see their chapters for details)

687: Manasseh, the anti-reformer

640: Josiah, the re-reformer

622: Deuteronomy's rediscovery; the Deuteronomistic History (DH 1.0) appears

612–605: Babylon defeats Assyria and Egypt

597: the first deportation of Judahites to Babylon

587: the Babylonian destruction of Jerusalem; the second deportation of Judahites

561: King Jehoiachin's release from captivity

ca. 550: the Deuteronomistic History (DH 2.0) appears

the family of Ahab and Jezebel, who are the principal combatants for Baal. In other words, on the surface the books of Kings may seem to be about human kings, but in reality their ultimate agenda is to promote the kingship of Yahweh—and Yahweh alone—as the true sovereign of the universe.

1 Kings 1–11: The United Kingdom under Solomon

The story opens with Solomon's accession and consolidation of power (1 Kgs 1–2), continues with his glorious deeds (1 Kgs 4–10), but after his death ends with the loss of ten tribes—the heavy penalty for his idolatry (1 Kgs 11). A chiastic structure may also underlie the presentation of the reign of Solomon: In this structure the central interest of 1 Kgs 1–11 clearly falls on the temple in Jerusalem, its construction (chs. 4–7), public dedication by Solomon (ch. 8), and its acceptance as God's "house" by Yahweh (ch. 9). Two theophanies play prominent roles: in the first, God gives Solomon wisdom (ch. 3), and in the second, Yahweh accepts the temple but warns the king of the high price Israel will pay for unfaithfulness to their covenant with God (ch. 9).

Diagram 15.1. Chiastic Structure of 1–2 Kings

A One Kingdom: Rise of the Davidic Dynasty	1 Kgs 1–11
B The Rise of the Northern Kingdom: Idolatry	1 Kgs 12–14
C Kings of Israel and Judah	1 Kgs 15–16
D Yahweh Battles Baal: Elijah and Elisha	1 Kgs 17–2 Kgs 11
C′ Kings of Israel and Judah	2 Kgs 12–16
B′ The Fall of the Northern Kingdom: Idolatry	2 Kgs 17
A′ One Kingdom: Fall of the Davidic Dynasty	2 Kgs 18–25

Diagram 15.2. Chiastic Structure of the Account of Solomon's Reign

A Solomon Takes Charge	1 Kgs 1–2
B Theophany: Wisdom Gift	1 Kgs 3
C Solomon in Charge: the Temple	1 Kgs 4–9
B′ Solomon's Great Wisdom: the Queen of Sheba	1 Kgs 10
A′ Solomon Loses Charge	1 Kgs 11

The Kingdoms of Saul, David, and Solomon

Aleppo

YAMHAD

Orontes R.

Euphrates R.

Tiphsah
(Thapsacus)

HAMATH

Hamath

Cyprus

Arvad

Tadmor

Kadesh on the Orontes

Lebo-hamath

Zedad

Byblos

Hazar-enan

Litani R.

*Mediterranean
Sea*

PHOENICIA

Sidon

Damascus

Tyre

Dan

ARAM

Acco

Hazor

Megiddo

Salecah

Beth-shan

Ramoth-
gilead

Jordan R.

Shechem

Joppa

Gezer

Rabbah
(Amman)

PHILISTIA

Gibeah

Ashdod

Jerusalem

Medeba

EASTERN DESERT

Gaza

Gath

*Dead
Sea*

Ziklag?

Raphia

Kir-hareseth

Beersheba

W. et-Arish

Tamar

MOAB

Bozrah

AMALEK

EDOM

Kadesh-
barnea

☐ Saul's Kingdom

▨ Kingdom of David and Solomon

▨ Area effectively under Solomon's
economic control

── Extent of Solomon's kingdom

N

SINAI

*Gulf of
Aqaba*

Ezion-geber

0   50   100 Miles

0   50   100 Kilometers

The David at center stage in 1 Kgs 1 is a stranger not seen in 2 Samuel. He's an old man suffering such poor circulation that a beautiful young woman named Abishag shares his bed at night just to keep him warm (but not to do anything else, in case you're wondering!). In the ancient Near East, monarchs traditionally designated which of their sons or near relatives would succeed them, sometimes effecting a smooth transition through a coregency of two kings serving together. Sadly, a now-elderly David has not indicated his choice—at least, not publicly—so, chs. 1–2 narrate an uneasy transition with factions of David's inner circle supporting either Adonijah (General Joab, Abiathar the priest) or Solomon (Nathan the prophet, Bathsheba, Zadok the priest, and Colonel Benaiah). When Solomon's half-brother Adonijah preemptively has himself crowned king, the Solomon-faction persuades David to order the immediate coronation of Solomon, his long-understood successor. In ch. 2 the aged David commands Solomon to be a strong king and also unwaveringly to do what pleases Yahweh, lest he jeopardize God's dynastic promise to their descendants. As the new king, Solomon implements his father David's death-bed advice by violently purging potential enemies, including Adonijah. Chapter 3 narrates both Solomon's marriage alliance with the king of Egypt and God's appearance in a dream granting him wisdom, wealth, and honor. Chapter 4 recounts his building of a regional empire whose wealth benefits both palace elites and ordinary Israelites—and grants him the leisure to write and collect proverbs, compose music, and study flora and fauna. In short, the narrative portrays a King Solomon who is reaping—indeed, maximizing to the full—the threefold promise granted him in the dream.

By devoting chs. 5–7 to Solomon's building of the temple, the narrative also casts this section as the capstone of Solomon's historical legacy. The storyteller regards the enormous, complex project as so historic that he links its foundation-laying to Year 480 after the Exodus (April–May ca. 966 BCE) and its completion to seven years later (i.e., October–November ca. 959 BCE). The temple's design compares with the long-house style of temple popular in the ancient world, and has the same general layout as the tabernacle's. Chapters 8–9 describe the national assembly's installation of the ark of the covenant in the temple, witnessing Yahweh's glory descending to occupy it, and receiving Yahweh's acceptance of it. The highpoint of the festivities, however, is Solomon's long, eloquent dedicatory prayer in ch. 8. The compilers of 1–2 Kings probably opted to report it in detail because it voices the theological themes and covenant concerns that drive their story of the monarchy (for their critical retrospective on why the Northern Kingdom failed to survive, see 2 Kgs 17). The key phrases that articulate Solomon's prime concerns are: "please hear the prayers" lifted here by kings and ordinary Israelites (1 Kgs 8:28-30) and, amazingly, even by visiting foreigners (vv. 41-43); "forgive their sins" (vv. 34, 36, 39); and "act" to answer their peititons. For example, God is to settle disputes between them (vv. 31-32), end droughts or famines, and enable them to defeat their enemies (vv. 33-39). Perhaps most tellingly, the climax of Solomon's prayer (vv. 46-50) anticipates that the Israelites' sins may drive God to exile them to foreign lands—exactly the fate with which 2 Kings ends. So the king petitions God to forgive them when they repent and to return them home—likely, a message aimed to instruct and encourage the exilic audience that 1-2 Kings addresses.

Like Balaam in the Torah (Num 22-24), another non-Israelite, the queen of Sheba (southern Arabia), testifies to the blessings of great wisdom and wealth with which God has blessed Israel under Solomon (1 Kgs 10). Annually, the palace welcomes a steady stream of international wisdom-seekers and tribute-payers, each honoring the king with luxurious gifts. Within the storyteller's exaggerated picture of Solomon's Midas-touch, however, lurks a not-so-subtle indictment that Solomon has run afoul of the Torah's Law of the King (Deut 17:14-20 [see Table 15.1]). In ch. 11 Yahweh announces that, when Solomon dies, his successors will rule only Judah and Jerusalem and that a man named Jeroboam will rule the other ten tribes. The prophet Ahijah of Shiloh symbolically acts out Jeroboam's ascent to royalty. When Solomon dies, his son Rehoboam succeeds him, and the foundational reigns of David and Solomon end. But, to the compilers of 1-2 Kings, Solomon's worship of foreign gods sets a bad precedent for the nation's spiritual health and possibly sows the single, small root from which the nation's later doom may spring. In short, the story of 1-2 Kings opens

Table 15.1. The Deuteronomistic Indictment of Solomon

Deuteronomy 17:16–20	1 Kings 10:23–11:5
The king is *not* to:	King Solomon:
1. Acquire great numbers of *horses* (v. 16)	1. Acquires 12,000 *horses* (10:26)
2. Get more horses from *Egypt* (v. 16)	2. Imports horses from *Egypt* (10:26)
3. Marry many *wives* (v. 17)*	3. Has 700 *wives* of royal birth (11:3)*
4. Accumulate lots of *silver and gold* (v. 17)	4. Accumulates lots of *silver and gold* (10:25)
5. Turn from *the law* in any way (vv. 18–20)	5. Abandons Yahweh for *other gods* (11:9–11)
***NB**: The reason: his heart will be led astray	***NB**: The result: his wives led him astray

with Solomon's accession and consolidation of power (1 Kgs 1–2), continues with his glorious deeds (1 Kgs 4–10), but after his death ends with the loss of ten tribes—the heavy penalty for his idolatry (1 Kgs 11). Even great, wise people can make big, dumb mistakes.

1 Kings 12–2 Kings 17: The Divided Kingdom

First Kings 12 through 2 Kgs 17 follows the story of the two competing kingdoms, Israel and Judah, over two centuries, with the Davidic dynasty in the person of Solomon's son Rehoboam ruling the latter (plus Benjamin) and Jeroboam the former. Sadly, both kings take actions that prove to be fatal missteps. This section's main subsections are: (1) the divided kingdom: the early decades (1 Kgs 12–16); (2) Elijah versus Ahab and Jezebel (1 Kgs 17–2 Kgs 1); and (3) Elisha and the legacy of Ahab (2 Kgs 2–17).

1 Kings 12–16: The Divided Kingdom: Early Decades

Chapter 12 narrates Rehoboam's misstep. The Davidic covenant (2 Sam 7) links Yahweh and David's family, but the sociological glue that binds the house of David and the tribes as united Israel is apparently a personal covenant between the monarch and the tribes. The succession of Rehoboam brings that covenant up for renewal at Shechem. Rehoboam needs to persuade the northern tribes to extend it, but he is bull-headed and rejects their precondition for renewal: the lightening of harsh royal policies. Foolishly, the new king even brags that he'll actually increase the burden, so the northern tribes angrily leave Shechem without an agreement, invoking an old political slogan as they depart (cf. 2 Sam 20: 1). The divided kingdom—Israel (the northern tribes) and Judah (plus Benjamin) as independent nations—is born. Chapters 12–14 go on to narrate Jeroboam's fatal misstep: he creates an alternate worship system to Jerusalem's; it is unauthorized by the Torah, is centered around golden calves at Dan and Bethel (echoes of the golden calf!), and is presided over by non-Levitical priests. Further, Jeroboam establishes an annual festival—not one the Torah authorizes—to replace the Feast of Tabernacles (which the Torah does authorize). The compilers of Kings brand this policy the "sin of Jeroboam," a criticism they'll repeat with all of Jeroboam's successors (see the sidebar on p. 186). Ahijah, the prophet who informed Jeroboam of his kingship, now announces that Yahweh will replace

Beirut

Sidon

PHOENICIA

Litani R.

Abana R.

Mt. Hermon

Damascus

Pharpar R.

Tyre

Dan

Kedesh

ARAM

Hazor

Mt. Meron

Acco

Mt. Carmel

Sea of
Galilee

Ashtaroth

Mt.
Tabor

Kishon R.

Yarmuk R.

Edrei

Megiddo

Mt. Moreh

Taanach

Beth-shan

Ibleam

Mt.
Gilboa

Ramoth-gilead

*Mediterranean
Sea*

Jordan R.

Jabesh-gilead?

Tirzah

Samaria

Mahanaim?

Mt. Ebal

Succoth?

Penuel?

R.-Mt. Gerizim

Shechem

Jabbok R.

Yarkon

Aphek

Joppa

Shiloh

ISRAEL

Bethel

Rabbah
(Amman)

Gezer

Jericho

AMMON

Aijalon

Jerusalem

Heshbon

Ashdod

Mt. Nebo

Gath

Bethlehem

Medeba

Ashkelon

Mareshah

Gaza

Hebron

Dibon

Gerar

*Dead
Sea*

Arnon R.

Raphia

JUDAH

MOAB

Beersheba

Kir-hareseth

PHILISTIA

Zered Br.

W. el-Arish

WILDERNESS

Besor Br.

Region
periodically
contested
by Judah
and Edom

N

Bozrah

Kadesh-
barnea

EDOM

WILDERNESS

| 0 | 10 | 20 | 30 Miles |
| 0 | 10 | 20 | 30 Kilometers |

The Sin of Jeroboam

Culturally, it is common for kings in the ancient world to effect changes in cultic matters, so Jeroboam's religious innovations are certainly within his royal purview (David exercised the same prerogative in bringing the ark to Jerusalem). Further, the Canaanites and Aramaeans often represent their gods as standing on calves or bulls. The animals symbolize the gods' fertility and strength — qualities people want their gods to have so they can bestow these same qualities on loyal worshipers. Jeroboam may have intended a similar notion for his calves but with a uniquely Israelite twist: the idea that Yahweh stands invisibly atop each calf. Alas, the king states that the calves represent "your gods" (plural), implying his attempt somehow to combine the worship of Yahweh with polytheistic ideas. The result is that people worship the calves, treating them as they would idols. In essence, knowingly or unknowingly, Jeroboam founds a new, idolatrous form of Yahwism (1 Kgs 13:26–33), an evil that his royal successors will fail to uproot.

him, Jeroboam (i.e., he'll not found a Northern dynasty), and will exile idolatrous Israel to a far-off eastern land. This sends the first prophetic signal in 1-2 Kings that the fledgling Northern Kingdom's ultimate destiny is bleak (for evaluation of all the kings, see Table 15.5).

In chs. 14-15, the story now weaves back and forth tracking the parallel royal reigns of the two new kingdoms. Under Rehoboam and his son, Abijam, idolatry also flourishes in Judah (less so under Rehoboam's grandson, Asa), but the narrator explains that for David's sake God keeps the royal dynasty alive and protects Jerusalem. The compilers of 1-2 Kings highlight the ongoing warfare between Israel and Judah that plagues the next four decades. The most highly contested territory lies in Benjamin along the strategic main north-south road not too far north of Jerusalem. In Israel, three violent coups undermine that nation's political stability; one king (Zimri) reigns only one week! Announcements by Ahijah the prophet had both appointed Jeroboam king and condemned him, and in ch. 16 an oracle by Jehu the prophet ended Baasha's father-son dynasty. This prophetic pattern of an announcement spoken to leaders and followed by fulfillment will persist throughout 1-2 Kings as one of the books' unique and dominant themes. The third and final coup by General Omri finally gives Israel an era of political stability— and new capital city, Samaria. In the end, however, the book's narrator rues Omri's unhappy legacy: his son Ahab, who with his wife Jezebel, a Phoenician princess from Sidon and devotee of the Canaanite god Baal, launch the Northern Kingdom on an irreversible, idolatrous course. The compilers of 1-2 Kings, however, feature two prophets, Elijah and Elisha, and picture them waging holy war against the royal pair's promotion of Baal worship. In the chiastic structure proposed above, that struggle constitutes the heart of the books (1 Kgs 17-2 Kgs 11), whose headline might be "Yahweh Battles Baal!" Theologically, the two prophets confront the reader with a twofold question: Who is Israel's God, and does Baal actually exist?

Table 15.2. Rulers of the United and Divided Monarchies

Saul?
Ishbaal (2 years)
David 1010–970
Solomon 970–931/930

	Israelite Ruler	Dates[a]	Dates[a]	Judahite Ruler
	Jeroboam	931/930–911/910	931/930–915/914	Rehoboam
	Nadab	911/910	915/914–912/911	Abijam
	Baasha	910/909–887/886	912/911–871/870	Asa
	Elah	887/886–886/885	871/870–849/848	Jehoshaphat
	Zimri	7 days		
	Tibni	5 years (rival to Omri)		
	Omri	886/885–875/874		
Dynasty of Omri	Ahab	875/874–853		
	Ahaziah	853–852	849/848–842	J(eh)oram
	J(eh)oram	852–841	842–841	Ahaziah
	Jehu	841–814/813	841–835	Athaliah (queen)
Dynasty of Jehu	Jehoahaz	814/813–806/805	841/835–796/795	Joash
	Joash	806/805–791/790	796/795–776/775	Amaziah
	Jeroboam II	791/790–750/749	776/775–736/735	Uzziah (Azariah)
	Zechariah	750/749	750–735/734	Jotham
	Shallum	1 month		
	Menachem	749/748–739/738		
	Pekahiah	738–737/736	735/734–715	Ahaz
	Pekah	737/736–732/731		
	Hoshea	732/731–722	715–687/686	Hezekiah
			687/686–642	Manasseh
			642–640	Amon
			640–609	Josiah
			3 months	Jehoahaz
			609–598	Jehoiakim
			598/597	Jehoiachin
			597–586	Zedekiah

a. Any proposed chronology of the Israelite and Judahite rulers is based on a number of variables such as coregencies, accession- or nonaccession-year dating, synchronism with external dates in the ancient world, and the usual problems associated with the textual data themselves. The difficulties are most acute for the second half of the eighth century. These dates are taken from K. A. Kitchen, *On the Reliability of the Old Testament* (Grand Rapids: Eerdmans, 2003), 30–33.

1 Kings 17–2 Kings 1: Elijah versus Ahab and Jezebel

Literarily, the story thrusts Elijah on stage in 1 Kgs 17, as it were, out of the blue and without background. Its real interest is the prophet's terse announcement that Israel will suffer a severe drought until Elijah says otherwise. Not surprisingly, this message so infuriates Ahab that Elijah seeks refuge with a poor widow in Phoenicia (modern Lebanon) where, through him, Yahweh works miracles: God sustains Elijah's impoverished hosts with food, and Elijah raises the widow's son from the dead. These events sound an important theme in 1–2 Kings: that Israel's God (not Baal) alone controls both the rain and the food it supplies, and even life itself. The same theme sounds in ch. 18, the classic, long-remembered contest atop Mount Carmel, a coastal ridge just southeast of modern Haifa and possibly a Canaanite cultic site. Statistics that the narrator provides portray Elijah as hugely outnumbered: Yahweh's lone prophet versus 450 prophets of Baal and 400 prophets of the goddess Asherah. Each of the two sides is to sacrifice on an altar and call upon its deity to send fire down. At issue is who is God—Yahweh or Baal—and thus worthy of Israel's worship and obedience? The storyteller starkly contrasts the competing rituals and their results: elaborate, day-long incantations by the clergy of Baal and Asherah elicit only dead silence, while Yahweh answers Elijah's short, simple prayer with fire dramatically falling from the sky to consume both the sacrifice and the altar. The stunning display drives the huge crowd to shout its confession of Yahweh, and the Baal clergy are executed. The episode ends with the long-awaited thunderstorm—the end of the drought—drenching Elijah and Ahab as they hurry toward Jezreel.

The narrator follows up Yahweh's decisive display on Mount Carmel with three scene-changes. The first (ch. 19) ushers Jezebel briefly on stage to send word threatening Elijah's life as revenge for the clergy slaughter. The message so terrifies Elijah that he flees through the barren Negev in southern Judah to the historic "mountain of God" (i.e., Horeb or Mount Sinai; cf. Exod 3:1; Deut. 1:6; 9:8; 29:1), far out of the angry queen's reach. In essence, Elijah's escape marks a kind of pilgrimage back to the site where Yahweh and Moses met. In this second scene—and in what smacks of a formal ceremony (note Yahweh's repeated questions and Elijah's repeated answers)—Elijah witnesses a series of violent natural phenomena but without Yahweh in them. Finally, Elijah hears "a gentle whisper" (TNIV), a startling, quiet sign of God's presence. Elijah's trip to Sinai proves a defining moment for him: after the drama, Yahweh graciously recommissions Elijah as his prophet to anoint new leadership—Hazael as king of Aram, Jehu king of Israel, and Elisha as his prophetic successor. In reality, Elijah completes only the latter, while Elisha carries out the other two anointings. The third and final scene-change returns the reader to Israel for three complex episodes in ch. 20, each of which ends with a prophet's condemnation of Ahab to a shameful death, and resumption of the Elijah-versus-Ahab theme in ch. 21. Condemned by Micaiah the prophet, in ch. 22 Ahab dies, fittingly felled by an archer's random shot that providentially penetrates his feigned disguise (see p. 12, also Table 2.5 on p. 22). Second Kings 1 features Elijah's last prophetic word: condemnation of Ahab's son and successor, Ahaziah, for seeking healing from a god other than Yahweh (2 Kgs 1). Like father like son.

Jerome T. Walsh and many others have noted the parallels between the lives of Moses in the Torah and Elijah in 1–2 Kings. These connections suggest that 1–2 Kings seek to portray Elijah at least as a prophet *like* Moses, if not the *new Moses* anticipated in Deuteronomy (Deut 18:15, 18). Both men flee their home country to escape a king's wrath (Exod 2; cf. 1 Kgs 17), and both do serious business with God at Horeb (Exod 33; cf. 1 Kgs 19). Because they appeal to Israel to worship Yahweh exclusively, a recent hypothesis reads Elijah and Elisha as an early (or the earliest) stage of a "Yahweh-alone movement," possibly the first step away from polytheism toward monotheism in Israel. Whatever the case, in the Bible Elijah represents the prophet *par excellence*: he represents the whole prophetic tradition on the Mount of Transfiguration (Matt 17:3), provides the paradigm for the new Elijah, John the Baptist (compare Mal 4:5–6; John 1:25; 2 Kgs 1:8; Matt 3:4), and exemplifies the power of prayer for all faithful believers (Jas 5:17; see also Rom 11:2–3).

A stele from Ugarit (modern Syria) depicting Baal, the Canaanite storm god and bringer of fertility, wielding a thunderbolt (15th–early 13th century BCE). In 1 Kings 17–18, Yahweh controls rain and life itself, discrediting Baal's alleged powers. On display at the Louvre, Paris. ©Mbzt (Wikimedia Commons, CC 3.0)

READING

Read 1 Kgs 1–2 Kgs 1 and formulate answers to the following questions:

1. Compare your impressions of the literary portrait of Solomon in 1 Kgs 1–11 with the portrait of David you read in 1–2 Samuel. What are the strengths and weaknesses of each? Which do you think biblical tradition seems to remember more favorably? What are your reflections about your own life with God after reading about them?

2. With what biblical character or situation after Solomon's death do you particularly identify? Why do you think that's the case? In what way(s), if any, does that character or situation help you in your own life with God? For example, does it explain something, challenge or encourage you, raise questions for you to consider, etc.?

3. What view(s) of Israel's God do people, Israelite and non-Israelite, show in their words and actions? How do they compare/not compare with your view of God? In what ways do they enrich or modify your view?

4. Which character(s) in 1 Kgs–2 Kgs 1 do you find most offensive? Why do you think that's so? What (if anything) do you learn from them about yourself?

5. The prophets play a prominent role in 1 Kgs 17–2 Kgs 1. What are some key aspects of that role? What do you see them trying to accomplish?

6. Read 1 Kgs 22. What do you see as God's involvement in the events? What is your response to the idea of God sending a "lying prophet"? How does that affect (if at all) your view of God?

BIBLIOGRAPHY

Avioz, Michael. "The Book of Kings in Recent Research (Part I)." *CurBR* 4 (2005): 11–55.
———. "The Book of Kings in Recent Research (Part II)." *CurBR* 5 (2006): 11–57.

Cogan, Mordechai. *I Kings: A New Translation with Introduction and Commentary*. AB 10. New Haven: Yale University Press, 2001.

DeVries, Simon. J. *1 Kings*. WBC 12. Waco, TX: Word, 1985.

Ellul, Jacques. *The Politics of God and the Politics of Man*. Translated by G. W. Bromiley. Grand Rapids: Eerdmans, 1972.

Greenwood, Kyle. "Late Tenth- and Ninth-Century Issues: Ahab Underplayed? Jehoshaphat Overplayed?" Pages 286–318 in *Ancient Israel's History: An Introduction to Issues and Sources*. Edited by Bill T. Arnold and Richard S. Hess. Grand Rapids: Baker Academic, 2014.

Knoppers, Gary N. *Two Nations under God: The Deuteronomistic History of Solomon and the Dual Monarchies*. 2 vols. HSM 52–53. Atlanta: Scholars Press, 1993.

Leithart, Peter J. *1 and 2 Kings*. Brazos Theological Commentary on the Bible. Grand Rapids: Brazos, 2006.

Lemaire, André, and Baruch Halpern, eds. *The Books of Kings: Sources, Composition, Historiography and Reception*. VTSup 129. Leiden: Brill, 2010.

Sweeney, Marvin A. *I and II Kings: A Commentary*. OTL. Louisville: Westminster John Knox, 2007.

Walsh, Jerome T. *1 Kings*. Berit Olam. Collegeville, MN: Liturgical Press, 1996.

2 Kings 2–17: Elisha and the Legacy of Ahab

Since Yahweh had named Elisha as Elijah's successor, in ch. 2 the compilers of 1–2 Kings portray the transition to Elisha with motifs portraying the fact that the Elijah-Elisha succession parallels the Moses-Joshua succession (see Tables 15.3 and 15.4) and is just as momentous and historic too. Elisha accompanies Elijah on a kind of farewell tour or formal leave-taking of the communities of prophets in Bethel, Jericho, and the Jordan River. Meanwhile, Jezebel and her children remain active, as does the worship of Baal among many Israelites. So the story of the prophets' holy war against that royal house continues. Finally, having said his goodbyes, Elijah dramatically crosses the Jordan on dry ground (but, unlike Joshua, Elijah is eastbound), where a single horse-drawn chariot of fire and a whirlwind whisk Elijah into heaven, leaving Elijah's cloak—symbol of his prophetic power—with his successor. The cloak opens the Jordan for Elisha to recross the river on dry land. The narrator reports the subsequent healing of salty water at Jericho and the cursing of insulting boys at Bethel to confirm that Elijah's spirit now inhabits Elisha—that he is a prophet with whom idolatrous Israel must reckon.

To narrate Elisha's ministry (chs. 3–13), the compilers string together a series of apparently independent stories that feature him. Most demonstrate his miraculous power, his clairvoyance, and his speaking for Yahweh to idolatry-prone Northern kings. Interestingly, the compilers have included episodes in chs. 4–6 that specifically parallel stories in 1 Kings that involve Elijah. The literary effect is to link the ministries of the two prophets and further confirm that Elijah's spirit also empowers Elisha. Each man multiplies oil for a widow (1 Kgs 17:8–16; 2 Kgs 4:1–7), resuscitates a boy (1 Kgs 17:17–24; 2 Kgs 4:8–37), performs a miracle that produces conversions (1 Kgs 18:20–39; 2 Kgs 5:1–27), and is pursued by someone under oath (1 Kgs 19:1–3; 2 Kgs 6:8–14, 31–32). On the other hand, Elijah had fled outside Israel to Zarephath, but in ch. 5 Elisha receives a surprise visitor in Samaria, the Aramaean General Naaman whom Elisha heals of his skin disease and who returns to Damascus committed to worshiping Yahweh there.

In chs. 6–7, the compilers include two episodes involving Aramaean military raids in Israel, scenes that contrast Elisha's firm reliance on Yahweh with the lukewarm faith and hostility toward prophets among Israel's leaders. In the first scene (6:8–23), the frustrated Aramaean king angrily

Table 15.3. Parallels between Moses and Elijah

Moses	Elijah
Power Symbol (Rod)	Power Symbol (Mantle)
Eastbound Crossing (Red Sea)	Eastbound Crossing (Jordan River)
Dry Land	Dry Land
Death outside Canaan	Death outside Canaan
Unknown Burial Site	No Burial Site

Table 15.4. Parallels between Joshua and Elisha

Joshua	Elisha
Preappointment by God	Preappointment by God
Power Symbol (Ark of the Covenant)	Power Symbol (Elijah's Mantle)
Westbound Crossing (Jordan River)	Westbound Crossing (Jordan River)
Dry Land	Dry Land
Acts Confirming Succession	Acts Confirming Succession

asks his military commanders why he can never find the Israelite army to attack it. His staff pins the blame on Elisha, who, they claim, informs Israel's king about Aram's whereabouts so that the Israelite army can completely avoid the Aramaeans. The king orders his troops to surround Dothan, Elisha's hometown, and capture the prophet. Early the next morning, the storyteller reports, Elisha's servant sees a frightening sight—the Aramaeans encircling the town—but Elisha replies confidently, "Don't be afraid. . . . Those who are with us are more than those who are with them." Then Yahweh enables the terrified servant to see something else: "the hills full of horses and chariots of fire all around Elisha" (2 Kgs 6:16–17 TNIV). At the prophet's request, Yahweh "blinds" the soldiers to Elisha's identity so that, ironically, Elisha takes *them* captive rather than the reverse—only to feed them and let them go, greatly frustrating the Israelite king, who's eager for revenge on his enemy! Elisha proves to be a prophet of miraculous powers, one whose prayers Yahweh answers, yet also a prophet who extends mercy to young GIs out to take his life. In the subsequent episode, at Samaria (6:24–7:20), Elisha reassures the Israelite king that Yahweh will decisively break the determined Aramaean siege, which has reduced the city to cannabalism. Sadly, defeatism not faith grips the king and his aide, so when four desperate lepers later announce their discovery of food in the now-abandoned Aramaean camp, the king thinks it's an Aramaean trick, not Yahweh's promised deliverance. The story further displays Elisha as a true prophet—and exposes the weak trust in Yahweh's power in the Northern Kingdom at the time.

Now, recall that in Israel kings receive their authority by being anointed by a prophet, so in chs. 8–10 Elisha fulfills Yahweh's commission to Elijah (1 Kgs 19:15–17) by anointing two kings: Hazael of Damascus, who will, much to Elisha's grief, violently attack Israel and Judah (see 2 Kgs 13); and Jehu of Israel, who will destroy and replace Ahab's dynasty, including Jezebel (see 1 Kgs 21:18–24). You may think it strange for an Israelite prophet to appoint a non-Israelite king, but the Bible consistently affirms Yahweh alone as Supreme King-Deposer and King-Appointer (compare Dan 2:21). Meanwhile, the story subtly introduces an especially ominous development for Judah: for the first (and only) time, marriage links the northern and southern monarchies. The result is that Ahab's idolatrous policy now has a royal patron in Judah. As noted, however, by accident Jehu meets both kings, killing Joram of Israel and fatally wounding Ahaziah of Judah—ironically, on property that once belonged to Naboth (1 Kgs 21) and thus fulfilling Elijah's prophecy that Ahab would pay for

A scene on the Black Obelisk of King Shalmaneser III (ca. 827 BCE) found at Nimrud and now in the British Museum (London). It may depict Jehu, king of Israel, giving tribute to the Assyrian king. The caption above the scene, written in Assyrian cuneiform, can be translated: "The tribute of Jehu, son of Omri: I received from him silver, gold, a golden bowl, a golden vase with pointed bottom, golden vessels, golden pails, tin, a staff for a king [and] spears." ©*Steven G. Johnson (Wikimedia Commons, CC-SA 3.0)*

Naboth's death (1 Kgs 21:18–24). The rest of Elijah's prophecy finds fulfillment in Jehu's bloody purge of what remains of Ahab's dynasty, including Jezebel (ch. 10). In Jerusalem, however, the last vestige of Ahab's family, his daughter Athaliah, siezes Judah's throne and nearly annihilates the Davidic royal family before the priest Jehoiada kills her (ch. 11). The compilers also honor Jehoiada for hiding David's lone descendant, the infant Joash, for mentoring the young king, and Joash for initiating a major temple renovation (ch. 12). Alas, Joash's long reign ends with his assassination by two palace officials, while in Israel, idolatry, Aramaean oppression, and divine rescue in answer to the king's prayer typify the reign of Jehu's son Jehoahaz (ch. 13).

Finally, the story rings down the curtain on Elisha with a tearful, unsettling scene in which he, through a symbolic action, informs Israel's King Jehoash that Aram will continue to trouble and perhaps even topple his kingdom. Even in death, Elisha retains his miraculous power, his bones reviving a dead man casually tossed into his tomb. Thus ends the remarkable Elijah-Elisha era and their ultimate victory over the house of Ahab.

In chs. 14–17, the compilers next turn to a series of formal, stylized regnal reports typical of 1–2 Kings to narrate the ultimate fate of the Northern Kingdom. Their formulaic presentation highlights four kings of Judah who please Yahweh (Amaziah, Azariah, Uzziah, and Jotham) and five kings of Israel that perpetuate the sin of Jeroboam (Jeroboam II, Zechariah, Menahem, Pekahiah, Pekah). An Assyrian invasion and the exile of Israelites under Tiglath-pileser III as well as three royal assassinations bode ill for Israel's future. In Judah, King Ahaz ends the string of four good kings by becoming a vassal of Assyria and by installing an idolatrous altar in the temple court (ch. 16). In ch. 17, the Northern Kingdom falls when King Hoshea's rebellion against Assyria sparks a three-year siege of Samaria that ends with its capture in 722 BCE and the exile of thousands of Israelites to northwestern Assyria and Media. King Sargon II imports into Israel people from Babylon and Aram, who come to worship both Yahweh and the gods of their homeland and, ultimately, become the people known as the Samaritans. To conclude, the narrator turns from storytelling to a long retrospective autopsy (2 Kgs 17:7–23) detailing the reasons for this disaster in light of Deuteronomy (compare with 1 Kgs 8). The unmistakable, fatal symptoms to which Israel failed to attend—its disobedience to covenant demands, persistent idolatry, and rejection of Yahweh's warnings through the prophets—explain its national death. In context, the autopsy serves to warn Judah as a national body to beware of such symptoms and to instruct the DH's exilic audience about "life-threatening mistakes to avoid." The success of their coming return to Judah hangs in the balance.

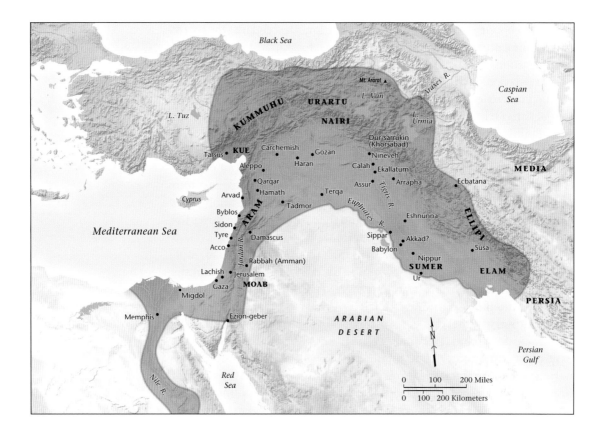

The Assyrian Empire

2 Kings 18–25: The Story of the Kingdom of Judah

In the story line of 1-2 Kings, the Kingdom of Judah is now the lone survivor of ancient Israel. A change of empires—from Assyrian to Babylonian—significantly shapes events in Judah during this period. The section's burning question is: will Judah also go down in flames and its people suffer exile as did their northern kinfolk? By way of orientation to this new era, the lists of dates on p. 179 summarize its important historical background.

Three kings—two religious reformers with an anti-reformer in between—typify this final period of Judah. Clearly, the compilers regard King Hezekiah as one of the royal good guys (chs. 18-20). In faithfulness to Yahweh and destruction of idolatry, he is head-and-shoulders above the other kings and is, in fact, the best king that Judah ever had (see the Deuteronomistic Grade Book, Table 15.5). He even boldly destroys the bronze snake personally made by Moses, to prevent the people from worshiping it as an idol. Yahweh rewards his faithfulness with success—victory over the Philistines and the courage to break his treaty with Assyria. Through the prophet Isaiah, Yahweh also rebuts Assyria's attempt in 701 BC to intimidate Hezekiah into surrender by devastating Judah's cities and by heaping scornful ridicule on Yahweh's sovereignty (2 Kgs 18–19). The compilers apparently regard this crisis as a memorable, signal event (see also Isa 36); they devote two-thirds of the Hezekiah section to it, including verbatim reports of messages exchanged between the two kings (see our comments on the parallel text, Isa 36–37, in ch. 22 below). In response, Yahweh promises to defend Jerusalem for David's sake, to deny King Sennacherib entry, and to send him back to Assyria. That night God sends an angel to decimate the Assyrian camp, forcing the Assyrian king to return home, where his two sons later assassinate him, ironically, in the temple of his own god (see the sidebar on the next page for the Assyrian account of these events in Sennacherib's Prism). Sadly, a century later, when Jeremiah announces Jerusalem's certain destruction if Judah fails to repent, Jeremiah's opponents cite the rescue of Jerusalem in 701 as evidence that Jerusalem will never fall. Ironically, that very counterargument dooms Jerusalem.

Indeed, in 2 Kgs 20 the compilers record a state visit by emissaries of the king of Babylon occasioned by reports he'd heard of Hezekiah's serious ill health (through Isaiah, Yahweh promised him healing). The king graciously gives his visitors a grand tour of the palace, including its storehouses, armory, and treasuries. Their visit elicits a chilling, ominous oracle from Isaiah: one day Babylon would plunder Jerusalem's treasures and exile some of its civic leaders. Literarily, the compilers include Isaiah's announcement to anticipate how the story of Judah is to end—unless, of course, in the meantime something changes in Judah.

Sadly, ch. 21 presents Hezekiah's successor, Manasseh, as the anti-reformer who reverses his father's policy. He is Judah's own

Table 15.5. The Deuteronomistic Grade Book of the Kings

King	Kingdom	Final Grade
Hezekiah Josiah	Judah	A
Asa Jehoshaphat	Judah	B
Jehu	Israel	C+
Joash Amaziah	Judah	C−
Everyone Else	Israel and Judah	F

A "Good, though not perfect"
B "Good, but . . ./except for . . ." [something serious]
C+ "Bad but . . ./except for . . ." [something positive]
C− "Good, but did evil at the end"
F "Did nothing good"

"As to Hezekiah, the Jew, he did not submit to my yoke. I laid siege to 46 of his strong cities, walled forts, and countless small villages, and conquered them. . . . I drove out 200,150 people, young and old, male and female, horses, mules, donkeys, camels, big and small cattle beyond counting, and considered them slaves. Himself I made a prisoner in Jerusalem, his royal residence, like a bird in a cage. . . . Thus I reduced his country, but I still increased the tribute and the presents to me as overlord . . . to be delivered annually. Hezekiah himself did send me, later . . . together with 30 talents of gold, 800 talents of silver, precious stones, antimony, large cuts of red stone, couches inlaid with ivory, nimedu-chairs inlaid with ivory, elephant-hides, ebony-wood, boxwood, and all kinds of valuable treasures, his own daughters and concubines. . . ."
(*ANET*, 288)

Ahab—as bad as Hezekiah is good. He not only restores what his father had banished, but he also introduces idolatry into the temple itself, an evil that the compilers of DH say exceeded the fabled Canaanites at their worst. Hence, the prophets forecast for Judah the same awful destruction and exile among enemies that devastated Samaria. When Manasseh dies, palace officials assassinate his son Amon two years later, and the "people of the land"—people who live in territory around (but not "in") Jerusalem—appoint eight-year-old Josiah to succeed him. The sharp contrast between Manasseh's religious policies and those of Josiah suggests that the transition marks a possible reaction to Manasseh's extreme idolatry by Yahweh loyalists.

The reign of the second (and final) reformer, King Josiah, is the focus of chs. 22–23. Some scholars think that Josiah was the climax of the compilers' first edition of DH—that this document may have originally aimed to support his reform. Josiah soon shows that he is cut from the same cloth as his great-grandfather Hezekiah. One of his first acts is to initiate repairs to the temple (compare with Joash in 2 Kgs 12), perhaps an early indicator of his preference for Yahweh over other gods (ch. 22). What interests the compilers, however, is the sequence of events sparked by the unexpected discovery during the renovations of a "book of the Torah" (probably some part of Deuteronomy; see ch. 9 above, p. 91). Its words jolt Josiah; he immediately recognizes that, given the book's serious covenant demands and severe penalties for disobedience, it's likely that a furious Yahweh may destroy Judah by imposing covenant curses. So, Josiah takes steps to forestall that disaster. Chapter 23 recounts the king's convening of a national assembly at the temple that leads the people to renew the covenant—that is, to recommit themselves to obey it. The king also launches a religious reform by purging all traces of Canaanite idolatry nationwide (including major Northern shrines such as Jeroboam's Bethel) and making the temple Judah's only legitimate religious center. Finally, he orders the people to celebrate Passover, a fundamental festival in Israel's worship life that had last been celebrated under Joshua (Josh 5). Thematically, however, DH's compilers regard Josiah's valiant endeavors as "too little, too late": they may postpone the disaster till the reign of a later king, but they cannot offset the irreversible damage done by Manasseh; Judah will still suffer the covenant curses (see 1 Sam 12:25; 2 Kgs 17).

In 609 BCE, Josiah dies at Megiddo under mysterious circumstances (compare with 2 Chr 35:20–24), futilely attempting to prevent an Egyptian force led by Pharaoh Neco from aiding Assyria, at the time under siege by the Babylonians. Again, the same "people of the land" appoint Josiah's son Jehoahaz to succeed him, but Neco imprisons Jehoahaz in Egypt (he later dies there) and installs as king another son of Josiah, renamed Jehoiakim. Alas, the puppet king must tax his subjects to pay the pharaoh's expensive tribute demands—and endure serious conflicts with the prophet Jeremiah as well (e.g., Jer 22:18–19; 36).

The compilers devote 2 Kgs 24–25 to recording the final stage of the monarchy's 400-year story. Judah limps to the finish line through two decades of evil puppet-kings imposed by the Egyptians (Jehoiakim) and the Babylonians (Jehoiachin, Zedekiah). Two invasions led by Nebuchadnezzar and his allies bracket the terminal events. In 597 BCE, with Egypt too weak to intervene, Nebuchadnezzar invades Judah, imprisons Jehoiakim's son Jehoiachin in Babylon, and also exiles there the cream of Judah's society—members of the royal family, much of its national leadership and military, as well as artisans and skilled workers. Historians call this incident the first deportation, and a second is soon to follow. Babylonian royal appointee Zedekiah (Jehoiachin's uncle) proves to be as evil as his predecessors and foolishly chooses to rebel against Nebuchadnezzar (see below; for his relations with Jeremiah, see Jer 37). As with 2 Kgs 17, in 2 Kgs 24 the compilers also diagnose the reasons for the nation's final disaster (24:2–4). They interpret the invasion as the fulfillment of what the prophets had long announced and an expression of God's anger over the idolatry rooted in the sins of Manasseh nearly a century before.

The story of Judah ends in 587 BCE, after a two-year siege, with the dramatic destruction of Jerusalem, the palace, and the temple by Babylonian forces, and with the second deportation: the exile of thousands of people to far-away Babylon. (Some, however, independently seek refuge in Egypt.) Interestingly, in ch. 25 the compilers furnish chronological details for each step in the disaster and mention key participants by name. Apparently, they regard this event as so historically important that they record its details for posterity. The Babylonians cruelly punish Zedekiah as he seeks to escape to the east. Samuel's early warning about Yahweh's severe penalty for idolatry proves true (1 Sam 12:25). The Babylonians plunder the temple's bronze and its worship vessels, execute temple and government officials, and appoint Gedaliah as provincial governor to be based in Mizpah. But an intriguing, brief epilogue reports that in 561 BCE, Nebuchadnezzar releases King Jehoiachin from prison in Babylon and permits him to eat at the king's table (compare Jer 52:31–34). Around the turn of the 20th century CE, excavations near the Ishtar Gate in Babylon found clay tablets thought to be part of Nebuchadnezzar's royal archives, including what are now called Jehoiachin's Rations Tablets (ca. 592 BCE). They list the king of Judah and his five sons among captives in and around the city authorized to receive food rations. The ending of 1–2 Kings sounds a hopeful note, implying that perhaps Yahweh's covenant with David remains in effect. The realization of that hope is the story that the postexilic books tell.

READING

Read 2 Kgs 2–25 and answer the following questions:

1. With what character(s) or event(s) in 2 Kgs 2–25 do you personally connect? Why do you think that's the case? In what way(s) do they address your own life situation or relationship with God?

2. Summarize the leadership traits, both positive and negative, that you observe in important characters in 2 Kgs 2–25. What implications might you draw from their examples for leaders of Christian communities today?

3. What picture of the religious life in Israel and Judah during this story segment do you see? In what way(s) does it compare to what you observe in church life today? With what hopes or concerns does it leave you?

4. In what way(s) do you see God involved in 2 Kgs 2–25? What evidences of God's grace, sovereignty, righteous anger, power, and so on do you see? What do you learn about the life of faith, including prayer, from these stories?

5. What attitude(s) toward foreigners does the reading reflect? What indicators of ethnic bias or ethnic openness, whether Israelite or other, do you read in it?

6. In retrospect, how "successful" do you think the monarchy was as an institution? That is, how does its overall performance compare to what Israel and Yahweh desired from it in the beginning?

7. What does 2 Kgs 2–25 contribute to your understanding of God's global vision for the world?

BIBLIOGRAPHY

Bronner, Leila L. *The Stories of Elijah and Elisha as Polemics against Baal Worship*. Leiden: Brill, 1968.

Cogan, Mordechai, and HayimTadmor. *II Kings*. AB 11. Garden City, NY: Doubleday, 1988.

Dharamraj, Havilah. *A Prophet like Moses? A Narrative-Theological Reading of the Elijah Stories*. PBM. Milton Keynes: Paternoster, 2011.

Ellul, Jacques. *The Politics of God and the Politics of Man*. Translated by G. W. Bromiley. Grand Rapids: Eerdmans, 1972.

Hobbs, T. R. *2 Kings*. WBC 13. Waco, TX: Word, 1985.

Kelle, B. E. "Judah in the Seventh Century: From the Aftermath of Sennacherib's Invasion to the Beginning of Jehoiakim's Rebellion." Pages 350–82 in *Ancient Israel's History: An Introduction to Issues and Sources*. Edited by Bill T. Arnold and Richard S. Hess. Grand Rapids: Baker Academic, 2014.

Leuchter, Mark, and Klaus-Peter Adam, eds. *Soundings in Kings: Perspectives and Methods in Contemporary Scholarship*. Minneapolis: Fortress, 2010.

Richter, Sandra. "Eighth-Century Issues: The World of Jeroboam II, the Fall of Samaria, and the Reign of Hezekiah." Pages 319–49 in *Ancient Israel's History: An Introduction to Issues and Sources*. Edited by Bill T. Arnold and Richard S. Hess. Grand Rapids: Baker Academic, 2014.

Smith-Christopher, Daniel. "Ethics of Exile." Pages 174–80 in *The Old Testament and Ethics: A Book-by-Book Survey*. Edited by Joel B. Green and Jacqueline E. Lapsley. Grand Rapids: Baker Academic, 2013.

Wray Beal, Lissa M. *1 and 2 Kings*. ApOTC 9. Downers Grove, IL: InterVarsity Press, 2014.

16 THE POSTEXILIC HISTORICAL BOOKS

JUDAH'S EXILE TO BABYLON (2 Kings 25) did not mark the end of Israel's long story. On the contrary, a new generation of writers record its next phase, the postexilic period, the story both of Israelites who returned home and those who did not. A few writers even offered their generation a fresh review of Israel's history from the very beginning. This chapter introduces readers to their writings.

The Fabulous Five

The next five Historical Books (counting Chronicles as two books) cover Israel's history from the creation of humankind (1 Chr 1:1) to the Jews' escape from annihilation at the hands of their Persian enemies (Esther). The sweep of this history—the breadth and detail of its knowledge—is magnificent, and so is its storytelling. Of course, we might wish for more details in some places, but in these books you will once again ride the historical ups and downs, successes and failures of Judah during the monarchy, the exile, and the first century of the postexilic period.

Each of the five books has its own unique identity, yet each helps to develop the larger story:

1. 1 Chronicles: How David, during his reign, authorizes the temple's construction and selects all the personnel needed to staff its various activities
2. 2 Chronicles: How David's descendants from Solomon to Zedekiah rule Judah

3. Ezra: How God brings his people back from exile and provides the priest Ezra to lead them to renew their commitment to worship Yahweh alone

4. Nehemiah: How God sends Nehemiah from Persia as governor of Judah to rebuild it as a nation

5. Esther: How two clever, courageous Jews rescue their people from annihilation by enemies and institute a new annual festival to remember and celebrate the event

The five books outline as follows:

1. At first glance, 1–2 Chronicles seem simply to offer a retelling of Samuel and Kings, but a closer look shows that in fact its message for postexilic Judah uniquely features David, the Levites, and the temple. A genealogical prologue traces the family lines of Israel from Adam to the twelve sons of Jacob (1 Chr 1–9). It treats the tribe of Judah and David's family line first (1 Chr 2–4) and furnishes more detail about the tribe of Levi than the other ten tribes (1 Chr 6). Further, Chronicles incidentally mentions kings of the Northern Kingdom, but its primary focus is on the Davidic monarchy (1 Chr 10–2 Chr 36:21), and some of those kings come off better in Chronicles than in Kings. Finally, Chronicles concludes with a brief epilogue in which King Cyrus of Persia publicly announces his acceptance of Yahweh's mandate to build God a temple in Jerusalem and his desire for the exiles to return to Judah (2 Chr 36:22–23).

2. Ezra begins where Chronicles ends—with Cyrus's decree (Ezra 1:1 = 2 Chr 36:22)—then carries the story line forward. In retrospect, it recounts the return of Judah from exile, the controversy over the rebuilding of the temple, its eventual completion and dedication, and the celebration of the first Passover since the return. Ezra debuts after a four-month journey from Babylon to Jerusalem (Ezra 7–8), and the book concludes with the controversy over mixed marriage between Jews and foreigners (Ezra 9–10).

3. Nehemiah opens with an autobiographical account of how he, the Persian king's food- and drink-tester in Susa, receives imperial authority and funding to rebuild the city of Jerusalem (Neh 1–2). A narrative report then details the rebuilding of the city's walls, including the strong local opposition to the project (Neh 3–4). At some point, he intervenes to end the oppressive profiteering by wealthy Jews from the

misfortunes of the poor and also waives his own right as governor to receive food supplies from the people (Neh 5). Nehemiah overcomes persistent obstacles by local non-Jewish officials and their Jewish allies, sees the wall to completion, its gates installed and their gate-keepers appointed, and registers all the families who have reoccupied Judah's towns (Neh 6-7).

At a large public gathering, Nehemiah, Ezra, and the Levites lead the people to renew their covenant with Yahweh (Neh 8-10). The reading of the Torah (Neh 8) drives the people to heartfelt confession of their sins (Neh 9) and to pledging to keep the Torah (Neh 10). Community leaders take steps to increase Jerusalem's population—especially priests, Levites, and musicians to staff temple services (Neh 11)—and the book's compilers supply comprehensive lists of them (Neh 11:1–12:26). Those clergy then lead the people in a dramatic public ceremony dedicating the city wall (Neh 12:27–47). They also respond obediently to a Torah passage read that day by removing foreigners from Judah (ch. 13). Finally, Nehemiah takes steps to ensure that the temple is properly used and not abused. He also implements other reforms to protect the temple from defilement, to ensure that the Levites receive financial support, to end abuses of the Sabbath, and to condemn marriages to foreign women.

4. The book of Esther narrates the rescue of Jews throughout the Persian Empire from the annihilation plotted by a Persian bureaucrat named Haman. The story has three main parts. The prologue (Esth 1-2) explains how Esther, a young Jewish woman living in Susa with her cousin Mordecai, becomes Queen Esther, wife of the Persian king Ahasuerus (or Xerxes). Part two (Esth 3-9) recounts, first, the story of the deliverance and, second, the establishment by Mordecai and Esther of an annual Jewish festival to remember it. Part three (Esth 10) imitates the royal style of 1-2 Kings to summarize the greatness both of the king and of Mordecai, whom the king promotes to be second in the kingdom.

The Context

Chronologically, the years 538-332 BCE constitute the OT postexilic period. It begins with the decree of Cyrus (538 BCE) that the temple in Jerusalem be rebuilt and that Jews return to their homeland; it ends with the victory of Alexander the Great over the Persians (332 BCE). The latter event ends the 200-year Persian period and ushers in the Hellenistic period. Table 16.1 provides (1) the dates within the Persian era of the events in the PostHB and (2) the dates of the composition of the PostHB. Politically, during both the Babylonian and the Persian Empires, the old Kingdom of Judah was the province of Yehud with its capital at Mizpah, a town seven miles north of Jerusalem (cf. 2 Kgs 25:22–25; the geographical area of the former Judah was somewhat smaller during the Persian period). But Jerusalem was an urban center (though small in population) and was located a few miles north of the Persian administrative center for Yehud at Ramat Rahel. So, Jerusalem first became the unofficial Jewish administrative center of Yehud, and when Nehemiah arrived (and with imperial approval), Jerusalem officially became the political capital of Yehud.

Judah's complex history had also resulted in Persian-period Yehud's becoming complex sociologically. The biblical story features immigrants who returned to Yehud after decades of living in Babylon, but among this group were both urban returnees who had spent the exile in cities such as Babylon and rural people exiled to small towns and farms across Babylonia. In addition, among the returnees were probably descendants of families that formerly belonged to and were exiled from the Northern Kingdom. The views of the past and the future would likely be different for each group, conditioned by different life experiences. A similar complexity would also be true of another group, the Jews who had remained in the land and not experienced exile. This would include descendants of families from both Judah and the northern tribes that once composed the Northern Kingdom. These groups would likewise include both rural and urban residents of the province of Yehud, and the above description does not exclude the possible presence of other complicating subgroups.

Recall that those exiled from Judah for the most part comprised the

Table 16.1. Overview of Postexilic Books

Books	Dates of Events	Dates of Composition
Ezra 1–6	538–515 BCE	ca. 400–300 BCE
Esther	483–474 BCE	ca. 400–300 BCE
Ezra 7–10	458–? BCE	ca. 400–300 BCE
Nehemiah	445–433 BCE	ca. 400–300 BCE
1–2 Chronicles	Creation–538 BCE	ca. 400–350 BCE

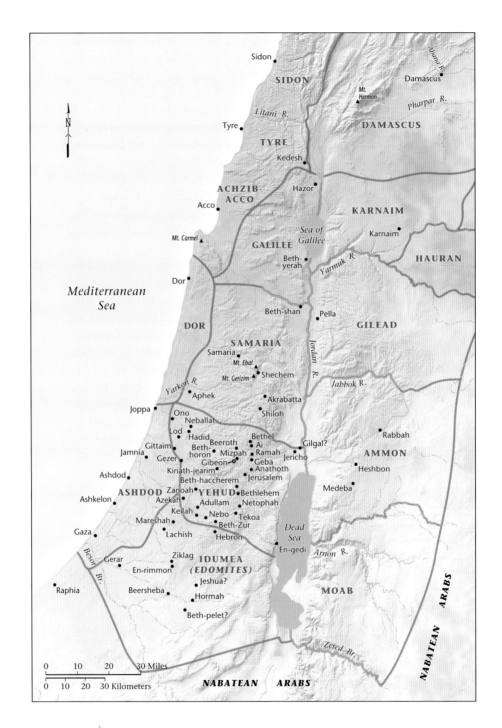

Persian Period
Yehud

Sidon

SIDON

Damascus

Mt. Hermon

Abana R.

Pharpar R.

DAMASCUS

Litani R.

Tyre

TYRE

Kedesh

Hazor

ACHZIB-
ACCO

Acco

KARNAIM

Karnaim

Mt. Carmel

*Sea of
Galilee*

GALILEE

HAURAN

Beth-
yerah

Yarmuk R.

Dor

*Mediterranean
Sea*

Beth-shan

Pella

GILEAD

DOR

Jordan R.

SAMARIA

Samaria

Mt. Ebal

Mt. Gerizim

Shechem

Jabbok R.

Akrabatta

Yarkon R.

Aphek

Shiloh

Joppa

Ono
Neballat

Lod

Hadid

Bethel

Rabbah

Gittaim

Beth-
horon

Beeroth

Ai

Gilgal?

Jamnia

Mizpah

Ramah

Jericho

AMMON

Gezer

Gibeon

Geba

Heshbon

Kiriath-jearim

Anathoth

Ashdod

Beth-haccherem

Jerusalem

Medeba

Zanoah

YEHUD

Bethlehem

ASHDOD

Ashkelon

Azekah

Adullam

Netophah

Keilah

Nebo

Tekoa

*Dead
Sea*

Mareshah

Beth-Zur

Gaza

Lachish

Hebron

Arnon R.

Gerar

Ziklag

En-gedi

IDUMEA
(EDOMITES)

En-rimmon

Beson Br.

Raphia

Beersheba

Jeshua?

Hormah

MOAB

Beth-pelet?

NABATEAN ARABS

0   10   20   30 Miles

0   10   20   30 Kilometers

NABATEAN   ARABS

Zered Br.

country's elites: the king and his entourage (e.g., the king's family, his advisers, administrators, servants, etc.), priests and Levites, artisans and skilled workers, and members of prominent wealthy families. You can easily imagine the tensions that would pit immigrants and permanent residents against each other—for example, if the newcomers expected the locals to recognize them as elite and to step aside to let them lead, since they had been in charge in Babylon. Undoubtedly, disputes over ownership of ancestral lands also arose. The population of postexilic Yehud was not only complex but numerically small. Roughly 10,000 Jews went into exile, but the population of Persian-era Yehud was roughly one-third of its preexilic number, and that of Jerusalem about one-fifth its preexilic number. We know that many also fled from Judah to Egypt shortly after the disaster of 587 BCE and remained there, and apparently many also remained in Babylon—and, if Esther is any guide, some also settled farther east in Persia. Geographically, most of Yehud's population occupied only the central mountain ridge west-to-east between the western lowlands and the Jordan valley and north-to-south from Bethel to Beth-Zur (ca. 15 miles south of the capital). You can imagine the enormous financial and labor challenges facing both returnees and residents in Yehud as they seek to rebuild their country.

The archaeological picture of Jerusalem in the postexilic period is also bleak. Early attempts by the immigrants to revitalize the city were apparently made (Ezra 1; 3:1–7) and, spurred on by the prophets Haggai and Zechariah, further steps were taken under the Persian king Darius I. But serious reconstruction awaited the arrival in Jerusalem of Nehemiah in the mid-fifth century—nearly one century after the return—appointed by Artaxerxes I to be Yehud's provincial governor. Daily life in postexilic Yehud was hard. Rubble was everywhere, so it took major effort just to settle down and secure homes and towns. There was no army to protect settlers from armed raids, so those residing in isolated, out-of-the-way places lived constantly on guard against such dangers. The ruins around them confirmed that the devastation about which the prophets had warned had come true and, worse, that they and their ancestors had brought it on themselves by not listening. A series of poor harvests caused food shortages that denied workers the full energy needed to rebuild and also took a toll on the morale of the populace. Besides the tensions noted above, persistent opposition to Jewish efforts by neighboring non-Jewish peoples further drained Jewish morale. Finally, and perhaps worst of all, the radical tension between the bright hope of a wonderful new day held out by the prophets and the harsh, unrelenting reality of the present day was disillusioning.

The timeline on p. 210 reveals the postexilic (and later) events, the historical contexts in which the PostHB would have been read (compare Tables 16.2 and 16.3 detailing the contemporary Persian and Hellenistic Greek rulers).

Table 16.2. Persian Kings

Name	Dates of Reign (BCE)
Cyrus	550–530
Cambyses	530–522
Bardiya	522
Darius I	522–486
Xerxes	486–465
Artaxerxes	465–424
Xerxes II	424
Sogdianus	424–423
Darius II	423–404
Artaxerxes II	404–358
Artaxerxes III	358–338
Artaxerxes IV	338–336
Darius III	336–330
Artaxerxes V	329

Table 16.3. Hellenistic Rulers: Alexander and Some of His Successors

Name	Dates of Reign (BCE)
Alexander I (Great)	336–323
Wars of Succession	323–305
Seleucus I (SYRIA)	305–281
Antiochus I Soter	281–261
Antiochus II Theos	261–246
Seleucus II Kallinikos	246–226
Seleucus III	226–223
Antiochus III Megas	223–187
Seleucus IV Philopator	187–175
Antiochus IV Epiphanes	175–164
Antiochus V Eupator	164–162
Demetrius I Soter	162–150

Name	Dates of Reign (BCE)
Alexander Balas	150–145
Demetrius II Nicator	145–140, 129–126
Antiochus VI Epiphanes	145–142
Diodotos Triophon	142–139
Antiochus VII Sidetes	139–129
Cleopatra Thea	126–123
Ptolemies (EGYPT)	
Ptolemy I Soter	306–282
Ptolemy II Philadelphos	284–246
Ptolemy III Euergetes	246–222
Ptolemy IV Philopator	222–204
Ptolemy V Epiphanes	203–180
Cleopatra I	180–177
Ptolemy VI Philometor	180–145
Cleopatra II	170–115

Table 16.4. The Hasmonean Family (the Maccabees)

167–164	Three brothers from a priestly family (Judas, Jonathan, Simon) lead a revolt against the Seleucid ruler of Palestine, Antiochus IV Epiphanes, because of his oppressive policies regarding the practice of Judaism. The initial struggle results in the freeing of the Jerusalem temple from Hellenistic control. Hanukkah is the festival that celebrates the cleansing and restoration of the temple ordered by Judas.
164–161	Judas leads struggles against continuing Seleucid control of the region.
161–142	Jonathan serves as high priest.
142–135	Simon serves as high priest and prince (ruler) of Israel, freed from Seleucid rule.
142–137	The Hasmonean family governs Israel and controls the high priestly office. Roman occupation, beginning in 63 BCE, reduces its political power.
37	Herod (the Great), from the region of Idumea, marries into the Hasmonean family and is appointed king of Judea by the Roman Senate.

539: The Medo-Persian army under Cyrus conquers Babylon and rules its vast empire.

538: Cyrus issues his decree permitting exiled Jews to return to their homeland and rebuild their temple.

522: Darius I begins to rule the Persian Empire.

520: Temple-rebuilding in Jerusalem gets serious.

515: Temple dedication and Passover celebrations take place in Jerusalem.

486: Xerxes I (or Ahasuerus) begins to rule the Persian Empire.

465: Artaxerxes I (Longimanus) begins to rule the Persian Empire.

332: Alexander of Macedon conquers the Persian Empire (beginning of Hellenistic era).

323: Alexander dies, and rival generals fight for control of the empire.

305: The Ptolemies in Egypt begin to rule Palestine and Syria.

198: The Seleucids wrest control of Palestine from the Ptolemies.

175: Antiochus Epiphanes IV begins to rule Palestine.

167: The Maccabees (Jewish) battle the Seleucids (Maccabean Revolt).

140: Hasmoneans (i.e., the Maccabees) begin to rule Judea as a semi-independent client state within the Seleucid Empire.

110: The Hasmoneans found a dynasty to rule Judea.

63: General Pompey of Rome conquers Palestine, the beginning of Roman rule there.

BIBLIOGRAPHY

Berquist, Jon L. *Judaism in Persia's Shadow*. Minneapolis: Fortress, 1995.

Briant, Pierre. *From Cyrus to Alexander: A History of the Persian Empire*. Translated by Peter T. Daniels. Winona Lake, IN: Eisenbrauns, 2002.

Japhet, Sara. *From the Rivers of Babylon to the Highlands of Judah: Collected Studies on the Restoration Period*. Winona Lake, IN: Eisenbrauns, 2006.

Kuhrt, Amélie. *The Ancient Near East c. 3000–330 B.C.* 2 vols. London: Routledge, 1995.

Moore, Megan Bishop, and Kelle, Brad E. *Biblical History and Israel's Past: The Changing Study of the Bible and History*. Grand Rapids: Eerdmans, 2011.

Veen, Peter van der. "Sixth-Century Issues: The Fall of Jerusalem, the Exile, and the Return." Pages 383–405 in *Ancient Israel's History: An Introduction to Issues and Sources*. Edited by Bill T. Arnold and Richard S. Hess. Grand Rapids: Baker Academic, 2014.

Williamson, H. G. M. "Exile and After: Historical Study." Pages 236–65 in *The Face of Old Testament Studies: A Survey of Contemporary Approaches*. Edited by David W. Baker and Bill T. Arnold. Grand Rapids: Baker Books, 1999.

Yamauchi, Edwin M. *Persia and the Bible*. Grand Rapids: Baker Books, 1990.

17 THE BOOKS OF 1–2 CHRONICLES

THE ENGLISH TITLE *CHRONICLES* DERIVES from the Christian theologian Jerome's remark (4th cent. CE) that the books offer "the chronicle (Gk. *chronikon*) of the whole of sacred history." That claim seems a little exaggerated, however, since Chronicles retells only the story of the Davidic monarchy and Judah, much as Samuel and Kings do but with a different beginning (genealogies from Adam to postexilic priests) and ending (the decree of the Persian emperor Cyrus in 538 BCE). About half the materials in Chronicles closely repeat parallels in Samuel and Kings, but in the other half the Chronicler's creativity reigns: he rewrites some parallels, completely omits others, writes new materials, and incorporates extrabiblical source materials not found in Samuel and Kings (see 1 Chr 29:29; 2 Chr 9:29; 20:34). The result is a work that is one-third longer than 1–2 Kings, making our treatment of it long as a consequence. If Joshua–2 Kings addresses an exilic audience in Babylon, Chronicles addresses a 4th-century audience in the Persian province of Yehud (or Judah)—and tells a somewhat different story (see below). It barely mentions Saul and the Northern Kingdom, spotlighting instead the Davidic dynasty and the tribes of Judah, Levi, and Benjamin as central to Israel's national life. It credits David (not Solomon) with the temple's construction plans, organization, and worship personnel (1 Chr 22–26) and gives expansive treatment to the religious reforms of Jehoshaphat (2 Chr 17, 19), Hezekiah (2 Chr 29–31), and Josiah (2 Chr 34–35). In our view, the composition of Chronicles was completed ca. 400–350 BCE.

Table 17.1. Biblical Sources for Chronicles

Genealogies (1 Chr 1–9)	Genesis, Exodus, Numbers, Joshua
Saul's Demise, David's Reign (1 Chr 10–29)	1–2 Samuel
Solomon, the Kingdom of Judah (2 Chr 1–36)	1–2 Kings

Table 17.2. Israel's Two Great Histories

The Deuteronomistic History	The Chronicler's History
Beginning: Death of Moses	Beginning: Adam & Genealogies
Conquest & Settlement	Conquest & Settlement Omitted
Judges	Judges Omitted
Saul as First King	Saul Barely Mentioned
David as Installer of Ark in Jerusalem, Solomon as Temple Builder	David as Founder of Temple and Cult
Primacy of the Prophets	Primacy of Priests and Levites
Ending: Release of Jehoiachin (560 BC)	Ending: Decree of Cyrus (538 BC)

How Did We Get This Second History – and Why?

1–2 Chronicles is clearly an anonymous work, neither explicitly identifying nor alluding to its author. But the aggregate of collected materials suggests that several hands probably wrote and/or compiled them, although we refer to these authors/compilers collectively as "the Chronicler." So why write another history of the monarchy? The simple answer is that the Jews living in 4th-century BCE Yehud no longer resonated with the old history. Their life is radically different from that of the exilic audience two centuries earlier, whose past mistakes the DH detailed to prepare them to return to Judah. The Chronicler's audience is already "home"—and under Ezra's leadership has avoided those mistakes. Further, Yehud has a far more complex makeup: the residents descend from both Northern and Southern Kingdoms, from those who remained in the land, and from those who returned from exile. Further, they live in a Persian province (Yehud), not the Israel and Judah of their ancestors, and their ruler is no longer a Davidic king but a Persian-appointed, albeit ethnically Jewish, governor. Their biggest challenge is to define and maintain their unique identity in a world where they daily rub shoulders with non-Jews who worship other gods. So, 1–2 Chronicles reformulates Israel's older traditions (e.g., the Pentateuch, Samuel–Kings, the Psalms, etc.) to stress: the primacy of Jerusalem over other historic cities such as Mizpah and Bethel; the unique, exclusive status of Jerusalem's temple and its priests and Levites; and the critical role that Judah, Levi, and Benjamin play in continuing the legacy of ancient Israel (see Table 17.1). Astoundingly, notwithstanding the importance accorded David, the Chronicler seems to argue that the Jewish community, temple worship under the Levites, and covenantal obedience fulfill the Davidic covenant rather than a ruling king (2 Sam 7).

BIBLIOGRAPHY

De Vries, Simon J. *1 and 2 Chronicles*. FOTL. Grand Rapids: Eerdmans, 1989.

Duke, Rodney K. *The Persuasive Appeal of the Chronicler: A Rhetorical Analysis*. JSOTSup 88. Bible and Literature Series 25. Sheffield: Almond Press, 1990.

———. "Recent Research in Chronicles." *CurBR* 8 (2009): 10–50.

Endres, John C. "The Spiritual Vision of Chronicles: Wholehearted, Joy-Filled Worship of God." *CBQ* 69 (2007): 1–21.

Evans, Paul S., and Tyler F. Williams, eds. *Chronicling the Chronicler: The Book of Chronicles and Early Second Temple Historiography*. Winona Lake, IN: Eisenbrauns, 2013.

Graham, M. Patrick, Kenneth G. Hoglund, and Steven L. McKenzie, eds. *The Chronicler as Historian*. JSOTSup 238. Sheffield: Sheffield Academic Press, 1997.

Graham, M. Patrick, Steven L. McKenzie, and Gary N. Knoppers, eds. *The Chronicler as Theologian: Essays in Honor of Ralph W. Klein*. JSOTSup 371. London: T&T Clark, 2003.

Hahn, Scott W. *The Kingdom of God as Liturgical Empire: A Theological Commentary on 1-2 Chronicles*. Grand Rapids: Baker Academic, 2012.

Japhet, Sara. *The Ideology of the Book of Chronicles and Its Place in Biblical Thought*. Winona Lake, IN: Eisenbrauns, 2009.

Jonker, Louis C. *1 and 2 Chronicles*. UTBC. Grand Rapids: Baker Books, 2013.

Klein, Ralph W. *1 Chronicles: A Commentary*. Hermeneia. Minneapolis: Fortress, 2006.

Knoppers, Gary N. *1 Chronicles 1-9*. AB 12. New York: Doubleday, 2003.

Throntveit, Mark A. "Chronicles." Pages 124-31 in *Theological Interpretation of the Old Testament: A Book-by-Book Survey*. Edited by Kevin J. Vanhoozer. Grand Rapids: Baker Academic, 2008.

The Story

1-2 Chronicles has two parts: the genealogical prologue (1 Chr 1-9) and the history of the Israelite monarchy (1 Chr 10-2 Chr 36). The latter historical section treats subtopics: (1) the reign of David (1 Chr 10-29); (2) the reign of Solomon (2 Chr 1-9); and (3) the Davidic monarchy (2 Chr 10-36).

The Book of 1 Chronicles

1 Chronicles 1–9: The Genealogical Prologue

Unlike DH, Chronicles begins its story by tracing Israel's ancestors from the beginning (from Adam) affirming theologically their election long ago by Yahweh. The succeeding genealogies trace Israel's ancestry:

1. from Adam to Abraham to Jacob (ch. 1)
2. of Jacob and Caleb (ch. 2)
3. of David and Solomon (ch. 3)
4. of Judah and Simeon (ch. 4)
5. of Reuben, Gad, and East Manasseh (ch. 5)

6. of Levi (ch. 6)
7. of Issachar, Naphtali, West Manasseh, Ephraim, and Asher (ch. 7)
8. of Benjamin (ch. 8)
9. of Israelites, priests, Levites and temple servants, the first to resettle in Judah after the exile (ch. 9)

Two theological assumptions are implicit in this list: first, that divine providence accounts for the family line's survival through seven centuries of threats and upheavals and, second, that everything David establishes enjoys divine approval. Though many of the places listed in fact lie outside Yehud, their inclusion here reflects the Chronicler's All-Israel theme—Israel's inclusiveness, indivisibility, and continuity with its storied past.

1 Chronicles 10–29: The Reign of David

The story of David's reign is foundational to the postexilic identity that the Chronicler seeks to cultivate. Chapter 10 makes brief mention of Saul—not his full career but only his death and burial (compare 1 Sam 31)—then introduces the story of David's reign. The Chronicler writes that the LORD put Saul to death for his disobedience and for his consultation with a medium rather than with the LORD himself (1 Sam 13, 15, 28). In DH, David first becomes king of Judah (2 Sam 2) and later also wins acceptance as king from the northern tribes (Israel; 2 Sam 5). Consistent with the Chronicler's All-Israel motif, ch. 11 reports David's coronation as a single event enacted by "all Israel," the same body that David leads to capture Jerusalem (not his elite troops). David's occupation and expansion of the city and the increase of his power, the Chronicler stresses, attest that the LORD is with David. Chapter 12 supplies further evidence that David rules "all Israel"—that is, the fact that his sizable, loyal army's roster features volunteers (not conscripts)

Table 17.3. Comparison of Samuel's and Chronicles' Presentations of the Davidic Covenant

2 Samuel 7:16	1 Chronicles 17:14
Your house and *your* kingdom will remain secure forever before me; *your* throne will be established forever.	I will appoint him over *my* house and *my* kingdom forever; *his* throne will be established forever.

drawn from all Israel's tribes. Chapter 14 quickly reviews a series of personal Davidic triumphs—the births of thirteen children, including Solomon, and the defeat (finally!) of the Philistines.

Chapters 15–16 recount that David and all-Israel welcome the ark of the covenant to his capital city with great ceremony. This is a terser version of 2 Sam 6 and David's wife Michal's displeasure with (in her view) David's excessive enthusiasm. Unlike the DH, the Chronicler underscores David's organization of the priests and Levites to facilitate the ark's dramatic arrival and to support its permanent role in Israel's worship life.

Chapter 17 introduces the Davidic covenant but tellingly rewrites the key promise (see Table 17.3, comparison, translation, and italics ours). The careful rewrite in Chronicles changes the statement from direct address to David by Yahweh, to Yahweh's indirect address, as though David were elsewhere ("Your . . ." versus "him, his . . ."), and also refers not to David himself but to his successors. It further underscores that the temple, kingdom, and royal throne belong to Yahweh, not to the king ("*my* house and *my* kingdom . . ."), and that royal authority over them derives from divine appointment not royal ancestry.

In chs. 18–20, additional military victories extend David's authority and good reputation outside Israel, bring in precious metals for the proposed temple, and grant the new nation peace and tranquility. More telling is the striking contrast between DH's account of the David-initiated census—customarily, a prelude to additional military ventures—and the divine judgment it incurs (2 Sam 24) and the Chronicler's expanded, revised version in 1 Chr 21–22. The latter first shifts the blame for the disaster from Yahweh to "Satan" (see the sidebar on p. 218 for background) and, second, makes the episode the prelude to if not the very moment when David initiates the building of the temple on the threshing floor where God mercifully ends the terrible plague. In short, unlike DH, the Chronicler credits David with selecting that threshing floor as the temple site and laying the necessary groundwork for launching the project—all, the Chronicler notes, before his death. Another expansion on DH is a prophetic

Stained-glass portrayal of the devil from the Cathedral of Saint-Étienne in Bourges, France, now in the Metropolitan Museum of Art in New York City. Thirteenth century CE.

oracle David cites to explain why the holy project will best be completed by Solomon (a man of peace) rather than himself (a man with blood-guilt). In chs. 23–27 the Chronicler also details David's organizational initiatives regarding the nation's cultic and civic leadership.

Finally, at a joyous, stately closing scene in chs. 28–29, David announces his generous donation of gold and silver for the temple and receives impressive donations (including jewels) from his assembled senior officials. He lifts a lengthy prayer in praise to Yahweh, and honors Yahweh with a huge number of sacrifices. Unlike the DH, in Chronicles the coronation of Solomon proceeds smoothly and is conflict free. Neither here nor elsewhere does the Chronicler mention Absalom's coup (2 Sam 15–18) or Adonijah's preemptive coronation and the faction of leaders who supported him (1 Kgs 1). Instead, the dignitaries together anoint Solomon as king and submit to his rule—and so, amazingly, do all of David's sons. Solomon formally sits on "the LORD's throne," and Yahweh also enhances the new king's splendor and popularity among the Israelites. Further, the Chronicler's portrait of David as dynamic, energetic, and fully in charge contrasts sharply with the frail, dying David in DH who requires a young virgin's body to keep him warm at night and who names Solomon his successor only after intervention by Bathsheba and Nathan (1 Kgs 1). In short, the Chronicler portrays a different David from Samuel and Kings; in Chronicles David is the brains behind both the temple building and Israel's ongoing worship life, and (we shall see) he is the nation's chief benefactor as well. Accordingly, the great king dies not from old age (so the DH account implies) but "at a good old age" (1 Chr 29:28), and the Chronicler honors his memory with a fitting regnal summary. Thematically, the proceedings underscore the vision that a vibrant, wealthy David ruling a peaceful, unified Israel stands behind the temple, its construction and staffing, and Solomon's peaceful accession.

READING

Read 1 Chr 1–29 and formulate answers to the questions that follow:

1. What literary, thematic, sociological, and/or theological impressions do the opening genealogies leave with you? What is the Chronicler trying to achieve by beginning the book with so much telephone-book-like detail?

2. With what impression of David as a character does 1 Chr 10–29 leave you? What differences do you observe between the David drawn in Chronicles and his portrait in Samuel and Kings?

3. What do you observe about God—his person, the role(s) God plays, the things God does—in 1 Chronicles? In what ways (if any) do your observations speak to your relationship with God?

4. List what main themes you sense the book emphasizing for its audience. In what way(s), if any, do they speak to your own life situation or relationship with God?

5. Read 1 Chr 22. What are your reflections or questions concerning David's explanation that Solomon, not he himself is to build the temple? Why do you think the Chronicler emphasizes that distinction?

6. What do you take away from 1 Chronicles that applies to your own life? What might 1 Chronicles have to say to the contemporary church? What does it contribute to the advance of the mission of God in the world?

BIBLIOGRAPHY

Braun, Roddy. *1 Chronicles*. WBC 14. Waco, TX: Word, 1986.

Graham, M. Patrick. "A Character Ethics Reading of 1 Chronicles 29:1–25." Pages 98–120 in *Character and Scripture: Moral Formation, Community, and Biblical Interpretation*. Edited by William P. Brown. Grand Rapids: Eerdmans, 2002.

Jarick, John. *1 Chronicles*. 2nd ed. Readings: A New Biblical Commentary. Sheffield: Sheffield Phoenix, 2007.

Table 17.4. Royal Grade Books: The Deuteronomist and the Chronicler on Judah's Kings

King	Final Grade (DH)	Final Grade (Chron)
Rehoboam	F	B
Abijah	F	C–
Asa	B	C–
Jehoshaphat	B	A–
Joash	C–	C–
Amaziah	C–	C–
Uzziah	F	C–
Jotham	F	C–
Ahaz	F	F–
Hezekiah	A	A
Josiah	A	A
Manasseh	F–	A
Everyone Else	F	F

A   "Good, though not perfect"
B   "Good, but . . . / except for . . ." [something serious]
C+   "Bad but . . . / except for . . ." [something positive]
C–   "Good, but did evil at the end"
F   "Did nothing good"

(2 Chr 21:20; 24:25; 28:27). What is startling, however, is the makeover that the Chronicler awards to some kings—either a simple makeover (to Abijah, Uzziah, and Jotham) or an extreme makeover (Rehoboam and Manasseh). Probably the makeovers seek to restore some of the luster to the Chronicler's ideal pious monarch and faithful temple-worshiper, patterned after his portrait of Solomon. He presents the David dynasty in as positive a light as possible because apparently, in his view, it is the foundation on which the temple-worship system and Yehud's future rest.

In chs. 10-12, to support the extreme makeover of Rehoboam, the Chronicler adds supplementary material beyond what DH supplies. It highlights Rehoboam's welcome of priests and Levites who defect from Israel to Judah and his humility and acceptance of prophetic reassurance during the invasion of the Egyptian king Shishak (compare 1 Kgs 14:25-28). In the end, however, the Chronicler joins DH in reckoning Rehoboam as "evil" because he fails to "seek the LORD," a key thematic phrase in Chronicles (see 2 Chr 12:14; 17:4; 31:21). What reduces the reformer Asa's Deuteronomic B to the Chronicler's C- is his preference for a military alliance with the Syrians rather than trusting in Yahweh, who had reassured him of victory through a prophet (ch. 16; cf. 1 Kgs 15). Another reformer, Jehoshaphat, earns praise in chs. 17-20 for his peaceful reign, his loyal devotion to Yahweh, his dispatching of Levites throughout Judah to teach the Torah, and his enacting of nationwide judicial reforms. His lone failure (the reason for his A-) is his ongoing alliance with Ahab and Israel (cf. 1 Kgs 22), a failing for which Jehoshaphat receives two prophetic rebukes (2 Chr 19, 20). Sadly, in Chronicles, after Jehoshaphat a string of two "bad" kings follows (Jehoram, Ahaziah), both of whom are kin of

Ahab and Jezebel, and they infect Judah with northern idolatry and die under divine retribution for it.

After a report about three good kings who go bad at the end and forfeit the honor of burial in the royal tombs (Joash, Amaziah, and Uzziah), ch. 27 fleshes out DH's brief portrait of a "good" king, Jotham (2 Kgs 15:32-38), highlighting his building projects and victory over the Ammonites. To the Chronicler, Jotham's faithful devotion to Yahweh compares with his father Uzziah's early years—before ch. 26 reports that Uzziah's pride led him to enter the temple, brashly perform priestly acts, and incur leprosy as punishment. Jotham's piety explains both his increased power and his burial with full royal honors—the first king since Jehoshaphat to receive this honor. Jotham personifies one of the Chronicler's key themes: faithfulness to Yahweh through Torah-obedience brings divine blessings. By contrast, Jotham's successor, Ahaz, receives one of the most unflattering royal accounts in Chronicles—worse even than DH's report about him. From the beginning, Ahaz shows himself to be a devoted Baal worshiper in the model of the Northern kings, not surprisingly (per the flip side of the theme just mentioned) bringing divine judgment on Judah: invasions by Aram and Israel. Ironically, the Chronicler contrasts Ahaz's idolatry with the respect for Yahweh shown by the Israelites—of all people!—by obeying a prophetic oracle during the attack. Also, how starkly different is Ahaz's response to a later Assyrian invasion: he seeks relief from their gods—a very obvious insult to Yahweh who is, in fact, the God responsible for the crisis (see 2 Kings 16). Through Ahaz, the Chronicler warns his audience that unbridled apostasy still poses an alluring threat to postexilic Judah and the Davidic ideal.

The reformer Hezekiah is clearly one of the Chronicler's heroes, and he devotes chs. 29-32 to Hezekiah's reign—a treatment in length second only to the accounts of David and Solomon (see 1 Chr 10-2 Chr 9). In chs. 29-30, the writer virtually rewrites 2 Kgs 18-20, adding long passages about the temple's cleansing and rededication and the celebration of the Passover by both north and south. The expanded narrative shifts the story's focus from political history (DH) to cultic history—a signal that the king (and the Chronicler) see a holy temple and proper worship as the kingdom's first priority and the key to its future. Interestingly, the king invites both north and south to celebrate the Passover and, notwithstanding some ridicule in some quarters, God opens people up to the idea. Eight tribes convene to celebrate a historic, two-week festival with a joy not seen in Jerusalem since David and Solomon—and, more importantly (says the Chronicler), a time when God hears the Levites' prayers. Religious reforms follow, the crowd destroying idolatrous sites on their way home and Hezekiah promoting new measures in Jerusalem, especially increased care of the clergy (ch. 31). In ch. 32, while suffering a fatal disease, the king exemplifies the Chronicler's ideal of a humble, repentant monarch—initially (and inexplicably) rejecting Yahweh's reassurance through a sign that he'd be healed, then humbly repenting of his ingratitude and, thus, sparing Judah terrible disaster (see 2 Sam 24). Fittingly, at his death, all Judah honors Hezekiah, and he is buried in the tombs of the kings.

But the Chronicler reserves his most impressive, extreme makeover for Manasseh. DH paints Manasseh as "the worst" king—Judah's version of Ahab (2 Kgs 21)—an opinion the Chronicler shares until reporting in 2 Chr 33 something that is absent in DH—Manasseh's genuine prayer of repentance, receipt of divine forgiveness, and implementation of religious reforms befitting a "good" king. Theologically, Manasseh's case again personifies the importance of humble, repentant petitions to God and affirms the nature of God as always willing to hear and answer them. Chapters 34-35 feature the last religious reformer—a "good" king of unwavering loyalty to Israel's God. Compared to DH, however, who makes Josiah the climax of his report, the Chronicler writes a noticeably shorter account that also describes a slightly different plot. In DH, it is the discovery of the law book (622 BCE) that sparks Josiah's subsequent purging of idolatry (2 Kgs 22), whereas in Chronicles the purging happens four years after the teenaged king Josiah first "seeks Yahweh" (628 BCE) and six years before the law book's discovery (2 Chr 34). In other words, in the Chronicler's hand Josiah exemplifies the compilers' ideal of people who devotedly and obediently pursue a close relationship with God. Understandably, the Chronicler omits blaming an idolatrous Manasseh for making Judah's subsequent demise inevitable (2 Kgs 23:26-27). Once again, the Chronicler displays his keen interest in the temple and proper worship in order to emphasize their fundamental importance for preserving postexilic Israel's identity within an ethnically and religiously pluralistic Persian Empire.

Finally, the Chronicler's inclusion of Yahweh's promise that Josiah will die in peace requires that the writer explain the king's surprising, violent death in a battle with Egypt. Sympathetically, he cites Pharaoh Neco's claim to be on a mission from God—that for Josiah to oppose him is to oppose God. Echoes of Ahab's death-scene—Josiah's use of a disguise and his death by an arrow—seem to imply that Josiah's resistance to Neco is disobedience. If so, the Chronicler apparently regards Josiah as a "good" but not "ideal" king; his death says that even good kings must remain obedient, as must all Israel.

The effect of this picture of Josiah is to substitute a positive but realistic version of his reign that distances the Chronicler's account from the elevated, climactic role that DH assigns Josiah. Further, with Judah's end in sight, the pace of the Chronicler's story quickens, ch. 36 covering more than two decades in a mere twenty-one verses (compare 2 Kgs 23:31–24:20). Under Josiah's "bad" royal successors (Jehoiakim, Jehoiachin, and Zedekiah), the Chronicler writes, increasing unfaithfulness, especially defilement of the temple and rejection of the prophets, typifies the nation. His report of the Babylonian destruction of the city and the temple is less detailed than DH's, with a focus on the plundering of the temple's metal vessels and the exile to Babylon of a "remnant" of Judah, the latter an important, illuminating metaphor for the Chronicler's own audience. To conclude, the Chronicler jumps ahead a half-century to the Persian conquest of Babylon, interpreting the half-century gap as the land enjoying the sabbath rests denied it by Judah (see Lev 26:31–35) and as the fulfillment of the seventy years of exile that Jeremiah announced (Jer 25:11–14; 29:10). In other words, the interim between exile and return satisfies both the teaching of the Torah and the preaching of prophecy.

2 Chronicles 36:22–23 — The Epilogue: The Decree of Cyrus

For his epilogue, the Chronicler sends the story from Judah to Persia and from the Davidic monarchy to the Persian monarch, Cyrus (the Chronicler omits the brief episode about Jehoiachin with which DH closes [2 Kgs 25:27-30]). A central theme in Chronicles, the temple, now marks the center of the brief episode with which the Chronicler's long story ends. (Remember: in the Hebrew Bible, this epilogue marks the final words in the whole canon.) In Cyrus's first year (538 BCE), the king issues a written proclamation throughout his Empire, an event that the Chronicler interprets theologically: by his own admission, Cyrus acts because of Yahweh's nudging; Israel's God ("the LORD") has also tasked Cyrus with building him a temple in Jerusalem. Finally, the king addresses "his [i.e., Yahweh's] people," wishing them God's nearness and, at last, permitting them to go home. That moment of liberation makes possible Jewish life in postexilic, Persian Yehud, where the Chronicler and his audience live. The closing plea ("Any of [Yahweh's] people may go up," v. 23 NIV) is ambiguous: it may call for diaspora Jews either to emigrate back to Yehud or simply to visit Jerusalem on religious pilgrimages.

Cyrus Cylinder. Written in Akkadian in cuneiform script, this ancient clay cylinder records a decree by the Persian king Cyrus the Great after his capture of Babylon (538 BCE). It confirms biblical reports that Persian policy authorized the return of Jewish exiles to Judah and of temple vessels to Jerusalem. *Photograph by Mike Peel (www.mikepeel.net) (Wikimedia Commons, CC-SA 4.0)*

I am Cyrus, king of the world, great king, mighty king, king of Babylon, king of Sumer and Akkad, king of the four quarters. . . . I returned the (images of) the gods to the sacred centers [on the other side of] the Tigris, whose sanctuaries had been abandoned for a long time, and I let them dwell in eternal abodes. I gathered all their inhabitants and returned (to them) their dwellings.

(COS 2.315)

READING

Read 2 Chr 1–36 and formulate answers to the questions that follow:

> 1. Read 2 Chr 1–9 and 1 Kgs 10–11. What marks the most significant accomplishments of Solomon according to the Chronicler? What do you think are Solomon's strengths and weaknesses as king? In what

ways does his portrait in 2 Chronicles differ from the view of him in 1 Kings?

2. Which one or two kings in 2 Chr 10–36 particularly impress you? What is it about them that you find memorable? In what way(s) do you especially relate to him (or them)?

3. Which one or two kings in 2 Chr 10–36 do you find the least impressive? What is it about them that you find less than impressive? In what way(s) do you especially relate to him (or them)?

4. Read 2 Kgs 21 and 2 Chr 33. How do the two portraits of Manasseh compare? In what way(s) are they alike, and in what way(s) do they differ? How do you explain the similarities and/or differences between the DH and the Chronicler?

5. What do you sense is God's involvement in the history of the Davidic monarchy? In what ways do you see God's involvement showing itself? (In your answer, include reflection on 2 Chr 35:20–24 and 36:22–23). What might God's involvement in the Chronicler's story say to people in postexilic Yehud? At what level of importance do you imagine they considered that involvement to be?

6. Other than kings, what leaders does God seem to use regularly? What special roles do they play in the story?

7. Read 2 Chr 30:1–27 and 35:1–19. The latter text praises Josiah's Passover celebration as the first to be held in 600 years, but the former text also reports one led by Hezekiah. What is it about Josiah's ceremony that merits the Chronicler's praise? In what way does it differ from the Passover led by Hezekiah?

8. Read 2 Chr 35–36. What memories of the prophet Jeremiah does the Chronicler incorporate into his book? According to the Chronicler, what contribution(s) does Jeremiah make to the unfolding story in the final two chapters of 2 Chronicles?

9. What are the theological implications of the fact that 1–2 Chronicles opens with Adam and closes with the Persian king Cyrus?

BIBLIOGRAPHY

Dillard, Raymond B. *2 Chronicles*. WBC 15. Waco, TX: Word, 1987.

Evans, Paul S. "Historia or Exegesis? Assessing the Chronicler's Hezekiah-Sennacherib Narrative." Pages 103–20 in *Chronicling the Chronicler: The Book of Chronicles and Early Second Temple Historiography*. Edited by Paul S. Evans and Tyler F. Williams. Winona Lake, IN: Eisenbrauns, 2013.

Jarick, John. *2 Chronicles*. Readings: A New Biblical Commentary. Sheffield: Sheffield Phoenix, 2007.

Johnstone, William. *1 and 2 Chronicles*. 2 vols. JSOTSup 253–54. Sheffield: Sheffield Academic Press, 1997.

Jonker, Louis C. *1 and 2 Chronicles*. UTBC. Grand Rapids: Baker Books, 2013.

Klein, Ralph W. *2 Chronicles: A Commentary*. Hermeneia. Minneapolis: Fortress, 2012.

Mabie, Frederick J. "2 Chronicles." Pages 286–393 in *1 and 2 Kings, 1 and 2 Chronicles, Ezra, Nehemiah, Esther*. Vol. 3 of *Zondervan Illustrated Bible Backgrounds Commentary*. Edited by John H. Walton. Grand Rapids: Zondervan, 2009.

Selman, Martin J. *2 Chronicles: A Commentary*. TOTC. Leicester: InterVarsity Press, 1994.

Wilcock, Michael. *The Message of Chronicles: One Church, One Faith, One Lord*. TBST. Leicester: Inter-Varsity Press, 1987.

18 THE BOOK OF EZRA-NEHEMIAH

Important Dates for Ezra-Nehemiah
539: the conquest of Babylon by Cyrus and the Medo-Persians
538: Cyrus's decree: return and rebuild the temple
the return's leaders, Sheshbazzar and Zerubbabel
522: Darius I rules the Persian Empire
520–515: Haggai and Zechariah are active in Jerusalem (see their chapters)
486: Xerxes (or Ahasuerus) succeeds Darius I
465: Artaxerxes I (Longimanus) succeeds Xerxes
458: the scribe Ezra comes from Babylon to Jerusalem
445: the governor Nehemiah comes from Babylon to Jerusalem

EZRA AND NEHEMIAH OFFER THE only record of Cyrus's decree and of events in postexilic Judah. The books probably originated in Judah, but not Jerusalem, ca. 400 BCE as a single work (Ezra-Nehemiah), since that is how they appear in Hebrew manuscripts. Indeed, it was not until the Middle Ages that Hebrew Bibles divided into two books what heretofore had been considered a single work. The book features two primary leaders, Ezra the priest and Nehemiah the governor, and highlights three rebuildings: the temple by Zerubbabel and the high priest Joshua (538-515 BCE), the Jewish community by Ezra (458-457 BCE), and Jerusalem's walls by Nehemiah (445-444 BCE). These three "buildings" give you a small glimpse of Jewish life in postexilic Yehud. Archaeological evidence and extrabiblical sources shed their own light on the period and generally fit well with the reports of Ezra-Nehemiah (see our introduction to the Postexilic Historical Books, ch. 16 above). The books stress the importance of the whole Jewish community, the crucial role of written documents (especially the Torah), and the holiness of both the temple and the whole city of Jerusalem.

How Did We Get These Books?

As with many such questions, the contents of Ezra-Nehemiah supply the primary data for sorting out the answer. Thankfully, the written source materials on which the compilers drew are more obvious in Ezra-Nehemiah than those thought to underlie other OT books. These include:

1. A historical prologue (Ezra 1–6)
2. Ezra's personal memoirs (Ezra 7–10 and Neh 8–10)
3. Nehemiah's personal memoirs (Neh 1–7 and 11–13)
4. Cyrus's empire-wide decree (Ezra 1:2–4)
5. Lists (e.g., Ezra 2; 7; Neh 3; 7)
6. Letters (e.g., in Ezra 4:11–22; 7:12–26)

These written sources certainly constitute the heart of the Ezra-Nehemiah book and, according to the persuasive case of H. G. M. Williamson, mark the first of three steps in its composition.

The historical prologue (see below) bridges the historical gap between the end of Chronicles (538 BCE) and the arrival of Ezra in Jerusalem (458 BCE); it supplies some information that is unavailable elsewhere in the Bible. With one exception (Ezra 7:12–26), the letters (correspondence in Aramaic between Persian officials in Samaria and the royal court in far-off Persia) fall within the historical prologue. Those written by the former officials seek to obstruct the Jews' ongoing rebuilding efforts, objections that the latter officials set aside. The memoirs of Ezra (EM) and Nehemiah (NM) offer an intriguing biblical rarity—first-person, contemporary accounts of events in their day and a few brief prayers. Finally, the lists

- inventory the temple vessels returned from Babylon
- tally the numbers of returnees per Judahite town
- genealogically certify Ezra's priestly credentials and describe his companions
- detail those responsible for rebuilding each section of the wall
- identify the signatories of the renewed covenant

- name (by tribe) the settlers of Jerusalem
- account for the priests and Levites who returned

Once the above were in writing, the second step—the joining of the original EM and NM by an editor—followed, producing four literary panels (Ezra 7–10; Neh 1–7; 8–10; 11–13). In the final step, an editor completed the Ezra-Nehemiah corpus by adding the historical prologue (Ezra 1–6) with its various lists and letters. As noted above, this three-step process probably ended ca. 400 BCE, bequeathing Ezra-Nehemiah as its special legacy.

The Story

Topically, Ezra-Nehemiah taken together comprises three parts: (1) reports on the implementation of Cyrus's decree (Ezra 1–Neh 7); (2) Judah's celebration of resumed community life under Torah (Neh 8:1–13:3); and (3) Nehemiah's report of his reforms (Neh 13:4–31).

The Book of Ezra

Read by itself, the book of Ezra has three parts: (1) the historical prologue (Ezra 1–6); (2) the report of Ezra's royal commission and arrival in Jerusalem (Ezra 7–8); and (3) the report about the controversy over mixed marriages between Jews and foreigners (Ezra 9–10).

The opening prologue of Ezra-Nehemiah (Ezra 1–6) looks back from the editor's vantage point (ca. 400 BCE) on events that unfolded in the period 538–458 BCE, the primary biblical record of that period. Chapters 1–2 identify Yahweh as the catalyst for all that follows, rousing Cyrus's spirit to issue a written decree that the temple in Jerusalem be rebuilt by returned Jews—a prompting that Cyrus himself acknowledges—to fulfill what Jeremiah had prophesied. The story tells all Jews who feel a similar divine "rousing-of-spirit" (the Hebrew terms are the same; compare Isa 45:13)—especially Judah, Benjamin, the priests, and the Levites—to join one of the two waves of returnees that follow. The first is a small group led by a Jew named Sheshbazzar, about whom little is known (Ezra 5:14, 16), but who carried back the sacred temple vessels taken from Jerusalem by Nebuchadnezzar. The second group, which was co-led later by Zerubbabel and Joshua, swelled the total number of returnees to more than 42,000 (Neh 7:66).

A bronze relief on the Knesset Menorah (1956) in Jerusalem by sculptor Benno Elkan depicts Nehemiah directing the rebuilding of Jerusalem. Nehemiah clutches Cyrus's decree (538 BCE), while an armed, modern Israeli (lower left) symbolizes the ties between returnees to Zion of both eras. (See p. 389 for a photograph of the whole menorah.) ©Tamar Hayardeni (Wikimedia Commons, CC 4.0)

Zerubbabel, the political leader, may have been a descendant of David (1 Chr 3:16-19; Matt 1:12-13) and was possibly the subject of messianic expectations (Zech 4:6-10; 6:9-14), while Joshua was the high priest. They both figure prominently as leaders of the returned community ca. BCE 520 in the books of Haggai and Zechariah (e.g., Hag 2:4; Zech 4:6). But Ezra-Nehemiah also implies that many Jews remained in Babylonia—the first phase of a new historical phenomenon that we know as the Jewish diaspora (i.e., Jews who choose to settle permanently outside the promised land). As noted earlier, the book of Esther attests that Jews had also settled farther east in Persia early in the fifth century BCE.

Not surprisingly, ch. 3 narrates how in the seventh month the newly settled returnees convene in Jerusalem to celebrate the Feast of Tabernacles, later appoint Levites to lead the temple rebuilding, and solemnly lay its foundation. However, news of the temple project spurs enemies in Samaria to send the Persian king a letter (copy included in Ezra 4) alleging that a rebuilt Jerusalem would become a hotbed of sedition in the empire's western provinces. Alas, the king's reply (copy provided) acknowledges the threat and orders the work to stop—and it does. But in chs. 5-6, the main story line resumes, circling back to the era of Darius I (550-486 BCE) and his written confirmation that Cyrus had, in fact, authorized its rebuilding, and Darius orders the project's opponents to facilitate the project with royal resources. The returnees soon finish the temple and suitably dedicate it in 515 BCE (seventy-two years after its destruction), formally install its clergy, and six weeks later celebrate Passover and the Festival of Flatbread as their ancestors did under Joshua (Josh 5; compare other historic celebrations in 2 Kgs 23:21-23; 2 Chr 35 [Josiah]; 2 Chr 30 [Hezekiah]). The present joyous celebration brings the historical prologue to a fitting close and sets the stage for the debut of Ezra and Nehemiah.

Chapter 7 introduces Ezra as a distinguished scholar and teacher of the Torah of Moses in Babylon, someone whose plans God has expedited. During the exile, Babylon had apparently replaced Jerusalem as the center of Torah study for Jews (cf. Jer 51), with Ezra a leading light prominent enough to receive written religious and political powers from the Persian king Artaxerxes (465–424 BCE), son of King Xerxes (or Ahasuerus; see the book of Esther). A four-month journey brings Ezra and his large entourage of clergy to Jerusalem in early August of 458 BCE with the emperor's written authorization and generous royal funding to assess Torah-obedience in Jerusalem—and specifically, to offer sacrifices there on the king's behalf. A long digression (ch. 8) lists the priestly families that accompanied Ezra, rehearses his organizational actions, especially his careful accounting of the valuables they are bearing to Jerusalem, and reports his official call on provincial officials. The lists in Ezra and Nehemiah may strike some readers as unnecessary, irrelevant detail, but to the returnees they preserved crucial historical records. They enabled leaders to adjudicate things such as membership in the religious community, claims to ancestral property, the right to live in Jerusalem, and which priests and Levites were qualified or unqualified to serve as temple clergy.

Finally, ch. 9 reports Ezra's distressing discovery that marriages link Jews (including priests and Levites) to non-Jews with detestable religious practices. The finding sparks his impassioned, tearful lament that his people, so recently recipients of unmerited divine mercy after an awful history of Torah-disobedience, have lapsed into it again. Chapter 10 relates Ezra's moves to remedy the situation, and his personal story ends with a long list of the priests and Levites who had entered into such marriages.

The Book of Nehemiah

Read by itself, the book of Nehemiah has seven parts: (1) Nehemiah's autobiographical report on how he receives imperial authority and funding to rebuild Jerusalem (Neh 1–2); (2) a report about the rebuilding of the city's walls against strong local opposition (Neh 3–4); (3) Nehemiah's autobiographical report that he ends oppressive profiteering by wealthy Jews (Neh 5); (4) his autobiographical report of how he completes Jerusalem's walls (Neh 6–7); (5) a report about the covenant-renewal ceremony (Neh 8–10); (6) lists of Jerusalem's residents and returned priests and Levites, and the report on the wall's dedication (Neh 11–12); and (7) Nehemiah's autobiographical report about how he removes foreigners from Judah and other reforms (Neh 13).

Nehemiah 1–2 finds the soon-to-be governor working in the fortress at Susa as the king's official food-and-drink taster—an ancient security measure for monarchs. The ancient city of Susa stands on an elevated plateau in southwestern Iran, and after impressive rebuilding by the current king's grandfather, Darius I, became one of three capital cities that were frequented by Persian emperors (besides Ecbatana and Persepolis). Nehemiah's unique position in the palace and his ongoing, personal contact with the king explain why Artaxerxes could recognize the grief written on Nehemiah's face that leads to their conversation about Jerusalem's shamefully ruined walls. Along with Nehemiah's lamentation and prayer for royal favor beforehand, his royal connection also explains why, at Nehemiah's request, the king commissions him to head the city's reconstruction and sends with him letters guaranteeing him safe passage and lumber supplies for the temple. But two officials in the province of Trans-Euphrates, Sanballat the Horonite and Tobiah the Ammonite, oppose Nehemiah's mission (the book calls them his "enemies").

Excursus: Who Were Nehemiah's Enemies, and What Were Their Motives?

When the Persians conquered the Babylonian Empire, they left in place the "Province beyond the (Euphrates) River," with Samaria as its administrative center. Its governor was one of Nehemiah's opponents, Sanballat (Akk. *Sin-uballit*), whose administrative authority apparently extended to Jerusalem and Judah, although the latter constituted the autonomous province of Yehud (Neh 2:10, 19). Archaeological evidence reveals Trans-Euphrates to be a thriving provincial economy with international connections, on the prosperity of which Yehud probably also depended (Neh 5:1–5). Some scholars read Sanballat's foreign name as evidence that he descended from a family that the Assyrians settled in Israel (8th cent. BCE; see 2 Kgs 17:24; Ezra 4:1–3), but several indicators suggest that he regarded himself as a faithful worshiper of Yahweh rather than of the Moon-God Sin. In papyri from Elephantine (near Aswan, Egypt) his sons' names incorporate "Yah-" for Yahweh; the qualifier "the Horonite" hints at a hometown among the towns named Beth-horon in Ephraimite territory. Further, his son-in-law was the grandson of the high priest Eliashib (Neh 13:28).

Nehemiah's second opponent is Tobiah the Ammonite, whose name ("Yahweh is good") implies that he also may have followed Yahweh, so "the Ammonite" refers to his home area rather than to his ethnicity. Ammon was a region along the Jordan's east bank roughly between the Arnon and Jabbok Rivers and centered in the city of Rabbah (modern Amman, Jordan), over which Tobiah may have exercised political leadership. Like Sanballat, he was related by marriage to Eliashib, who permitted him to lodge within the temple area during Nehemiah's absence (13:4–9). Nehemiah 6:17 depicts him as an ally of the nobles in Judah, and later he headed the Tobiads, one of the two families vying to control Jerusalem in the Hellenistic period. Nehemiah's third opponent was Geshem the Arab, who may have been the king of Kedar mentioned in an inscription from north Arabia.

In short, the three opponents were probably regional governors under the king of Persia who headed groups that had traditionally intervened in the internal affairs of the unwalled villages and towns left over from former Judah under Babylon. They may have resented Nehemiah's governorship over the province of Yehud as a royal intrusion into their exclusive, profitable domains. They may also have regarded the rebuilding of Jerusalem's walls as a precursor to the reestablishment of the Davidic monarchy, which in their view was a harbinger of a treasonous revolt against the king (Neh 6:6–7) and a personal threat to their own wealthy, regional hegemonies. They probably feared the imperial fallout that might engulf them if their worst fears materialized.

In Neh 3–4 the theme of opposition to Nehemiah's mission twice surfaces in ridicule heaped by Sanballat and Tobiah on his efforts to rally the Jews to begin rebuilding the walls and in the governors' scheme to undermine it. Ezra-Nehemiah's record of the individuals responsible for each segment of the wall testifies to the dedicated, popular support the project enjoys and to their devout prayers for God to stymie the opposition. But two tense scenes in ch. 5 sound three subthemes: the fear of a surprise, violent attack against unarmed workers, Nehemiah's courageous antidote to it (the time-tested Israelite conviction about God's fighting on their side), and the Torah-based ethical demand that bankers return land taken from Jews in default and not charge other Jews interest. The chapter concludes with an aside that illustrates Nehemiah's own self-sacrificial spirit—his waiving of financial support due him as governor and his prayer that Yahweh reward his efforts. Finally, in ch. 6 the enemies' final ploys to stop Nehemiah fail, and they and their coconspirators never enter the story again.

With the wall rebuilt and its gates in place, ch. 7 turns to genealogical research to separate out families among the first wave of returnees whose ancestors had served the temple in Jerusalem from those who hailed from other towns. Obviously, its purpose is to determine who settles in Jerusalem or its environs to resume temple service and who settles in ancestral towns elsewhere. Chapter 8 reports that on Day 1 of Month 7 everyone attends a dramatic national assembly at which, by popular demand, Ezra reads the Torah to the crowd. The historic significance of this event merits underscoring. First, it marks the first time in the book that Ezra and Nehemiah appear together as a united leadership. Second, it marks the debut of the Torah as a completed document, presumably edited by Ezra; of Ezra as it primary teacher; and of the Levites as either its translators or its interpreters, fanning out through the crowd. We can imagine small groups clustering around them, hungry to absorb the meaning and import of Ezra's reading. This division of roles between Torah-teachers (scribes or rabbis) and their assistants (Levites) persists into the NT period. When King Josiah first heard the book of the Torah read, he grieved about Judah's failures, and Ezra's reading likewise reduces this audience to tears. But Nehemiah urges the people to celebrate the day as a day of great joy, not mourning—and they do, immediately celebrating the seven-day Feast of Booths as the Torah instructs them for Month 7, with a daily Torah-reading—the first joyous celebration of this sort since Joshua's day.

Chapters 9-10 add that two weeks later the Levites also lead the people, both lay and clergy, in confessing their sins in a long prayer that reviews Israel's sorry history of unfaithfulness, pleads for God to take seriously their present slavery to foreign kings, and announces the renewal of their covenant commitment to Yahweh. It gives readers insight into how the residents of Yehud understood their national history—its successes, failures, and lessons to be learned. Another long list (the names of everyone agreeing to the covenant) briefly interrupts the prayer, and ch. 11 adds the list of families selected to live in Jerusalem—mostly descendants of temple staff or civic officials but some chosen by lottery. (At the time, the city had few residents since houses inside the walls had not yet been rebuilt.) Chapter 12 recounts the elaborate, joyous dedicatory procession on the wall, and ch. 13 the community's obedient exclusion of all foreigners from the assembly, an action that ends the use by Tobiah the Ammonite of temple storerooms. This policy may mystify, if not offend, some modern readers, but it is important to understand that, at the time, the residents of Yehud were living in survival mode. They were surrounded by hostile, powerful political enemies, faced with temptations to revert to the sins of their ancestors, and navigating a daunting demographic complex of competing interests within their population. Their conservative stance is best understood against that background.

READING

Read Ezra-Nehemiah and formulate answers to the questions that follow:

1. With what main impressions does your reading of Ezra-Nehemiah leave you about what daily life was like in early postexilic Judah? What one word summarizes your perception of that era?

2. Why do you think Ezra-Nehemiah includes so many lists? What do they contribute to the book's message, or do you consider them to be distractions?

3. In your opinion, what lies behind the conflicts between Ezra and Nehemiah and their so-called enemies? What are your thoughts about the way Ezra and Nehemiah respond to them? In what way(s), if any, do you think they model appropriate or inappropriate responses for Christian leaders today?

4. The first-person "memoirs" of Ezra and Nehemiah play an important role in the book. With what picture of each of the two leaders do they leave you? Why (or why not) do you think you might have followed their leadership had you lived back then?

5. What do you sense is the spiritual condition of the people in postexilic Judah according to Ezra-Nehemiah? What evidence in the book suggests that their condition improved or declined during this period? In what way(s), if at all, do you think the situation in postexilic Judah compares with your perception of the spiritual condition of the Christian community of which you are currently a part? What ways to improve its spiritual life or avoid its decline does Ezra-Nehemiah suggest to you?

6. What role do you see the written Torah playing in the lifetimes of Ezra and Nehemiah? What does this teach us about the role that our written Scriptures might play in our worshiping communities and personal lives today?

7. What is your response to the strict policy of Ezra and Nehemiah that people, especially religious leaders, married to foreign women must

divorce them? What do you think is at stake in that policy, and what might it teach us about Christian marriage today?

8. What does Ezra-Nehemiah contribute to your understanding of God's mission in the world today?

BIBLIOGRAPHY

Boda, Mark J., and Paul L. Redditt, eds. *Unity and Disunity in Ezra-Nehemiah: Redaction, Rhetoric, and Reader.* Hebrew Bible Monographs 17. Sheffield: Sheffield Phoenix, 2008.

De Troyer, Kristin. "Zerubbabel and Ezra: A Revived and Revised Solomon and Josiah? A Survey of Current 1 Esdras Research." *CurBR* 1 (2002): 30-60.

Eskenazi, Tamara Cohn. *In an Age of Prose: A Literary Approach to Ezra-Nehemiah.* Atlanta: Scholars Press, 1988.

Lemaire, André. "Fifth- and Fourth-Century Issues: Governorship and Priesthood." Pages 406-25 in *Ancient Israel's History: An Introduction to Issues and Sources.* Edited by Bill T. Arnold and Richard S. Hess. Grand Rapids: Baker Academic, 2014.

Leung Lai, Barbara M. "'I'-Voice, Emotion, and Selfhood in Nehemiah." *Old Testament Essays* 28 (2015): 154-67.

Levering, Matthew. *Ezra and Nehemiah.* Brazos Theological Commentary on the Bible. Grand Rapids: Brazos, 2007.

Magen, Yitzhak. "The Dating of the First Phase of the Samaritan Temple on Mt. Gerizim in Light of Archaeological Evidence." Pages 157-212 in *Judah and the Judeans in the Fourth Century B.C.E.* Edited by Oded Lipschitz, Gary N. Knoppers, and Rainer Albertz. Winona Lake, IN: Eisenbrauns, 2007.

Southwood, Katherine E. *Ethnicity and the Mixed Marriage Crisis in Ezra 9-10: An Anthropological Approach.* Oxford Theological Monographs. Oxford: Oxford University Press, 2012.

Too Shao, Joseph, and Rosa Ching Shao. *Ezra-Nehemiah.* Asia Bible Commentary Series. Singapore: Asia Theological Association, 2007.

Williamson, H. G. M. *Ezra, Nehemiah.* WBC 16. Waco, TX: Word, 1985.

19 THE BOOK OF ESTHER

Important Dates for Esther	
486: Xerxes I (or Ahasuerus) rules the Persian Empire	
483: Xerxes' six-month reception at Susa; Queen Vashti's removal on its final day	
479: a new (Jewish) queen	
472: Haman's plot to annihilate the Jews	
	Esther's intervention and countermanding decree

NAMED AFTER ITS MAIN CHARACTER, Esther reports how a remarkable escape from annihilation (mid-5th century BCE) leads Jews to celebrate a new festival, Purim. Its story is set in Susa, one of several capitals among which Persian emperors rotated their residences. The book's familiarity with Persia, its court and customs, and its lack of Greek influences suggest a Jewish author in the 4th–3rd centuries. A major theme of the book is role reversal (called *peripety*): from domination to downfall (Vashti, Haman, the Jews' enemies) and from certain doom to victory (Esther, Mordecai, the Jews). Though the book never mentions God, in our view the coincidences and reversals that drive the plot imply the hidden hand of divine providence at work.

The Story

The story of Esther has two main sections: the report concerning the origin of Purim (chs. 1–9) and an epilogue concerning Mordecai's relationship with

Ruins of the palace at Persepolis, one of the great centers of the Persian Empire. ©*Hansueli Krapf (Wikimedia Commons, CC-SA 3.0)*

the king (ch. 10). The long opening section recounts the deliverance of the Jews initiated by Mordecai and accomplished by Esther and ends with their decrees to establish Purim as an annual Jewish festival (9:18–32).

Chapters 1–2 set the scene with a description of the Persian Empire's geographical immensity and dazzling images of its diversity, imperial grandeur, and fabulous wealth. They introduce three of its four characters—King Ahasuerus (or Xerxes), a minor royal official named Mordecai, and Mordecai's cousin Esther, a beautiful, pleasant girl whom Ahasuerus selects to be his new queen. Beforehand, Mordecai and Esther had secretly agreed that her Jewish identity should remain a secret. Chapters 3–7 narrate the palace intrigue in which Mordecai and Esther secretly scheme to stop the annihilation of all Jews that has been decreed in the king's name by the story's villain, Haman, who is the Empire's new prime minister and descendant of an ancient Israelite enemy (1 Sam 15). The counterscheme begins in ch. 4 when, prodded by Mordecai, Queen Esther agrees to intervene with the king, accepting the mission's great risk with the memorable words, "If I perish, I perish." Thankfully, when approached, the king kindly grants Esther an audience and, more importantly, he and Haman attend three intimate banquets as her guests. At the third, Esther finally exposes Haman as the mastermind of the plot against the Jews, her own people, and the once-oblivious king angrily sentences Haman to be hanged on the very gallows the villain had prepared for Mordecai. Haman's execution marks the climactic, humiliating reversal of his fortunes after his success in manipulating the king to approve an annihilation plan.

Under Persian law, however, the original decree cannot be voided, so chs. 8–9 recount how decrees issued in the king's name by Mordecai and Esther save the Jews not only from Haman's plot but also from their other known enemies. Finally, in ch. 10 the story ends as it began except for a new wrinkle: Ahasuerus still sovereignly rules a vast Empire, but Mordecai, the once-despised Jew, now also enjoys prominence and influence in the royal court.

Esther in Recent Contexts

Recently, feminism and the Holocaust have raised two important questions: How are we to interpret Esther in light of feminist concerns? And how does the Jewish experience of the Holocaust during World War II impact interpretation of the book of Esther today?

Feminists interpret the book as both sexist and racist: its plot features the violent oppression of women and Jews. Ambivalence about the character of Esther also prevails. Some writers suggest that modern women honor and emulate her piety, beauty, and political intelligence; some esteem Esther as a hero like Deborah, whose seizure of leadership (see 4:11) produces positive results. But for others Esther embodies a "good citizenship" model for women living under oppression—that they seek to get along with rather than to oppose present male power structures. Instead, they find a more robust and desirable heroine in Vashti and her beauty, independence, and pride. Her refusal to serve as a royal sex-object on display models a strong female character more congenial to the concerns of modern women. Finally, feminists propose that an intriguing dialogue underlies the three versions of Esther: the Hebrew version (MT) mirrors a male perspective and promotes the submission of women to men; the first Greek story (LXX) exposes and critiques that hidden male bias; but the second Greek story (the so-called "A-Text") reflects the MT's more sexist view.

The experience of the Holocaust (or the *Shoah*) has now made the book of Esther the most difficult biblical book for Jews. The primary problem is that God did not providentially save them from annihilation in 20th-century Europe as he did in 5th-century BCE Persia. As a result, Marvin Sweeney calls for a radical rethinking of how we theologize about Esther. From the book's secular and vengeful nature, he suggests its main point: when God fails to intervene, humans are responsible to seek the defeat of evil as God's partner in creation. In his view, the book also challenges Christian readers to choose whether to acquiesce in the destruction of Jews and Judaism or to identify themselves with Jews even to death. He asks Christians to reckon with the Jewishness of the OT and to make the acceptance of the legitimacy of Judaism and of the Jewish people an axiom of Christian theology.

What about All the Violence?

Christians may have a hard time with this book and what strikes readers as vengeful Jewish nationalism that foments the slaughter of tens of thousands of "innocent" people. Such misgivings are understandable: the deadly danger that drives the book probably lies outside most people's experience, and the very idea of violence by God's people bumps up against Jesus's teachings against it. In fairness, however, we recommend that readers take seriously how often in history Jews have faced just such death-threats from non-Jews. Recognize also that, according to the book, the Jews only killed their "enemies" (i.e., those who threatened them) and that they also kept no plunder (i.e., there was no profit motive in play). Recall, further, that Purim celebrates not the destruction of other people but the providential deliverance of the Jews from annihilation specifically by those hostile to them. One could argue, along with many Jewish scholars, that the book actually narrates an act of justice in defense of a beleaguered Jewish community, an act rooted in the universal human right of and responsibility for endangered people to protect themselves. In short, we suggest that readers interpret Esther within the context of ancient Persian society and from a Jewish perspective.

Is Esther Historical?

You may find this question surprising—and you may even reply, "Of course it's historical. It's in the Bible!" Of course, much of the Bible narrates history (we argue, literarily in the narrative form of story), but we caution readers to leave open the possibility that Scripture may reflect a variety of literary forms. The danger that the default setting of "history" poses to our reading of the Bible is that it may lead us to filter out important—even crucial—dimensions of the text intended by original writers.

So, why do most scholars treat Esther as fiction? First, they allege that Esther has some historical discrepancies that create doubt regarding its historicity. For example, Esth 1:1 says that Ahasuerus ruled 127 satrapies (*medinot*), whereas in Herodotus, a Greek historian (ca. 400 BCE), the number is 20, and 23–30 in an inscription of the king's father, Darius (compare with Dan 6:1, where the figure is 120). On the other hand, in Hebrew *medinot* also designates "provinces" (see Ezra 2:1; Neh 1:3; 7:6), so the higher number in Esth 1:1 probably counts "provinces" within the 20–30 satrapies. Second, scholars argue that the book invokes literary devices more typical of fiction than sober history-writing (e.g., stereotyped characters, hyperbole, irony, and humor).

Nevertheless, we think it reasonable to assume that some actual historical event stands behind the origin and celebration of Purim as told by the Esther story. Without the story, what would Purim celebrate, and why would people later accept a made-up story that originally had no ties to Purim? In our view, Esther is historical in that it passes on Jewish testimony of a remarkable moment of salvation back in history, albeit in a unique, novelistic form. Its telling cleverly embellishes the story's historical core for edification and enjoyment. We describe its genre as novelized history—the memories of historical events reported as a traditional, clever story. As Karen Jobes notes, the real question which the book poses to us is not whether the story is history or fiction but how are we to understand it as both.

READING

Read Esth 1–10 and formulate answers to the questions that follow:

1. Describe your perception of the book's main characters (King Ahasuerus, Haman, Mordecai, and Esther). What's their family back-

PART 4

The Prophets

20 WHAT IS HEBREW POETRY?

POETRY COMPRISES ABOUT ONE-THIRD OF the Bible, most obviously in the "poetical books" (Job, Psalms, Proverbs, Ecclesiastes, and Song of Songs), but also in the prophets. Further, narratives prominently feature several long poems—the Song of the Sea (Exod 15) and the Song of Deborah (Judg 5)—along with smaller snippets such as the "Song of the Well" (Num 21:17-18). The prominence of poetry in the OT makes an understanding of Hebrew poetry an important tool for any Bible reader.

What Is Poetry?

Most readers can spot biblical poetry by its most obvious feature—the extra white space around it in our Bibles. But what is it? Basically, poetry is a form of oral or written communication with highly structured, brief sentences and vivid, evocative words. Prose has its own structures, and it may also use brief sentences and evocative words, but poetry uses them to a greater degree than prose. So, we should think of prose and poetry not simply as opposites but as the ends of a continuum (see Table 20.1). In general, the more structurally compact, emotionally intense, and metaphorically worded a composition is, the closer it approaches the poetry end of the spectrum. By the same token, the more discursive, abstract, and prosaic the composition, the closer it comes to the prose end. Two unique dynamics of poetry—its use of words and the structure called parallelism—underlie its unique power to communicate. Indeed, unlike prose, poetry's evocative words and images appeal to the imagination rather than the mind, and it touches our emotions as well. Before examining it further, however, we might ask how Hebrew poetry compares to the English poetry most familiar to us.

How Hebrew Poetry Compares (or Doesn't) to English Poetry

In some ways, English poetry and Hebrew poetry are much alike (see Table 20.2). They both have the same basic elements, the single poetic lines that, when strung together in a series, compose a poem. Both wield vivid language and wordplays, and both seek to communicate abstract ideas through concrete images. Both employ *rhythm* (or *meter*) and *rhyme* but in different ways. Basically, English poetry produces its *meter* by alternating within a poetic line between stressed and unstressed syllables according to fixed patterns. In an *iambic* pattern, for example, each line combines two-beat (unstressed-STRESSED) sounds with the stress on the second syllable—as in "I SAW three SHIPS come SAIL-ing IN on CHRIST-mas DAY, on CHRIST-mas DAY . . . ." *Trochaic* meter, by contrast, features the opposite pattern: that is, STRESSED-unstressed—as in "MA-ry HAD a LIT-tle LAMB, its FLEECE was WHITE as SNOW. . . ."

Instead of fixed meter patterns, however, Hebrew poetry shows a kind of loose meter we might call free rhythm. Its poetic lines combine stressed and unstressed syllables but not in a discernible, standard, fixed pattern.

Table 20.1. The Prose-Poetry Spectrum

Poetry	Poetic Prose	Prose
Ps 97:1–2 (TNIV) The LORD reigns, let the earth be glad; let the distant shores rejoice. Clouds and thick darkness surround him; righteousness and justice are the foundation of his throne.	*Ruth 2:12 (authors' translation)* May the LORD repay you for what you've done. May your wages be paid in full by the LORD, the God of Israel, under whose wings you have come to take refuge.	*Gen 1:1–3 (authors' translation)* In the beginning God created the heavens and the earth. Now the earth was a vacant wasteland; darkness was over the surface of the deep, and the Spirit of God was hovering over the waters. And God said, "Let there be light," and there was light.

Also, the lines have similar but not the exact same length. In other words, Hebrew poetry typically avoids pairing a very long line with a very short line (and vice versa). Unlike English poetry, Hebrew poetry does not have end-rhyme, in which the final words of poetic lines rhyme. (Sometimes Hebrew poetic lines end with rhyming words but not as a rule.) Instead, Hebrew poets love to use rhyming words—that is, puns or sound plays—between similar-sounding words in the same line and in the immediately following line. Their puns often include alliteration (the same or similar consonant sounds) and assonance (the same or similar vowel sounds). Note Isa 1:24 (TNIV), for example:

Ah,	I will vent my wrath	on my foes
hoy	*'ennakhem*	*mitsaray*
and	avenge myself	on my enemies.
ve	*'innaqemah*	*me'oyevay*

Notice the pairing of both line-initial and line-ending rhyming sounds (*'ennakhem mitsaray // 'innaqemah me'oyevay*). Note also the use of both alliteration (initial "*en-*" and "*m-*" sounds) and assonance (two -*ay* and one *oy* sounds).

In Isa 5:7 (TNIV) two key rhyming wordplays in the final two lines enhance the rhetorical power:

Table 20.2. The Characteristics of Poetry

Poetic Feature	English Poetry	Hebrew Poetry
Structure	Poetic line	Poetic line
Meter	Yes	"Free rhythm"
End rhyme	Yes	No (but rhyming words)
Rhetorical strategy	Abstract ideas through concrete images	Abstract ideas through concrete images
Metaphor	Yes	Yes
Special word use	Vivid language Wordplays	Vivid language Wordplays
Style	Word variation	Word repetition
Parallelism	No	Yes

between lines A and B (see below). It also shows the insights to be observed in reading the text slowly. Slow reads permit us to reflect on the words and their connotations—and especially the "binocular" sense they convey when taken together. It's like the difference between slowly savoring the flavors of a delicious meal and thoughtlessly gulping it down and rushing off to the day's next event. Rich insights and inspiration follow the slow savoring of poetry's words and their deliciously combined flavors.

Two-line couplets are typical of proverbs, but most Hebrew poems continue for many lines (i.e., lines C, D, E, etc.). Shortly, we will suggest the three major ways in which parallel lines interrelate, but for now, consider two examples of three-line parallelism (triplets):

	a	b	c	
A	those who seek	my life	lay their snares;	
	a'	b'	c'	
B	those who seek	to hurt me	speak of ruin,	
			c''	d
C	and	( )	meditate treachery	all day long.
				(Ps 38:12 NRSV)

The evidence that parallelism forms this verse is obvious. Structurally, each of the first two lines composes a complete sentence that begins with the same subject ("those who seek . . ."). Semantically similar terms ("snares," "treachery") also confirm parallelism's presence, as does their presumed common setting of conspiracy and danger. "To hurt me" in B voices the malevolent purpose of the snare-laying in A and the "treachery" in C. The three lines play off each other, thus briefly sketching the speaker's perilous situation. At first glance, "speak of ruin" in B seems to allude to public accusations against the victim, but since "lay their snares" and "meditate treachery" both concern secret scheming, "speak of ruin" may instead refer to confidential planning-discussions among coconspirators. Finally, the lone unparalleled element (d), a brief time reference ("all day long"), underscores the relentless obsession that drives the enemies. Again, read together, the three lines sketch out a situation of inescapable personal peril, their emotive language leading the reader to feel the speaker's fear and despair.

Psalm 130:5 offers a more complex triplet compared to the above example, most strikingly in its structure:

		a	b	c		
A		I	wait	for the LORD,		
		a′	b′	c′		
B		my whole being	waits,	( )		
				c′	a″	b″
C	and			in his word	I	put my hope.

(Ps 130:5 TNIV)

Line A and B are virtually synonymous (e.g., "wait," "waits"), but two differences distinguish line B. First, an ellipsis at the end (i.e., nothing parallels "for the LORD") makes it noticeably shorter than line A. Second, in line B the simple pronoun "I" becomes "my whole being," implying that the speaker's "waiting" is active rather than passive. No multitasking here! Rather, the wait fully engages the psalmist's whole being; it is focused and wholehearted. Interestingly, the ellipsis of line B carries over into line C, whose initial parallel link is with the last part of line A rather than with anything in line B ("for the LORD" // "in his word"). Line C thus introduces a new insight, the important role of Yahweh's "word"—God's spoken declarations, assurances, promises, and so on—in the waiting process. The main sentence follows and brings the whole triplet to an end ("I put my hope"). Those final words parallel the verbs in A and B ("wait," "waits"), and the result is that C reverses the word order of A and B. Such reversals produce an example of *chiasm*, a common phenomenon in biblical poetry and elsewhere (the literary device is called a *chiasm* because the reversed parallels form an imaginary *X*, the letter *chi* in Greek). The chiasm has two literary effects: on the one hand, it makes the motif of hope the triplet's closing thought; on the other, it poetically connects the verbs "wait"/"waits," and "hope" to associate their meanings. The poem understands that for the speaker to "wait" is to "hope" and to "hope" is to "wait." In other words, to "wait" means not passively to let time pass but actively to live with a firm sense of expectancy. Once again, to pause and savor the binocular view of parallelism enriches the reader's understanding of the poem.

Ways That Lines A and B (and C, D, E, etc.) Interrelate

The discussion above focused on recognizing the parallelism of words and phrases within lines and their contribution to the meaning. At this point, the question is: what is the relationship between poetic lines A, B, C, D, and so on as wholes? To answer this, we draw on Susan Gillingham's useful suggestion (pp. 78–87) that three main types of relationship bind poetic lines.

Type A = B. In the first type, lines A and B are interchangeable. That is, B in some way either echoes (i.e., repeats, restates, etc.) or contrasts with A (i.e., makes a different, if not opposite, point). Diagram 20.3 provides examples of both types with their parallelism scanned. Proverbs 14:15 clearly contrasts ("but") the dangerous gullibility of clueless folks who believe (and act!) on everything they hear without the prudent caution that guides the actions of the wise. In the example of simple restatement (Ps 95:1-2), all four lines feature cohortative verbs ("let us . . ."), all of which call for noisy actions directed to Yahweh

Diagram 20.2. Three Main Types of Parallelism

1. A = B

2. A > B

3. A < B

A, then B

Diagram 20.3. Line A Equals Line B

A = B   (A equals B)

Simple Restatement:		a	b	c	
	A	Come,	let us sing for joy	to the LORD;	
			b′	c′	d
	B	( )	let us shout aloud	to the Rock	of our salvation.
			b″	c″	d′
	C		Let us come	before him	with thanksgiving
			b‴	c‴	d″
	D and ( )		extol	him	with music and song.
	(Ps 95:1–2 TNIV)[a]				

Contrast:		a	b	c
	A	The simple	believe	anything,
		−a′	−b′	−c′
	B but the prudent		give thought to	their steps.
	(Prov 14:15 TNIV)[b]			

a. The absence of a parallel word or phrase is common in poetry. It is called *ellipsis*.
b. The "minus" signs indicate that line B offers a contrast to line A (i.e., it opens with "but").

(lines A, B) or concerned with Yahweh. Line A identifies Yahweh by name, while the parallel identifier in line B invokes a metaphorical nickname, the "rock of our salvation"—the always reliably secure place to which we flee to escape life-threatening dangers. Subtly, the rock metaphor hints at the reason undergirding the calls for shouts of praise: Yahweh's reputation as Israel's protector in danger. Another subtlety is a shift in focus from the identity of the addressee (lines A, B) to the means by which to praise Yahweh: with thanksgiving. And what is the means of giving thanksgiving? Line D clarifies the form by which one gives thanks: through music and songs.

Type A > B. With this parallelism, line A states the main idea, while B qualifies it in some way, thus bringing the main thought of A to a fuller completion. Grammatically, B is subordinate to A. As Diagram 20.4 sug-

Diagram 20.4. Line A Is Greater Than Line B

A > B (A Is Greater than B)   A = Main Clause, B = Subordinate Clause

A = Statement B = Time Clause	A	a By the rivers of Babylon,	b there we sat down	c and wept	
	B	a′ when	b′ we remembered		d Zion.
	(Ps 137:1, translation ours)				
A, B = Statement C, D = Reason	A	a Place me	b like a seal	c over your heart,	
	B	b′ ( )	like a seal	c′ on your arm;	
	C for	a love	b is	c as strong	d as death,
	D	a″ its jealousy	( )	c″ unyielding	d′ as the grave.
	(Song 8:6 TNIV)				
A = Statement B = Implication	A	a The LORD	b is	c my shepherd,	
	B	a′ I	b′ lack nothing.		
	(Ps 23:1 TNIV)				
A = Statement B = Result	A	a Mockers	b resent	c correction,	
	B	a′ so they	b′ avoid	c′ the wise.	
	(Prov 15:12 TNIV)				

gests, line B serves various functions to produce that completion. Sometimes it supplies a time reference to locate the statement of line A chronologically (Ps 137:1) or offers the motivation for its main thought (Song 8:6). Others draw out the implications (see Ps 23) or cite the result that flows from the main statement (Prov 15:12). The examples in the diagram in no way exhaust the possible ways in which B may support A, but they at least sample the variety of forms that fit this type of parallelism. Careful reading of poems will yield an even wider range of relationships between parallel poetic lines.

Several of the examples require additional brief comment lest their savory nuances be missed. Notice that Song 8:6 pairs two couplets (A + B, C + D), each with the A = B type of parallelism. Repeated or synonymous words clearly bind each of the line pairs as parallels. Their interrelationship with each other, however, follows the A > B pattern since C + D supplies the reason for what A + B affirms. More important, subtle differences between parallel elements enrich the overall sense we are to gain. In A + B the speaker asks her lover to, as it were, seal her on both his "heart" and his "arm," a combination implying his whole being (i.e., inner, outer)—or, in modern terms, "body and soul." A "seal" in the ancient world asserted the sealer's ownership and authority over its bearer, thereby symbolically declaring the sealed item off-limits to would-be intruders. The lover's twofold plea thus seeks the exclusive, loving devotion and public identification of her beloved with her. As the reason for this request, C points to the power of love—it is inexorably as powerful as death. As follow-up to C's general comment, however, D's words evoke a more specific image, comparing the reverse side of love ("jealousy") to a specific place, "the grave" (Heb. *she'ol*), the place where the dead reside. Also, if "death" (in general) is "strong," D pictures "jealousy" as "unyielding" (lit., "hard")—obstinate and tenacious. In short, true love demands the kind of tenacious, resolute devotion and belonging that say "no" to others and promise the beloved absolute, exclusive, loyal devotion.

The striking thing about Ps 23:1 is that line B is noticeably shorter than line A (three syllables versus five in Hebrew). One expects the parallel lines to compare in length, so the missing two syllables in line B give the verse an abrupt ending—in effect, a two-syllable silence in which to ponder line B's claim ("I lack nothing"). Literarily, the wordless moment allows the reader to meditate on the implication of having Yahweh as one's shepherd: incredible goodness and generosity. Finally, the Hebrew of Prov 15:12 lacks the word "so," but it is clear that line B reports the logical result of the mocker's aversion to correction: the mocker (lit.) "doesn't go to the wise" for advice.

Type A < B. In this type of parallelism, line A introduces an idea that line B further develops by expanding, complementing, or completing it. Grammatically, A is subordinate to B. Diagram 20.5 presents three subtypes of this pattern, which create comparison, dramatic effect, and continuation, respectively.

In Ps 103:13 the comparison juxtaposes a compassionate human father with compassionate Yahweh, line B asserting that the latter is just as compassionate as the former. But the objects of their compassion differ: a father's compassion extends to his "children," whereas Yahweh extends compassion to "those who fear him." In one sense, the Yahweh-fearers far outnumber the number of children in any given family, so the couplet may implicitly praise how much Yahweh's compassion surpasses that of a hu-

Diagram 20.5. Line A Is Less Than Line B

A < B   (A Is Less Than B)   A = Subordinate Clause, B = Main Clause

A = Comparison B = Statement			a	b	c		
	A	As	a father	has compassion	on his children,		
			a′	b′	c′		
	B	so	the LORD	has compassion	on those who fear him.		
	(Ps 103:13 TNIV)						

A = Statement B = Dramatic Effect			a	b	c	d	
	A	How	could	one man	chase	a thousand,	
				b′	c′	d′	
	B	or		two	put to flight	ten thousand?	
	(Deut 32:30a, italics and translation ours)						

A = Statement B = Continuation		a	b	c	d		e	f
	A You who bring good news	to Zion,						
	B			go up	on a high mountain.			
		a′	b′					
	C You who bring good news	to Jerusalem,						
	D			lift up your voice	with a shout,			
				c″			don't be afraid;	
	E			lift it up,				
				c‴	b″			
	F			say	to the towns of Judah,			
	G							"Here is your God!"
	(Isa 40:9 TNIV)							

man father. From another angle, the juxtaposition of "children" and "those who fear him" seems to imply that Yahweh reckons the latter as his children. In other words, what makes people Yahweh's children? High respect for God typifies them. Deuteronomy 32:30a lines up increased numbers in lines A and B for dramatic effect: a twofold increase in troop strength (line A "one" // line B "two") results in an astounding, tenfold rise in the number of troops routed ("a thousand" // "ten thousand"). The context, the Song of Moses, makes this point: the only way to account for the stunning defeat of a mighty army (Israel) by a hopelessly outnumbered force (their enemies) is that Israel's Rock, Yahweh, took the enemies' side. Between A and B, the escalation of numbers gives line B its dramatic, climactic effect.

Finally, though it is complex poetry, Isa 40:9 offers an example of continuation. Continuation occurs when subsequent lines in poems continue a sequence of events or thoughts begun by the preceding lines. It is the prominence of a sequence pursued through succeeding poetic lines that distinguishes this poetic strategy from simple restatement (A = B) or the juxtaposition of main and dependent clauses (A < B). Lines A and C are clearly parallel since both identify those addressed: a female messenger who brings good news to Zion/Jerusalem. As do all messengers, this one reaches Jerusalem from elsewhere—from wherever Yahweh is—to report the news and, most importantly, to announce the arrival there of God in person (see the last line). Lines B, D, E, and F are parallel because each features an imperative action by the messenger—and in the same position within each line. Two phrases, "Don't be afraid" and "Here is your God!" lack apparent parallels and consequently contribute uniquely to the theme of the poem. The former reassures the messenger lest her fears prevent her from speaking loudly, and the latter closes the verse and marks its unexpected climax. A close look at the verbs reveals that the lines commission the messenger to pursue the following sequence:

1. Ascend a high mountain;
2. then shout loudly (i.e., the twofold "Lift up [your voice]");
3. say specifically, "Here is your God."

In short, succeeding poetic lines in Isa 40:9 feature a continuation, instruction about what specific steps the messenger is to take to position herself and to shout loudly so that the cities of Judah listening below can hear.

Where Was Poetry Used?

Old Testament poetic sayings or songs arise primarily in connection with common life experiences and over time became the genre or wording used to mark those occasions. Births of children occasion poetic birth announcements—private news delivered to an expectant father (Jer 20:15; cf. Ruth 4:16) or public notice given to the expectant subjects of a royal family (Isa 9:6). Marriages also lead families and even whole towns to invoke poetic blessings on brides and grooms, and poems from the Song of Songs probably were sung at weddings (Gen 24:60; Ruth 4:11-12; compare Ps 45; Judg 14). Israelites also sing victory songs to commemorate national turning points and to extol Yahweh's invincible military prowess (Exod 15; Judg 5; compare Samson's boast, Judg 15:16). When work beckons, work songs such as the Song of the Well (Num 21:17-20) energize laborers doing construction or harvesting crops. Popular proverbs familiar to ordinary Israelites find their way into the public rhetoric of prophets (Jer 31:29; Ezek 18:2), who also coin their own sayings (e.g., Amos 3:8). Dirges give grieving Israelites the words with which to mourn the tragic deaths of children, comrades in arms, and even whole cities (Job 1:21; 2 Sam 1:17-27; Ezek 19; Lam 1, 2).

Finally, prophets creatively turn standard poetic genres on their heads to spring rhetorical surprises. Sung by Isaiah, a love song for some public occasion suddenly turns into an announcement of judgment on the audience (Isa 5:1-7). In Jeremiah's hands, a communal lament seeking the expected "yes" answer from Yahweh instead receives an emphatic, disappointing "no!" (Jer 14:1-12). As if standing before a coffin, Amos invokes a lament over Israel's national death as if it were already a reality (Amos 5:2). Finally, for his purpose, Joel reverses the popular "swords-into-plowshares" line of Isaiah and Micah (Isa 2:4; Mic 4:3) to read "plowshares into swords" (Joel 3:10). In short, Israelite poets understand the rhetorical power of poetry, including its creative reversal. Knowledge of the unique dynamics of poetry will enable the careful reader—slowing down, of course!—to savor the clever, imaginative words of Israel's poets and to feel the powerful grip of their poems. (For cultic poetry and royal psalms, see our ch. 32 on the Psalms; for wisdom and prophecy, see the appropriate introductory chapters.)

BIBLIOGRAPHY

Alter, Robert. *The Art of Biblical Poetry*. Rev. ed. New York: Basic Books, 2011.

Berlin, Adele. *The Dynamics of Biblical Parallelism*. Rev. ed. Grand Rapids: Eerdmans, 2008.

Boda, Mark J. "Poethics? The Use of Biblical Hebrew Poetry in Ethical Reflection on the Old Testament." *CurBR* 14 (2015): 45–61.

Dobbs-Allsopp, F. W. *On Biblical Poetry*. Oxford: Oxford University Press, 2015.

Eissfeldt, Otto. *Introduction to the Old Testament*. Translated by Peter Ackroyd. New York: Harper & Row, 1965.

Gillingham, Susan E. *The Poems and Psalms of the Hebrew Bible*. OBS. Oxford: Oxford University Press, 1994.

Heim, Knut. "How and Why We Should Read the Poetry of the Old Testament for Public Life Today." Pages 16–21 in *How and Why We Should Read the Old Testament for Public Life Today*. Edited by Ryan P. O'Dowd. Hamilton, ON: Cardus, 2011.

Klein, William W., Craig L. Blomberg, and Robert L. Hubbard, Jr. *Introduction to Biblical Interpretation*. 3rd ed. Grand Rapids: Zondervan, 2017.

Kugel, James. *The Idea of Biblical Poetry: Parallelism and Its History*. Baltimore: Johns Hopkins University Press, 1998.

Petersen, David L., and Kent H. Richards. *Interpreting Hebrew Poetry*. Guides to Biblical Scholarship. Minneapolis: Fortress, 1992.

Stewart, Anne W. *Poetic Ethics in Proverbs: Wisdom Literature and the Shaping of the Moral Self*. New York: Cambridge University Press, 2016.

21 WHO AND WHAT ARE THE PROPHETS?

I N CLASSICAL JUDAISM, THE THREE large scrolls of Isaiah, Jeremiah, and Ezekiel, along with a fourth scroll combining the smaller works of Hosea, Joel, Amos, Obadiah, Jonah, Micah, Nahum, Habakkuk, Zephaniah, Haggai, Zechariah, and Malachi comprise the Latter Prophets division. These complement the Former Prophets of Joshua, Judges, 1-2 Samuel, and 1-2 Kings in the Hebrew Bible. Judaism has traditionally understood these narrative books as representing a prophetic perspective in their presentation of Israel's history with God. The three large scrolls of Isaiah, Jeremiah, and Ezekiel are designated the Major Prophets, and the twelve works of the fourth scroll collectively constitute the Minor Prophets. There is a reference to the "Book of the Twelve" in the deuterocanonical book The Wisdom of Ben Sira (49:10), a Jewish work dated to the mid-2nd century BCE, which is the earliest reference to the fourth scroll noted above

Some of these terms and arrangements were taken over into the Christian tradition. The OT includes these fifteen books in its prophetic section, with the three Major Prophets followed by the twelve Minor Prophets in the same order. The one qualification to this statement is the inclusion of the book of Daniel between Ezekiel and Hosea. Daniel is also one of the Prophetic Books, but in the Hebrew Bible it is placed in the category known as the Writings (see ch. 25 below on Daniel). The books of Joshua, Judges, Samuel, and Kings are similarly kept together in the Christian OT and have traditionally been considered Historical Books (see ch. 13 on Ruth). This is not to deny a prophetic perspective to the narrative presentation in these books, but it does reflect a different category in the Christian canon (see Table 37.2 on pp. 478-79).

The Vision of Zechariah, by an unknown artist. Ca. 1300. The medieval painting depicts the first vision of the prophet Zechariah in 1:7–17.

What Is a Prophet?

The brief description above of the prophetic books in the OT does very little to define them. We are better off by first asking and addressing the basic question of what is a prophet in ancient Israel before returning to the exploration of the prophetic books.

There is no universal agreement about what a prophet is in the OT or in the ancient world generally. We should begin, however, with the vocabulary and characteristics of prophetic activity in the OT itself, recognizing that the data are but a subset of prophetic activity in ancient Israel. Our task is made a bit more difficult by later communities of faith that attributed the title or the function of *prophet* to any number of figures in the OT, even if there is little evidence to conclude that those persons understood themselves as a prophet. Nevertheless, this is an important factor for us to keep in mind when assessing the prophets. A figure is deemed a prophet, at least in part, because others think this about him or her.

First some basic vocabulary. The Greek word for *prophet* that underlies the English word refers to someone who speaks on behalf of another. The etymology of the Hebrew word *navi'*, typically translated "prophet" in English, is obscure but perhaps refers to a person who is calling or being called. We should not put much stock in the etymology of either word, because the established usage of terms is more important, but it is the case that speaking on behalf of God (or another deity) is a primary activity of a prophet in the OT. Two other terms for prophets support this basic profile. One is "man of God" (1 Sam 9:6 = Samuel; 1 Kgs 17:18 = Elijah), and the other is "seer," referring to the perception of the prophet in receiving a message from God (1 Sam 9:9; Amos 1:1; 7:12; Isa 2:1), whether in a vision or some other medium such as a dream. Anthropologists and sociologists often describe a prophet as an intermediary between the divine and human worlds. This fits the profile of a prophet in Israel. Some would also use the term "diviner" to describe a prophet. Although helpful for comparative purposes, that term includes a wide range of ritual practices that are not attested in the OT or are even forbidden (cf. Deut 13:1-11).

Prophets are known among Israel's neighbors as well (Num 22-24; 1 Kgs 18:19). Indeed prophets and prophetic activity had a recognized place in the broader ANE society. There are references to them in extrabiblical texts, but no corpus of prophetic texts survives that matches the scope of the prophetic literature in the OT.

One may compile a basic profile of a prophet from the narrative descriptions of them. Three passages are helpful in this regard.

1 Kings 22. Note that the various prophetic figures in 1 Kgs 22 did not agree with one another! Micaiah ben Imlah, a prophet among others in the account, was called on by the kings of Israel and Judah to speak a word from the LORD regarding a decision to go to war with the Aramaeans. Prophets were important for discerning the will of God for Israel's leaders. Micaiah claims that he was privy to the Lord's conversation with his heavenly council (1 Kgs 22:1-28) and that he knows God's disposition regarding the Israelite king. He even reports that the prophets who have advised the king that he will succeed in war have a lying spirit sent by God! This visionary report would qualify him as a "seer" and in modern anthropological terms also as a diviner (he was able to discern a message from the divine world). Note also that another prophet, Zedekiah, made horns and used them to illustrate his message that the Israelite king would prevail in battle. Prophets sometimes illustrated their messages with symbolic acts.

2 Samuel 11:1-12:15. Note the language of "sending" in 2 Sam 11-12. Various figures in the story "send" a person or message in order to accomplish a task. David's crimes displeased the Lord, who "sends" Nathan to confront the king and to announce that there would be consequences to his acts of murder and adultery. Nathan is, in effect, the Lord's representative, sent to deliver his message. We might compare this to the vision report in 1 Kgs 22:19-23, where the Lord sends one of the host of heaven (= angels) to carry out a task on earth. Interestingly, the writers do not reveal in the account how Nathan knew of the plan to have Uriah killed.

Amos 7:10-17.   Amaziah is a priest, which means that he too speaks on behalf of God. So how does he see his role vis-à-vis Amos? Amaziah claims that the land of Israel cannot bear Amos's prophecies, which were indeed harshly critical of King Jeroboam II. He urges Amos, whom he calls a "seer" (7:12), to leave Bethel so that he can prophesy for money elsewhere. Amos seems to deny that he is a prophet in the professional sense of seeking remuneration, but he insists that the Lord has commissioned him to prophesy. Two conceptions of prophecy, both of which can be illustrated from the OT, are thus set before the reader. Amaziah understood prophecy to be a fee-based vocation, perhaps akin to fortune-telling or personal advice on religious matters (compare 1 Sam 9:5-8). After all, he too was a religious professional, serving at the sanctuary supported by Jeroboam II and receiving income from the tithes and offerings brought to Bethel. Amos labored under the conviction that God had shown him a message (see Amos 1:1; 7:1-9; 8:1-3) and that he must deliver it in Israel, regardless of personal or professional matters.

It is certainly true that other figures (who aren't called prophets) speak for God in the OT and in the ancient world. Priests, for example, speak for God in cultic matters and officiate at sacrificial ceremonies. They too can be prophets (e.g., Moses, Samuel, Jeremiah, Ezekiel). The priesthood in the temple, however, was limited to male Levites and was an inherited office. Prophets also spoke about matters of sacrifice and worship or the requirements of Torah, but they could be male or female and were not limited to the tribe of Levi. Moreover, the phenomenon of prophecy, although it was a recognized institution in Israel like the priesthood, did not need to be an inherited office or associated with a sanctuary. Prophets such as Nathan could serve at the royal court, which means that they held an "office" or fulfilled an officially designated role of prophet. Other prophets, such as Micaiah ben Imlah (or Elijah and Elisha) and Amos, stood over against the ruler of the day and sometimes against other court-supported prophets and priests. One of the primary characteristics of the prophetic books in the OT is the amount of critical assessment of Israel and Judah they contain.

How to Tell a "True" (versus a "False") Prophet

A "true" prophet . . .

1. Announces God's true message because he/she personally heard it decided at the "heavenly council" (Jer 23:18, 22)
2. Does not lead people away from worshiping the Bible's God (Deut 13:1–3; Jer 23:13)
3. Points out the sins of God's people (Mic 3:8) rather than supporting evildoers (Jer 23:14)
4. Mainly announces doom (Jer 28:8)
5. When announcing hope, can only be verified by waiting to see if his/her announcement comes true (Deut 18:22; Jer 28:9)
6. Does not tailor his/her message to please either the audience addressed or the one paying for it (Mic 3:5)

Prophecy in Israel and Judah: A Quick Overview

It is wrong to think of prophecy as originating in Israel with the individuals named in the prophetic books, even though a figure such as Isaiah or Jeremiah typically comes to mind when modern readers think of an OT prophet. The earliest person called a prophet in the OT is actually Abraham (Gen 20:7), and his prophetic act was that of an intercessor with God. Intercession with God was certainly a prophetic activity (see Jer 15:1) although, again, prayer was not limited to prophets. This is the only reference in the OT to Abraham as a prophet, and it is instructive for at least two reasons: (1) It illustrates the fact that a person may act prophetically at a particular time but not be widely known or thought of otherwise as a prophet. And as noted above, (2) there were several biblical figures who were subsequently understood to speak or act prophetically, whether or not this was their self-understanding or the perception of many of their contemporaries. In the later communities of Judaism, Christianity, and Islam, many persons in the OT, Abraham included, are considered prophets, or something about their life is understood as having been prophetic (see Acts 2:30).

In Deuteronomy Moses is depicted as a prophet, indeed the paradigm of a prophet (Deut 18:15; 34:10). He was also receptive to others who were prompted by the Spirit of the Lord to engage in prophetic activity (Num 11:26–29). Moses combined mediation of God's Torah with insight into its ongoing application, plus he projected what Israel's future would entail, given its disobedience (Deut 30; 32 = a prophetic song). The warnings in Deuteronomy about syncretism and apostasy are the mirror-opposite of faithfully consulting the Torah in covenant obedience. Authentic prophecy in Israel should follow Moses's example.

Deborah, one of the judges of Israel, was also a prophetess (Judg 4:4–5). There is no elaboration in the text on her prophetic activities; perhaps they are associated indirectly with her judicial and administrative functions. Possibly her victory song celebrating the defeat of Sisera (Judg 5:2–31) may be understood as prophetically inspired. Miriam, the sister of Moses, is called a prophetess in the context of her singing the "Song of the Sea," a poetic hymn celebrating the defeat of Pharaoh's army at the Sea of Reeds (Exod 15:1–18, 20–21). Several of the judges were seized by God's Spirit (3:10; 6:34; 11:29; 14:6; 15:14) and were used to deliver the people. Since spirit possession can also be a characteristic of a prophet (Num 11:26–29; 1 Sam 10:11; 19:23–24), including ecstatic behavior, Deborah's prophetic identity could have been related to the charisma of the Spirit.

Table 21.1. Prophets in the Preexilic Historical Books

Prophet	Date	Person Anointed/ Appointed	Person Advised[a]	Scripture
Samuel	10th c.	King Saul	King Saul	1 Sam 3:20; 9:9
		King David	King David	1 Sam 16
Gad	10th c.		King David	1 Sam 22:5; 2 Sam 24:11
Nathan	10th c.		King David	2 Sam 7; 2 Sam 12; 1 Kgs 1
Ahijah of Shiloh	10th c.	King Jeroboam I (Israel)	King Jeroboam I (Israel)	1 Kgs 11:28–39; 1 Kgs 14
Jehu	9th c.	King Baasha (Israel)	King Baasha (Israel)	1 Kgs 16:7, 12
Elijah	9th c.	King Hazael (Aram)	King Ahab (Israel)	1 Kgs 17–19
		Prophet Elisha		1 Kgs 19:15
		King Jehu (Israel)		1 Kgs 19:16
			King Ahaziah (Israel)	2 Kgs 1
Micaiah ben Imlah	9th c.		"King of Israel"	1 Kgs 22
			King Jehoshaphat	
Elisha	9th c.		Prophets from Jericho	2 Kgs 2:15–18
			People of Jericho	2 Kgs 2:19–22
			Boys at Bethel	2 Kgs 2:23–25
			King Joram (Israel)	2 Kgs 3
			King Jehoshaphat (Judah)	
			Prophet's Widow	2 Kgs 4:1–7
			Woman of Shunem[b]	2 Kgs 4:8–37
			The Prophets	2 Kgs 4:38–41
			His Servant	2 Kgs 4:42–44
		King Hazael (Aram)[c]	"The king of Israel"	2 Kgs 5
		King Jehu (Israel)[c]	Prophets	2 Kgs 6:1–7
			"King of Aram"	2 Kgs 6:8–23
			"King of Israel"	
			"The king" and "the officer"	2 Kgs 6:24–7:20
			King Hazael (Aram)	2 Kgs 8:7–15
			King Jehu (Israel)	2 Kgs 9
			King Jehoash (Israel)	2 Kgs 13:14–21

Prophet	Date	Person Anointed/ Appointed	Person Advised[a]	Scripture
Jonah	8th c.		Jeroboam II (Israel)	2 Kgs 14:25
			King of Assyria	Jonah 3
Isaiah	8th c.		King Hezekiah (Judah)[d]	2 Kgs 19–20
Huldah	7th c.		King Josiah (Judah)	2 Kgs 22:14

a. We mean by the word *advised* a range of interactions, including appointments and confrontations, promises and condemnations, and so on.
b. See 2 Kgs 8:1–6.
c. Apparently, although Elisha actually anointed the kings, the compiler of 1–2 Kgs understands Elisha's actions as implementing the earlier commission to Elijah.
d. For Isaiah's interaction with King Hezekiah's predecessor, King Ahaz (Judah), see Isa 7; compare Isa 14:28.

It is with the rise of the monarchy that frequent references to prophets begin (see Table 21.1). On the one hand, readers are at the mercy of their sources, and both Kings and Chronicles evidence prominent roles for prophets during the united and divided monarchies. On the other hand, this fits with a recognized pattern in the ancient Near East, where prophets provided theological warrant and guidance for monarchs. One has only to think of Samuel, the priest/judge and prophet, in his relationship with Saul, or of Nathan, David's candid adviser, noted previously. It is also the case that Samuel and Kings present prophets as independent messengers of the cosmic Lord who might speak in judgment on or opposition to royal policies (as did Elijah, Micaiah, and Elisha). Thus, with the rise of figures such as Amos and Isaiah, whose prophetic work resulted in scrolls preserving their words and bearing their name, the institution of prophecy was not in its infancy but in full-blown strength. The prophets of the 8th–7th centuries BCE frequently challenged Israel and Judah corporately, predicting judgment to come upon the people and major social institutions, and on occasion announced judgment on the evil of the enemies (e.g., Nahum).

Prophecy continued after the political demise of Israel (722 BCE) and Judah (587 BCE). In the postexilic or Second Temple period, prophets (Haggai and Zechariah) urged the rebuilding of the temple, and others criticized (Joel and Malachi) their contemporaries for their lack of piety and for their disobedience to divine command. There are also at least two new "tones" or emphases among the postexilic prophets: (1) their language of judgment on Judah and Jerusalem does not typically have the full-blown corporate harshness of their preexilic counterparts; (2) their language and style of presentation has more symbolism and a broader eschatological horizon than their preexilic counterparts, although this is more a matter of degree than kind in both cases.

The postexilic books of the Latter Prophets all date to the period of Persian hegemony (538-330 BCE), with the possible exception of the last chapters of Zechariah, which some interpreters suggest come from the early period of Greek control. Josephus, a Jewish author in the first Christian century, likely reflected a common understanding of his day in claiming that an "exact succession" of the prophets in Israel ended during the time of Persian rule (*Against Apion* 1.38-41). This view should not be pressed to mean it was popularly believed among later Jews that prophecy had ceased altogether in the Persian period. Josephus more likely is providing his take on the ending of the prophetic collection (and the end of what became the Hebrew Bible), but with sporadic prophetic activity continuing into his own day.

Prophetic Speaking and Acting

The writing down of prophetic messages appears for the most part to be a secondary activity, although it was integral to the writings' reception as an authoritative collection. A number of passages in the prophetic books begin with "hear" or "listen," still preserving the predominantly oral nature of the prophetic enterprise as originally carried out. But whether oral or written, prophetic discourse was typically delivered in forms recognizable by their contemporaries and intended to convict or persuade an audience. Skills in the rhetoric of a culture are important to public communicators who want to be "heard" or "read" by their contemporaries. Those who want to be heard have a better chance of success if they are keen observers and have learned the implicit communication skills of a culture. Of course, being heard and being persuasive are two different things!

A statement that begins "thus says / has said the Lord. . ." is patterned on the speech of messengers commissioned by a master to speak on his or her behalf (see Gen 32:3-5; Amos 1:3, 6, 9, 11, 13; 2:1, 4, 6). A word that begins "the Lord has a case against ___" plays on the language of the judicial court (see Exod 23:2-6; Deut 1:12; 19:17; Mic 6:1-5; Isa 3:13). A prophet could use a song (Isa 5:1-7), a psalm (Isa 12:1-6), an interrogative lament (Jer 12:1-6; Hab 1:2-4), or a funeral cry (Amos 5:1-2). Prophets could draw on the language and ritual of public worship (Joel 2:12-17) or on the task of a watchman (Hab 2:1). The question of going to war in antiquity was not only an issue of political strategy but also of seeking the will of the gods. As noted above, prophets, among others, were consulted (see 1 Kgs 22:3-6). Prophetic oracles against other nations (of which there are many in the prophetic books) or predictions about a future decisive "day of the Lord" may be rooted in the deliberation about war and the seeking of the divine will.

Although prophets could use prose discourse, much of what is preserved about their public speaking is poetry. Poetry was a public art form, a rhetorical style that is common to the great hymns and prayers of the Psalter and prophetic speech (see ch. 20 above on poetry). Prophets were public communicators, rhetoricians who crafted their public speech for dramatic effect and ease of remembrance.

Prophets also enacted or embodied aspects of their message. Their (symbolic) acts were an extension of their rhetorical strategy, designed first as dramatic embodiments of their message and second to persuade observers of the truth of their message. Zedekiah, one of the prophets who served Ahab, wore a pair of iron horns to illustrate his conviction that the Lord would give the Aramaeans into Ahab's hand, so that the king would "gore" them (1 Kgs 22:11). Isaiah of Jerusalem went naked and barefoot for three years as a sign to Egypt and Judah (Isa 20:1-6) that their current plans would lead to disaster and the stripping of Judah's inhabitants. Jeremiah wore a yoke as a sign that the Lord had yoked Judah and its neighbors in servitude to Nebuchadnezzar (Jer 27:1-22). Ezekiel undertook several bizarre acts as illustrations of Judah's failure, the siege of Jerusalem, and the judgment of exile (Ezek 4:1-5:17). Prophets' families were even used as signs. Hosea and Isaiah named children as signs of their message (Hos 1:2-9; Isa 7:1-9; 8:1-4). And Ezekiel did not mourn the death of his wife, as custom and propriety required, so that her death and his reaction would be a sign to his contemporaries (Ezek 24:15-27).

We would be amiss to think of the prophets as "lone rangers," even if the conclusion of "eccentric" or "strange" for some of them seems inescapable. Unfortunately, little is preserved about prophetic communities, disciples, and other support systems, but they surely existed. During the time of Elijah and Elisha there are references to the sons of the prophets or the company of the prophets (2 Kgs 2:1-5). Moreover, on occasion the writers simply report that an unnamed prophet from one of the communities carried out a function (1 Kgs 20:35-43). Isaiah's book preserves a reference to his disciples (8:16), and Jeremiah's life and written legacy would have

ment through the historical process—from the individual oracle or saying through to its representation in a written, edited collection. Both emphases have borne fruit for the understanding of prophetic activity. In recent years there has been more attention given to the shape and function of a prophetic book as a document. This is essentially a *synchronic* approach: taking the book as a whole and investigating the shape of its presentation for readers. Less attention is given to the historical figure of the prophet or to the stages of the book's formation, though these things are not necessarily ignored. Moreover, increased attention has been paid to what can be called *reception history*: the way in which people past and present have interpreted the book.

Introducing a Prophetic Point of View: Eschatology

Before turning to individual prophetic books, we may find it profitable to reflect on the phenomenon of OT prophecy through the lens of one of its pronounced characteristics—namely, depictions of the future. This will assist us yet again with an angle of vision toward what makes an OT prophetic book "prophetic." In popular imagination, prophets are the persons who predict the future. For a number of people, religiously inclined or not, this is the basic definition of a prophet. So pronounced has been this view that religious progressives in the 19th and 20th centuries countered its influence by saying that the OT prophets were as much *forth-tellers* as foretellers. That allowed them to underscore what is indeed a core value in the prophetic books, the importance of justice and righteousness among God's people and the societies in which they live. Think of the great quotation of Mic 6:8 that is so often used in this regard:

> What does the Lord require of you, but to do justice, to love kindness, and to walk humbly with your [our!] God?

It is also the case that Micah, like most of the prophetic books, projects a future for readers that is unlike their present (or ours). We can call this a form of forth-telling, in that it moves forth initially from the circumstances of the prophet's contemporaries and provides a future perspective for their consideration. It could entail judgment, as in 3:12, where judgment on Jerusalem is announced because of the city's wickedness, or it could portray future peace among various peoples, as the Lord's justice is meted out among the nations to ensure a peaceful existence (4:1–5). We could also call this a form of *foretelling*, since it depicts a time and type of existence that are not yet evident (then or now) and that depend on divine activity.

The prophetic books are unique among the OT writings in the emphasis given to depictions about a future that the Lord will bring to pass. We can obtain a better overall grasp of their particular profile in the OT, therefore, with some attention to this emphasis. It is also the case that the prophetic books are the primary written sources for the depictions of the future in classical Judaism and the NT.

The Term Eschatology

The English word *eschatology* is derived from a Greek term meaning "the last things." It is a term widely used in theological discourse to refer to conceptions about future hope, judgment to come, the transformation of the world, and even eternity itself—all topics with biblical roots. And so interpreters can use the term to describe prophetic conceptions of the future, although strictly speaking, not all of the relevant prophetic texts concern the last things as understood in later Judaism and Christianity. Prophetic texts may simply refer to a decisive change to come at some future point. Such change may be imminent (e.g., return from exile) or remote (e.g., the gathering of nations to Mount Zion). Moreover, relatively little is said in prophetic texts about resurrection from the dead, a key component of "last things" as they touch on eternity itself, though quite a bit is said about God's transforming acts to come in the ongoing historical process. One can compare the prophetic announcements of judgment on Israel and Judah to a death sentence and the future that the books project to a new gift of life (see Ezek 37). So we use the term *eschatology* broadly in reference to prophetic depictions about the future and, particularly, to decisive, fundamental changes in the future such as new temples, new covenants, and even new heavens and a new earth. Perhaps we might think of the prophets' future projections as deriving from "baptized imaginations," that is, from people whose intuitive and imaginative abilities are touched by God in order to represent spiritual truth in profound and unexpected ways.

The prophetic eschatological texts are primarily announcements of salvation, predictions of future change/transformation, and vision reports full of symbolism. The defeat of evil and even death itself, however, also entails struggle and judgment. The prophets do not present eschatological doctrine in systematic form. One can move from the data to formulating some broad lines of development in prophetic claims about the future, but precision in such matters, particularly in seeking to reconstruct a linear development of eschatological thinking, is not possible. Part of the problem comes with the process of compiling the prophetic books (see above). In their portrait of a prophet's life and words, ancient editors compiled, shaped, and augmented the materials at hand. In re-presenting the prophets, the books have somewhat dehistoricized them, on occasion submerging the "original context" of some texts and placing them in a new context for readers. In their historical analysis, modern scholars have made distinctions in the portrait (particularly in the oracles about the future) between what they think original to the prophet and what they surmise is the work of the editors in "updating" a message for a new audience. This is a necessary and worthwhile effort, but as might be expected, interpreters have not always agreed on the extent to which prophetic projections about the future derive from the prophets themselves or from editors. Indeed, such interpretive discussions vary significantly from book to book, but it must be kept in mind that the issues of dating and authenticity are particularly acute for the oracles concerning the future.

In the final analysis, historical dissection and the quest for the authenticity of oracles are not the final word about the value of the material in a prophetic book, as if the work of an editor is less valuable than the work of the prophets themselves. Jewish and Christian communities of faith have accepted the books as they stand, not the hypothetical reconstruction of their literary prehistory, however valuable the quest for origins and the dating of individual oracles might be.

The Example of Jerusalem

Isaiah personified the Jerusalem of his day as a prostitute, a city with corrupt leadership, but a city that would again become a center of justice (1:21–27). This portrayal of Jerusalem assumes the city had a positive role in the past (during David's time?). Isaiah (2:2–4) shares with Micah (4:1–5) a vision that the Jerusalem of the future will be a place of pilgrimage for nations that will come to the city to receive instruction from the Lord and to rid themselves of the implements of war. The holy mountain of Jerusalem, where the temple was located, is the place Jesse's greater son will rule, and the wolf will lie down with the lamb (Isa 11:1–9; cf. 9:1–7). Isaiah represents yet another eschatological tradition for Jerusalem: that of renaming it in the future as evidence of its transformation (Isa 1:26; cf. Jer 33:16; Ezek 48:35). Jerusalem's metaphorical transformation from widow and divorcee to the mother of returning exiles and the place of pilgrimage for others is a prominent theme in Isa 40–66. These are the prophecies of the Second and Third Isaiah. To signify its change of status and its still-future transformation, Jerusalem receives new or additional names (Isa 60:14; 62:1-12). Joel predicts that armies will gather for battle but that Jerusalem will be the center of the new commonwealth that the Lord will establish (Joel 2:28–3:21).

In the symbolic visions of Ezekiel (40–48), an angel shows the prophet a Jerusalem the topography of which has vastly changed and in which a new temple is set. The visions come after a time of conflict between Israel/Judah and the wicked forces of Gog (a symbolic name in Ezek 38–39). As a prophet from the exile, Ezekiel describes visions designed to give hope to those who long for restoration; however, the Jerusalem of the vision is obviously not the city and sanctuary of the postexilic period (when the book of Ezekiel is compiled). The visions, therefore, of Ezek 40–48 are best understood as eschatological in scope—another form of the larger tradition of a peaceable kingdom yet to come. They are also the source of several items in John's vision of a heavenly Jerusalem that will come down and of the new heavens and earth in Rev 21–22.

Zechariah's last three chapters contain descriptions of the future day of the Lord, with strife and convulsions engulfing Jerusalem and its inhabitants. These chapters may stem from editorial work done to supplement Zech 1–8 and 9–11. The symbolism in them is as pronounced as that in Ezekiel, with travail in the ascendancy until God's victory is revealed. A restored and purified Jerusalem is the climax/conclusion of the prophecies. The symbolic, allusive language, with angels and visions, and the pronounced struggle between good and evil, of which the last chapters are but a part are rooted in an apocalyptic mind-set and literary expression. An apocalyptic mind-set understands the human community as being involved in a larger cosmic struggle between good and evil, with God's people under threat or oppression; but God will be victorious at the end, and the world will be transformed. Readers see elements of this literary style and mind-set as early as the book of Ezekiel, with portions of Joel and Zechariah following suit, and Daniel is strongly shaped by them.

One can sense from this brief survey that the prophetic texts pulse with visions and portrayals of a future that only God can bring about.

What Do the Prophetic Books Do for Israel?

We noted above that the prophetic books provide readers with words and deeds from the past because they remained relevant for subsequent generations. Many of them explained the past, accounting for such things as the fall of Israel to the Assyrians and that of Judah to the Babylonians. They showed that in time of crisis, the Lord had raised up messengers to point out failure, announce pending judgment, and convey the need for change. Subsequent generations could learn from these things, finding negative examples to avoid and positive examples to follow.

The prophetic books helped Israel and Judah come to grips with failure. In doing so, they also offered the people various insights into an expanded sense of identity as God's people in the world. Political defeat and exile brought an end to certain kinds of corporate existence but became the basis for other ways of continuing on as the people of God.

The prophetic books encourage readers to act responsibly on their faith commitments. Some of the books advocate for justice and righteousness, others for holiness and resolve in the face of difficulties. The prophetic books also offer hope for a transformed future for the people of God and the community of nations. They remind readers that God is a moral judge, whose past and present acts in history are a prelude to more-fundamental change.

READING

After reading this chapter, please formulate answers to the following questions:

1. Having looked at 1 Kgs 22; 2 Sam 11:1–12:15; and Amos 7:10–17, how would you define the role of a prophet?

2. Are there prophets in the modern world? If so, how are they similar to what you have encountered in your reading of the OT, and how are they different?

BIBLIOGRAPHY

Ben Zvi, Ehud, and Diana V. Edelman, eds. *The Production of Prophecy: Constructing Prophecy and Prophets in Yehud*. London: Equinox, 2009.

Blenkinsopp, Joseph. *A History of Prophecy in Israel*. Louisville: Westminster John Knox, 1996.

Boda, Mark J., and J. Gordon McConville, eds. *Dictionary of the Old Testament: Prophets*. Downers Grove, IL: InterVarsity Press, 2012.

Clements, Ronald. *Old Testament Prophecy: From Oracles to Canon*. Louisville: Westminster John Knox, 1996.

Cook, Stephen L. *Prophecy and Apocalypticism: The Post-Exilic Setting*. Minneapolis: Augsburg Fortress, 1995.

Day, John, ed. *Prophecy and the Prophets in Ancient Israel: Proceedings of the Oxford Old Testament Seminar*. New York: T&T Clark, 2010.

Gordon, Robert, ed. *The Place Is Too Small for Us: The Israelite Prophets in Recent Scholarship*. Winona Lake, IN: Eisenbrauns, 1995.

Gowan, Donald G. *Eschatology in the Old Testament*. 2nd ed. Edinburgh: T&T Clark, 2000.

————. *Theology of the Prophetic Books: The Death and Resurrection of Israel*. Louisville: Westminster John Knox, 1998.

Grabbe, Lester L., and Martti Nissinen, eds. *Constructs of Prophecy in the Former and Latter Prophets and Other Texts*. Atlanta: Society of Biblical Literature, 2011.

Hays, J. Daniel, J. Scott Duvall, and C. Marvin Pate. *An A-to-Z Guide to Biblical Prophecy and the End Times*. Grand Rapids: Zondervan, 2012.

Matthews, Victor. *The Hebrew Prophets and Their Social World*. Grand Rapids: Baker Academic, 2012.

Nissinen, Martti. *Prophets and Prophecy in the Ancient Near East*. Atlanta: Society of Biblical Literature, 2003.

O'Brien, Julia M. *Challenging Prophetic Metaphor: Theology and Ideology in the Prophets*. Louisville: Westminster John Knox, 2008.

Rad, Gerhard von. *The Message of the Prophets*. New York: Harper & Row, 1967.

Sawyer, John F. A. *Prophecy and the Biblical Prophets*. New York: Oxford University Press, 1993.

Stökl, Jonathan. *Prophecy in the Ancient Near East: A Philological and Sociological Comparison*. Leiden: Brill, 2012.

Sweeney, Marvin. *The Prophetic Literature*. Nashville: Abingdon, 2005.

VanGemeren, Willem. *Interpreting the Prophetic Word*. Grand Rapids: Academie, 1990.

Westermann, Claus. *Basic Forms of Prophetic Speech*. Philadelphia: Westminster, 1967.

Wilson, Robert R. *Prophecy and Society in Ancient Israel*. Philadelphia: Fortress, 1980.

22 THE BOOK OF ISAIAH

Important Dates for Isaiah of Jerusalem (First Isaiah; Isa 1–39)
735: Israelite/Aramaean pressure on Jerusalem
724–720: fall of Samaria and exile of Israelites to Mesopotamia
701: Assyrian attack on Judah and siege of Jerusalem

Important Dates for Second Isaiah (Isa 40–55)
597–538: Judahites in Babylonian exile
539: Cyrus conquers Babylon

Important Dates for Third Isaiah (Isa 56–66)
538–520: some Jews return to Judah and Jerusalem
520–515: rebuilding of temple in Jerusalem

THE BOOK OF ISAIAH IS one of three Major Prophets in the OT. Like Jeremiah and Ezekiel, it comprised a scroll of its own among the sacred Scriptures of Judaism. The book begins with a call to the heavens and earth as witnesses to the surprising stupidity of God's people (1:2-3), and it concludes with announcements about a new heaven and earth to come, with a chastened and renewed Israel secure in the care of the Lord (65:1-66:24). One might think of the book, then, as prophecies in a cosmic context, where God's wayward people are refined in judgment and exile, nations are weighed in the balance of God's justice, and those who survive are brought to a point of expectation about future transformation. This

profile-in-movement reflects a broader, three-part pattern that one can see in several prophetic books: (1) the prophet's contemporaries are evaluated negatively; (2) God's judgment and/or refining justice reaches Israel and other nations; (3) and future deliverance and transformation are predicted for God's people and remnants of the nations.

The book does not unfold in linear fashion. Like many of the other prophetic books, its contents are grouped by theme and related vocabulary, including some narratives (e.g., 7:1-9; chs. 36-39) but mostly poetic prophetic speech. Major subunits can be identified as follows:

The Great Isaiah Scroll (1QIsaᵃ). A portion of a scroll of Isaiah dating approximately to 100 BCE, found in 1947 in a cave near the northwestern corner of the Dead Sea.

Judah and Israel in Crisis, Isa 1-12
Oracles concerning Other Nations, Isa 13-23
Convulsions in History and Salvation to Come, Isa 24-27
Judgment and Future Promise, Isa 28-33
Transformation after Judgment, Isa 34-35
Assyrian Attack against Judah and Hezekiah, Isa 36-39
God and His Servant People, Isa 40-55
Repentance, Judgment, and Future Transformation, Isa 56-66

The matter of identifying the prophet of the Isaiah book is more complicated than for the other prophetic books. This is only partly because Isaiah is a large work. It is due mostly to historical analysis of its contents and the conclusion that the book addresses audiences in different geographical (Judah, Babylon) and chronological contexts (8th–6th/5th centuries BCE). Since the heading of the book indicates that Isaiah carried out his tasks during the reigns of Uzziah, Jotham, Ahaz, and Hezekiah in Judah (the second half of the 8th century BCE), some interpreters have concluded that the entire book should be attributed to him and that God gave Isaiah the ability to speak in detailed fashion to a future generation about its life in exile in Babylon. The majority of modern scholars, however, have concluded that the book developed over a period of time (see Table 28.2). They have, therefore, proposed multiple authors who followed in the wake of the great Isaiah of Jerusalem as his disciples, reinterpreting and applying older material and providing new prophecies as well. The canonical title "The Book of Isaiah" (not "Isaiahs") commends all of its contents, materials both by Isaiah himself and by his prophetic disciples, as Isaiah's prophetic legacy (see also Jer 1:1).

The book is an epitome of the OT's prophetic literature, a marvelous compendium of prophecies that spans much of the 350-year period of the Latter Prophets (ca. 750–400 BCE). The following descriptions reflect the language used by modern scholars in referring to sections of the book. Apart from the information that can be gleaned about Isaiah of Jerusalem, the figures represent convenient shorthand for the work of anonymous prophets influenced by the great work of the "first" Isaiah, who like him addressed timely oracles to their contemporaries.

I. Isaiah of Jerusalem (First Isaiah) prophesied during the reigns of Uzziah, Jotham, Ahaz, and Hezekiah (Isa 1:1). This is a time span of fifty years or so. The army of the expanding Assyrian Empire marched

Table 22.1. The Composition of Isaiah

	Isaiah 1–39	Isaiah 40–55	Isaiah 56–66
Author	Isaiah I	Isaiah II	Isaiah III
Nickname	"First Isaiah"	"Second (Deutero-) Isaiah"	"Third (Trito-)Isaiah"
Location	Jerusalem	Babylon	Judah
Period	Preexilic	Exilic	Postexilic
Dates	742–688 BCE	550–538 BCE	538–515 BCE

through the states of the eastern Mediterranean region repeatedly, eventually defeating Israel and making Judah a vassal. Much of the material in Isa 1–39 is attributed to him.

II. An anonymous figure known as Second (or Deutero-)Isaiah is assigned the material in Isa 40–55 (and often Isa 34–35). Those chapters presuppose a setting in Babylon for Judahite exiles, who are addressed and urged to see the hand of the Lord at work in preparing the way for a return to Judah. The Persian general Cyrus is mentioned by name (Isa 45:1, ca. 540 BCE).

III. Another prophetic figure, again anonymous, is often described by modern scholars as Third (or Trito-)Isaiah and considered to be responsible for Isa 56–66. Those chapters presuppose a setting in early postexilic Jerusalem and have a tone and emphasis somewhat different than those of chs. 40–55. Thus, many interpreters have concluded that the person responsible for them is different from Second Isaiah. There are also those who interpret chs. 40–66 as essentially the work of one figure or group. In terms of chronology and setting, it is possible for one person to have been present in Babylon in the middle of the 6th century BCE and then to have returned to Jerusalem with one of the early groups in the last third of the century. Such a person could well be responsible for compiling the book as a whole.

IV. Some interpreters have discerned yet another prophetic figure or contributor to the book known as Fourth Isaiah, who would have been responsible for Isa 24–27. Some among them simply describe these four chapters as the Isaianic Apocalypse, having concluded that they originated in the postexilic period and reflect an apocalyptic mind-set.

There are two current trends at work in the above genetic analysis of the book. One is a reaction against the view that the book comprises large segments of material, each with an identifiable date—with the latest simply being added to the previous one(s). As noted above, updating was probably at work in the earlier segments, as new material was added to the collection. Moreover, a preoccupation with identifying single individuals as authors may underplay the work of communities of transmitters who preserved and updated the texts that were foundational to their identity. The second trend is an emphasis on the impact of the book as a finished product—irrespective of previous editions (which are acknowledged)—and a literary work in its own right. Two good examples of this type of analysis on Isaiah are the works of Brevard Childs and Rolf Rendtorff.

A Phoenician ivory carving of a widespread ancient iconographic theme, "the woman at the window," from Assyrian Nimrud (9th–7th centuries BCE). It depicts a woman, possibly a sacred prostitute of the goddess Astarte or Ishtar, peering out a window. It illustrates the wealth, international reach, and cultural sophistication of Assyria, the military nemesis of Israel and Judah during this period. Excavations in Ahab and Jezebel's palace in Samaria uncovered a similar example (cf. 2 Kgs 9:30–33). ©*Osama Shukir Mohammed Amin FRCP(Glasg) (Wikimedia Commons, CC-SA 4.0)*

Isaiah of Jerusalem

The eighth-century prophet Isaiah was apparently a well-connected member of Judahite society. Some may want to use the modern terms *upper class* or *patrician* to describe him. He was certainly well educated; his poetry is superbly crafted and includes an impressive vocabulary. The narrative of his encounter with King Ahaz during a time of crisis presupposes someone well known in his day (7:1–9). Not everyone who wants to talk with the head of state, especially during preparations for war, gets an audience!

Isaiah was married to a prophetess. This is the most likely way to interpret the report that he had sexual relations with "the prophetess," who bore a son (8:3). At least two children of his are given symbolic names to illustrate aspects of his preaching about the future (7:3; 8:1–4). With respect to the broader setting of his prophetic activity, he lived during the last half of the 8th century and through some of the most tumultuous decades of Israel's and Judah's history. The earliest dated event in the book takes place in the year that King Uzziah died (6:1–13; ca. 745 BCE). Not long after that the Assyrians repeatedly campaigned in the region, taking

Table 22.2. Assyrian Campaigns in the 8th Century BCE Related to Israel and Judah

Tiglath-pileser III (a.k.a. Pul)	Tribute paid by Menachem, king of Israel (2 Kgs 15:17–22; Assyrian annals)	ca. 738
Tiglath-pileser III	Attacks Israel and Aramaeans (Damascus) Pekah killed and Hoshea made king in Israel Ahaz pays tribute and Judah becomes vassal (2 Kgs 15:29–16:9)	734–732
Shalmaneser V	Besieges Samaria (2 Kgs 17:1–6; Assyrian annals)	724–722
Sargon II	Takes Samaria and exiles some inhabitants (Assyrian annals)	720
Sargon II	Attacks Philistines, perhaps some cities of Judah (Isa 20:1–6; Assyrian annals)	715–711
Sennacherib	Attacks Judah and lays siege to Jerusalem (2 Kgs 18–19; Isa 36–37; Assyrian annals)	701

over cities, territories, and states (see Table 22.2 on Assyrian campaigns). At one point in a tense situation, the Israelite king and the king of Damascus plotted to overthrow Ahaz (7:1–9). Eventually Assyria would take over the Northern Kingdom of Israel and devastate Damascus (732–721 BCE). King Ahaz of Judah became an Assyrian vassal (ca. 732 BCE), probably avoiding the more somber fate of several neighbors, including Israel. In the 14th year of King Hezekiah (701 BCE), the Assyrians laid siege to Jerusalem after devastating the countryside (Isa 36–39; 2 Kgs 18–19). There is a late and legendary tradition contained in the Martyrdom of Isaiah, a Hellenistic-Roman work, that the prophet was executed during the reign of Manasseh.

Isaiah had disciples, but unfortunately, little is known about them. At one point during the simultaneous crises with Assyria, Israel, and Damascus, the prophet was rebuffed, wrote down his prophecy as a testimony for the future, and gave it to his disciples (8:16–17). Perhaps this was the humble beginning of the book of Isaiah, a process of disciples at work that continued for decades (see 30:8–9) and ultimately became multigenerational.

Isaiah 1–12

The first chapter of Isaiah sets the tone for the various charges of moral and spiritual failure leveled throughout the book as well as for the expectation that God will redeem and transform his people. The heavens and earth are called as witnesses to the folly of Israel, God's people. "Israel" is used in the sense of the whole people of God rather than as a designation for the Northern Kingdom in contrast to Judah. The call to the heavens and the earth has the Lord speaking like a prosecuting attorney to a jury. Israel's stupidity is greater than that of domesticated animals, since the latter learn to recognize the work of their masters, but Israel seems clueless. Theirs is, furthermore, a culpable stupidity. God's people are sinful and weighed down with iniquity, having rejected the Lord. Daughter Zion (= personified Jerusalem) is vulnerable and alone. "Like Sodom and Gomorrah" is the charge against the people (see Gen 18-19)! Their worship of the Lord in the temple is more an abomination than a delight. An appeal is made for them to do what is right and just or to face the consequences. The chapter ends with a poetic sketch of Jerusalem's past, present, and future. Its past was glorious, its present is like that of a prostitute, and its future can be that of restoration to something of its former glory and even beyond that.

Note the exaltation of Jerusalem in the vision of the "latter days" in Isa 2:2-4. It expands on the positive reversal of the city's current state as announced in 1:26. Essentially the same prophecy is presented in Mic 4:1-4. Indeed, the future exaltation of Jerusalem/Zion is a frequent theme in prophetic texts, not least in Isa 40-66. In the latter days of ch. 2, the nations will stream up to the Temple Mount in Jerusalem and learn the instruction of the Lord. That will result in an era of peace, when the implements of war will no longer be needed.

Chapter 6 is dated to the death of Uzziah in the middle of the 8th century BCE. Since this is the earliest date provided in the book, some interpreters conclude that the account is about Isaiah's call to be a prophet. That is plausible but uncertain. What is palpably clear in the account is an emphasis on the holiness of the Lord, whose revealed presence actually supersedes the earthly temple, which is intended to represent him as being present to the people. Perhaps the threefold cry of the seraph choir that the Lord is *holy* reflects a hymn or chant that was used in the temple liturgy by an earthly choir. That God is holy—that is, transcendent, set apart from impurity and corruption, majestic, glorious, and thus threatening to those who are not—is a theme that runs through the book of Isaiah. God is "holy" (6:3; 57:15), the "Holy One" (10:17; 40:25; 43:15;

49:7), and above all the "Holy One of Israel" (1:4; 5:16, 19, 24; 12:6; 17:7; 29:19, 23 [Jacob]; 30:11-12, 15; 31:1; 37:23; 41:14, 16, 20; 43:3, 14; 45:11; 47:4; 48:17; 49:7; 54:4-5; 60:9, 14).

The holiness of the Lord evokes the response in the prophet that neither he nor the people are holy. The prophet receives the gift of purification and answers the call to go to God's people with a message. The message will not be received, however; it will instead confirm the obduracy of the people and result in a refining judgment.

The Calling of Isaiah, by Giovanni Battista Tiepolo. Ca. 1726. Tiepolo painted this scene in the ceiling of the bishop's palace in Udine, Italy. It is his interpretation of Isaiah 6:6–9.

Readers should note carefully that the message to the people in 6:9-10 is not "do not listen or understand." *Deaf* and *mute* will be the characteristics of the people's reception of Isaiah's message, not what his message will urge them to be! Anyone who heard the prophet and believed his announcement of judgment would want to make changes in hopes of avoiding rather than incurring judgment. In this passage readers will recognize one of the purposes of the prophetic books, which was to explain to later readers why Israel and Judah fell. Israel and Judah fell because they refused to hear and obey the prophets that the Lord raised up.

The section of the book that follows (7:1-9:7) gives an illustration of how Isaiah was rebuffed in his attempt to persuade King Ahaz of a course of action during a crisis. The Israelite king Pekah, son of Remaliah, and Rezin, king of Damascus, conspired to replace Ahaz (descendant of David) with someone more to their liking. A date is not given, but one can be approximated on the basis of the names of the rulers (ca. 735 BCE). Isaiah famously advises Ahaz to seek a sign from the Lord that the Lord will protect the house of David from the two conspirators. The feckless ruler hesitates, however, whereupon Isaiah informs him that a sign will be given—the birth of a child named Immanuel (7:1-17).

There are many questions raised by this account. Whose child is Immanuel? Is his mother a virgin or a young woman, as 7:14 is variously translated? Is the birth to happen soon, or is this something to happen centuries later? Some readers will know the reference to a virgin with child because of Matthew's Gospel and the Christmas story of Jesus's conception

tween Judah and Moab in the multiple references to Moabite place-names. The poetry, while harsh in tone against Moab, is also exquisite in performance, using sarcasm and parody to portray Moab as undone by judgment in the historical process.

Isaiah 24–27

As noted above, Isa 24–27 are sometimes called the Isaianic Apocalypse. This is because of its more pronounced eschatological tone, employing the language of cosmic convulsion and radical future change (see the discussion on the word *apocalyptic* in ch. 25 below). For readers of Isaiah, these chapters follow the oracles regarding other nations as an expanded presentation of judgment and deliverance. When God deals with the folly and hubris of nations, including that of Israel and Judah, then both judgment and transformation take on a cosmic profile. This same theme recurs with the announcement of a new heaven and a new earth in Isa 65–66.

Isaiah 25 speaks of God's overcoming of several limitations inherent in human existence. One is his expansive provision of a banquet for his people (25:6). Another is his overcoming of death (25:7-12), a theme that reoccurs in 26:19, with its reference to the dead coming alive (resurrection). God will deal with all unruly powers, even that of Leviathan (27:1), perhaps a type of sea monster but certainly a power that only God can vanquish. Note that the last two verses in this section (27:12-13) project the restoration of Israelite and Judahite exiles, worshiping in peace in Jerusalem. Again, this is the same hope of Isa 56–66 and is consistent with the proclamation of 19:18-25—testimony to the unity that the completed book of Isaiah achieves.

Isaiah 28–33

Isaiah 28–33 contains a variety of poetic oracles of both critique and future promise. Note the movement from criticism, with references to Ephraim (the Northern Kingdom of Israel), Jerusalem, and Egypt in chs. 28–31, to more-expansive descriptions of threat and future redemption in chs. 32–35. These latter chapters have material similar to that in Isa 40–55. Chapters 28–29 reflect the tumultuous times of armed campaigns and sieges during the Assyrian presence in the eastern Mediterranean. Isaiah portrays the

Lord at work in judgment and surprising deliverance. Note the reference to the Lord's "strange work" in 28:21, which recognizes the complexity of discerning divine activity!

With the Assyrian campaigns in the region, Judah was sorely tempted to seek alliances with neighbors. The prophet opposed alliances with unreliable neighbors because of the inevitable compromises required, but most of all because they showed a lack of trust in the Lord. Chapters 30–31 contain oracles against relying on Egypt for help against the Assyrian menace. In Isa 31:1–3 the prophet pronounces "woe" on those who go down to Egypt seeking military aid. The final verse has paired lines contrasting Egypt and the Lord: those seeking and those receiving help.

> The Egyptians are human, not God;
> Egyptian horses are flesh, not Spirit.
>
> The Lord will stretch out his hand;
> the *helper* will stumble and the *helped* will fall [a pun in Hebrew].
> Together they will come to an end.

Isaiah 34–35

Isaiah 34–35 presents a broad contrast among the nations that the Lord will engage in future judgment. In ch. 34 the Edomites are singled out for judgment. This is not the only place in the prophetic books where Edom is distinguished as a future recipient of judgment on a day of the Lord's vengeance (v. 8). The small book of Obadiah is devoted to the description of Edom's judgment. Note also the raw emotion expressed in Ps 137:7 regarding Edomite complicity when the Babylonians destroyed Jerusalem. Chapter 35 also speaks of the Lord's vengeance (v. 4), this time in vindication of his people, whom he will bring back to Judah and Jerusalem to be renewed in their ancestral land. The material in these chapters is similar to that in Isa 40–55.

Isaiah 36–39

The same account of an Assyrian attack on Judah and siege of Jerusalem appears with minor variations in Isa 36–37 and 2 Kgs 18–19. They are narrative

The large Judahite site of Lachish had a strongly fortified gate and entrance into the city during the 8th century BCE. This stone wall runs along the roadway leading to the entrance at the top of the photograph. ©*Oren Rozen (Wikimedia Commons, CC-SA 3.0)*

presentations, and the fact that this material occurs in two different biblical books suggests that the account of the Assyrian attack existed in some form as an independent source and was subsequently incorporated into a larger work by different editors. Since the annals of the Assyrian king Sennacherib also preserve information on parts of the campaign against Judah, and there is relevant archaeological material to consider from Mesopotamia and Palestine, the event has drawn considerable interest from both biblical scholars and historians. Interpreters compare and contrast the lines of evidence coming from the biblical texts, Assyrian texts and archaeology, and the excavation of the city of Lachish (see Isa 37:8) southwest of Jerusalem (note the comments on 2 Kings in ch. 15).

Much of the account is taken up with the taunting lines of the Assyrian general who seeks the surrender of Jerusalem. Hezekiah, king of Judah, humbled himself before the Lord, and Isaiah encouraged him to stand firm (37:14–35). Unlike Ahaz at an earlier time, Hezekiah is more receptive to the prophet's counsel. Three central themes of Isaiah's ministry are evoked in his words. "Virgin daughter Zion" (= Jerusalem) is depicted as behaving scornfully toward the Assyrians, rejecting their claim to take her as their own (37:22). The Assyrian king is charged with arrogance toward God, the Holy One of Israel (37:23-25). In turn, God will put a hook in the nose of the Assyrian and turn him away from Jerusalem (37:29). The Assyrian will not enter Jerusalem, "for my sake and for the sake of my servant David" (37:35).

Isaiah could be critical of both Jerusalem and the Davidic incumbent on the throne, but as noted above, he stood in the tradition that Zion and David were the Lord's chosen vessels. In metaphorical terms, Zion was the Lord's "daughter," and the king was his adopted "son." The Holy One of Israel would defend his own against the Assyrian oppression. Sennacherib's army decimated much of the countryside and took Lachish, the second largest city of the realm. In his palace in Nineveh, Sennacherib later dedicated a room to the taking of Lachish. He was unable to take Jerusalem, however, a fact attributed to divine intervention by the biblical writers (Isa 37:36-38; cf. 31:4-9). As a result of this event, some in Judah concluded that Jerusalem was inviolable and that God would always rise to defend the city. Such a viewpoint was anathema to Jeremiah, who assumed God's freedom to judge and to deliver and who struggled fiercely against this wrong thinking in his day (Jer 7:1-15; cf. Lam 4:12).

The conclusion to the reign of Hezekiah reports (Isa 39) that envoys from Babylon paid a visit to Jerusalem. This account helps transition to the perspective of chs. 40-55, most of which presuppose a Judahite community in exile in Babylon after the fall of Judah and Jerusalem in 587 BCE.

Second Isaiah (Isaiah 40–55)

The opening lines of Isa 40 set an expectant tone with the command to "comfort my people" and "speak to Jerusalem's heart" that her punishment phase is coming to an end, "for she received from the Lord a double measure for her sins." What most Jews considered to be the problem—the punishment of exile—Second Isaiah sees as an opportunity for God's saving sovereignty to be manifested in the historical process and in a location far from Judah. By analogy one could say that the exiles found themselves in uncharted waters, fearing that they had been abandoned by God and worried that their resources would not be able to sustain them. Second Isaiah, however, creatively employs the traditions of God's past dealings with Israel to demonstrate his conviction that God has not abandoned the people but is about to do a "new thing" (43:19; cf. 42:9) in the ongoing story of his covenant mercies.

The prophet announces that God's people will be able to return to Judah and Jerusalem from their places in exile, a return that is depicted in the language of a new exodus (43:14; 49:10; 51:9-11). Just as God defeated the power of Egypt, made a way for the escaped slaves in the wilderness, and brought them first to Sinai and then to the promised land, so the Lord will take the exiles from the power of Babylon and make a way for the return to Zion.

Languishing exiles are urged to look to the rock from whence they were hewn—namely, Abraham and Sarah (51:1-2; cf. 41:8). God had made covenant promises to them, including the building of a great nation from their descendants. Those covenant promises were not obsolete, regardless of what many had surmised about God's intentions. Noah is cited as an example of someone who was caught in perilous times but whom God embraced with a promissory covenant of peace (54:9-10). The people corporately are encouraged to think of themselves as recipients of the "sure mercies" of David, even if there is no son of David any longer on the throne in Jerusalem (55:1-5). Readers will recognize that each of these figures from the past was the recipient of covenant promises. The prophet creatively reinterprets them for the circumstances of his day and the "new thing" that God is doing.

Moses and the Sinai covenant are not mentioned by name in these chapters. This is not because they were unknown, but likely because of the way in which the covenant curses for disobedience had been used. Both Israel and Judah had been charged by earlier prophets with failure to maintain obedience to God's revealed standards. The Sinai/Horeb covenant had been understood by analogy to marriage. That was a fundamental point of Hosea's theology in 8th-century Israel and was taken up by Jeremiah as well (Jer 2:2; 31:32). The brief covenant formulary, "I will be their God and they will be my people" (Exod 19:4-6; Lev 26:12; Jer 24:7; 31:33; Ezek 11:20; Zech 8:8), is similar to the affirmation that husbands and wives make to one another. In metaphorical terms, unfaithfulness to the covenant was infidelity or adultery, and God's judgment upon Judah and Jerusalem was a divorce. Second Isaiah represents Zion as grieving over her "divorce" from the Lord (Isa 50:1-3; 54:1-8), but speaking for God, the prophet denies that the "divorce" is permanent. In one of the most astounding metaphors in all of Scripture, the prophet represents God as assuring Zion (= the "mother" of the people) that, far from abandoning her, he has "inscribed her on the palms" of his hands (49:16). As with a tattoo, this is assurance of a permanent connection.

Israel/Jacob is repeatedly named God's "servant" people (41:8-9; 42:1; 43:10; 44:1-2, 21; 45:4; 48:20). Part of the "new thing" announced by the prophet is that God intended for his servant people to bear witness to his name and glory among the nations. As noted above, what most exiles thought was a terrible problem—being exiled from Judah and Jerusalem and forced to live among other peoples—was an opportunity to further God's wider purposes. Israel was called to "bring justice (*mishpat*) to the nations," to be God's "covenant" to them, and a "light" among them (42:1-6; cf. 49:6). These exalted tasks for the servant people are perhaps a further outworking of the promises to Abraham that all the families of the earth would be blessed in his seed (Gen 12:3; 22:18). We should also note that Isaiah of Jerusalem accused the people of his day of "no justice" (*mishpat*) in Isa 5:7 but also projected that a future Jerusalem would be redeemed by justice (1:27). His visions of the future foresaw the exercise of justice in the hands of David's greater son (9:6-7; 11:1-6), mediated from Jerusalem (2:2-5).

The "Servant" in Isaiah 40–55

There are references to a servant who has a ministry to perform with the servant people (Isa 49:1-8): "It is too little for you merely to be my servant in reestablishing the tribes of Jacob and in restoring Israel. I will make you a light to the nations to be my salvation to the ends of the earth" (49:6). "Salvation" in this context means deliverance from threat or oppression, the instituting of justice, and the maintaining of peace. This mysterious servant is also described as a "covenant to/for the people" (49:8). Since neither a person nor a people can literally be a covenant, the term is probably shorthand for a covenant mediator. And even more mysteriously, two other passages about God's servant depict him as afflicted, suffering vicariously, and ultimately killed (50:4-11; 52:13-53:12). Of whom does the prophet speak? Is this a way of talking about Second Isaiah himself, an otherwise anonymous figure with a crucial role to play in the exilic community, Zerubbabel (Jehoiachin's grandson and descendant of David), or a righteous remnant with a ministry on behalf of the larger people of God?

The angle of vision in the last servant poem represents the surprise of people who realize that the servant's death was a sacrifice for their trans-

A typical Israelite lamp from the Iron II period (8th–7th centuries BCE). *Photo by Ken Baumheckel. Used with permission, courtesy of the Ancient Coin Club of Los Angeles. accla.org.*

gressions—that is, his suffering was vicarious, in that the servant bore what was due to them (53:4-7, 10-11). Since the servant's death on behalf of others was God's will, God mysteriously vindicates him postmortem. All in all, the portrait of the mysterious suffering servant is powerful but allusive, leaving many to wonder, with the Ethiopian in the book of Acts (Acts 8:26-35): "How can I understand this without help?" Were it not for the NT adoption of this suffering servant as a prophetic portrait of Jesus's affliction and death, discussion of the servant's mysterious identity would not draw the massive attention it has received! As it is, early Christianity saw in the suffering servant of Second Isaiah a prophetic portrayal of the suffering of Christ, just as it did of the innocent sufferer in the psalms of lament. Virtually every verse in Isa 53:1-12, either whole or in part, is reflected in one or more of the NT writings. In light of this history of interpretation, modern readers have a dramatic example of the ways in which a historical and a theological reading differ. The identity of the suffering servant is most certainly a legitimate question of historical investigation. Who came to the mind of the earliest hearers/readers of the prophet? No matter how dramatic and compelling the description, the answer is nevertheless unclear. The fact that later Jews (and then Gentiles) saw in the prophetic depiction a portrait of Christ's suffering and death is, finally, a testimony to the inspired imagination of both prophet and readers.

Second Isaiah, traditionally described, ends with ch. 55 and a passage about the efficacy of God's word. How appropriate for one who announced the end of exile, new light from God for the nations, and a vicarious sacrifice for the transgressions of God's people.

Third Isaiah (Isaiah 56–66)

The historical setting of chs. 56-66 is Palestine and Jerusalem in the aftermath of Cyrus's decree and the return of some exiles to their families' homeland. Jerusalem was in the Persian province of Yehud (a form of the word *Judah*). They had returned, and a modest temple had been built, spurred on by Haggai and Zechariah, but no eschatological dawning of a new day had occurred. The dramatic words of Second Isaiah were behind them. God had indeed brought them back! Now what?

The prophetic voice of 56-66, often referred to as Third Isaiah, picks up the familiar role of critically examining his contemporaries, while pointing forward to God's transforming work still to come. There are idolatry and immorality in postexilic Yehud (57:1-10), and the Sabbath is not taken with the seriousness it deserves (56:2, 5-6; 58:13). And certainly there is not enough justice and righteousness to go around (56:1; 58:6-7; 59:15-21; 61:1, 8). Chapter 64 even presents portions of a liturgy of repentance by the people. As one would expect, the role of the (recently rebuilt) temple is emphasized. The well-known line regarding the temple, "a house of prayer for all peoples" (56:7; cf. Matt 21:13) appears in the context of a prophecy to encourage "foreigners" to join themselves to the Lord (Isa 56:6-8). In the broader context, it is not clear how broadly one should take the term *foreigners*, but the prophet represents an openness not shared by all. Possibly the prophet is motivated by the eschatological vision of Isa 2:2-5 and seeks a provisional display of God's instructional blessings to the nations.

Chapters 56-66 preserve the people's moments of eschatological expectation, even if the return from exile had placed them under Persian control. There is much in these chapters about the restoration of Jerusalem. This is a continuation of a theme running through the book. The prophet represents God's poetic address to Jerusalem describing the glory that will come to the city (60:13-14):

> To make beautiful the place of my sanctuary;
> And I will make the place of my feet glorious.
> Descendants of those who assaulted you will come and bow before
> you;
> Those who rejected you will prostrate themselves at your feet.
> They will call you "the Lord's city,"
> "Zion of the Holy One of Israel!"

Readers of Ezra and Nehemiah will know that the rebuilding and reorganization took quite some time after the initial waves of returning exiles. The temple was completed in 516, a modest structure in light of the First Temple, and the old city of Jerusalem did not have an intact wall around it until 445 or later. So the encouraging words about the temple and Jerusalem should be heard against the background of difficult times and disappointments. Jerusalem is described as a crown in the Lord's hand, and:

No longer will it be said to you "Forsaken,"
Nor your land be termed "Desolate";
Instead you will be called "My Delight Is in Her!"
And your land [will be called] "Married!"

. . .

As the bridegroom exults over the bride,
So your God rejoices over you. (Isa 62:4–5)

The prophetic voice is eager in describing the work of the Lord in calling
him and the community that inhabits Zion. He understands that he has
been given "good news" for those who are broken in spirit, oppressed, and
held as prisoners. God's Spirit is upon him to proclaim an "acceptable year
of the Lord" (61:1–3), a time of new beginnings like the years when debts are
forgiven and the poor can begin with a clean slate.

The prophet projects from the meager circumstances to a time of a
new heavens and earth, when the land produces enough for all, there is
security for all, and even a youth will live to be 100 years old (65:17–25).
This is an eschatology that one might call "back to the future!" Such a future is like the garden of the beginning in Gen 2. The book of Isaiah, itself
a compendium of Israel's classical prophecy, points to the confession that
all things God has made can be transformed. The prophetic book strains at
what can only be hinted: death itself can be defeated for the most complete
of all transformations (compare Isa 26:19). This can only be hinted at until
one comes who can both say and demonstrate that the "acceptable year" of
the Lord has arrived (Luke 4:16–21).

READING

Read Isa 1–66 and formulate answers to the following questions:

1. How do you understand the harsh criticism of worship in Jerusalem
   in Isa 1:10–17? Do you think that the prophet, speaking in God's name,
   condemns formal worship and sacrifice as such, or is he depicting a
   corrupt form of public worship?

2. Read Isa 6:10. How would you explain the verse's significance in light
   of your reading of the book of Isaiah as a whole?

3. Jerusalem is mentioned many times in the book of Isaiah. What depiction of the city in the book is most surprising to you and why?

4. According to Isa 37:1, King Hezekiah tore his clothes and covered himself with sackcloth. As you read this description in context, what do you think those actions represent, and why do you think he did those things?

5. Read Isa 40:25. The prophet represents God as asking the people, "To whom will you compare me?" Is it wrong to compare God to people or things? If so (or not), why?

6. The prophet represents God as saying that his thoughts are not the people's thoughts, and his ways are not their ways (55:8). How do you think such a statement impacted the people's self-understanding and their understanding of God?

7. How important is the matter of the book's authorship for interpreting its significance? Why is it important or why not?

BIBLIOGRAPHY

Berges, Ulrich F. *Book of Isaiah: Its Composition and Final Form*. Sheffield: Sheffield Phoenix, 2012.
———. *Isaiah: The Prophet and His Book*. Sheffield: Sheffield Phoenix, 2012.
Block, Daniel I., and Richard Schultz, eds. *Bind Up the Testimony: Explorations in the Genesis of the Book of Isaiah*. Peabody, MA: Hendrickson, 2015.
Childs, Brevard S. *Isaiah: A Commentary*. Louisville: Westminster John Knox, 2001.
———. *The Struggle to Understand Isaiah as Christian Scripture*. Grand Rapids: Eerdmans, 2004.
Gallagher, William R. *Sennacherib's Campaign to Judah: New Studies*. Leiden: Brill, 1999.
Goldingay, John. *The Message of Isaiah 40–55: A Literary-Theological Commentary*. New York: Continuum, 2005.
———. *The Theology of the Book of Isaiah*. Downers Grove, IL: InterVarsity Press, 2014.
Grabbe, Lester L., ed. *"Like a Bird in a Cage": The Invasion of Sennacherib in 701 BCE*. JSOTSup 363. Sheffield: Sheffield Academic Press, 2003.

Ezekiel was a contemporary who was taken into exile to live near Babylon and received his "call" to prophesy there in 593 BCE. His book takes up several of the same concerns as the book of Jeremiah (see Table 23.1).

Jeremiah: The Book and the Person

The book of Jeremiah likely reached a stable form not long after Jehoiachin's death in Babylonian captivity (52:31-34), although *stable* does not mean "uniform." Even during the lifetime of Jeremiah, there were collections of his prophecies (Jer 36) and reports of the exchange of letters between him and Judahites taken to Babylon (Jer 29). Jeremiah also carried on a prophetic ministry in both Judah and Egypt. All this suggests multiple editions of traditions about Jeremiah in Egypt, Babylon, and Judah, and the earliest forms of the book in Hebrew and Greek still preserve some differences. The Greek version of the book is 1/8 shorter than the Hebrew and begins its primary collection of foreign oracles in ch. 25, not ch. 46, as in the Hebrew and modern English versions.

There are three characteristics of the book that distinguish it from other prophetic books. The first is the amount of biographical material devoted to Jeremiah. Percentage-wise, it is higher than in any other prophetic book. The second follows from this. There are quite a number of references to his contemporaries in the prose accounts, as Jeremiah conducted much of his prophetic work in the public arena. Modern research has discovered extra-biblical references to several of these contemporaries. For purposes of broader historical reconstruction, Jeremiah (and the book) would have been the most documented figure from Judah in his day. The third characteristic is Jeremiah's laments, or even complaints—attributed to him in response to oppressive and vindictive treatment. In this characteristic, Jeremiah follows the profile of the Psalter, with its many individual laments regarding unjust treatment.

The book can also be described in terms of three types of literature, going back to analysis done by Sigmund Mowinckel. As noted above, there are prose accounts about the prophet. Second, there are poetic passages (public oracles, prophecies against nations, etc.). These are genres common to other prophetic books and to the public speaking of prophets. Third, there are some prose "sermons," similar in tone and emphasis to the material in Deuteronomy (e.g., Jer 11:1-13; 44:1-14). Interpreters are divided over the extent to which this material goes back to the prophet himself. Some propose that his editors presented Jeremiah as a latter-day Moses who preached

Table 23.1. Historical Table for Jeremiah and Ezekiel

Event	Date	Scripture
13th year of Josiah; call of Jeremiah	627	Jer 1:2
18th year of Josiah; discovery of book of law; reform of temple, etc.	622	2 Kgs 22
Fall of Nineveh	612	
Death of Josiah; 3-month reign of Jehoahaz; 1st year of Jehoiakim; Jeremiah sermon	609	2 Kgs 23:29–36; Jer 26:1–24; probably 7:1–34
Carchemish battle; Nebuchadnezzar made king	605	Jer 36:1; 25; 46:2–12
Nebuchadnezzar attacks Ashkelon	604	Jer 36:9
Jehoiakim becomes vassal of Babylon	604/3	2 Kgs 24:1
Babylonian defeat on border of Egypt	601	
Jehoiakim revolts against Babylon	ca. 601	2 Kgs 24:1
11th year of Jehoiakim/his death	598 (Dec?)	
3-month reign of Jehoiachin; Jerusalem besieged and surrenders; king and people taken into exile	597	2 Kgs 24:8–16
Zedekiah made king by Nebuchadnezzar	597	2 Kgs 24:17–18
Regional conference in Jerusalem; Zedekiah revolts against Babylon	ca. 594	Jer 27; 2 Kgs 24:20
Call of Ezekiel	593	Ezek 1:2–3
Visions of Jerusalem	592	Ezek 8–11
Ezekiel and elders of Israel	591	Ezek 20:1–44
Babylonians besiege Jerusalem	588	Jer 39:1–2; 2 Kgs 25:1; Ezek 24:1–2
Jeremiah imprisoned	587	Jer 32–34
Ezekiel prophesies against Egypt/Pharaoh and Tyre	587	Ezek 26:1–21; 29:1–16; 30:20–26; 31:1–18
Jerusalem falls in 11th year of Zedekiah; Gedaliah appointed governor by Babylonians	587	2 Kgs 25:3–11; Jer 39:2; 40:5; 2 Kgs 25:22; Ezek 33:21–22
Gedaliah assassinated	586?	2 Kgs 25:25; Jer 41
Jeremiah and Baruch taken to Egypt	586?	Jer 43
Lament for Egypt		Ezek 30; Ezek 32:17–32
Lament over Pharaoh	585	Ezek 32:1–16
Another group taken into exile	582/1	Jer 52:30
Ezekiel's prophecy against Egypt	571	Ezek 29:17–21
Jehoiachin released from house arrest	561	2 Kgs 25:27; Jer 52:31
Babylon falls to Cyrus	539	Ezra 1:1

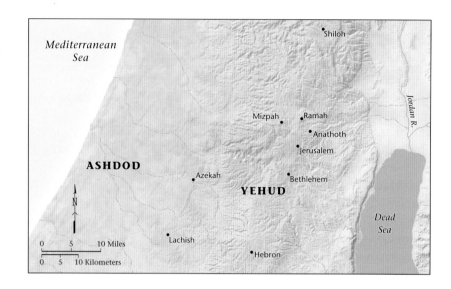

Anathoth and Mizpah. Anathoth was Jeremiah's home, Mizpah the capital of Judah/Yehud after Jerusalem fell.

to his contemporaries just as Moses did to Israel shortly before the people crossed into Canaan. After all, it was likely an early form of the book of Deuteronomy that was discovered during the temple repairs of Josiah's reign (2 Kgs 22:1–23:3), a book that stated that the Lord would raise up a prophet like Moses for Israel after his death (Deut 18:15–19). Others such as Holladay conclude that the prophet himself adopted and adapted the style of "Deuteronomic" presentation for rhetorical purposes.

Like the large books of Isaiah and Ezekiel, the prose and poetic materials in Jeremiah do not unfold in linear fashion but are collected topically and thematically.

The Presentation

The book of Jeremiah can be subdivided into two major portions: (1) chs. 1–25, and (2) chs. 26–52. There are more poetic oracles in the first portion and more biographical accounts in the latter.

Jeremiah 1–25: A Collection of the Prophet's Oracles and Prayers

The form of Jeremiah's call (1:4–10) has similarities with the form of the call of Moses at the burning bush (Exod 3:1–15). As noted above, there are other similarities with the Deuteronomic Moses traditions in the portrait of Jeremiah, particularly in the latter's prose sermons in Jer 7:1–8:3 and 11:1–14. The verbs in 1:10 that summarize Jeremiah's commission are used in several places in the book (e.g., 18:7–9; 24:6; 31:28; 42:10). Much of the material in the book intends to "pluck up" or "tear down" Judah's self-sufficiency and thereby offer critical assessment of the nation. Correspondingly, the prophecies of forgiveness and restoration fill out the verbs of "building" and "planting."

Chapters 2–6 are largely poetry, containing shorter prophecies that have been placed together by theme or similar phraseology. The opening oracle sees Israel's history by analogy to marriage, with the people in the role of faithless covenant partner to the Lord (2:2–13). In brief fashion it represents much of the prophet's message to Judah and Jerusalem: God had given Israel the promised land; the people had made it an abomination, with their leadership coming under withering criticism. Four different terms are used to portray Judah's failed leadership.

> The *priests* did not say, "Where is the Lord?"
> The *handlers of Torah* did not know me;
> The *rulers* [lit., "shepherds"] transgressed against me;
> And the *prophets* depended on Baal and pursued worthless things.
> (Jer 2:8).

Chapters 3–4 have calls for repentance as well as announcements of judgment (3:12–14), although the tone is largely accusatory. In 3:6-13 Jeremiah develops a metaphorical portrayal of Israel and Judah as wayward sisters. Ezekiel has related portrayals of Israel and Judah, or Samaria and Jerusalem (Ezek 16, 23).

Two celebrated "sermons" of Jeremiah are located in the temple courtyard (Jer 7/26; 36). The latter was actually delivered by Baruch, a scribe and companion of the prophet, because Jeremiah had been barred from preaching at the temple after his earlier effort! The book preserves portions of the "first" sermon in two different forms. In 7:1-34 readers have its longer form, while 26:1-6 offers a shorter version that, unlike the longer rendition, is followed by a description of the crowd's reactions (26:7-24). In the sermon Jeremiah announces that God will make the Jerusalem temple like Shiloh— that is, enemies of the people will overrun it as the Philistines did during the time of Eli and Samuel (1 Sam 1-7). In a refrain emphatic with sarcasm, the prophet urges the people:

> Don't trust in these deceptive words, "This is the temple of the
> Lord, the temple of the Lord, the temple of the Lord." (Jer 7:4)

Apparently it was popularly believed that when all was said and done, the
Lord would act to protect his temple from violation. Although Jeremiah's
audience does not say it, this belief may go back to Sennacherib's previous
assault on Jerusalem (Isa 36–37), when the city was spared, or to a psalm
of Zion such as Ps 46 and its claim that "God is in her midst, she will not be
moved" (Ps 46:5).

Jeremiah opposed any magical associations with the temple and argued instead that the mere presence of God's temple in Jerusalem would
not be enough to preserve the people. His comparison of the temple with
a "den of robbers" (Jer 7:11) would be taken up by another prophetic figure
(Matt 21:13; Mark 11:17).

Chapters 11–20 contain Jeremiah's laments over harsh treatment and
rejection of his prophetic word. As noted above, his prayers of anguish were
similar to those attributed to David and others in the Psalter who pray under threatening circumstances. These prayers are sometimes called Jeremiah's "confessions," which may be a misleading term to some contemporary
readers, who may be unfamiliar with the *Confessions* (i.e., autobiographical
reflections) of St. Augustine. What Jeremiah mostly "confesses" is not his
sin but his anguish and anger, so the term *confession* is intended as a reference to the prophet's personal reflections. We might say that Jeremiah not
only knew the hymns and prayers of Israel that existed in his day but that
he found his identity as a prophet and faithful person in them. As with
all people, there were limits to the frustration and abuse Jeremiah could
endure. Jeremiah's limit was reached on more than one occasion. After his
beating and public humiliation in the stocks, his lament begins as follows:

> Lord, you seduced me and I was deceived;
> You have overcome me and triumphed!
> I am the object of derision all day;
> Everybody mocks me.
> Every time I speak, I cry out,
> I call out "violence" and "destruction."
> For me the word of the Lord has become a reproach and humiliation.
> But if I said, "I will not remember him,
> Nor speak again in his name,"
> Then in my heart it becomes like a burning fire

Within my bones;
I am weary of constraining it,
And I can no longer endure it. (Jer 20:7-9)

Jeremiah's abuse comes as a result of his public role. His laments provide a window to the personal cost he bore as a result of his prophetic activities— something that he may have anticipated in his reluctance to accept God's call to serve as a prophet. His experience recapitulates that of other prophetic figures such as Moses, Elijah, and Elisha, who were beset with difficulties because they sought to be obedient to God's call.

Chapters 21-22 contain withering criticism of Judah's kings. A classic prophetic invective against royal pretensions is found in one of the oracles directed to Jehoiakim:

Woe to him who builds his house without righteousness,
    And his upper chambers without justice;
    Who takes his neighbor's labor without pay
    And gives no wages. . . .
Are you a king to compete in cedar furnishings?
Did not your father eat and drink, and do justice and righteousness?
Then it was good for him.
He judged the cause of the poor and needy.
Then it was good.
Isn't that what it means to know me? declared the Lord. (Jer 22:13-16)

In this devastating critique the foundational terms *justice* and *righteousness* are repeated. Jeremiah draws on the normative traditions that the Davidic king should uphold justice and righteousness in his realm (see Ps 72), as these are central to God's own rule (Ps 97:2). Jeremiah's poetry also reflects respect for Josiah and his combination of a royal life with concern for his people. When projecting the rule of an ideal Davidic king, Jeremiah sees the commitment to justice and righteousness as central (Jer 23:5-6; cf. Isa 9:6-7).

The book gives repeated indications of conflict between Jeremiah and other prophetic figures of his day. A collection of oracles in 23:9-40 provides Jeremiah's side of the argument about the state of the people and the roles of prophetic adversaries. The basic conflict is reflected in the refrain "Peace, peace, when there is no peace" (Jer 6:14; cf. 23:16-17).

Jeremiah presents Babylon and Nebuchadnezzar as instruments of God's judgment on faithless Judah and Jerusalem. Historically, that judgment took the form of Judah's military and political defeat, along with the destruction of Jerusalem, the removal of the Davidic king Zedekiah, and the forced migration or exile of thousands of Judahites (Jer 52:1-30). According to 25:8-14 the exile would last seventy years, a figure that the book of Daniel will adopt and expand on as a way to grasp God's unfolding drama in history (Dan 9). Note the way Jer 25:13 refers to the contents of Jeremiah's book: God will bring upon the land all the words he uttered about it as prophesied by Jeremiah. This is a comment (in the book!) that understands the book itself as a witness to help readers understand the significance of Judah's fall and to see the future as a medium through which God will continue his work with future generations.

Jeremiah 26–52: Biography, Hope, and Judgment on Nations

The second half of the Jeremiah book contains a number of biographical accounts, one collection of hopeful oracles, another of oracles against various nations, and ends with a historical summary of Jerusalem's fall to the Babylonians. This last-named historical summary is similar to the material in 2 Kgs 24-25. In fact, the books of 2 Kings and Jeremiah have essentially the same conclusion: a report that Jehoiachin, the exiled king of Judah, was released from imprisonment (compare 2 Kgs 25:27-30).

Chapters 26-29 portray various ways in which the prophet was caught up in controversial events and exchanges with people. One of his temple sermons (Jer 7) received a negative reaction on the part of hearers, and ch. 26 narrates in some detail their response. The description of Jeremiah's "trial" provides a good portrait of the social dynamics of his day, with the priests and prophets as his accusers, royal officials as presiding judges, and the people of the land speaking in his defense. Note also that Jeremiah was not the only prophet to have harsh things to say about Judah and King Jehoiakim. A certain Uriah was put to death for his prophetic activity and his body thrown into the paupers' grave (26:20-23). Jeremiah predicts an even worse fate for Jehoiakim (22:18-19)! The chapter's concluding reference to Ahikam, a member of one of the distinguished families of Judah, indicates that Jeremiah had some support in influential circles. Ahikam's father was a high official under Josiah (2 Kgs 22:3), and his brother Gemariah's office was the location where Baruch read Jeremiah's prophecies to the worshipers in the nearby temple courtyard (Jer 36:10).

Like other prophets, Jeremiah enacted his message in symbolic public acts (see Jer 13:1-11; 19:1-13). Chapters 27-28 portray him wearing a yoke to represent visually his message that the Lord had yoked Judah and Jerusalem in servitude to Nebuchadnezzar. Based on the dating provided by the two chapters, Jeremiah played this public role after Jerusalem surrendered to the Babylonians in 597 BCE, when the young king Jehoiachin was taken into exile, along with sacred vessels from the temple and other leaders. Were these things just a simple "slap" on the wrist, with a turnaround coming soon, or was Judah still deeply mired in problematic, self-destructive behavior? Note the actions of Hananiah in ch. 28, as he opposed Jeremiah. His language and symbolic act (breaking Jeremiah's yoke!) fit the profile of a prophet. He spoke in the name of the Lord as well, but his personal fate implicitly indicts him as a false prophet.

Chapter 29 provides evidence of letters that went back and forth between the Judahites who had been taken into exile in 597 BCE and those who remained in the land. One should compare Jeremiah's words to the exiles in this chapter with the vision of good and bad figs in 24:1-10, which announces that Judah's future lies with these exiles. His hopeful words to them lead into a collection of prophecies known as "the book of consolation" (chs. 30-32).

The prophecies of forgiveness and restoration in chs. 30-32 refer to a larger audience than the first wave of exiles. Note the references to Israel (as distinct from Judah), Samaria, and Ephraim (30:4; 31:4-6, 18-20). The Northern Kingdom suffered two waves of exile at the hands of the Assyrians in 734-32 and 722-20 BCE. Some interpreters propose that these are prophecies from an earlier time in Jeremiah's ministry, when Josiah sought to bring remnants of the former Northern Kingdom into Judah. Whatever their historical setting, they show a broader concern for the communities of exiles formed from both the Assyrian and the Babylonian campaigns in the area. Note also that the restoration passages regarding Judah are inclusive regarding the future. They presuppose that Judah will fall as an entity and that the Lord will work through historical circumstances for its future restoration.

The Prophetic Way of Sorrow

Some years ago Gerhard von Rad called the biographical accounts of Jeremiah's suffering (Jer 26–28; 36–44) the prophet's *via dolorosa* ("way of sorrow/suffering"), echoing the description of Jesus's passion. These biographical accounts of Jeremiah's anguish illumine his prayers or "confessions" and vice-versa. To call Jeremiah's experience of rejection and persecution a *via dolorosa* does not mean that Jeremiah's suffering was somehow redemptive in the way that Jesus's suffering was in the Christian faith. It more likely reveals something of the cost of acting publicly on unpopular convictions. The pattern of a rejected prophet may also indicate something of the background to understanding Jesus's humiliation and passion on the part of the Gospel writers. Much of Jesus's public ministry, including his rejection, follows the pattern set out in the OT prophets.

Both Jeremiah and Ezekiel struggled with the questions of justice and proportionality regarding corporate judgment. Both books quote a proverb to the effect that when an earlier generation sins, a later generation is unfairly held responsible (Jer 31:27-30; cf. Ezek 18:1-32). This matter is noted along with additional comments in the discussion of Ezekiel.

One of the best-known passages in the book is the prophecy of a coming "new covenant" (Jer 31:31-34). That term is unique in the OT, but its referent has a few parallels elsewhere. Other prophets speak of a future covenant that the Lord will make with his people after their breach of the national covenant mediated by Moses (Exod 19:3-8; Deut 29-30). Hosea, for example, projects a covenant that is like a remarriage between divorced spouses (Hos 2:14-23), and Ezekiel predicts an "everlasting covenant" (Ezek 16:59-63; 37:26) to overcome the effects of Israel's brokenness and sin, a term that Jeremiah also uses elsewhere (Jer 32:40). It is one of the OT ways of speaking about grace and mercy, whereby God provides for his people what they are unable to do for themselves. Jeremiah's unique phrase has had quite an impact in history. Its promise of reconciliation with the Lord and forgiveness of sins was taken over by Jesus and the early Christian community and applied to the gospel message (Mark 14:24; 1 Cor 11:25; Heb 8:8-13). Eventually the term *new covenant*, taken from the OT, became the heading for the collection of authoritative Christian writings that the Christian Church recognized as a New Testament (Lat., *Novum Testamentum*) to go with its OT documents (see ch. 37 on canon).

Jeremiah 32 narrates a symbolic act carried out by Jeremiah from imprisonment. He buys a field from his cousin (who apparently needed money) during the time when the Babylonians were in the region and had besieged Jerusalem. The city would fall some months later. Given the stark and foreboding circumstances, it was not a good time to be buying property. His purchase came with the message that fields would again be bought and sold, for God would be at work to restore Judah after judgment. This is one of several accounts of Jeremiah's incarceration at the hands of Judah's leadership (20:1-6; 37:11-21; 38:1-28). According to ch. 36, Jeremiah instructed Baruch, his secretary and companion in public activities, to deliver his prophetic oracles at the temple. Je-

Collecting the Prophecies of Jeremiah

King Jehoiakim destroyed an early copy of Jeremiah's oracles, and a second scroll was written with additional oracles (36:11–33). In addition to his continued speaking in Jerusalem, the prophet wrote letters to exiles in Babylon (29:1–32). He also delivered oracles to exiles in Egypt (43:8–44:30). Perhaps we should think of the collecting of Jeremiah's oracles and stories about him as taking place in at least three different locations before the book associated with him reached a final form later in the postexilic period.

hoiakim was king at the time and reacted negatively to them. Note in the account the interest taken in whether these came from Jeremiah or not, as if oracles from him would merit serious attention. The king's response to the prophetic scroll used by Baruch was the opposite of his father's reaction to the book of the Torah discovered during temple repairs (2 Kgs 22). There is recognition in the account that more than one form of Jeremiah's oracles had been in circulation.

The last section of biographical accounts (chs. 39–44) covers the time from the fall of the city to the Babylonians (while Jeremiah is under arrest) to the forced settlement of Jeremiah and Baruch in Egypt after the assassination of Gedaliah, the Judahite governor of the land appointed by the Babylonians. Gedaliah was the son of Ahikam, who had kept Jeremiah from an angry crowd after one of his temple sermons (Jer 26:24; 40:5). It is not clear how long Gedaliah's tragic rule lasted, but it was likely only a few months in duration. The last thing recorded about Jeremiah is that he and Baruch were taken to Egypt against their will by Judahites anxious to escape the difficulties in Judah after Gedaliah's murder. The tradition of Jeremiah's prophetic ministry lived on to such an extent that in later Judaism there was speculation that God would send him again to Judah. Apparently the reasoning was that God would not give up on Jeremiah after his years of work, any more than God could abandon John the Baptizer after his execution. Jesus's disciples, when asked who people were saying he was, replied that "Jeremiah" was one of the answers being given (Matt 16:14).

The book of Jeremiah ends with a collection of oracles against various nations, the last and longest being against Babylon, and a historical résumé of Judah's defeat. Note the multidimensional portrayal of Babylon in the book. Nebuchadnezzar and Babylon are servants of the Lord, employed to do his historical bidding (25:8–14). Babylon is the home of exilic communities and worthy of their prayers for peace (29:1–14). And in Jer 51–52, Babylon will be the object of God's judgment, like other nations who operate unjustly and oppress others.

Both Jeremiah and Baruch were popular figures in early Judaism. The OT Apocrypha contains two later works associated with them, Baruch and the Letter (or Epistle) of Jeremiah, both likely products of the Maccabean period. Additionally, there are two lesser-known, noncanonical works, 2 and 3 Baruch, that emerged even later. Perhaps we can say that all these works are the "aftereffects" of the book or the results of its continuing impact on the imagination of later readers. In any case, Baruch is noted explicitly for his writing (Jer 36:4, 18); hence, the three works under his name. And with

This clay seal impression reads "Gedaliah son of Pashhur." An opponent of Jeremiah by the same name is mentioned briefly in Jer 38:1. An Israeli archaeologist, Eilat Mazar, found this impression in her excavation work in the Old City of Jerusalem. The impression was formed from a stone seal and was likely used to seal a leather or papyrus document. Several seals or seal impressions have been discovered in recent decades with names of Jeremiah's contemporaries. ©Eilat Mazar. Photo by Gabi Laron. Used with permission.

regard to letters, Jeremiah sent one to the early wave of exiles in Babylon (29:1-32); thus, the separate Letter of Jeremiah of later tradition.

READING

Read Jer 1–52 and formulate responses to the following questions:

1. Read Jer 13:1-11, an account of a symbolic act performed by the prophet. How does it illustrate his message for Judah? Does it make Jeremiah seem unbalanced or eccentric in your assessment? Why?

2. The bitter reflection regarding the day of Jeremiah's birth in 20:14-18 has similarities to the harsh language of Job (3:1-19). Why do you think that these figures speak of their birth in such negative terms? Is it frustration, despair over life itself, or something else?

3. If you tried to summarize the sermon of Jer 7:1-15 in a couple of sentences, what would you say?

4. The word *covenant* is an important term in the OT, and it represents several significant concepts in ancient Israel. In light of Jer 33:19-26, how would you define the term?

5. What are some of the characteristics of the prophets that Jeremiah opposes in Jer 29? Should we call these figures false prophets, and if so why or why not?

BIBLIOGRAPHY

Allen, Leslie. *Jeremiah*. Louisville: Westminster John Knox, 2008.
Brueggemann, Walter. *The Theology of the Book of Jeremiah*. Cambridge: Cambridge University Press, 2007.
Hall, Christopher A., ed. *Commentary on Jeremiah: Jerome*. Ancient Christian Texts. Downers Grove, IL: InterVarsity Press, 2012.
Holladay, William L. *Jeremiah*. 2 vols. Hermeneia. Philadelphia: Fortress, 1986, 1989.
Longman, Tremper, III. *Jeremiah, Lamentations*. Peabody, MA: Hendrickson, 2008.

Lundbom, Jack R. *Jeremiah*. 3 vols. Anchor Bible. New York: Doubleday, 1999–2004.

McConville, J. Gordon. *Judgment and Promise: The Message of Jeremiah*. Winona Lake, IN: Eisenbrauns, 1993.

Mowinckel, Sigmund. *Zur Komposition des Buches Jeremia*. Oslo: Dybwad, 1914.

Rad, Gerhard von. *Old Testament Theology*. 2 vols. New York: Harper & Row, 1965.

Seitz, Christopher R. "The Prophet Moses and the Canonical Shape of Jeremiah." *ZAW* 101 (1989): 3–27.

Wright, Christopher H. *The Message of Jeremiah*. Downers Grove, IL: InterVarsity Press, 2014.

24 THE BOOK OF EZEKIEL

Important Dates for Ezekiel
597: surrender of Jerusalem to Babylonians and the exile of King Jehoiachin and other Judahites to Babylon, including the priest Ezekiel
592–587: Ezekiel begins prophetic activities in Babylon and has visions of life in Jerusalem
587: defeat of Judah, destruction of Jerusalem, and exile of additional Judahites to Babylon
571: the latest dated oracle in the book of Ezekiel (29:17)

LIKE MOST PROPHETIC BOOKS, THIS one also bears the name of its central human character, a priest from Jerusalem who was exiled to Babylon in March 597 BCE, along with Judah's king and other leaders. According to the opening of the book, the prophet received his call to prophetic tasks in the fifth year, fifth month of Jehoiachin's exile, which would be summertime 593 BCE. Ezekiel contains a higher number of dated oracles than other prophetic books, with the latest coming nearly twenty-two years later (29:17), in the year 571 BCE. There are likely later texts in the book—certainly editorial arrangement and elaboration continued—but these two dates provide the parameters of the dated oracles and confirm the profile of the book as an interpretation of Judah's defeat at the hands of the Babylonians and a purveyor of visions of a new age that the Lord would usher in at a future time.

Ezekiel: The Book and the Person

The book is frequently compared to that of Jeremiah for several reasons. Each originally constituted a large scroll of material and sought to interpret Judah and Jerusalem's crushing defeat by the Babylonians. Both prophetic figures came from priestly families, although only Ezekiel is described as a priest. Ezekiel is typically described as Jeremiah's younger contemporary. He may have been age thirty in 593, if the reference to the year thirty in Ezek 1:1 is to the beginning of his prophetic activity (see Table 23.1 on p. 303).

The book of Ezekiel describes scenes in both Babylonia and Jerusalem, with the prophet's physical location set "among the exiles at the Chebar River" in Babylonia and more particularly the settlement of "Tel-abib" by the river (Ezek 1:1; 3:15). The Chebar is probably the *ka-ba-ru* waterway mentioned in the Murashu archives from Nippur (5th cent. BCE), a city southeast of Babylon. The canal ran from Nippur past the capital's east side and formed part of a complex division of the flow of the Euphrates near Babylon for irrigation and transport purposes. Interestingly, in 1910 CE, Jewish immigrants to Palestine chose the name *Tel Aviv* from the book of Ezekiel as the name of their growing community, now the second largest city in the modern state of Israel. This is an illustration of the impact that the Babylonian exile and the book of Ezekiel had on Jewish identity. While living in the exilic community, Ezekiel's visionary experiences transported him, as it were, to several locales. He describes being moved by the hand or Spirit of God to behold in a vision the Jerusalem of his day (Ezek 8:3; 11:1), a valley of bones (37:1), and the transformed land of Israel (40:1-4).

The prophet's literary style is heavy on symbolism. Ezekiel describes a complex chariot throne of the Lord (Ezek 1:4-28), portrays history in the form of eagles and a vine (17:1-24), compares Jerusalem and Samaria to adulterous sisters (23:1-49), and addresses strange entities such as Gog and the land of Magog (38:1-2). To illustrate his message, the prophet undertakes several symbolic acts such as eating a scroll, lying on his side for months, and cutting his hair and burning it in a fire (chs. 3-5). Such elements raise questions for readers, ancient and modern, about the mental state of Ezekiel and how we are to interpret such involved literary presentations. Perhaps the best approach is to begin with the recognition that such forms of speaking and writing emerged from a vivid imagination and reflect the horror of Judah's demise. Their bizarre-

ness is an attempt to engage the attention of an audience and to represent the gravity of Judah's circumstances. In spite of others' attempts to analyze his personality, we find it better to acknowledge that the prophet's inner life cannot be reconstructed from the book in any significant way. We have the text but no viable means to get behind it to evaluate his mental state. We can accept or reject the claims that the book is the result of the prophet's religious experience with God, but it is not possible to get behind it to assess the "real" Ezekiel. We may have a modern illustration, however, for the book's visionary symbolism in the phenomenon of virtual reality. Ezekiel's encounter with God produced intricate literary portraits of prophetic activity akin to the alternate worlds that digital artists create in the present.

Miniature of a twelfth-century illuminated manuscript of the Bible, currently in the Bibliothèque nationale de France. The image depicts Ezekiel eating a scroll in preparation for prophesying to the Israelites (Ezek 3).

The Presentation

The book of Ezekiel has three major subsections that follow a basic chronological/thematic scheme: (1) Chapters 1–24 concern Israel and Judah and address them before the fall of Jerusalem to the Babylonians in 587 BCE. The old covenant name *Israel* is frequently used to refer to Judah as the people of God. (2) Chapters 25–32 address various foreign nations, particularly as they too deal with the advancing Babylonian power and as the prophet sees their judgment unfolding in the historical process. (3) Chapters 33–48 deal with the effects of the Babylonian defeat of Judah and depict ways in which the Lord will overcome Israel and Judah's exile and bring in a transformed age.

Ezekiel 1–24: Symbolic Acts and Oracles before Jerusalem's Fall in 587 BCE

The initial chapter sets the tone for much of the involved literary style of the book. It contains descriptions of a chariot throne and the divine presence associated with it. The remarkably detailed symbolism underscores the transcendence of the Lord over his creation and his freedom of mobility in it. For all the specificity of portrayal, note the language of approximation at the conclusion: "This was the appearance of the likeness of the glory of the Lord" (1:28). The Lord's glory is set over against Judah's sinfulness and the prophet's humanity and is a theme that runs throughout the book. In ch. 2 Ezekiel is first addressed as "Son of man," or as the NRSV states it, "Mortal." It confirms his finitude before the living God, who frequently uses the term in addressing Ezekiel.

What we might describe as Ezekiel's "call" is followed by a series of symbolic acts. He is to act as a "watchman" or "sentinel" (3:17) and to communicate with God's people in word and deed. Judah is frequently called by the old covenant name of *Israel*. Ezekiel undertakes strange tasks assigned to him by God (chs. 4–5) to illustrate the continuing sinful state of Judah and judgment to come, even after the city of Jerusalem surrenders to the Babylonians in 597 BCE. Ezekiel was one of a number of other Judahites taken into exile after the city's surrender. This did not, however, prove to be the "wake-up call" and national soul-searching that Ezekiel believed it should have been.

Interpreters have looked for modern analogies to the bizarreness of Ezekiel's acts and suggested, among other ideas, the phenomenon of street theater. It is true that modern street theater and pantomime can have strong countercultural elements and a pronounced social critique. Prophetic sign-acts may have been ancient counterparts. However we assess such depictions as Ezekiel lying on his side for over a year or constructing models of a future siege of Jerusalem, they comport with the prophecies of judgment that follow in chs. 6–7. Note the chilling finality to the claim in 7:2 that the "end" has come upon the land of Israel. Amos offered essentially the same comment regarding Israel and Samaria as the result of a vision (Amos 8:2). The recording of the symbolic acts and the oral prophecies appear to have at least two goals. One is to convince readers that the Lord provided plenty of warning that time was indeed up and that judgment was imminent. A second goal appears with the repeated wish that Israel would "know (= learn) that the Lord is God" (Ezek 7:4, 27). Such "knowing" is not intellectual assent but more a wholehearted, transformative acknowledgment of God's person and work. There is no question, according to the book, that the Lord brought judgment on the land in order to display his glory and holiness, however difficult that may be to contemplate in ancient or modern times.

Visionary elements predominate in chs. 8–11, where an angelic figure serves as a palpable agent of God's Spirit in bringing Ezekiel to Jerusalem.

The prophet "sees" idolatrous worship underway in the temple precincts and learns (again) that God will undertake judgment on these matters. Note the marks given to those who grieve over Judah's failures (9:3-6). They are to be spared, but other people caught up in the idolatry of the day and in doubting the activity of the Lord (9:9) are slain in the vision. This is all a prelude to the central visionary matter in these chapters, which is God's shocking departure from the temple, the result of the people's defiling activity. Ezekiel's theology is rooted in the conviction that God was present to his people in the temple. The ark of the covenant in the inner sanctum was the visible throne of the invisible Lord (see Ps 132:13-14). Ezekiel "sees" God's glory arising, with the rustling noise of the cherubim as the chariot throne gets underway. God is on the move, as in the initial vision of the book. The Lord heads east toward the community in exile, and the fate of the unprotected city is sealed. The final, extended vision of the book corresponds to this section and presents another "visit" to the holy city and temple, this time completely transformed for appropriate worship and possessed of a new name, "The Lord Is There" (chs. 40-48).

Ezekiel 13 reveals conflict with other prophetic figures. Such conflict was inevitable. One sees similar material in Jeremiah (Jer 23:9-40; 28:1-17). The two books even share a common refrain: "peace, peace, when there is no peace" (Ezek 13:10; Jer 6:14). It is clear from the vocabulary that Ezekiel's opponents used similar forms of expression such as vision reports to present their message that Jerusalem's restoration was soon to come.

Ezekiel repeatedly uses the figure of a vine to portray Judah and Jerusalem and the history of the people (15:1-8; 17:1-24; 19:10-14). A vine symbolizes cultivation, fruitfulness, and value. Its destruction represents a judgment on lack of fruitfulness and the tragedy of the vine's not fulfilling its intended function. Ezekiel also uses eagles to portray the machinations of leaders such as Nebuchadnezzar, Zedekiah, and the Egyptian pharaoh (17:1-10). His imagery is described as a riddle and parable. Some translations use the term *allegory* (e.g., the NRSV) to describe the detailed symbolism, but Ezekiel's message is not hidden behind seemingly unrelated items; it is just complex with comparisons due to his chosen figures of speech.

In chs. 16 and 23 Judah and Israel's history is portrayed using the metaphors of Jerusalem as wife and Samaria and Jerusalem as sisters and wives. Again, these are not allegories but something akin to complex parables. In ch. 23 the two cities are given symbolic names. Both chapters employ figural language to portray a history of disobedience to God, comparing it to adultery, prostitution, and promiscuity. The capital cities, representing the people, are the Lord's wives. This is by way of the analogy between covenant and marriage (as in Hosea and Jeremiah). Their failures at covenant fidelity are compared to marital infidelity, and their punishments are harsh. A well-known Israeli scholar once remarked in conversation that these two chapters are "pornographic" in the sense that they use sexually explicit language for exaggerated effect. Note, for example, the following:

> [Oholibah/Jerusalem] lusted after lovers in Egypt whose male members were like those of donkeys and whose seminal emissions were like those of stallions. (Ezek 23:20)

Such language is shocking and offensive and was designed to be so. It reflects an attempt to explain defection from the Lord in coarse terminology, using the language of emotional and physical estrangement and personal affront. The book of Hosea presents a similar portrayal of Israel's failures

Table 24.1. Examples of Symbolic Names

Name	Translation	Message
Jedidiah (2 Sam 12:25)	"Yahweh's beloved"	David's adultery forgiven
Jezreel (Hos 1:4–5, 11)	"God sows"	God effects judgment/salvation
Lo-ruhamah (Hos 1:6)	"not pitied"	expect no divine mercy
Lo-'ammi (Hos 1:9)	"not my people"	covenant to end
Immanuel (Isa 7:14; cf. Matt 1:22–23)	"God is with us"	good: salvation for Jerusalem, bad: Assyria en route
Maher-Shalal-Hash-Baz (Isa 8:3–4)	"Swift is booty, speedy is prey"	Damascus & Samaria doomed — and soon!
Tsemakh Tsadik (Jer 23:5–6)	"righteous branch"	future, upright king
Oholah (Ezek 23)	"(cult) tent owner" (Samaria)	sanctuaries ≠ sanctuary
Oholibah (Ezek 23)	"my cult tent is in her" (Jerusalem)	
Jesus (Matt 1:21, 25)	"savior"	his mission = forgiveness

Names could be an important indicator of identity in ancient Israel. Like Hosea, Isaiah gave symbolic names to children (Isa 7:14; 8:3–4; 9:6). Jeremiah gave a symbolic name to a future ruler (Jer 23:5–6), and Ezekiel gave symbolic names to Samaria and Jerusalem (Ezek 23:1–49).

an interesting phenomenon, since Jehoiachin had only a brief time on the throne of Judah before being taken to Babylon as an exile. They do not occur in chronological order. The dated prophecies run from a time before the fall of Jerusalem to the Babylonians in 587 BCE to the year 571, the twenty-seventh year of Jehoiachin's "reign" (29:17). Although he was in exile, years are still dated according to his reign. As with the prophecies against Tyre, Ezekiel uses various literary forms, including the funeral lament in ch. 32 over the predicted defeat of Egypt.

Ezekiel 33–48: More Turmoil and the Final Vision of a Transformed Community

Ezekiel is described as a watchman or sentry (3:16-21; 33:1-9). This is one way to describe the prophetic roles that he undertook. It was his appointed task to cry out regarding the imminent danger to the nation that he saw in vision and dream as well as to portray a future time of wholesale change. These chapters, therefore, continue the sharp critique of the prophet's contemporaries but also move beyond them to prophecies and visions of a broader, positive future.

Good leaders should be like shepherds to their people. Chapter 34 contains strong criticism of Judah's leaders who failed the people. Their failures are one reason for the judgmental prophecies in the book. But Ezekiel also offers hope for the future, based first on the conviction that God is the true shepherd of Israel and will thus rescue his people, and second that God will raise up a second "David" to care for them and be their ruler.

Beginning with ch. 36, Ezekiel turns toward the future restoration and transformation of Israel that culminates in the detailed visions of a new holy city and land. This follows a pattern noted in the introduction to the prophetic books. In these last chapters of Ezekiel, Israel's restoration is for the sake of God's name and glory, not because the people have somehow earned their renewal. Note, for example, the vision of the valley of dry bones in ch. 37: Ezekiel is asked whether such bones "can live." The biological answer, of course, is "no!" Ezekiel's reply, however, leaves the fate of the dry (and defiling) bones with God, who commands him to prophesy to them. The resurrection of the bones into living beings represents the renewal of the people in exile and their restoration in their homeland. Resurrection is not a self-generated act but a gift provided by God. Their restoration in a homeland, however, is prelude to even grander visionary

Depiction of Ezekiel's vision of the valley of dry bones (Ezek 37) from the Luther Bible, published in 1534 with several hand-colored woodcuts.

matters. The covenant that Israel broke will be restored, the Lord will take up residence among them by means of his Spirit in a new sanctuary, and a new David will be their prince (= ruler). The conclusion to ch. 37 is a good summary, and it sets the stage for the climactic vision in 40–48:

> The nations will know that I, the Lord, am sanctifying Israel,
> when my sanctuary is among them forever. (Ezek 37:28)

Here the prophet's vision has moved beyond the geography of restoration to the renewal of the people in their covenant relationship with God. It is a "new temple" theology: as the Lord was once present with his people through the medium of the First Temple, so the Lord will be even more a sanctifying presence among them in the eschatological future.

Evil and human fallibility have staying power, however! This appears as a theme in chs. 38–39. Interpreters are divided on whether these chapters about threats to Israel should be read in linear sequence to an accomplished restoration in chs. 36–37 or whether they are intended to speak in kaleidoscopic fashion—that is, circling around to another set of images dealing with the same subject. In any case, evil and warfare are resilient, and the mysterious figures of Gog and Magog, apparently peoples from the far north of Israel in Asia Minor, are on the predatory move. Eventually their forces are destroyed. Reading these chapters between the restoration passages in 36-37 and the transformed land in 40-48 can be a jarring experience. Gog and Magog represent a hitherto-unknown power and come from a greater distance than Israel's previous enemies. Whatever their historical setting, they represent the continuing struggle with evil until the book's grand conclusion. This is the way, for example, that John the seer portrays Gog and Magog in Rev 20:7-10, as prelude to the descent of the heavenly Jerusalem.

The last nine chapters of the book comprise the longest single visionary account in the book and, indeed, in the OT. They are best read in light of the book as a whole, as these last chapters are shaped by the same priestly concerns and themes that brought the other Ezekiel materials together. There are two items to keep in mind in reading through them. The first is the visionary material in chs. 8-11, where the prophet is taken to Jerusalem to see the idolatrous worship in the temple complex and to behold the departure of the Lord's presence from the temple. The second is the declaration in ch. 37 that the Lord will set his sanctuary again among his people and that the nations will know that he sanctifies Israel. What will a newly (or re-) sanctified city and land look like to a priest in an eschatological age to come? Chapters 40-48 are a literary portrait in answer to that question.

The vision is dated some twenty-five years after Ezekiel was taken into exile. He is transported again (compare with 8:3) to a high mountain with a city to the south. Although not named specifically, this is a transformed Mount Zion with the new city of Jerusalem to the south. An angel guides the prophet again (see 8:2), and he is to report what he sees to the house of Israel. First, Ezekiel walks through the temple complex, noting its measurements and layouts (chs. 40-43). Chapter 44 contains a discussion of the roles of the prince (a future Davidic ruler), Levites, and priests, along with a matter-of-fact statement that Ezekiel saw the glory of the Lord filling the temple (44:4)! As noted, God's presence in this eschatological temple reverses the vision of God's departure in chs. 10-11 and fulfills the promise of God's residence among the people in chs. 36-37. Moreover, just as the finished tabernacle (Exod 40:34-38) and the finished temple (1 Kgs 8:10-13) were filled with God's presence, so will the new temple be filled with God's presence in the coming eschatological age. The last verse of the book states it succinctly: the future name of the holy city is "The Lord Is There" (48:35). Second, although Ezekiel is not through reporting about the temple complex and services, including sacrifices and offerings (chs. 45–46), he also "sees" a transformed landscape of Canaan. There are new dimensions for the holy city, expanded and redrawn boundaries for the tribes of Israel, and water from the temple that flows eastward to the Dead Sea and makes even it suitable for life. This is the eschatological home of the house of Israel as "seen" in a vision.

It is important to note that all of this is provided for Ezekiel. Unlike the First (and Second) Temple in Jerusalem, he constructs nothing and sees nothing built. Everything—temple, city, and reconstituted landscape—is simply "there" upon his visionary arrival. This is essentially the pattern in John's final vision in the NT book of Revelation (Rev 21–22). In his case, however, he "sees" the holy city coming down out of heaven as the center of the new heavens and earth (from Isa 65–66). Nothing is built (i.e., made by human hands), but everything is provided.

Ezekiel's final vision has been variously interpreted in Christian and Jewish communities. Granted that his final chapters describe a perceived eschatological future, what is their connection to Israel's future as a nation or as a people? Some interpreters are content with the recognition that Ezekiel's vision reflects the prophet's vivid imagination. There is no anticipation of a concrete, earthly filling out of the vision to come but appreciation for the prophet's skill in portraying a restored, priestly-oriented community and his conviction that God's faithfulness extends to the future of the people. Some Christians believe that Ezekiel's vision is taken up and expanded in John's final vision (Rev 21–22), with God and the Lamb taking the place of a physical temple, and that is the fulfillment of Ezekiel's prophetic hope. Others find in Ezekiel's vision an indication that a future temple should be built in Jerusalem. For example, there are Christian interpreters who propose that the millennial rule of Christ depicted by John (Rev 20:1–6) will have a literal fulfillment on this earth, complete with a temple in Jerusalem, animal sacrifice, and new Jewish settlement patterns in the eastern Mediterranean, as described by Ezekiel. There are also some Jewish interpreters who believe that a future temple will be built in Jerusalem, whether in an eschatological age or not, and they use Ezekiel's visions for support. There are even male descendants of the tribe of Levi preparing to serve as priests in a rebuilt temple, should such a structure be rebuilt.

The topic of a new Jewish temple in a future Jerusalem evokes quite a passion among those who believe that Ezekiel's visionary account points to it. Others, as noted above, may well appreciate the grandeur of the prophet's portrayal of a transformed city and temple but do not see it as requiring a literal rebuilding of the temple. We recommend some resources to consult for further information on this matter of biblical interpretation:

Price, Randall. *The Temple and Bible Prophecy: A Definitive Look at Its Past, Present, and Future*. Eugene, OR: Harvest House, 2005. [Price believes there will be a future temple built in Jerusalem.]

Beale, G. K. *The Temple and the Church's Mission: A Biblical Theology of the Dwelling Place of God*. Downers Grove, IL: InterVarsity Press, 2004. [Beale believes that the prophecies in the OT regarding a future temple in Jerusalem are fulfilled in John's visions of a new Jerusalem in Rev 21–22.]

"The Temple Institute." http://www.templeinstitute.org/. [The Temple Institute is a Jewish organization that believes a temple will be built in Jerusalem and is working toward that end.]

READING

Read Ezek 1–48 and supply answers to the following questions:

1. Read Ezek 37:1–14. How do you understand the claim in v. 11 that the bones are "the whole house of Israel"? Is this a reference to a people or a political entity (nation)? What kind of restoration of Israel is depicted in the coming to life of the bones?

2. Read Ezek 16:1–63. On what parts of Israel and Judah's previous histories does Ezekiel draw? Do you think that the prophet's depiction of the people's faithlessness is too harsh or fairly depicts their failures? What covenant is in mind in 16:60?

3. Read Ezek 4–5. Which of Ezekiel's symbolic acts do you find the most surprising and why? How do you understand the purpose of these acts?

4. Read Ezek 34. In what ways have Israel's leaders shown themselves to be false or failed shepherds? In what ways will God demonstrate that he is the true or faithful shepherd? What implications for Christian leadership might you draw from this chapter?

5. Read Ezek 40–48. How do you interpret these chapters? Are there other biblical passages that you find similar?

BIBLIOGRAPHY

Beckwith, Carl, ed. *Ezekiel, Daniel.* Reformation Commentary on Scripture. Downers Grove, IL: InterVarsity Press, 2012.

Block, Daniel I. *The Book of Ezekiel: Chapters 1–24.* NICOT. Grand Rapids: Eerdmans, 1997.

———. *The Book of Ezekiel: Chapters 25–48.* NICOT. Grand Rapids: Eerdmans, 1998.

Block, Daniel I., and Jacob Milgrom. *Ezekiel's Hope: A Commentary on Ezekiel 38–48.* Eugene, OR: Wipf & Stock, 2012.

Davis, Ellen. *Swallowing the Scroll: Textuality and the Dynamics of Discourse in Ezekiel's Prophecy.* New York: Continuum, 1989.

Joyce, Paul M. *Ezekiel: A Commentary.* London: T&T Clark, 2007.

Klein, Ralph W. *Ezekiel: The Prophet and His Message.* Columbia: University of South Carolina Press, 1988.

Sweeney, Marvin A. *Reading Ezekiel: A Literary and Theological Commentary.* Macon, GA: Smyth & Helwys, 2013.

Wright, Christopher J. H. *The Message of Ezekiel: A New Heart and a New Spirit.* Downers Grove, IL: InterVarsity Press, 2001.

Zimmerli, Walter. *Ezekiel.* 2 vols. Hermeneia. Philadelphia: Fortress, 1979, 1983.

25 THE BOOK OF DANIEL

Important Dates for Daniel
605–539: Babylonian rule
539: Belshazzar dies, Cyrus conquers Babylon
538–332: Persian rule
332–164: Greek rule of Alexander and his successors
175–164: rule of Antiochus IV Epiphanes
167–164: Maccabean (Hasmonean) revolt

THE BOOK OF DANIEL, NAMED for its central character, typically evokes both wonder and puzzlement among readers. It has some of the best-known stories and some of the more puzzling visionary depictions in all of the OT. On the one hand, there are the accounts written in third person: the Hebrew youths in the fiery furnace, Daniel in the lions' den, and the mysterious handwriting that just appears on a palace wall. On the other hand, there are depictions of strange beasts and a mysterious statue made of various metals and feet comprising a mixture of iron and clay. As discussed below, much of the visionary material is formulated in apocalyptic style and written in first person, as Daniel's own accounts.

Daniel is also one of the books that is assigned to different sections in collections of the Scriptures. In the Hebrew Bible, Daniel comes in the third category of books, the Writings or the Hagiographa, not in the Prophets. Perhaps this is because the book was not completed until after the collection of the prophetic books in the Hebrew Bible was compiled or because Daniel was reckoned among the wise by Jewish readers and thus placed with books such as Proverbs and Ecclesiastes. In the Christian Bible, however, Daniel is placed right after Ezekiel and before the Twelve Minor Prophets. In other words, the book is paired with Ezekiel, representing yet another figure from the Babylonian exile, and considered prophetic (cf. Matt 24:15). This placement reflects one arrangement of the books in the Septuagint (LXX), an originally Jewish translation of the Hebrew Bible into Greek that became the Scriptures of early Christianity. And as if to confirm Daniel's wonderful peculiarity, about 40 percent of the book was originally written in Aramaic (2:4–7:28).

The Book of Daniel and the Figure of Daniel

Ezekiel's prophecy against the ruler of Tyre compares that ruler's wisdom to the wisdom of a figure named Daniel (28:3). The spelling of the name Daniel (*Dan'el* in 28:3) is slightly different from that in the book of Daniel. This leads many interpreters to see Ezekiel's reference, not to the Daniel of the OT book, but to a legendary wise figure mentioned in Ugaritic literature from the second millennium BCE named *Dan'el*. In any case, wisdom is a common description of these named figures.

Daniel was a popular figure among Jews and Christians, and thus several additions to the book by his name circulated among Greek-speaking Jews and Christians. Three of these are: The Prayer of Azariah and the Song of the Three Young Men, Susanna, and Bel and the Dragon. The first document actually appears between 3:23 and 3:24 in some Greek translations of Daniel. The other two are also written in Greek, but they circulated separately from the Greek translations of the larger book. All three works are part of what is known as the OT Apocrypha and thus read in many Christian traditions (see ch. 37 below on canon and text). Additionally, there are some fragmentary texts among the Dead Sea Scrolls that are known as part of a Pseudo-Daniel cycle. Expanded traditions about the figure of Daniel in Judaism have parallels with those about Jeremiah, Baruch, and Ezra. The comments that follow deal with the book of Daniel held in com-

> ### Danel and Ugarit
>
> The writings from ancient Ugarit offer a number of similarities to the OT and Israelite culture. They date to the Late Bronze Age, ca. 1500–1200 BCE. One of these similarities is the figure Danel (a name closely related to the Hebrew name Daniel), who is mentioned in the document called the Epic of Aqhat. Danel was the father of Aqhat and a revered figure in the story, who judged fairly for widows and orphans (see Jeremiah's injunction in Jer 7:6 to care for widows and orphans).

mon by the Hebrew Bible and the Protestant OT. (For additional information about the popular Greek additions to that book, see the bibliography in our ch. 37.)

Apocalyptic Literature and Eschatological Symbolism

Part of Daniel's peculiarity results from its genre (= literary type). It has the basic characteristics of a historical apocalypse. The term *apocalypse* is taken from the Greek noun meaning "revelation." An apocalypse is

> a genre of revelatory literature with a narrative framework, in which a revelation is mediated by an otherworldly being to a human recipient, disclosing a transcendental reality which is both temporal, insofar as it envisages eschatological salvation, and spatial insofar as it involves another, supernatural world. (Collins, *Apocalypse: The Morphology of a Genre*, p. 9)

In addition to the angel role, an apocalypse may contain visionary accounts, highly symbolic language, numerology, or a dualism between light and dark, good and evil. Daniel shares all these characteristics. There are also apocalyptic traits in prophetic books such as Ezekiel and Zechariah, but Daniel is the best example of this literary style in the OT. Table 25.1 compares prophetic characteristics with apocalyptic characteristics.

The dualism and emphasis on eschatology may be keys not only to the book's literary style but also to the social forces that birthed the book. Daniel and some other apocalypses are rooted in historical contexts of persecution. They could be considered countercultural to some readers, even in the host culture. In Daniel's case, the symbolic language can function as a code to instruct and to encourage Jewish readers under persecution as well as to conceal or at least obscure things for the dominant, oppressing culture.

Apocalyptic Symbolism and the Setting of the Book in Times of Persecution

The narratives of the book place Daniel and other exiled Hebrews in Babylon from the reign of Nebuchadnezzar until that of Cyrus, King of the Medes and Persians. There are references in it to a siege of Jerusalem in the third year of King Jehoiakim (Dan 1:1), the death of Belshazzar in Babylon (Dan 5:30), a brief reign by Darius the Mede (Dan 5:31; 9:1; 11:1), and the third year of Cyrus (Dan 10:1). This is a period of approximately seventy years. At present, there are historical difficulties in accounting for a siege by Nebuchadnezzar on Jerusalem in Jehoiakim's third year and for the figure of Darius the Mede. To illustrate: Nebuchadnezzar was not made king of Babylon officially until Jehoiakim's fourth year (605 BCE) in the typical mode of record keeping in Judah. Second, there is no corroboration for an assault on Jerusalem in the year 605 BCE in other ancient sources. Possibly the reference to Jehoiakim's third year assumes what is called accession-year dating, in which the partial first year of a new ruler is not counted in his years of reign. In this accounting, a ruler's years are reckoned from the first full year of reign after the death of the predecessor. This type of dating was used in Mesopotamia. In this scheme, 605 would indeed be Jehoiakim's third year; nevertheless, we still lack corroborating sources for an attack on Jerusalem or the exiling of Hebrew youths at this time.

With respect to the figure of Darius the Mede, surviving sources do not list a Darius the Mede as a ruler in Babylon between the fall of the city and the declaration of Cyrus as its ruler. Some interpreters have suggested that Darius was another name of Cyrus or another name for a high official of the time who served in an appointed capacity immediately after Nabonidus,

Table 25.1. Prophecy versus Apocalyptic

Prophecy	Apocalyptic
Repentance from sin	Sin too great, destruction inevitable
God's displeasure with his evil people	People's displeasure with evil, desire for God's intervention
Call for God's people to repent	Call for a faithful remnant to persevere
Divine intervention by natural or human means	Direct divine intervention by supernatural means
Direct speech by God	Mysterious, symbolic, indirect speech by intermediary
Prediction of imminent and future events	Prediction of cosmic, final solutions

This table is simplified from D. Brent Sandy and R. L. Giese Jr., eds., *Cracking Old Testament Codes* (Nashville: Broadman & Holman, 1995), 178–79.

the last Babylonian king. When one adds the use of Aramaic for a middle portion of the book of Daniel, some terms for musical instruments in 3:5 that have Greek origins, and the detailed knowledge of the rule of Alexander the Great and some of his successors (11:2–45), interpreters frequently conclude that the book, whole or in part, was written considerably later than the early Persian period.

At this point, we should also note that the book presents a series of coming empires through the following images: a statue composed of various metals (2:31–45); four beasts, the last of which has ten horns (7:2–28); a ram and a he-goat with four horns (8:1–26); the princes of Persia and Greece and their supernatural forces (10:13–21); and various rulers who succeed a strong king from Greece (11:1–45). Taken together, it seems that the series ends with the successors to the empire established by Alexander the Great (died 323 BCE). Most of the attention in the various descriptions of the kingdoms is given to the fourth and last kingdom (see the sidebar). These characteristics lead many interpreters to see the book as originating in the 2nd century BCE, and more particularly, in the time of Antiochus IV Epiphanes, the Greek ruler (175-164 BCE) who defiled the temple in Jerusalem and persecuted the Jews who rose up in revolt against him for that desecration. In this scheme Antiochus is the arrogant small horn of the goat (8:8–25) as well as the pretentious king of the north (11:20–45) who wreaks havoc for a time and who will set up an abomination in the holy place (9:27; 11:31). The books of 1 and 2 Maccabees, two works from the 2nd/1st century BCE, provide many details on the fierce persecution of Jews by Antiochus IV, his defiling of the temple in Jerusalem, and the revolt led by the Maccabees (Hasmonean family) against him. The Jewish festival of Hanukkah originated in celebration of the successful cleansing of the temple after Antiochus's forces were pushed out of the city. (For details, consult the appropriate tables at the conclusion to chapters 10 and 16 on Neo-Babylonian rulers, Persian kings, Hellenistic rulers, and the Hasmonean family.)

Modern readers face two basic options with respect to the book of Daniel. (1) One option is to take seriously the exilic/early postexilic setting of the narratives as an indication of when the book was written and to assume that the depictions of the Greek Empire are supernatural knowledge granted to Daniel by God. This option should not be rejected out of hand, but it doesn't answer the question of the "historical difficulties" in the description of Nebuchadnezzar and Darius the Mede or the literary characteristics (e.g., words of Greek origin) of the Aramaic text. As noted above, the reference to "Danel" in Ezek 14:20 could be evidence for the well-known Daniel in sixth-century Babylon. While this is possible, Ezekiel's Danel is more likely a king from the second millennium BCE who is known from ancient texts discovered at Ugarit in northern Syria (see the sidebar on p. 329). This latter identification would fit the references to Noah and Job in Ezek 14:20, who were sages from earlier times. (2) The other option is to take seriously the depiction of Antiochus IV Epiphanes in Dan 11 as the historical location of the author, who adopts older traditions about the persecution of the ancestors in exile and recasts them in his current context of intense persecution. This is preferable to a third option, which is that the book of Daniel is completely the creation of an author who lived during the time of the Maccabean revolt (167 BCE and following). There are several things about the third-person narratives of the Hebrew youths that are more likely older traditions about life in exile that are subsequently adapted by a later author. The first-person visions similarly follow a pattern of depicting world empires that is recast in the Maccabean period in yet another period of persecution. In what follows, the second option is assumed.

Prophecy, Wisdom, and Eschatology in Daniel

Neither Daniel nor his companions are called prophets in the book, but they have certain characteristics that are associated with prophetic activity. They are, however, explicitly grouped in the category of the wise (Dan 1:18–20; 2:13) and share certain characteristics of sages. According to ch. 2, Nebuchadnezzar was unhappy with his magicians and sorcerers and sought to destroy those who could not interpret his dreams. In Israel, interpreting dreams was one activity of a prophet (Deut 13), although Joseph, who is

Reconstruction of the original bricks of the Ishtar Gate, the eighth (or northern) gate to the inner city of Babylon built by Nebuchadnezzar (ca. 575 BCE), in the Pergamon Museum, Berlin. ©Radomir Vrbovsky (Wikimedia Commons, CC-SA 4.0)

not called a prophet, interpreted Pharaoh's dream (Gen 41). Daniel had the wisdom and the theological insight from the God of heaven to describe and to interpret Nebuchadnezzar's dream. And thus, like Joseph of old in Egypt, he rises to a place of prominence in Babylon. He is wise in a court setting where other magicians and sages are located. The superiority of his insight is illustrative of the supremacy of the Lord, the God of Israel, over the Babylonian deities. Like Ezekiel and Zechariah, Daniel had interaction with angels, intermediaries from God who made sure that their human audience knew what God intended to reveal about the future. Moreover, it is in reflection on the prophetic word of Jeremiah about a seventy-year period of exile that Daniel is graced with insight about seventy weeks of years to come (Dan 9:1–27).

Thus Daniel represents a combination of the characteristics of prophets and court sages. Sages sought to understand mysteries, and prophets sought a defining word from the Lord. Daniel represents both in the court setting of a foreign culture. What he adds to both prophecy and wisdom is a heightened eschatological awareness. He can speak of a kingdom that is eternal (Dan 2:44), of the resurrection of the dead to either everlasting life or to eternal contempt (12:2), and even of the "end of time" (12:4). God's sovereignty is such that Daniel can speak about times and seasons and the ways in which the Almighty has granted pagan empires periods of rule. Nebuchadnezzar, the most powerful person of his day, went mad and ate grass like an animal. This was to confirm that the Most High held sway over the affairs of people and nations and that his kingdom would be an everlasting dominion (4:28–37).

The Story

The book of Daniel has two major subsections: (1) third-person narratives about Daniel and his friends (Dan 1–6), and (2) first-person accounts of Daniel's visions (Dan 7–12). The Aramaic portions of the book appear mostly in the first section but extend into ch. 7.

Daniel 1–6: Daniel and His Friends

Daniel and his companions may be exiles in Babylon, but their primary identity is not that of defeated exiles but of servants of the Most High, the God of heaven. In ch. 1 the Hebrew youths do not eat the food of the Babylonian court but food that is in accord with their laws and culture. The question of diet and of acceptable food was something that every exile faced, plus the dietary customs of Judaism took on added importance in the later Second Temple period. Here is testimony that the dietary practices of Judaism were divinely willed and capable of nourishing God's people in a hostile culture.

Nebuchadnezzar's dream depicted a statue of various metals and feet of clay and iron (2:31–45). Daniel's wisdom surpasses the insight of the court sages in that he knows both the dream's contents and their symbolic significance. The statue represents a series of four empires, beginning with Babylon, which comes to an end. The stone (not made by human hands) that knocks down the statue and then fills the earth represents God's eternal kingdom. As noted above, this succession of empires, including God's eternal kingdom, is depicted several times in symbolic form (Dan 7:1-27; 8:1-26; 10:13-21; 11:1-45). Most interpreters take their initial clue in identifying the pagan empires by comparing these references. The first empire, of course, is Babylon itself (2:36-38), while the second and third are the Medes and Persians (2:39). The powerful and oppressive fourth is that of the Greeks under Alexander the Great and his successors (2:40-43). Some interpreters have interpreted the four great empires as (1) Babylon, (2) Media-Persia, (3) Greece, and (4) Rome, seeing the ultimate fulfillment of Daniel's coming kingdom during Rome's rule, when Jesus announced the rule of God as "at hand." It is very likely that both Jesus and early Christians saw the hopes of Daniel's eternal kingdom fulfilled in the kingdom that Jesus announced and embodied, but this is a different matter from a precise enumeration of the four world empires portrayed in ch. 2.

Three youths were thrown into a fiery furnace because they refused to worship the golden image (Dan 3:1-30). This was an issue that Jews would face periodically from the exile onward. Bowing to honor a pagan ruler was a difficult thing, but pagan worship was another, more defiling matter. The latter was not acceptable to practicing Jews, although the threat of persecution caused some to compromise. To the three youths the choice was obvious: whether God saved them or not, they would not bow down to an idol. Note the poignancy and the perseverance of the Hebrew youths expressed in 3:16-18. There would be (and have been) times when Jews were put to death for their refusal to participate in various religious requirements of a Gentile government. Antiochus Epiphanes set up an idol in the Jerusalem temple courtyard and forbade certain Jewish practices, provoking both outrage and revolt on the part of Jews—all of which led to his fierce persecution of Judaism (see Dan 9:26-27; 11:31; 1 Macc 1:10-2:41; 2 Macc 5:15-7:42; Matt 24:15).

Daniel faced a similar situation in the command of the king that for thirty days everyone was to pray to the image of the king (6:1-27). Daniel had the habit of praying toward Jerusalem, and he continued that practice, even after the edict. This posture of prayer toward Jerusalem apparently increased as a result of the Babylonian exile and the dispersion of God's people. The decision was clear, both for Daniel and for the officials who wanted to trap him. Even though Daniel had an exalted place in the administration of Babylon, they persuaded the king that he should be thrown to the lions because his religious convictions ran counter to those of the Empire.

Nebuchadnezzar's second dream (ch. 4) shows that his sovereignty ultimately comes from the God of heaven whom Daniel (whose Babylonian name is Belteshazzar) worships. There is no extrabiblical confirmation of an

illness for Nebuchadnezzar, but an interesting document among the Dead Sea Scrolls (4Q242, The Prayer of Nabonidus) refers to the healing powers of a Jewish diviner during the reign of the last Babylonian king. Some interpreters suggest that the Prayer of Nabonidus and the account in Dan 4 derive from similar traditions.

Chapter 5 provides a dramatic narrative regarding the fall of Babylon and the end of the Babylonian Empire. "King" Belshazzar was a caretaker regent over Babylon when the last official king, Nabonidus, was away for some years in the Arabian Desert. The Medo-Persian forces under Cyrus did take the city in a quick operation. As noted above, the figure of Darius the Mede, who takes over from Belshazzar (5:31), cannot be verified by surviving historical records. There were, however, three different Persian rulers with the name Darius who succeeded Cyrus.

Daniel 7–12: Accounts of Daniel's Visions

The second half of the book primarily contains vision reports. In the context of a vision of beasts representing the Gentile kingdoms of the world, Daniel sees the Ancient of Days seated on the throne. This is a theophany,

Belshazzar's Feast, by Rembrandt. 1635. Rembrandt depicts here the famous writing on the wall described in Daniel 5:5–29.

a depiction in visionary language of the presence of God and a foretaste of the eternal kingdom to come (7:1–14). Here readers encounter the majestic theology of the cosmic king who will receive worship and honor from all peoples. The Gentile nations are not simply fodder for the fire of judgment; they include people capable of worship and service in the eternal kingdom. Readers should compare this visionary scene in Dan 7:1–14 with that of the throne-room scene of God and the Lamb in Rev 4–5. In the latter, people from every tribe, language, and nation are deemed "saints" and "priests" in God's kingdom (Rev 5:9–10). For the author of Daniel, those who love and serve the Lord, even in exile or under persecution are "saints of the Most High." "Saints" may include angels (cf. 8:13), but here the reference is to faithful humans. Moreover, representing the people of God is one "like a Son of Man" (7:13–14), who is granted an exalted place by God. If beasts represent the dominant Gentile empires to come, the one like a "Son of Man" represents the people of God and the eternal kingdom. There is a clear allusion to this scene in Mark and Matthew's depiction of Jesus on trial before the high priest. When asked whether he is the Son of God or not, Jesus refers to the "Son of Man coming on the clouds with power" (Mark 14:60–62; Matt 26:63–66; cf. Dan 7:13). The phrase *Son of Man* can mean more than one thing—sometimes it means nothing more than a mortal or human being (see Ezek 2:1)—but the allusion to Dan 7:13 demonstrates that the regal and representative role of the Son of Man in Daniel was understood by early Christians specifically to portray the work of the Messiah.

Although the book of Daniel has a robust view of God's sovereignty and his will for a transformed future, it is also realistic about the resilient power of evil that opposes God. Throughout the book the contrasts are starkly drawn. Evil throws the saints into the fire or the lions' den. Troubles will continue for weeks of years before the advent of eternal righteousness. Angels too wrestle with the power of evil. The powers of evil can manifest themselves in the successive kingdoms of this world. The eternal kingdom represented in the book is known by promise and faith, but it is not yet manifest to all. That is, God's dominion is not recognized by all until the end of times and seasons, when evil has run its course. The book of Daniel has a pronounced eschatological tint to it, representing the coming rule of God as the decisive change for all of history. In these matters the book portrays themes that will strongly influence Judaism, Christianity, and even Islam. Judgment and salvation are God's acts, which can only be completed in the world to come.

Chapter 8 continues the portrayal of Gentile kingdoms and the difficulties to come. Daniel's vision again includes animals and their characteristics as representative of the kingdoms. Note that an angel named Gabriel assists Daniel in interpreting his vision. Daniel is the one book in the OT that has named angels (see Michael, 10:13; 12:1). Gabriel also brings a message to Mary in Nazareth (Luke 1:26), and in Islamic tradition he commands Muhammad to recite God's revelation to him.

Daniel reflects on the meaning of Jeremiah's prediction of an exile lasting seventy years (Dan 9:1–27; cf. Jer 25:11–12). His reflection takes the form of a prayer of confession. The angel Gabriel comes again to him to say that while the exile is to last seventy years, God has determined that seventy weeks of years will pass until the coming of the eternal kingdom. The number seven connotes completeness in Israelite thought, so seventy sevens are an intuitive representation of completeness extending over a considerable amount of time. Other aspects of the time period described are more difficult to determine precisely. It is likely, for example, that the period of sixty-nine weeks runs from the restoration of Jerusalem under Persian rule until the rise of the prince who is to come (Antiochus Epiphanes), who subjects Jews to persecution. That persecution under Antiochus is part of the last week and

The prophet Daniel depicted in a 12th-century stained glass window in the Augsburg Cathedral in Germany. ©Hans Bernhard (Wikimedia Commons, CC-SA 3.0)

26 THE BOOKS OF HOSEA, AMOS, AND MICAH

THE THREE MINOR PROPHETS OF the 8th century, Hosea, Amos, and Micah, are preserved to explain why Israel fell to the Assyrians, to explain what lessons readers might take from that, and to indicate ways in which the Lord is still at work in the world. The burning question the books address is: how does one explain in theological terms the demise of Israel as an independent state, Judah's vassal status to Assyria, and the success of the Assyrians in controlling the region? According to each prophetic book, God raised up a prophet to speak a timely word of judgment, discipline, and renewal in the midst of international turmoil.

All three books were compiled after the fact by disciples and editors. In the cases of Hosea and Amos, their prophetic activity was largely, if not exclusively, in Israel, but the final compiling and circulation were done in Judah. Micah was a Judahite who addressed both Israel and Judah. Amos too was a Judahite, even though he traveled north to Israel to carry out his prophetic tasks. There are some rather complicated theories about the editorial compiling of each book, based on careful analysis of vocabulary and perceived audience. On the one hand, readers should reckon with the possibility of updating and elaboration until sometime in the postexilic period, particularly in the case of Micah. On the other hand, these are relatively short books and may have reached their essential form in the generation that succeeded the prophets themselves.

What Was Going On at the Time of Their Prophetic Work?

In the 9th–7th centuries BCE, the Assyrian Empire eventually overwhelmed all the states in the eastern Mediterranean region, including Egypt for a time. States and tribal groups were defeated and annexed, forced into various stages of subservience as vassals, or otherwise made to comply with Assyrian designs (see Table 22.2 on p. 285).

The heartland of Assyria was northern Mesopotamia, which is today northern Iraq. Part of an old civilization, the Assyrian expansion began in the early 9th century. Ahab of Israel and his regional coalition partners struggled fiercely against Shalmaneser III, who carried out several military campaigns to his west as one part of Assyrian expansion. Interestingly, this is known from Assyrian records (see Table 2.5 on p. 22). The treatment of Ahab in 1 Kings does not mention his opposition to the Assyrians. The first half of the 8th century saw something of a respite for the eastern Mediterranean states, but it was simply the lull before the storm. In the year 745 BCE, the vigorous ruler Tiglath-pileser III came to power. Before he died in 727, his forces had taken over approximately two-thirds of Israel (2 Kgs 15:29), leaving Samaria and the Ephraimite hill country as something of a rump state, and forcing Judah under Ahaz to become a vassal state. His successor Shalmaneser V would bring an end to Samaria's independence in 722 BCE, and his successor Sargon II would send thousands of the inhabitants of Samaria and its environs into exile. Sargon too would campaign in the region after the end of the independent state of Israel. And finally, his successor Sennacherib would concentrate his forces on a devastating campaign against Hezekiah (who had withheld tribute after the death of Sargon) and Judah. They surrounded Jerusalem, but the siege was broken, and Hezekiah survived on the throne (Isa 36–39; 2 Kgs 18–19). It had been quite a half-century!

One way or another Judah slipped back into the status of vassal as the Assyrian Empire reached its greatest expanse in the first half of the 7th century. Even Lower Egypt fell to Esarhaddon, the Assyrian king. Manasseh's long tenure as king came in the shadow of Assyrian might. The decades-long Assyrian control of the eastern Mediterranean would ease in stages, beginning with the death of Assurbanipal in 627 BCE and concluding with the fall of Nineveh in 612 BCE.

The Book of Hosea

Hosea is the first of the Minor Prophets in the Hebrew Bible, following the three Major Prophets of Isaiah, Jeremiah, and Ezekiel. Daniel, although not considered one of the twelve Minor Prophets in Judaism, comes between Ezekiel and Hosea in Christian Bibles. There are at least three plausible reasons for Hosea's placement at the head of the twelve smaller prophetic books. He may have been considered the earliest of the prophets in the collection. Modern scholars often assign that spot to Amos, Hosea's contemporary, but the superscriptions place both prophets in the reign of Jeroboam II in Israel. Hosea is also the largest book of the Minor Prophets, and its subject matter forms a good introduction to the works that follow.

Hosea's superscription lists four kings of Judah (Hos 1:1: Uzziah, Jotham, Ahaz, and Hezekiah), whose combined reigns covered most of the 8th century; Jeroboam II is the only Israelite king who is named here. Jeroboam was a contemporary of Uzziah; he died about mid-century, and a period of instability ensued, including multiple assassinations of a reigning monarch (2 Kgs 14:23–15:31). The list of Judahite kings implies that the book of Hosea was edited in Judah after the fall of Samaria. A number of "refugees" from Israel came to Jerusalem and Judah in the final years of the Northern Kingdom, among them possibly Hosea himself, or more likely, his anonymous disciples.

The book of Hosea has two main subsections, chs. 1–3 and 4–14. The theme of the first subsection is the marriage and family life of Hosea as illustrative of God's relationship with Israel. The second and larger subsection contains poetic prophecies against the folly of Israel, concluding with portions of a repentance liturgy and affirmations that Israel is still precious to the Lord. Both sections of the book are informed by a central metaphor: Israel is God's household or family.

Hosea 1–3: Marriage and Family

The first three chapters of Hosea are concerned with the prophet's wife, Gomer, and their three children, although this is not a simple report about the prophet's family. The family details in them are a part of a prophetic proclamation designed primarily to portray Israel as rebellious and estranged from the Lord. Gomer and the children represent Israel, and Hosea represents the Lord. The names of the three children, Jezreel, No-Compassion, and Not-My-People, symbolize a breach between Israel and God. Four commands to Hosea by the Lord are cited: first, to marry Gomer, and then to name the three children that she bore (1:2–9). Hosea 1:10–11 has a reversal motif, contrasting the historical failure of Israel with God's resolve to bless and renew Israel in the future. The two parts of ch. 2 show this same pattern: 2:1–13 depicts judgment on Gomer/Israel, and 2:14–23 her restoration in the future. Chapter 3 is a first-person account of the prophet, who purchases an adulteress as a sign that God intends to reconcile with his wayward people.

There are numerous questions for readers that arise from such a shocking beginning. Did God actually command such a marriage, or is the description retrospective, the prophet's way of portraying Israel's faithlessness by analogy with his wife's faithlessness? What is meant by the terms *harlotry* and *whoredom*? Do they refer to commercial prostitution or sacred prostitution to ensure fertility on Gomer's part, or are they metaphorical references to Israel's "adultery" against the Lord? And what about the children and their names? Commentators ancient and modern have wrestled with these and related questions. They should be consulted for a history of discussion and additional details.

Here are some suggestions to consider: The commands in Hos 1:2–9 portray a prophet carrying out symbolic acts (compare Isa 8:1–4). Israel is personified by Gomer and is also represented by the adulterous "land" in 1:2. The prophetic family drama conveys that Israel has broken its loyalty to the Lord. Thus, the command for a prophet to marry a woman of harlotry is intended to shock an audience with a portrayal of God's unfaithful people. The term *harlotry* is complicated, since prostitution is frequently used metaphorically in the OT to describe the breaking of faith or trust.

That becomes its basic meaning in several contexts, including the description of Gomer in Hos 1–2, rather than a specific reference to some form of sexual activity. Nevertheless, some scholars have suggested that Gomer was involved in some form of explicit sexual activity such as prostitution or a form of Canaanite fertility religion in which ritual sex was a component. The latter option cannot be demonstrated conclusively from ancient parallels or the OT itself. On the other hand, it cannot be ruled out. Perhaps it is best simply to say that Gomer was involved in a form of marital infidelity, but it has receded into the background of the text and its details cannot be recovered. Primarily she is an Israelite who represents the people who are collectively estranged from the Lord. The names of the children similarly do not represent themselves in any particular activity except that they are offspring of a harlot/adulteress. Their names are intended to represent Israel's status as guilty and judged before the Lord.

Chapter 2 presents the dynamic of Israel's relationship to the Lord through the metaphor of divorce (2:1–13) and a second marriage (2:14–23). Gomer and the children are mentioned at the beginning, but soon the hearer/reader intuits that Israel in covenant disobedience and in a new restored covenant is what is in fact at issue in this story. Chapter 3 preserves the first-person report of a response to the divine command "to go, again love a woman loved by her husband, though she is an adulteress, just as the Lord loves the children of Israel, though they turn to other deities" (3:1). The symbolic analogy between man and woman, God and Israel, is explicit in this text. But is Gomer the unnamed woman of ch. 3? And if so, had she fallen into debt slavery as a result of the divorce from Hosea? Since the woman is not named, one cannot be sure, but contextually the argument is strong that it is Gomer, regardless of the circumstances that led to her servitude. Restoration for Israel would come in the future. The reference to seeking "David their king" (3:5) is seen by many scholars as an editorial comment, assuming that the northern prophet himself would not have taken a Judahite perspective on the role of the Davidic dynasty. That may well be; if Hosea himself held such a view of the Davidic dynasty, it would put him in the minority in northern Israel. If it is an editorial update, it reflects the circles who put the book together in Judah after the fall of Samaria.

Hosea is sometimes described as the first "biblical person" to use the analogy between the Sinai covenant and human marriage. This is because one can date the prophet and his context to a specific time in Israel's history, whereas scholars have increasingly concluded that dating the contents of the narrative portions of the OT can vary widely from passage to passage. On balance, it is unlikely that Hosea is the originator of such a metaphor. He simply assumes it as a point of presentation to his audience.

In recent years the metaphor of the Sinai covenant as marriage has come under increasing criticism, primarily from feminists and others, who find the role of Gomer to be an unfortunate stereotype, indeed demeaning toward women. Some interpreters have also expressed reservations about the metaphor, since it reinforces a male persona/identity for God.

And finally, there are those who see the treatment of Gomer in 2:1-13 as abusive, especially the possibility that Gomer was stripped of her clothes and forced to leave her family as part of a punitive divorce (cf. 2:3, 10). With respect to Gomer's expulsion, one can say that it is certainly more humane than the penalty of execution for adultery, which was an option in ancient Israel (Lev 20:10; Deut 22:22).

Traditionally, however, the metaphor of covenant as marriage has been considered one of the high-water marks of the OT. It is unique to Israel among the nations of the ancient Near East. No other culture claims this intimate analogy for the divine-human relationship. Rather than casting the covenant between God and Israel strictly in legal or contractual terms, the metaphor of marriage places the emphasis on the personal and the intimate. In marriage, *personal* and *intimate* correspond also to an exclusive sexual relationship. It is precisely in the covenant of marriage where such matters as love, loyalty, and fidelity take on their sharpest hue and where their absence can have the most devastating consequences. Although the metaphor is popularly associated with Hosea, it is also employed by other prophets (Jer 31:32; Ezek 16:1-63; Isa 50:1), and it is the source of the metaphor in the NT that the church is the bride of Christ (2 Cor 11:2; Rev 21:2).

Hosea represents God in anthropomorphic terms as someone jealous/zealous for the covenant relationship with Israel and emotionally distraught, even quite angry at the thought of Israel's infidelity. Indifference toward God's people and the created world is not something to be associated with the God of Israel.

Hosea 4–14: Condemnation and Forgiveness

The poetry that comprises Hos 4-14 is among the most allusive in the OT. Absent are any references to Gomer, prophetic children, or the marriage metaphor in the first subsection, although there are references to a broken covenant (8:1) and Israel collectively as God's "son" (11:1). The chapters contain a variety of accusations and figures of speech defining Israel and its self-destructive actions. For example, in the complaint that "they have made kings, but not by me" (8:4); or that "all their kings have fallen, yet none call on me" (7:7; cf. 13:9-11), readers may see the twenty years or so since the death of Jeroboam II being portrayed as a series of tragedies and political intrigues. In the call to "blow the trumpet and sound an alarm" (5:8), readers may sense a reaction to one or more of the battles that raged in and around Israel during that same time period. In the sarcasm "Ephraim is like a silly dove, without sense; they call to Egypt and travel to Assyria" (7:11; cf. 12:1), readers may sense some of the desperation of power-politics as the smaller state of Israel (characterized by its central tribe, Ephraim) sought alliances or agreements with larger states simply to stay afloat. The prophet apparently thought of these efforts as futile and as evidence of a lack of trust in the Lord (8:8-10).

The prophet is fond of metaphors and similes. Already mentioned is the comparison of the people with a clueless dove (7:11). They are also like a wild donkey (8:9), a disappearing early morning fog (6:4), grapes in the wilderness (9:10), a fruitful vine (10:1), a trained cow (10:11), a heated oven (7:6), and a half-baked pancake (7:8). God also is described through simile and metaphor. God is an attacking lion (5:14), a leopard and bear (13:7-8), the rains that replenish (6:3), a loving parent (11:3-4), and a fertile tree (14:8).

One of the most dramatic texts in all of the OT is the representation of God in an anguished soliloquy. Given Israel's propensity to rebel against God, who is represented as a loving parent, God speaks to himself as a wounded parent considering the effects of a "tough-love" approach toward an incorrigible child:

> How can I give up on you, Ephraim?
> How can I let you go, Israel?
> Should I give you over like Admah?
> Can I treat you like Zeboiim?

(Admah and Zeboiim are cities associated with Sodom and Gomorrah and the wickedness there; Gen 14:2, 8; Deut 29:23.)

> All my compassion is heated up!
> I will not act on my fury;
> I won't destroy Israel again!
> After all, I am God, not a human being,
> Indeed the Holy One in your midst;
> And I will not come in fury. (Hos 11:8–9; authors' translation)

In chs. 4–14, Hosea alludes or refers several times to God's previous dealings with Israel. From what is now the book of Genesis, the prophet cites the destruction of the cities on the plain (Hos 11:8; Gen 18; Deut 29:23) and the cycle of stories about Jacob (Hos 12:12; Gen 27–33). He affirms that God had redeemed Israel his "son" from Egypt (Hos 11:1), mentions the "prophet" (= Moses) who brought Israel up from Egypt (Hos 12:13), recalls divine providence in the wilderness wandering (Hos 13:5–6), and that Israel had sinned at Baal-peor (Hos 9:10; Num 25). Hosea uses these references to remind his audience of its primary identity as God's people and thereby to point out incongruities with their present actions.

The last chapter has a fascinating combination of language about repentance and the desire of God to "heal" (Hos 14:4) wayward Israel. Note also the comparisons of God with such natural phenomena as "dew" (important for sustenance in agricultural work in the summertime) and an evergreen tree. God's sustaining interaction with his people is strikingly portrayed in language not used elsewhere in the OT for divine presence.

The book concludes with an emphasis on wisdom and discernment:

> The ways of the Lord are right; the righteous walk in them,
> but those who rebel against the Lord stumble in them. (Hos 14:9;
> authors' translation)

This is an editorial comment that is reminiscent of wisdom literature and commends a thoughtful reading of the prophetic book. It represents Hosea's book as providing an exposition of the ways of the Lord and of Israel's stumbling in its rebellion against those ways.

Read Hos 1–14 and prepare answers to the following questions:

1. How do you understand the role of Gomer in Hos 1–3?

2. Read Hos 4:1–3. How might we understand the reference to the land's "mourning" in v. 3?

3. Read Hos 6:4–6. How does this brief passage interpret the work of prophets?

4. What do you sense about God's role in relation to Hosea, his family, and Israel? What (if any) implications do you draw for yourself from this book?

BIBLIOGRAPHY

Dearman, J. Andrew. *Hosea*. NICOT. Grand Rapids: Eerdmans, 2010.

Emmerson, Grace I. *Hosea: An Israelite Prophet in Judean Perspective*. Sheffield: JSOT Press, 1984.

Macintosh, Andrew A. *A Critical and Exegetical Commentary on Hosea*. ICC. Edinburgh: T&T Clark, 1997.

Sherwood, Yvonne. *The Prostitute and the Prophet: Hosea's Marriage in Literary-Theoretical Perspective*. Sheffield: Sheffield Academic Press, 1996.

The Book of Amos

The work of Hosea's contemporary, Amos, is preserved in a book of nine chapters with three sections. An initial section is composed of oracles against various neighboring states and concludes with the book's first accusations against Israel for unrighteousness and injustice (Amos 1:3–2:16). The second and largest section is addressed to Israel and its failures to uphold the standards of the covenant with the Lord (3:1–9:10). This material is almost exclusively judgmental in evaluating Amos's contemporaries. The book concludes, however, with a brief third section that projects a transformed future for Israel (9:11–15).

Amos's work in Israel is dated by the superscription (1:1) to the reigns of Uzziah in Judah and Jeroboam II in Israel—that is, at the mid-point of the 8th century. It also mentions an earthquake at the time of his prophetic work. There are indications in the book, however, that the prophet's work continued past the death of Jeroboam, such as the reference in Amos 6:2 to the fate of the Syrian city of Calneh (which fell to the Assyrians in 738 BCE). The prophet was a shepherd from Tekoa (south of Bethlehem in Judah), who was convinced that God had told him, "Go, prophesy to my people Israel" (7:15). There are at least two notable things in this comment: The first is that someone from the state of Judah would go north to prophesy in Israel. One can explain the effort easily enough by appeal to divine compulsion: "God told me to do it!" But why send someone from Judah? Was there no one in Israel for God to raise up? The second thing to note about the command in 7:15 is the first-person pronoun *my*. The Israelites are God's people. In their separation from Judah and in their disobedience to the covenant stipulations of justice and righteousness—in short, in their rebellion—they are still God's people and worthy of a prophet's efforts at uncovering the truth before them.

The book of Amos has a Judahite editorial hue to it. The opening verse proclaims that "the Lord roars from Zion" (1:2), and the transformed future envisioned at the conclusion is built on restoring the rule of the Davidic dynasty (9:11). Some have supposed that the references to the Lord in Zion and to the Davidic dynasty are editorial—that is, they were added by those who compiled the oracles of the prophet in Judah after the fall of Israel. On the other hand, what if Amos represented a Judahite point of view while in Israel: namely, that the Lord, the God of Israel, was spiritually present in the temple in Jerusalem and that David's line had an important role to play in the future governing of God's people? This might explain one reason that a Judahite felt called to go and prophesy to Israel: it was in service to the ideal of the twelve-tribe covenant confederation, headed by a son of David.

Amos 1–2: Oracles against Nations

Amos is concerned with the meaning of history and the fate of nations, even as the book bears down on Israel and the particularities of its failure to God in a historical moment. Amos 1:3–2:16 contains oracles against the unrighteous behavior of eight nations/city-states, including Judah and Israel. A

The section begins with Amos's central message for Israel (3:2):

> You only have I known of all the families of the earth;
> therefore, I will bring all your transgressions upon you. (authors'
>   translation)

This is election and covenant-responsibility language, not the language of simple cognition, as if God didn't know any of the other peoples! The verb *know* is used in the sense of intimacy and expected integrity, not that of simple factual knowledge. One might compare the claim in Amos 9:7 that Israel is like the African Cushites (i.e., from the standpoint of nationhood, a faraway people and nothing spectacular). Yes, God brought up Israel from Egypt, but—and here Amos seems to depend on traditions known to his audience—God also brought up the Philistines from Caphtor (= Crete) and the Aramaeans from Kir (= perhaps northern Syria). Some among Amos's audience believed that God's rescue of their ancestors from Egypt made them unique, but according to the prophet, the exodus is not the basis for Israel's unique relationship with God. God knows and is known among the nations, but God entered into a covenant with Israel that had expectations that Israel has not met. Thus the chilling logic of 3:2: precisely because God has entered deeply into Israel's history and defined the people for himself, they must suffer the consequences of their actions. The last clause of 3:2 is usually rendered "I will punish you for all your iniquities" (e.g., NRSV); but the more literal translation given above indicates that the "punishment" is the bringing of Israel's transgressions upon itself.

Amos is at one with Isaiah, Jeremiah, and other prophets in his caustic critique of public worship in Israel. His criticism is not that services are sparsely attended with little enthusiasm but that the corporate life of Israel belies its identity (5:21-24). The well-known word pair "justice and righteousness" is at the center of Amos's critique. What good is Israel's worship when injustice and unrighteousness are the order of Israel's day?

Amos 9:11–15: Hope for the Future

The book ends with hope for the future, specifically the raising up of David's dynasty to rule and, eventually, marvelous agricultural bounty for the people. Is it possible, some interpreters have asked, for Amos to move from announcing judgment to predicting future transformation, or should we think instead of editors who updated/supplemented the prophet's somber critique with a positive portrayal of the future? Perhaps the answer to that question, valid though it may be, is less important than the juxtaposition of these two aspects of divine activity now within one prophetic book. After all, in the historical process God cannot be a redeemer without also being a judge on that which opposes his purposes. And the reverse is also part of God's freedom: in carrying out judgment, God has the option also of preparing for redemption. It is part of the monotheistic tradition that the one God of heaven and earth is at work on multiple levels. The stern little book of Amos is a salutary reminder that God's people are not exempt from judgment, but also God's "no" can be followed by a graceful "yes" in God's good timing.

The reference to possessing the "remnant of Edom" in Amos 9:12 provides a link with the prophecy of Obadiah, the small book that follows Amos. Obadiah's primary focus is to address Edom with a timely judgment. See the discussion about Edom, including some references to Amos 9:11-12, in the section on Obadiah. We should note also that Amos 9:11-12 are cited (from the Septuagint) in the apostolic meeting described in Acts 15:15-18.

READING

Read Amos 1–9 and offer answers to the following questions:

1. Read Amos 3:2 and 9:7. How do you understand the claim that God has uniquely "known" Israel (3:2) in light of the claims that Israel is like the Cushites and that God also acted in exodus-like events for the Philistines and the Aramaeans (9:7)?

2. The prophet pronounces that an "end" has come upon Israel (8:2). What does that mean historically and theologically? Would you compare it, for example, to the divorce that Hosea mentions?

3. The prophet offers a number of criticisms of Israel (and Judah). How do you think that he might define the justice and righteousness for which he calls in 5:24?

4. What might a modern counterpart to Amos say and do?

BIBLIOGRAPHY

Andersen, Francis I., and David Noel Freedman. *Amos.* AB 24A. New York: Doubleday, 1989.

Barton, John. *The Theology of the Book of Amos.* Cambridge: Cambridge University Press, 2012.

Paul, Shalom. *Amos.* Hermeneia. Philadelphia: Fortress, 1990.

Hubbard, David A. *Joel and Amos.* Downers Grove, IL: InterVarsity Press, 2009.

The Book of Micah

The prophet Micah was from Moreshath-Gath, a town to the southwest of Jerusalem, where animal husbandry and farming were primary activities. The superscription (1:1) makes him a contemporary of Isaiah of Jerusalem and active in the last third of the 8th century BCE. He prophesied about "Samaria and Jerusalem," meaning that the two capital cities are addressed as representing their respective states. Micah's work thus begins before the fall of Samaria in 722 BCE, but when it concludes is less clear. Perhaps he lived through the assault on Judah by Sennacherib in 701 BCE.

The outline of Micah is less clear than that of Amos. Judgment/destruction and salvation/deliverance prophecies are interspersed throughout the book in alternating fashion. Chapters 1–2 criticize the audience but end with a word of hope for a surviving remnant (Mic 2:12–13). Chapter 3 offers scathing judgment of Israel and Judah, while ch. 4 projects restoration in days to come. Chapter 5 presents one from David's line as a ruler in the time of restoration. The Lord presents a case against the people in 6:1–5, which is followed by several responses in 6:6–7:20. Although the Assyrian threat is explicit in the book (5:5–6), Babylon is also mentioned in 4:10. This follows the pattern of the book of Isaiah and suggests an editing process that continued until the postexilic period.

Micah 1–3: Judgment and a Glimpse of Hope

Micah follows the convention of other 8th-century prophets in his critical evaluation of the public life of Israel and Judah and in his announcement of judgment to come in the historical process for both of them. And like others', his imagery is fearful and unforgettable. For example, Micah re-

The Elah Valley is located southwest of Jerusalem and is one route from the coastal plain to the Judahite hill country. The famous confrontation between David and Goliath (1 Samuel 17) took place in the Elah Valley. Moresheth, Micah's hometown, lies just south of it. ©Ian Scott (Wikimedia Commons, CC-SA 2.0)

fers to leading citizens and rulers of Israel as cannibals devouring their own people (Mic 3:1–3) and venal prophets as those who cry "peace" when they are given food in payment but "war" when there is no present—that is, payment—for their services (3:5). The fierce judgment announced for Jerusalem in 3:12 was remembered years later by the elders in Jerusalem, who noted that King Hezekiah responded to Micah's preaching with acts of repentance (see Jer 26:16–19).

Micah 4–5: Promises of Blessing

Note the text Mic 4:1–5. Much of it appears also in Isa 2:2–4. The passage portrays Jerusalem "in days to come" as an instructional center, where nations come to the temple to receive instruction in walking in the ways of the Lord. In Micah's version a peaceful life is where people can sit under their vines and fig trees in security. When God's rule is made manifest, there is no need for the implements of war. Note also that later in the same chapter, there is a description of "Daughter Zion" fighting against oppressive nations assembled against her who would otherwise plunder the city (4:11–13; cf. 5:7–9). Micah also follows the pattern of several prophetic books in portraying the rule of a future descendant of David in a restored Israel. The reference to Bethlehem as the home of David's family (5:2) is unique in the prophetic literature.

Micah 6–7: Condemnation, Repentance, and Hope

In a prophetic "lawsuit" (6:1-5), Micah recites elements from the Lord's prior history with Israel to charge the people with failure to respond to the "saving acts" of the Lord. Here again one sees a pattern, along with Hosea and Amos, in which a story line about the past is used selectively to make a point to apply to the generation at hand. Like Amos and Isaiah, Micah opposes separating the worship of God, on the one hand, from a life of commitment to the well-being of people and the exercise of personal integrity, on the other hand (compare Isa 1:10-20; Amos 5:21-24). This comes through in the answer to his rhetorical question of how best to present himself before God (6:6-8). His mode of presentation is perhaps based on the language used to enter the temple precincts in Jerusalem (see Ps 15). The series of questions in Mic 6:6-7 establishes an ascending value of commitment (burnt offering, a yearling, thousands of rams, ten thousand rivers of oil) that culminates in the sacrificial gift of a child. In the ancient Near East, the gift of a child to a deity, whether literally in sacrifice or in some other form of dedication (e.g., Samuel), was understood as a supreme act of devotion. The conclusion to the question of what will please God is not a criticism of ritual or sacrificial practice per se but an answer that places these things in the larger context of personal piety:

> So what does the Lord require of you but to do justice, to love kindness (*hesed*), and to walk circumspectly with your God? (Mic 6:8)

The final chapter of Micah contains first-person laments and reflections about future deliverance. The content does not seem to be a single poem; it contains both singular and plural voices. An initial voice mentions the heavy hand of judgment that has come upon the people. It is not the last word, however, which comes in two parts: the first is an expression of trust (7:8), and the second is a rhetorical affirmation that God is unique (7:18-20). God's uniqueness is not in the task of judging but in the twin tasks of pardoning and removing the impediments that sin has spawned. In Judaism, these last three verses are part of the synagogue liturgy on the Sabbath Eve service before the Day of Atonement.

> Who is a deity like you, pardoning iniquity,
> And overcoming the transgression of the remnant of his inheritance?
> He does not maintain his anger forever; instead, he delights in
>   lovingkindness.

He will have compassion on us; he will overcome our iniquities.
You will cast all our sins into the deep sea.
You will show steadfastness to Jacob, lovingkindness to Abraham,
Just as you swore to our ancestors,
From days long ago.

This last sentence reminds readers of the promises that God made to the ancestors before there was a nation of Israel or Judah, promises that provide hope in the midst of defeat and exile (see Isa 51:1-3).

READING

Read Mic 1-7 and formulate answers to the following questions:

1. Read Mic 3:9-12 in the context of ch. 3. How would you interpret the prediction that Jerusalem will become a pile of ruins? Note how this passage in interpreted in Jer 26:16-19.

2. Read Mic 6:6-8. What is the role of sacrifice in the worship of God in light of this passage? How would you summarize the characteristics listed for Israel in v. 8?

3. Read Mic 7:8-10. How are judgment and deliverance related in this passage? Who or what might be the enemy?

4. Read Mic 7:18-20. Reflect on the meaning of each metaphor in these verses. How and why is forgiveness achieved?

BIBLIOGRAPHY

Allen, Leslie. *The Books of Joel, Obadiah, Jonah and Micah*. NICOT. Grand Rapids: Eerdmans, 1976.

Andersen, Francis I., and David Noel Freedman. *Micah*. AB 24E. New Haven: Yale University Press, 2006.

Prior, David. *The Message of Joel, Micah and Habakkuk*. Downers Grove, IL: Inter-Varsity Press, 1999.

Waltke, Bruce K. *A Commentary on Micah*. Grand Rapids: Eerdmans, 2007.

27 THE BOOKS OF ZEPHANIAH, HABAKKUK, AND JOEL

Important Dates for Zephaniah
640–609: reign of Josiah in Jerusalem

Important Dates for Habakkuk
605–598: defeat of Egypt at Carchemish and beginning of Babylonian rule
598: Jehoiakim rebels against vassalage to Babylon

Important Dates for Joel
515–400: postexilic life in Yehud and Jerusalem

ZEPHANIAH AND HABAKKUK WERE JUDAHITE prophets from the 7th century BCE. Their work was carried out at a time of transition and uncertainty in Judah. The small state of Judah sought to maintain itself amid the changes wrought in international affairs: first, as Assyrian control waned after the death of Assurbanipal in 627 BCE; and second, as the Babylonians and Egyptians sought to assert themselves in place of the Assyrians after the sacking of Nineveh, the Assyrian capital, in 612 BCE. The date of Joel is uncertain. Like Zephaniah and Habakkuk, a setting in Judah and Jerusalem is presupposed in the book, as is worship at the temple. The balance of probability is a postexilic date for Joel, sometime in the Persian period, perhaps in a time similar to that of Malachi (ca. 400 BCE). All three books have explicit and implicit references to other nations caught up in the international struggles of the times, along with prophecies about the place of Judah and Jerusalem in those struggles and in the future beyond them. For this reason they can be read profitably together. Zephaniah and Joel are also similar in that each book moves from judgment on Judah and Jerusalem to the exaltation of them in an era to come.

Two kings ruled in Judah during most of the 7th century: Manasseh (687-642) and Josiah (640-609). Manasseh had the longest reign in Judah's history, given the likelihood of a period of his coregency with Hezekiah, his father. Apart from notice of a later repentance (2 Chr 33:12-19), both Kings and Chronicles report evil for his reign. His reign also coincided with the greatest expanse of the Assyrian Empire. Josiah inherited the polytheism and syncretism of Manasseh's reign, plus the status of vassal to the Assyrians. He was only eight years old when made king. As he reached maturity, the power of Assyria began to wane, and Josiah moved toward religious reform and greater political freedom (2 Kgs 22-23; 2 Chr 34:3). When Josiah died in 609, a struggle ensued between Egypt, which was eager to reassert itself in regional affairs, and the Babylonian rebels, who sought to take over Assyrian holdings. Judah, of course, was caught in the middle. Egypt initially forced tribute from Judah and in 608 placed Jehoiakim, a compliant son of Josiah, on the throne of Judah (2 Kgs 23:31-37). The Babylonians under the young general Nebuchadnezzar defeated the Egyptians in 605 at Carchemish in northern Syria. Subsequently Judah and Jehoiakim were forced to become a Babylonian vassal. Jehoiakim withheld tribute from the Babylonians, and they responded with a siege of Jerusalem. Jehoiakim died, and his son and successor Jehoiachin surrendered to the Babylonians in 597. Tragedy would repeat itself some ten years later, when the Babylonians captured and largely destroyed Jerusalem and then took portions of the population into exile.

The Book of Zephaniah

In distinction from other prophets, Zephaniah is given a four-generation lineage (1:1). The reason for this is not stated, but a plausible reason is the name of his great-great-grandfather Hezekiah, which suggests descent from the royal house. If so, that would make him the lone Israelite or Judahite prophet with known royal ancestry. His work is set during the reign of Josiah, probably in the first half of his rule (640-625 BCE), since the polytheism and syncretism opposed by Zephaniah (1:4-6) was something that the adult Josiah also opposed in his reforming efforts. The prophecy against Assyria in 2:13-15 fits best in a time when that Empire was in a weakened state.

The book of Zephaniah has four sections: (1) an announcement of the coming day of the Lord (ch. 1); (2) a call for Judah to seek the Lord humbly before that day (2:1-3); (3) oracles against foreign nations (2:4-15); and (4) an announcement to Jerusalem of coming judgment and blessing (ch. 3).

Zephaniah 1–3

The harsh assessments of Judah in the first chapter assume judgment on the horizon for the nation. Zephaniah employs a common prophetic motif, the coming day of the Lord (1:14), as the basis for a critique of his contemporaries. This is terminology for a decisive future event, whether judgment on evil or the advent of a time of peace. The book actually has various depictions of a "day of the Lord" (cf. 3:1-7). The language is dark, jarring, and cosmic as the divine warrior approaches in judgment. Idolatrous practices (1:4-6) are one reason for the judgment on Judah. Chapter 2 begins with a call to the discerning "humble" among the nation to seek the Lord before the day of wrath is revealed (2:1-3). Judgment from the Lord, the cosmic judge, will also fall on the Philistines (2:4-7), the taunting Moabites (2:8-11), the Cushites (2:12), and even Assyria (2:13-15). After additional depictions of judgment (3:1-7; 8-13), Zion is called to shout with joy at her role as the centerpiece of divine rule (3:14-20). The last verse of the book reminds hearers/readers that this is something yet to be accomplished.

Zephaniah offers a particular take on what modern people call spirituality and spiritual discipline. There are two references to the "humble" ('ani), whom the Lord seeks (and is even forming) through Judah's difficult circumstances (Zeph 2:3; 3:11-13). Perhaps there is even a sense that humility is what the crucible of difficulties in the prophet's day will bring about. On the one hand, the humble take "refuge" in the Lord. As a category of people, the "humble" are known particularly in the Psalms (Ps 7:1; 18:31; 36:7; 57:1; cf. Nah 1:7), and the word speaks to personal devotion to the Lord and dependence on him. On the other hand, it also refers to those who may have a low socioeconomic status but who seek righteousness and integrity in their lives.

Zephaniah depicts two sides in his portrayal of God as a warrior. One side shows the Lord moving against the failures of Judah. The other side is portrayed succinctly in Zeph 3:17, where the Lord is a "warrior who saves." This theology of the divine warrior is behind the judgment of nations (Judah as well as others) and the eventual reversal of Jerusalem's sad state of affairs on a decisive "day" to come in the future.

READING

Read Zeph 1–3 and formulate responses to the following questions:

1. How do you understand the references to the "humble" in chs. 2–3?

2. The conclusion to the book affirms that the Lord is a "warrior who saves." Are there other places in the Bible that describe God as a warrior or as a savior? How does this warrior image fit with other images (example: God as shepherd) for God in the OT?

The Book of Habakkuk

The prophet Habakkuk's name appears twice in his short work, since the book contains two superscriptions (Hab 1:1; 3:1). The Chaldeans (= Babylonians) are mentioned in 1:6 as a force that the Lord is raising up to discipline his people. This one reference is the primary key to dating the book. It seems to originate in the time period after the fall of Nineveh in 612, as the Babylonians asserted themselves in taking over from the Assyrians, and before the Babylonian destruction of Jerusalem in 587. With the defeat of the Egyptian army in 605, the Babylonians began asserting pressure on states in the region such as Judah, and Habakkuk's prophecies may reflect the worry and unease brought about with this shift in political power. Popular knowledge of Babylonian military prowess and colonial policies may underlie this anxiety as well.

The book has three sections: (1) Habakkuk's psalm-like dialogue with God (1:1–2:4); (2) a series of woe speeches (2:5–20); and (3) Habakkuk's prayer (ch. 3).

Habakkuk 1–3

A number of interpreters have proposed that Habakkuk was a cult prophet, meaning that he was associated in some way with the work of the temple in

Habakkuk Pesher. Among the better known of the Dead Sea Scrolls, the Habakkuk Pesher dates to approximately 50 BCE. *Pesher* is the Hebrew word for "interpretation" or "comment." The Habakkuk Pesher is one of the earliest examples of a biblical commentary, where a line from the biblical book is quoted and then brief comments about its meaning are provided.

Jerusalem. If this is correct, he may have also been a priest or a Levite. One reason for the proposal is that Habakkuk's language and forms of expression are similar to the hymns and prayers (laments) of the Psalter. For example, the opening line of his prophecy, "How long, O Lord, shall I call for help?" is similar to the first two verses of Ps 13. The format that follows in the book—Habakkuk's questions and the Lord's answers—compares to the common cultic process thought to govern prayers of lament. The song/prayer in ch. 3 also has its own superscription, which introduces a "prayer of Habakkuk the prophet." It is very similar to the headings to individual psalms (see Ps 7). The prayer even has the term *Selah* (Hab 3:3, 9, 13), which is often used with compositions in the Psalter and is a performance notation meaning something like "refrain" or "crescendo." The concluding line of the book is a direction "to the choirmaster," yet another term from the Psalter. Perhaps the prayer even circulated as a separate composition before its employment in the prophetic book. Note also the acclamation to the hearers/readers that the "Lord is in his holy temple; let all the earth keep silent" (Hab 2:20). One might compare that command to the injunction in a psalm of Zion to "be still and know that I am God" (Ps 46:10).

Habakkuk also plays the role of a watchman (2:1), a crucial task for a city or company of people in a time of threat (see Ezek 3:17; 33:7). The superscription to the book (Hab 1:1) describes the contents as an oracle that the prophet "saw." We might say that the prophet was a visionary (see 2:3) who used the traditional language of worship to emphasize his prophetic message. Some interpreters have suggested that the prayer in ch. 3 alludes to a prior vision, which is what lies behind the prophet's dialogue with God in chs. 1–2.

In the first chapter the presence of the strong and hasty Babylonians is seen as threatening. They were the historical agents of the overthrow of the hated Assyrians, but their actions suggest to the prophet that their cure is as bad as the Assyrian disease. The Babylonians are portrayed as hunters relentlessly reeling in their defenseless prey with nets and hooks (Hab 1:15–17). Habakkuk cries out to God like one of the psalmists, questioning how the evil foe could be part of God's just judgment, as it targets a comparatively more righteous people (1:13)!

Perhaps the best-known line in the book is "The righteous [person] shall live by his faithfulness" (Hab 2:4). This short affirmation raises several questions, but in context it describes the opposite of a proud person. A righteous person is faithful, not haughty or proud, and maintains integrity in spite of adverse conditions. It is language similar to that used in Zephaniah about the humble who seek righteousness (Zeph 2:3). It is also a text with a fascinating impact on subsequent interpreters. In the Babylonian Talmud (b. Makkot 23b-24a; ca. 500 CE), Hab 2:4 is cited as a summary of the commandments in the Torah. A Rabbi Simlai states that Moses gave 613 commandments in the Torah; 248 are positive and 365 are negative. Others note that in Ps 15 David had reduced the number to 11 commandments; Isa 33:15-16, to 6; Mic 6:8, to 3; Isa 56:1, to 2; Amos 5:4, to 1 (although one rabbi suggested that "seek God and live" could be two principles). But with Hab 2:4, the commands were distilled to one. A righteous person should live by faithfulness to God's revealed will in the Torah.

In the NT, Hab 2:4 is cited by Paul as the scriptural proof for being justified (made right with God) by faith in Christ and Christ's faithfulness (Rom 1:17; Gal 3:11). As in the later talmudic discussion, the text serves as a summary statement of a posture or approach toward life before God. Habakkuk 2 continues with a series of "woe speeches" against injustice and violence. It is difficult to tell if they all describe the same culprit, but they seem to describe the Babylonians as haughty and greedy, perhaps following up the claim in Hab 1:11 that they worship their own strength as their god.

Habakkuk's prayer (3:2-19) contains visionary elements representing the Lord as marching from the south in martial form, struggling with the various powers of the cosmos, but finally victorious over them. It concludes with first-person reflections appropriate to a somber moment in history. Even though the yield of fields and flocks be insufficient,

> I will nevertheless exult in the Lord,
> I will rejoice in the God of my deliverance.
> The sovereign Lord is my strength!
> He set my feet like the deer;
> He makes me walk on my high places. (Hab 3:18-19, authors'
>   translation)

As noted above, there is a reference to a choirmaster or conductor at the end of the book. This indicates that Habakkuk's prayer (psalm) was probably performed—that is, sung or chanted. We don't know whether this is a composition by Habakkuk himself or was adopted by him. Possibly it describes the vision (or part thereof) mentioned in 2:2–3. The prayer also raises the question of the use of the prophetic book after its completion and whether other parts of it were also publicly presented. The book does place an emphasis on responding to tumult and difficulty with measures appropriate for divine worship and personal piety.

Habakkuk's brief prophecies may have been made into a book as a result of the command in 2:2–3 to write down a vision that might wait a fair amount of time for fulfillment. The book would then serve at least two related functions. One would be to preserve Habakkuk's words to inspire perseverance until the vision/prophecy was fulfilled, and the second would be to provide hope in the interim for a suffering people.

READING

Read Hab 1–3 and formulate responses to the following questions:

1. As noted above, the prophecies of Habakkuk share vocabulary and themes with the prayers in the Psalms. Does this connection cause you to see Habakkuk differently from other prophets? If so, how and why?

2. As noted above, the prophet's affirmation that the righteous "live by faith" (Hab 2:4) has been influential in both Jewish and Christian communities. How do you understand this affirmation?

3. With what new ideas or challenges does the book of Habakkuk leave you?

The Book of Joel

In three chapters Joel moves from the devastation of a locust plague, to Judah and Jerusalem's need for repentance, to judgment on nations, and to the eventual exaltation of Jerusalem. It is a pattern similar to that of Zephaniah, although the expressed need for repentance is more pronounced in Joel. It is implicit in Zephaniah, given his stress on humility. In his emphasis on the future exaltation of Jerusalem, Joel is similar to Ezek 40–48 and

Zech 12–14, and he also shares the language of the "day of the Lord" with Zephaniah, Zechariah, and others. In the concern for worship and heart-felt response to the Lord, the prophet is similar to Habakkuk. Interpreters have suggested that Joel also (along with Habakkuk) was a cultic prophet, someone linked closely to the temple service and the liturgy employed there. If a Persian period setting is correct for the prophet, then the service in question was that of the Second Temple. A devastating locust plague (Joel 1:4–12) was the occasion for the prophet to reflect on the need for change among God's people.

The book has three sections: (1) calls for mourning and repentance before the coming judgment on Judah (Joel 1:1–2:17); (2) the Lord's announcement of Judah's salvation (2:18–32); and (3) a vision of coming judgments on the nations (ch. 3).

Joel 1–3

For a short book, Joel has much to say about both repentance and judgment in the historical realm. He is often remembered as the prophet who speaks about "rending hearts and not garments" (Joel 2:13). This memorable phrase is best seen in context, where it is part of a hoped-for response to an imminent day of the Lord's judgment. The first chapter contains calls to priests and people alike to wear sackcloth and utter lamentations, along with fasting (1:13–14). Chapter 2 begins with a call to sound the alarm, for the day of the Lord is coming. Its dark and dangerous advent is described and then followed by the rhetorical question (Joel 2:11), "Who can endure it?" The text continues:

> "Even now," says the Lord, "return to me with all your heart, with fasting, weeping, and mourning.
> "Rend [Heb. qar'a] your hearts and not your garments.
> "Return to the Lord your God, for he is gracious and compassionate, slow to anger and abundant in lovingkindness, and one who turns from evil." (Joel 2:12–13, authors' translation)

It may not occur to modern readers that this language of mourning and returning is likely taken from repentance liturgies and temple rituals. Fasting, weeping (Joel 2:17), mourning, and the rending of garments were recognized acts at such events as national crises and funerals. Josiah tore

(Heb. *qarʿa*) his garments after reading the recently discovered Book of the Covenant, which apparently listed a number of curses for disobedience (2 Kgs 22:1-13). After the Babylonians destroyed the temple, Israelite pilgrims with torn clothes journeyed to the site to mourn its loss (Jer 41:4-7). The prophetic injunction to "rend hearts," therefore, was to underscore the solemn significance of penitential rituals. Such outward acts should represent a whole-hearted movement toward the God of judgment and forgiveness, and away from those practices that God abhors. Moreover, the prophet also quotes the fundamental Israelite affirmation of God as "gracious and compassionate" (Exod 34:6-7; Num 14:18; Deut 4:31; Neh 9:17; Ps 86:5, 15; 103:8; 145:8; Jonah 4:2). This too was probably recited in worship and temple liturgies. For Joel it was the basis on which human repentance could receive a proper reception.

The book of Joel portrays visionary elements that had interesting influence on later communities. One vision for future transformation includes the prediction that God will pour out his Spirit on humankind with the result that whoever "calls on the name of the Lord will be delivered" (Joel 2:28-32). This text is cited in the book of Acts to explain the phenomenon of speaking in tongues on the Day of Pentecost (Acts 2:17-22). That experience of early Jewish Christians was understood as a fulfillment of Joel's prophecy. Another vision in Joel portrays a climactic day of judgment for nations in the valley next to Jerusalem (Joel 3:2-17). The prophet uses its name—the valley of Jehoshaphat (meaning "the Lord is judge")—to speak of God's "judgment" of peoples, beginning at that spot. Such a play on words is a mnemonic device to underscore the importance of the vision's contents. One result of this visionary proclamation in subsequent history has been the burial of Jews, Christians, and Muslims on the slopes of the valley located east of the old city of Jerusalem.

Joel shares with Amos the marvelous imagery of the hills dripping with sweet wine (Joel 3:18; Amos 9:13). It is likely one reason that the two books are set next to each other among the Twelve. It is not Joel's last word, however, as it is Amos's. There are prophecies of judgment against Egypt and Edom and the final affirmation that the "Lord dwells in Zion" (Joel 3:19-21).

Winepress. Grapes were crushed in stone installations like this one to collect their juice in vessels, so that fermentation could begin in the process of making wine. *Photo by Anat Harrel, Israel Tour Guide, 2014. Used with permission.*

READING

Read Joel 1–3 and formulate responses to the following questions:

1. The prophet emphasizes the need for Judah's repentance in approaching God. How would you explain Joel's understanding of repentance to someone who asked for clarification? How would you define the term *repentance* and its role in religious practices today?

2. Joel depicts the nations gathered before the Lord in judgment (3:2, 12). Of what other prophetic texts where nations will gather before the Lord does this remind you? How is the depiction in Joel 3:1–3, 11–16 similar to and different from the gathering of peoples before the Lord in Matt 25:31–46?

3. Summarize the lasting impression(s) that Joel leaves with you. What do you take away from reading this book?

BIBLIOGRAPHY

Allen, Leslie. *The Books of Joel, Obadiah, Jonah and Micah*. NICOT. Grand Rapids: Eerdmans, 1976.

Andersen, Francis I. *Habakkuk*. AB 25. New York: Doubleday, 2001.

Baker, David W. *Nahum, Habakkuk, and Zephaniah*. Downers Grove, IL: InterVarsity Press, 2009.

Berlin, Adele. *Zephaniah*. AB 25A. New York: Doubleday, 1994.

Bridger, Gordon. *The Message of Obadiah, Nahum and Zephaniah*. Downers Grove, IL: InterVarsity Press, 2010.

Hubbard, David A. *Joel and Amos*. Downers Grove, IL: InterVarsity Press, 2009.

Prior, David. *The Message of Joel, Micah and Habakkuk*. Downers Grove, IL: InterVarsity Press, 1999.

Sweeney, Marvin. *Zephaniah*. Hermeneia. Philadelphia: Fortress, 2003.

28 THE BOOKS OF JONAH, NAHUM, AND OBADIAH

Important Dates for Jonah and Nahum

750: Jonah prophesies during the reign of Jeroboam II (2 Kings 14:25)

700: Sennacherib expands the old city of Nineveh and makes it the capital of the empire

612: Nineveh falls after a siege by the Medes

Important Dates for Obadiah

587–400: bad relations between Edomites and Jews

THE THREE SHORT BOOKS OF Jonah, Nahum, and Obadiah share a common theme: each is concerned with the Lord's work in dealing with foreign nations. Jonah and Nahum are both concerned with Nineveh, which was one of a series of Assyria's capitals. Obadiah addresses the Edomites, who live southeast of the Dead Sea. He is not the only prophet to address them (see below). Both the Assyrians and the Edomites were repeatedly involved in hostilities against Israel and Judah. How does one see the enemy and the oppressor in light of God's unique claim on Israel, when one believes that God is the creator of the world and relates to other nations as well? There is, of course, no single answer to such a complex question, as the prophetic texts make clear.

As we noted in the introduction to Amos, prophecies about other nations are a constituent part of the prophetic books. They occur sporadically as individual oracles or (the majority of them) in a given book are collected together in one section. The Major Prophets, Isaiah (13–23), Jeremiah (46–

provides him with a near-death experience, often the kind of thing that causes dramatic change in a person's life. Jonah praises God for his survival and then goes on to preach the shortest sermon recorded in the Bible: "Forty days and Nineveh will be overthrown" (3:4). Nevertheless, the whole city responds with repentance to a message that does not even contain an explicit call to repent. Even the cattle are given sackcloth to wear (3:8)! And finally, God changes his intention to destroy the city (3:10), leaving Jonah to complain bitterly that his suspicions all along have been that God does not want to destroy the Ninevites (4:1-2). In Jonah's judgment the Assyrians deserve annihilation, and his anger is such that he prefers death to Nineveh's survival (4:8).

Jonah's message to Nineveh, which was a succinct announcement that judgment was coming soon, offers opportunity for reflection on prophetic predictions. Was Jonah somehow a false prophet because what he announced/predicted did not come to pass in forty days? Prophets were certainly capable of calling for repentance, but repentance was only implicit in what Jonah actually said. Perhaps one of the functions of the story of Jonah was to make the point that prophetic prediction was not necessarily the announcement of an unalterable fact but a word always at the disposal of the sovereign Lord in working out his larger designs. In Jonah's case, the one-sentence prophecy was hilariously effective and served God's greater purpose—though it remained unfulfilled in a literal sense.

Another function of the book, whether intended by the writer(s) or not, appears in a comparison of it with Nahum's prophecy. This is an important feature of reading a book as part of a collection and not simply as a stand-alone work. The two books are different in form—Jonah is a short story and Nahum an extended prophecy against a nation—but both should be read as reflections on the character of God. On the one hand, Jonah 4:2 is an exposition of the fundamental confession (Exod 34:6-7) from Mount Sinai that God is "merciful and gracious, slow to anger and abundant in lovingkindness," and not just with regard to the covenant people (see Joel 2:12-13). Such mercy can be extended even to the wicked and to oppressors. On the other hand, Nahum is an exposition of the confession that God is a defender of the oppressed and "will not leave the guilty unpunished" (see Deut 5:9-10/Exod 20:4-6). The prophet Jonah wanted Nahum's justice to come quickly, while the book of Jonah ends with God's query: "Should I not be concerned about Nineveh?" In neither book is there a question of Nineveh's guilt or of God's commitment to his people. Both are assumed. Together they exhibit a sovereign freedom in the ways of the Lord, including the audacious extension of the mercy promised Israel to one of Israel's cruelest enemies.

Read Jonah 1–4 and formulate responses to the following questions:

1. The comments above suggest that Jonah is a parable. How adequately do you think that term describes the book? If not, what other term would you prefer and why?

2. Why was an Israelite such as Jonah so upset at the repentance of the Ninevites? What evidence suggests that he was also upset with God?

3. How would you retell the story of Jonah using contemporary characters?

The Book of Nahum

Nahum's three chapters are essentially an expansive prophecy against Nineveh, possibly formulated on the eve of the city's fall and subsequent destruction at the hand of Babylonian rebels in 612 BCE. Most oracles against nations in the OT are briefer than Nahum, but it was not every day that the heretofore most-influential city in the known world was defeated and overrun. We might compare Nahum briefly with the book of Zephaniah, which is similar in size and date, to get a sense of Nahum's profile. In its three chapters, Zephaniah addresses Judah and various other nations. Some of the latter are unnamed and are mentioned collectively. Chapter 2 has a series of prophecies against Judah (Zeph 2:1–3), the Philistines (2:4–7), Moab and Ammon (2:8–11), the Cushites (2:12), and Assyria and Nineveh (2:13–15). Nahum, by comparison, has but one focus: God's triumph over the tyrant Nineveh and the display of justice to the nations freed from its control. What Zephaniah portrays in three verses, Nahum expands upon and savors in three chapters.

Nahum's three chapters indicate its basic structure: (1) an announcement of Nineveh's imminent fall (Nah 1); (2) a vivid poetic account of the battle for Nineveh (Nah 2); and (3) a woe speech against the city (Nah 3).

Nahum 1–3

The city of Nineveh is personified as a woman in various profiles (queen or princess, harlot, and sorceress), following a broad cultural convention and recognized poetic usage. Jerusalem and other cities are similarly personified elsewhere in the OT (e.g., Isa 1:26-27; 47; 60; Ezek 16; Lamentations). Nineveh represents Assyrian might and prestige, just as Washington and Beijing do currently for the United States and the People's Republic of China in current international relations.

Nineveh's perch at the pinnacle of power was the result of a might-makes-right policy. It is described as a "bloody city, full of deception and booty" (Nah 3:1), a harlot and sorceress (3:4). There was no limit to its treasures (2:9)—which, of course, had been plundered from others. In a bitter comparison, Nineveh and its rulers have been like a pride of lions, killing and eating what they please (2:11-12).

Nahum's poetry also presents once-mighty Nineveh in various postures of humiliation. She is to be stripped and carried off (Nah 2:7), plundered (2:9), and her garments lifted over her head in disgraceful exposure (3:5). In one graphic metaphor, the city will be consumed the way fruit is eaten by hungry people (3:12). Fire will ravage the city, and the sword will find its inhabitants (3:15). The concluding line of the book represents jubilation over the report that it has fallen, for its "relentless evil has crossed through" nearly everyone (3:19).

God is portrayed as the divine warrior, whose advance upon the enemy throws up cosmic convulsions (Nah 1:2-8). In the Sinai covenant God's self-identification is that of a jealous God who judges unto the third and fourth generation but shows compassion unto the thousands of those who love him (Deut 5:9-10/Exod 20:4-6; cf. Exod 34:6-7). The opening portrayal of the Lord in Nahum is based on this rendering of the divine character: "A jealous and avenging God is the Lord" (Nah 1:2). "To avenge" is a fair rendering of the Hebrew verb *naqam* used in Nah 1:2, although it can also be translated "vindicate." This latter sense is another side of the frightful depiction of the divine warrior, because Nahum describes the Lord as "good, a 'stronghold' in a time of trouble," and moving on behalf of "those taking 'refuge' in him" (1:7). Here Nahum reflects the language of the Psalter that the Lord is the "refuge" and "fortress" of the righteous (Pss 5:11; 7:1; 11:1; 16:1; 17:7; 18:2; 25:20; 37:40; 64:10; 71:1; 118:8-9; 141:8; 144:2). The defeat of Nineveh, the haughty harlot, is the vindication of those who had been her unwilling slaves.

It is interesting to read Nahum in the context of modern liberation theology, which emphasizes God's taking the side of the poor and oppressed in

their struggles for dignity and freedom. Does not Nahum resonate with this approach, at least in the condemnation of Assyrian oppression? On the other hand, Nahum reflects no pity for Nineveh/Assyria, only contempt. That gives pause, even to those who can rejoice at the fall of a murderous tyrant. Perhaps we can say that Nahum represents a "bottom-up" theological viewpoint: those on the bottom of an oppressive history celebrate the fall of an evil colossus. Pity for the death and destruction wrought on Nineveh may come later. Judgments and vindications in the historical process are often messy and violent affairs, and the fall of Nineveh was no exception. People of faith are caught in something of a dilemma, since either God is involved at various levels in the process and thus a part of the mess and violence, or God is aloof and thus merely a spectator. The consistent biblical witness is that God interacts in and through creation and history and is not indifferent to human suffering.

Nahum does not weigh the pros and cons of divine activity in a violent world as a kind of philosophical exercise, any more than it weighs options

A palace wall relief at Nineveh (7th century BCE) depicts victorious Assyrian soldiers piling up booty to divide. Nahum announces that Nineveh, the greedy plunderer, will itself be plundered (2:9, 12; 3:1). ©*Marie-Lan Nguyen (Wikimedia Commons, CC-2.5)*

for human response to a tyrant's fall. The book is not sweeping Judah's failures under the rug but is simply announcing that at this historical moment, God is on the side of the oppressed, using the historical process to bring down a tyrant and showing God to be the refuge of God's people. Indeed, at the news of Nineveh's fall, Judah is called to celebrate its feasts (Nah 1:15).

As indicated above, reading Nahum and Jonah together is an enlightening exercise in biblical interpretation. The two books offer different takes on the great confessional claim that God is gracious and compassionate but will not leave the guilty unpunished (Exod 34:6–7). One seizes on the compassion of God and the miracle that even the wicked can repent (compare Matt 12:41); the other demonstrates God's active opposition to evil. Can one be right without the other? Or should we acknowledge that both have something timely and disturbing to say?

Assyria (though not Nineveh specifically) is part of an intriguing prophecy in Isaiah (19:23–25) regarding the worship of the Lord. The prophet speaks of a "day" to come (see below on Obadiah) when Israel, Egypt, and Assyria will be a blessing in the midst of the earth and when Assyria will be called "the work of [God's] hands." This comes at the end of several prophecies about judgment on Egypt (Isa 19:1–17)! It is a reminder that while the prophecies against the nations are part of the prophetic claim that God is the moral judge of the world and vindicator of his covenant people, the blessing that God intends for creation includes peoples who from time to time have experienced judgment in the historical process. The last book of the NT is emphatic on this point, noting in a series of visionary catastrophic judgments that there are people from every tribe and tongue (Rev 5:9; 7:9–10) who comprise the blessed people of God.

READING

Read Nah 1–3 and formulate responses to the following questions:

1. We suggest that it is important to read Jonah and Nahum together. Do you think that is true? Helpful, but overrated as a way to understand the book?

2. We also suggested that Nahum is an example of a theology that sides with the oppressed (in this case Israel and Judah). Do you think that is true? Helpful, but overrated as a way to understand the book?

The Book of Obadiah

The shortest of the Minor Prophets is essentially an oracle against the nation of Edom. In this regard it is similar to Nahum and its prophecy against Nineveh. Edom and the Edomites are frequent subjects of prophetic oracles of judgment (Amos 1:11-12; Isa 21:11-12; Jer 49:7-22; Ezek 32:29). As noted above, Edom cooperated with Babylon in the downfall of Judah (Obad 10-14). That activity was preceded by the settlement of Edomites and related clans in the southern reaches of Judah, and their expansion continued after the fall of Jerusalem. The perfidy of the Edomites is painful in that it comes from a "brother" (Obad 10; cf. Amos 1:11). Edom traces its heritage back to Esau, the brother of Jacob.

The dating of the book is a difficult matter. In the sequence of the twelve Minor Prophets, it comes after Amos. This suggests to some interpreters that the book originated in the 8th century BCE. It may be, however, that its placement after Amos was topical, since Amos 9:12 refers to the future possession of the remnant of Edom by the people of Israel, and the short prophecy of Obadiah is all about the coming fall of Edom. The majority of scholars date the book of Obadiah to the postexilic period, after the hated behavior by Edom at Jerusalem's fall. Some also suggest that, as Nahum marked a celebratory prophetic response to Nineveh's demise, so Obadiah may offer a hope-inspiring antidote to worries over Edomite encroachment northward into southern Judah.

The Presentation

Edom's destruction is put in the context of a coming "day of the LORD" (Obad 8, 11, 15), when nations will be judged. Obadiah follows a prophetic motif in projecting dramatic change on a "day" or on "days" to come (Amos 5:18-20; 9:11; Zeph 1:7-18; Jer 31:31). This was a common way to influence or persuade an audience, by announcing that God's future actions would effect fundamental change. The terminology was taken over into the NT (Matt 24:36; Acts 2:17-21; 1 Thess 5:1-3).

The Day of the LORD

Several prophetic books refer to a future "day" or "day of the LORD." A few references are Amos 5:18; Joel 3:14–15; Obad 15–16; Mic 4:6; and Zeph 1:7–18. The references seem less directed toward a particular day, in the sense of a 24-hour chronological reference, and more directed toward decisive actions that God would undertake for Israel and the world. Amos, for example, warned his audience against looking forward to the day of the LORD. Apparently the people thought it would just be a time of judgment on Israel's enemies, while Amos thought it could also include judgment on Israel for its sinfulness. Zephaniah too saw the day as a time of widespread judgment, to be followed by the restoration of God's people (Zeph 3:14–20).

This three-horned female figure was found at Horvath Qitmit in southern Israel and dates to the 7th or 6th century BCE. The best cultural parallels suggest that she represents an Edomite goddess. ©Chamberi (Wikimedia Commons, CC-SA 3.0)

In Obadiah's usage, the "day of the Lord" is judgment that employs a reversal motif: "What you have done will be done to you" (Obad 15; cf. Ps 137:7-9). Edom's terrible response to Judah's "day" of distress (Obad 12) sets in motion its own day of distress, when, as Obadiah puts it, Edom's deeds will "return on its head." Judgment comes when the "house of Jacob will be a fire . . . and the house of Esau will be stubble" (Obad 18).

Although a day for Edom's judgment is the focus of Obadiah's prophecy, it is set in the context of a broader day, when God takes decisive action against nations who have wronged Israel and Judah (Obad 15-16). It is also a decisive day, when Zion/Jerusalem is exalted (Obad 21). This too follows the reversal motif, and it is part of a larger prophetic expectation about Judah and Jerusalem as being the center of a renewed world (cf. Joel 3:9-21; Zeph 3:14-20; Isa 2:2-4; 66:5-24; Ezek 40-48; Zech 12-14).

Readers can see in Obadiah's words and related prophecies virtually unrelenting doom for Edom. Nevertheless, as with the topic of Nineveh and Assyria, it is more complicated and dynamic for Edom than this, when one compares other biblical texts. In the order of the Twelve, Obadiah follows Amos and thus provides one way to illustrate the final portion of Amos 9:11-15, where David's booth (= his dynasty and rule from Jerusalem) is raised up and possesses the remnant of Edom and other nations that are called by the Lord's "name." We might call this a type of "remnant theology," where the brotherhood connection between Judah and Edom plus the claim that the Lord will bring blessing to the nations through Abraham's seed (Gen 12:3) mean more than a simple defeat of Edom. Furthermore, the Greek translation of Amos 9:12 sees in this context a claim that the nations belong to the Lord and will be ruled by David's son. The LXX reads the consonants of Heb. *Edom* as the consonants and vowels of *'adam* (= humankind) and translates the text as saying David will possess the "remnant of humanity." At a still-later time, that same Greek text is cited by Jewish Christians as scriptural proof that Gentiles (= humankind) will be incorporated into the rule of David's greater son, the Messiah (Acts 15:1-20).

One can cite other occasions in the prophetic texts when the dominant announcement

Remnant Theology

Despite all of the judgment on Israel and Judah that was announced by the prophets in the historical process, the prophets also held to the belief that God would preserve a remnant of his people. For example, the Lord told Elijah that in spite of Israel's failures, there were 7,000 people who had not worshiped Baal (1 Kgs 19:18). The name of one of Isaiah's children was Shear-jashub, which means "a remnant shall return" (Isa 7:3). Micah predicted that the lame and rejected would form a transformed remnant in the land (Mic 4:7). See also Zeph 3:13-14. Haggai addressed those who returned from exile as a "remnant" of the people (Hag 2:2), as do the postHB in the following century (2 Chr 34:21; 36:20; Ezra 9:8, 13; Neh 1:2).

of judgment on a nation—for the most part a result of bitter relations—is tempered by the claim that a changed and blessed future is also part of God's design. As noted above, this is the case with Egypt, a nation with multiple prophecies of judgment against it in the various prophets (Jer 46; Ezek 29-30). One can also see this tempering at work in the prophecies regarding Moab (and Ammon). At the conclusion of extended announcements of judgment on Moab, Jeremiah simply states on behalf of the Lord: "In the latter days I will restore the fortunes of Moab" (Jer 48:46; cf. 49:6).

READING

Read Obadiah and formulate responses to the following questions:

1. As noted, Obadiah claims in places that the evil done by Edom will also be done to Edom. Do you think this is an example of an "eye-for-an-eye" philosophy? How do you think that judgment on Edom serves the cause of justice?

2. We suggest that it is important to compare the various places where a subject such as Edom or Assyria is addressed in the Bible. Do you think that this is an important matter, or is it more important to let Obadiah be Obadiah and to have his say independently of other writers?

BIBLIOGRAPHY

Alexander, T. Desmond. "Jonah and Genre." *TynBul* 36 (1985): 35-59.

———. *Obadiah, Jonah and Micah*. Downers Grove, IL: InterVarsity Press, 2009.

Allen, Leslie. *The Books of Joel, Obadiah, Jonah and Micah*. NICOT. Grand Rapids: Eerdmans, 1976.

Baker, David W. *Nahum, Habakkuk, and Zephaniah*. Downers Grove, IL: InterVarsity Press, 2009.

Bridger, Gordon. *The Message of Obadiah, Nahum and Zephaniah*. Downers Grove, IL: InterVarsity Press, 2010.

Christensen, Duane. *Nahum*. AB 24F. New Haven: Yale University Press, 2009.

Kim, Hyun Chul Paul. "Jonah Read Intertextually." *JBL* 126 (2007): 497-528.

Raabe, Paul R. *Obadiah*. AB 24D. New York: Doubleday, 1996.

Sasson, Jack M. *Jonah*. AB 24B. New York: Doubleday, 1995.

29 THE BOOKS OF HAGGAI, ZECHARIAH, AND MALACHI

Important Dates for Haggai and Zechariah
522: Darius I begins to rule in Persian Empire
520: rebuilding of temple begins in Jerusalem
515: temple dedication and Passover celebration in Jerusalem

Important Dates for Malachi
515–400: period of Persian rule over Jerusalem and Yehud

BY CONSENSUS, HAGGAI, ZECHARIAH, AND Malachi are postexilic books. Even so, readers will encounter a range of proposals for their origins. Haggai is the most straightforward of the three, and its dating is closely related to that of Zechariah. Haggai essentially comprises four oracles dated to the 2nd year of the Persian king Darius (1:1 [compare v. 15]; 2:1, 10, 20). The subject matter—the rebuilding of the temple in Jerusalem—indicates that it is Darius I (ruled 522-486 BCE) who is in mind, since there was more than one Persian monarch with that name (see Table 16.2 on p. 209 for a list of Persian kings). We learn from scattered details in Ezra 6 that the modest Second Temple was finished in Darius's 6th year (515 BCE). Haggai's references to Darius's 2nd year correlate with the year 520 BCE, according to the modern Western calendar. The book of Zechariah has three dated oracles (1:1, 7; 7:1) from Darius's reign, and the subject matter of Zech 1-8 closely overlaps that of Haggai. Zechariah's first two dated prophecies are also from Darius's 2nd year, and the third oracle is from the king's 4th. The dating and context for the second half of Zechariah, chs. 9-14, are most likely later than the reign of Darius I (see below). In the case of the book of Malachi, its internal evidence strongly suggests the Persian period for its origin, with a plausible setting at virtually any point in the 5th century BCE.

Jews who returned to Jerusalem and Yehud in the late 6th century BCE faced several problems, which readers of Ezra and Nehemiah will recognize. On the one hand, they returned to a city mostly in ruins and in need of rebuilding. This is in addition to the difficulties that they faced in finding and sustaining their own living conditions. On the other hand, they faced opposition from local inhabitants and the need to stay in the good graces of the regional Persian officials. These three prophetic books deal primarily with problems internal to the Jewish community in navigating these difficulties and in discerning the will of God in such circumstances.

Haggai and Zechariah are often joined together by interpreters because their prophetic work overlapped. Indeed, listing the two figures together is an ancient phenomenon. They are named together already in the book of Ezra (5:1). Cyrus the Great had brought an end to the hegemony of Babylon (539 BCE), laying claim to its holdings, while proclaiming change for the peoples of the region (Ezra 1:1–4). Some prophetic figures encouraged Jews to return to Jerusalem and the province of *Yehud*, an Aramaic term related to the Hebrew word for *Judah*. Several groups of people returned during the years of Persian control, although the majority of exiled Jews did not. As Ezra 5:1–2 indicates, the prophets Haggai and Zechariah prophesied to the returnees and particularly to two leaders of the early community, Zerubbabel and Jeshua (sometimes written as Joshua). These two figures led the efforts to rebuild the temple in Jerusalem. According to a genealogy preserved elsewhere (1 Chr 3:19), Zerubbabel was the grandson of Jehoiachin, the king of Judah exiled to Babylon in 597. The Persians made Zerubbabel the governor of the province (Hag 1:1; 2:2). This was likely meant to pacify the inhabitants by acknowledging their previous history. As a descendant of David, Zerubbabel would have been popular with the former exiles, but as a Persian appointee, he would have been expected to keep order and to be cognizant of Persian interests. The Jeshua of Ezra 5:2 is the Aramaic form of the Hebrew name Joshua, referring to the high priest and son of Jehozadak (Hag 1:1; Zech 3:1).

The Book of Haggai

The prophet Haggai is referred to as "the messenger of the Lord" (Hag 1:13), who offers encouragement to rebuild the temple and trust that the Lord is among the people to form them into a holy community. Structurally, the book has four sections, each with an oracle (or oracles): (1) a series of short oracles concerning temple rebuilding (1:1–15); (2) an oracle of encouragement about the rebuilt temple's glory (2:1–9); (3) an oracle concerning uncleanness (2:10–19); and (4) an oracle of promise for Zerubbabel (2:20–23).

Haggai 1–2

The short book of Haggai begins with a notation that the word of the Lord came through Haggai to Zerubbabel, governor of Yehud, and Joshua, the high priest, in the 2nd year of Darius the Persian king (1:1). The other dated oracles in the book follow within four months' time. As noted above, the addressees are the twin leaders of the Jewish community recently returned to Jerusalem. The people with them are referred to as the "remnant people" (1:12), who are encouraged to rebuild the house of the Lord. Note also the claim that the Lord is "with them" and that they should not fear. This is a different tone from what is typically used by the preexilic prophets, who frequently castigated their contemporaries. Interestingly, Haggai's work is referred to in the third person. The book is a report about his words from someone else. In 2:1–9 Haggai contrasts the glory of the former house (which was considerable) with that of the current ruins facing the remnant people who have returned to Jerusalem and Yehud. Drawing on an eschatological vision for the future, the prophet proclaims that the wealth of nations will come to the rebuilt (Second) Temple (cf. Isa 60:10–18; 66:12; Zech 14:14). In 2:10–19 the sad and unclean conditions of the people are described. They are real and debilitating, but the restoration of the temple and its sacrificial worship will be an antidote.

In the last oracle (2:20–23), the prophet turns again to a vision of the future, referring to the shaking of the cosmos and of nations. At this time there were some rumblings of disorder and rebellion elsewhere in the new Persian realm, so the prophet may have seen these rumblings as precursors to more dramatic change to come. Zerubbabel is once again front and center, described as the Lord's "servant" and "signet ring." The latter reference is a metaphor signifying that Zerubbabel will act with the authority and

approval of the Lord. Readers should consider this description of Zerubbabel in light of the same term used for judgment on his grandfather, the exiled king Jehoiachin, in Jer 22:24–30. In that text Jehoiachin would have been (and was) cast away as ruler (and deemed childless), even if he had been a signet ring on the Lord's hand. Haggai, as it were, reverses the ongoing effects of that judgment with the announcement that Zerubbabel is integral to the Lord's plans for rebuilding the temple and reconstituting life in Jerusalem and Yehud. The prophecy may have also encouraged Zerubbabel in his leadership role and buttressed his authority among dissenters. Whether this prophecy intended to bestow messianic expectations on him is a matter of discussion. See below regarding his fate.

The Temple Mount of the Old City of Jerusalem looking to the southwest. The gold-roofed Dome of the Rock is a Muslim shrine originally constructed in the late 7th century CE. It was built over or near the ruined foundation stones of the Jewish Second Temple. *©Andrew Shiva (Wikimedia Commons, CC-SA 4.0)*

READING

Read Hag 1-2 and respond to the following questions:

1. Read Hag 2:1-9. There seem to be a few people who saw the former temple before it was destroyed by the Babylonians. How do you think they would have felt, standing near its ruins, and hearing the words of Haggai?

2. If you were Zerubbabel, how would you interpret the prophecy from Haggai that the Lord was about to shake the heavens and earth and destroy kingdoms (Hag 2:20-23)? Would that be good news or bad news for the community in Yehud?

The Book of Zechariah

Zechariah is one of the longest of the Minor Prophets and shares with Ezekiel a penchant for visions and symbolic description. It has two basic parts: (1) chs. 1-8 and (2) chs. 9-14. Much of the first section is a series of night visions. The material in chs. 9-14 is also visionary, with symbolic and apocalyptically oriented rhetoric. In this regard chs. 9-14 have some similarities with Daniel as well.

As noted previously, some interpreters have concluded that the visionary materials in Zech 9-14 are later than the early Persian period and are the editorial result of continued reflection on the announcements of the prophet from that time. In that sense, the present book's origin compares with the process suggested for the book of Isaiah. Whereas Zech 1-8 has dated oracles and material related to the rebuilding of the Jerusalem temple, the latter half of the book is structured around two expanded "oracles" or "sayings" (see the headings at Zech 9:1 and 12:1). In chs. 9-14 the eschatological future of Jerusalem is symbolically depicted in the context of international and cosmic travails. The reference

---

Postexilic Number 70s

Jer 25:11: Judah and other nations will serve Babylon for 70 years.

Zech 1:12: The 70 years of judgment lasts from the destruction of the First Temple until the building of the Second Temple.

2 Chr 36:20-21: The land had lain desolate as a Sabbath rest for 70 years, from the destruction of the temple to the rise of the kingdom of Persia.

Dan 9:1-27: The 70 years of exile announced by Jeremiah are part of a pattern of 70 weeks of years in which Israel's history shows continued judgment and the defeat of a prince who attacks Jerusalem.

to struggles with Greek soldiers in 9:13-14 may indicate a time after the conquest of Alexander the Great (died 323 BCE). Because of the involved symbolism and eschatological imagery, it is difficult to define a firm historical context or contexts for these last six chapters.

Zechariah 1–8

Readers will want to compare the visionary and symbolic descriptions in Zech 1-8 with the short book of Haggai. Zechariah too encourages the leadership of the fledgling community in and around Jerusalem to build the temple and a community faithful to the Lord. Throughout, the prophet is a master of visionary drama. In one evening he has a series of night visions that include such things as colored horses (1:7-17; 6:1-8) and a flying scroll and basket (5:1-4, 5-11). These vision reports and the angelic commentary that accompanies them are the heart of these chapters. The initial vision in 1:7-17 sets the tone for what follows. The prophet encounters an angelic rider, something like a patrol officer, whose trip results in a cry to the Lord, "How long will you hold back mercy for Jerusalem and Judah?" The answer is that the Lord will have compassion on them. The second vision (1:18-21) portrays the enemies of the people as horns that will be shattered. Vision three (2:1-13) shows that the city limits of Jerusalem will be expanded and promises that God will again dwell in its midst. A fourth vision (3:1-5) shows the high priest Joshua in dirty clothes and accused by the satan (probably an angelic adversary as in Job 1 or a symbolic depiction of an earthly adversary; see the sidebar on p. 218). According to the angel who accompanies Zechariah in his visions, the high priest Joshua will be cleansed and prepared to lead the people. Moreover, God's servant the Branch (3:8; cf. 6:12-13; Isa 11:1; Jer 23:5), which is almost certainly a reference to Zerubbabel, will assist him in this work.

Zechariah's fifth vision combines references to a lampstand and olive trees (4:1-14). The lampstand is of gold and represents sacred things. The two olive trees are Zerubbabel and Joshua. In the midst of the visionary account is an encouraging word from the Lord to Zerubbabel: "Not by might nor power, but by my Spirit" (Zech 4:6). To quote it out of context is to make it seem like a slogan; in context it is a reminder that the Persians have the dominant political power and military might but that God's life-giving Spirit is at work in bringing about a new chapter in the history of his people. Haggai spoke similarly (Hag 2:4-5). Zerubbabel, who for a short time received such fanfare, suddenly disappears from the surviving sources of the period. No one knows what happened to the descendant of David whom the Persians appointed governor. Was he removed by the power of the Persian government? Did he suddenly die? His mysterious absence paradoxically becomes all the more evidence for the truth of Zechariah's word to him, in that the temple was rebuilt and the community did persevere in the context of multiple difficulties.

The sixth vision (5:1-4) is of a flying scroll! It represents a curse on perpetrators of theft and swearing falsely in Yehud. The seventh vision (5:5-11), equally astonishing, depicts a woman in a basket named Wickedness who is taken away by two winged women and set in the land of Shinar (Babylon). While some of the details are obscure, the point seems to be the removal of sin from Judah and its placement in the former land of exile.

The eighth and last installment (6:1-8) of the night visions circles around to the themes with which they began. There are four chariots patrolling the earth, which represent the powers of the four winds. God's Spirit settles in the north country, perhaps signifying the extension of his sovereignty in a formerly hostile region. The last item in ch. 6 reverts from vision report to a description of the coronation of Joshua the high priest and of a crown for the Branch, who will build the temple.

Chapters 7-8 address matters of fasting and religious identity in Jerusalem, given that descendants of the exiles sent away in punishment have now returned. Note particularly the reference to the Lord's jealousy for Jerusalem in Zech 8:2 and his promise to dwell in Jerusalem (Zech 8:3-9; cf. 1:14-16). With the rebuilding of the temple, the theological claim from the past is renewed. God is among his people. This also has implications for the nations, because they too will come to Jerusalem to seek the favor of the Lord (Zech 8:20-23; cf. Isa 2:2-4).

Zechariah 9–14

The last six chapters of Zechariah contain two headings (9:1; 12:1). Much of the material concerns eschatologically oriented symbolism of struggles between Jerusalem and surrounding nations. The texts portray birth pangs, as it were, toward an age of peace. As noted, there are similarities in tone and emphasis between Ezekiel and Zech 9-14, both of which have a transformed Jerusalem at center stage in a new age to come, after travail among the nations.

The Knesset Menorah, by Benno Elkan. 1956. This sculpted model of the ancient temple's menorah is located in front of the Israeli Parliament building known as the Knesset in Jerusalem. ©*Posi66* (*Wikimedia Commons, CC-SA 3.0*)

In the context of judging nations, there is an announcement of a peaceful ruler who will enter Jerusalem on a donkey (Zech 9:9–10). The imagery is that of a triumphal entry celebrating peace. The horse was a symbol of war, but the donkey symbolized humility and peace. For the first readers of Zechariah, this imagery was a reminder of the still-unfulfilled promises to the Davidic line that a realm of peace and justice was Israel's heritage. Interestingly, the Gospels of Matthew (21:5) and John (12:15) quote Zech 9:9 in describing Jesus's entry into Jerusalem during the week before the Passover sacrifice. To do so was to say that Jesus was the king of Jerusalem whom the prophets foretold and that the kingdom he represented was one of deliverance and peace. There are, furthermore, a remarkable number of allusions to the last chapters of Zechariah in the accounts of Jesus's last week.

Chapters 10–11 have a similar theme, God's criticism of corrupt leadership ("shepherds"), similar to the critique of Judah's leaders in Ezek 34:1–10. Chapter 10 is poetry and also contains the theme of restoring Judah and Israel. The language of restoration describes the people coming back from Assyria and Egypt, which suggests either that the chapter includes older material regarding Assyria that is now being updated, or that Assyria is a symbolic reference to the land of exile. In any case, there is something of a new exodus theme sounded in the description of passing through the sea in 10:11. Some of the most obscure imagery in the book appears in 11:4–17 as part of the critique of corrupt leadership. The reference to named shepherd staffs (11:7) indicates a figural, if not allegorical, presentation. Note the

Gospel writer's adaptation of the thirty pieces of silver from Zech 11:12-13 (Matt 27:3-10).

The last three chapters have repeated references to decisive events on the historical horizon as the prophet perceives them. There are multiple references to a "day" when the Lord will act to effect change (e.g., Zech 12:3-4; 13:1; 14:1). The centerpiece of the collected prophecies is Jerusalem, which will be purged and transformed. Nations will surround and threaten the city, only to be thwarted. Note the repeated references to the "house of David" in ch. 12. The precise referent is not clear, but in context it refers at least to the triumph of Judah, David's tribal inheritance (Zech 12:7), if not more specifically to the vindication of David's descendants, who are not otherwise named. We might compare this material to the prophecy in Isa 55:3, where the Lord makes an everlasting covenant with the people in exile (= the "you" is plural) to give them the sure mercies promised to David.

There is a dramatic description of mourning for someone pierced (Zech 12:10-14). At this distance from the writer's context, it is difficult to know who is in mind. It could be the prophet himself or another figure representing the community. Interpreters have long noted the parallels with the suffering servant of Isa 53. In any case, the mourning is for someone dear to the community of Judah and Jerusalem.

Chapter 13 begins with a reference to flowing water from Jerusalem, a sign that a new age will come into play (compare Zech 14:8). This material has similarities with the vision of Ezek 47 and the miraculous flow of water from Jerusalem to the Dead Sea. The advent of a new age for Jerusalem comes with considerable difficulty, a theme also congenial to prophets such as Ezekiel, Zephaniah, and Joel, as well as the book of Revelation in the NT. Note the reference to the striking of God's shepherd and the death of two-thirds of the inhabitants of the land (13:7-9), a theme that continues into the last chapter.

The turmoil of battle is finally turned when the Lord goes forth to fight on behalf of his people (Zech 14:3). The last chapter reveals something of the changes that ensue. The survivors then live in a city without cold and frost and without night. God's kingly rule over the earth is centered in Jerusalem, and the land around the city undergoes change, as in Ezekiel's climactic vision. Rebellious nations are finally defeated, and peoples are drawn to Jerusalem to worship the Lord. Reading the last chapter is similar to viewing a series of photos or drawings that provide impressionistic data for the imagination. It is neither a blueprint nor a comprehensive description of the future, but it sketches out a stubborn confidence in God's ability to vindicate his people and to bring to pass his eschatological promises. It is no wonder then that Zechariah's visionary symbolism was frequently drawn upon by the prophet John in the book of Revelation.

READING

Read Zech 1–14 and answer the following questions:

1. Read Zech 1:7–17. What roles do the angels play in representing the Lord to the prophet? Does this passage remind you of other biblical scenes with angels? If so, what are some of the similarities and differences between them?

2. Both Zerubbabel and Joshua are called "Branch" (Zech 3:8; 6:12). How do you interpret that term? Note some references given above to the term elsewhere in the OT.

3. The OT prophets have visionary statements about future blessings and future difficulties to fall on Jerusalem. How do you understand the depictions of attacks on Jerusalem and the changes in the life of the area portrayed in Zech 14:1–11? Do they remind you of other OT texts?

The Book of Malachi

Malachi is the last named text in the Book of the Twelve. For most modern readers, this also means that Malachi is the last book of the OT. This "ending" status is because the prophetic books come last in virtually all forms of the Christian Bible. The pattern in the Hebrew Bible differs, where the collection known as the Writings follows the Torah and the prophetic books, and 1–2 Chronicles is the last work. Because the prophets are placed last, their representation of a transformed future gets the last word in the OT collection, as if to say that God's good work has not come to completion yet.

The name *Malachi* in 1:1 is the Hebrew phrase meaning "my messenger." The same term is used in 3:1, though this latter reference may be to a different figure than in the book's heading. Some have wondered, therefore, whether the book is from an unnamed messenger rather than a person named Malachi. In any case, the OT preserves nothing else about a prophet named Malachi. The book probably dates to ca. 400 BCE, and its four chapters combine an emphasis on God's expectations for righteous living with an expectation that a day of refining God's people will come.

Structurally, the book of Malachi has two parts: (1) a series of eight disputation speeches on various topics (Mal 1:1–4:3); and (2) a closing exhortation (4:4–6). In a disputation speech, a speaker (e.g., a prophet) argues a truth claim, rebuts his audience's anticipated objections to it, and provides additional arguments (cf. Isa 28:23–29; Amos 3:1–8). Some scholars suggest that audience unresponsiveness to earlier prophetic oracles was behind the prominence of the disputation speech in Malachi's rhetoric.

Malachi 1–4

Malachi denies that the sad circumstances of the people in and around Jerusalem indicate that God has forsaken his people. He points to the recent judgment on Edom as evidence that the God of justice has not abdicated his role (Mal 1:2–4). In one of the disputations, Malachi singles out the priests for particular criticism. His criticism is more direct (transparent) than the critique of the shepherds in Zechariah. Their lackadaisical efforts mislead the people, whether it be in performing the temple service or in offering the best of the herds for the sacrificial ritual (1:6–14). The prophet also cites God's covenant with Levi as the basis for the significance and the solemnity of levitical duties (2:1–8). In another disputation, the prophet cites God's opposition to the practice of divorcing the wife of one's youth (2:13–16), along with the memorable claim that God "hates divorce" (2:16). Readers should keep in mind that such a sweeping statement probably does not intend to do away with the option of divorce per se (divorce is recognized in Deut 24:1–4; cf. Matt 19:3–9). It does underscore the importance of marriage and rejects the practice of older men divorcing their wives for the purpose of marrying younger women.

Malachi's social-theological critique of his contemporaries and his projection of judgment and transformation to come are all rooted in a common confession: the God of Israel is a God of justice. Apparently some of the prophet's contemporaries denied that God was just or interested in their affairs (Mal 2:17; 3:13–15). They may also have been only nominally committed to their covenant. Malachi was confident, however, that God would prevail over their failures and any other form of opposition. In his appeal to his contemporaries, he commends those who "fear" the name of the Lord, for the "sun of righteousness shall rise with healing in its wings" (4:2). A winged sun disc was a recognized royal symbol in Israel and among some of its neighbors. The reference may be a veiled messianic prophecy that a ruler from David's line would come forth in the future or a reference to God's cosmic rule soon to be manifest in the historical realm.

The tone of the last chapter is a fitting conclusion to a collection of prophetic books. It begins with yet another prophecy about a coming "day of the Lord"—in this case a prophecy that signifies judgment such as a "burning furnace" (Mal 4:1) and the vindication of a faithful remnant of Israel over the forces of wickedness. Before the advent of that day, however, readers are enjoined to remember the Torah of Moses given for all Israel. This is similar to the conclusion of Ecclesiastes (12:13) that to fear God and keep his commandments is the basic posture of God's people, since the future is known fully only to God. Malachi also mentions the coming of Elijah the prophet (4:4–6). Elijah was taken to heaven in dramatic fashion (2 Kgs 2:1–25), and consequently, expectations developed over time that God would send Elijah back to warn the faithful before a cataclysmic day of judgment. After all, announcing and interpreting the future are prophetic tasks. Who better to take up the task of pointing to dramatic change on the horizon than Elijah? In the Gospel narratives of the NT, John the Baptizer is equated with Elijah— that is, John carries out Elijah's role in announcing the dawn of judgment and deliverance (Matt 11:1–14).

In Christian Bibles, the juxtaposition of Malachi and Matthew portrays the salvation-historical scheme of promise and fulfillment that is basic to Christian theology. Malachi points toward judgment and transformation to come, representing the essential claims of prophecy at the end of the OT. Matthew begins with a genealogy of 42 generations, running from Abraham and concluding with the birth of Jesus, the dawn of a new chapter in the history of God's people.

READING

Read Mal 1–4 and answer the following questions:

1. The subject of divorce is a sensitive matter in any culture. How do you interpret Malachi's claim that "God hates divorce" (2:16) in the context of 2:10–16? What does it mean to the discussion of faithful actions in 2:10–16 that everyone has "one father" (= God)?

2. According to Mal 3:6, the Lord "does not change." As you read the book of Malachi, what kind of change do you think is envisioned in this reference? How does this affirmation about God connect with the passages where God does react to circumstances and seems to change (for example, Gen 6:5-8)?

3. In Mal 1:6-14, the prophet complains about the poor attitude in Jerusalem toward the offering of sacrifices. In reading the criticism, what would you consider to be the right attitudes and practices at the Second Temple in Jerusalem? How might we translate those values into modern culture, where there is no animal sacrifice?

4. We noted that Malachi's intended audience may have been "nominally committed to its covenant." With what impression(s) of that audience, positive and/or negative, does the book leave you, and do these impressions support or rebut this characterization?

BIBLIOGRAPHY

Adam, Peter. *The Message of Malachi*. Downers Grove, IL: InterVarsity Press, 2013.

Baldwin, Joyce. *Haggai, Zechariah and Malachi*. Downers Grove, IL: InterVarsity Press, 2009.

Hill, Andrew. *Malachi*. AB 25D. New York: Doubleday, 1998.

Klein, George L. *Zechariah*. NAC 21. Nashville: Broadman & Holman, 2008.

Meyers, Carol, and Eric L. Meyers. *Haggai, Zechariah 1-8*. AB 25B. Garden City, NY: Doubleday, 1987.

Verhoef, Pieter. *The Books of Haggai and Malachi*. NICOT. Grand Rapids: Eerdmans, 1987.

Webb, Barry G. *The Message of Zechariah: Your Kingdom Come*. Downers Grove, IL: InterVarsity Press, 2003.

PART 5

The Poetry

30 WHAT ARE THE WISDOM BOOKS?

B Y GENERAL AGREEMENT, THE WISDOM books consist of Job, Proverbs, and Ecclesiastes. Occasionally interpreters have questioned whether Job is a wisdom book, since it differs from the other two in providing a narrative account of a renowned figure from east of Canaan. Most interpreters, however, find the topical similarities between the conversations in Job and the short sayings and brief discourses that comprise the majority of Proverbs and Ecclesiastes to be decisive in grouping these three books together. In the larger scriptural canons of the Roman Catholic and Orthodox Churches, there are additional wisdom books. They are Ecclesiasticus, also known as the Wisdom of Jesus Son of Sirach, and the Wisdom of Solomon (see our ch. 37 on canon and text). Their titles are evidence of their traditional association with "wisdom" in God's world.

What Is Wisdom?

According to Prov 1:7, the "fear of the Lord is the beginning [= starting point or chief portion] of wisdom/knowledge." Additionally, according to the same verse, fools reject wisdom and the beneficial instruction that it contains for life. There are similar sentiments in Job 28:28 and Eccl 8:12-13, and they help in briefly defining wisdom in these three books. Wise persons hold God in awe and reverence, and seek to pattern their lives on ways that acknowledge God and are congruent with God's purposes for life and well-being. One may define wisdom more broadly as the "art of steering" among life's choices, to use a phrase that works for both the theologically based "fear of the Lord" counsel and the more secular-oriented instruc-

The Lord Is My Shepherd,
by Eastman Johnson. 1863.
It depicts the intense
meditation required for
one to gain wisdom.

tions also included in Proverbs and Ecclesiastes. This definition would also cover much of what would be considered wisdom in modern Western societies, whether originating from a familiar source such as a grandparent or from people who are consulted in the larger society, such as counselors or experts in a given subject. *Secular-oriented* simply refers to the wise sayings and discourses that comprise the wisdom movement but that do not refer explicitly to God. Such counsel and advice may well assume that life and health come ultimately from a wise creator, even when reference to deity is absent. That would certainly be the case for the biblical materials. The wise person, therefore, as presented in Proverbs, learns from observation, experience, and tradition what works to preserve life and health in the world created by God. The fool does not.

Proverbial wisdom comes in the form of brief, poetic sayings. Such sayings are often contrastive in style (antithetical parallelism), so that terms are defined by their opposites. Thus, in reading through the book of Proverbs one can get a basic idea of what comprises wisdom and who is a wise person, while at the same time compiling a profile of their opposites—that is, the things that are not wise. Here is a brief list from the beginning of the book (Prov 1:2–7 NRSV) of desirable or positive things that help define wisdom:

Instruction
Understanding
Wise dealing
Righteousness
Justice
Equity
Shrewdness
Knowledge
Prudence
Fear of the Lord

Some of these have moral and spiritual connotations, and others, such as shrewdness or knowledge, are morally neutral but valuable nonetheless for achieving positive outcomes. These same verses provide characteristics that are not wise, whether morally neutral (but in danger of making mistakes) or dangerous in application. They are:

Simple (naïve)
Young (inexperienced)
Foolish (heedless of instruction/helpful knowledge)

One can see the contrastive style of presenting wisdom and its opposite in the following two poetic proverbs. They are typical in both form and content as part of the wisdom movement in ancient Israel. The bold terms are reinforcing negatives; the italic terms are reinforcing positives.

Treasures gained by **wickedness** do not profit, but *righteousness* delivers from **death.** (Prov 10:2 NRSV)

Doing wrong is like a sport to a **fool**, but *wise conduct* is pleasure to a *person of understanding.* (Prov 10:23 NRSV)

Short sayings and brief discourses in the wisdom movement sometimes portray a type of Two-Way Doctrine, which understands God as the overseer of a system in which blessing results from human actions that conform to divine standards, and curse or failure is the result of human folly. We might also call this perception the Act-and-Consequence Connection. The sayings traditions in Proverbs primarily orient readers to the Two-Way Doctrine and affirm its value for steering in life. So, for example, Prov 12:18 affirms that the speech of a wise person brings healing, but careless words do harm. These phenomena can be observed over and over again in human interchange. Ecclesiastes takes the certainty that some derive from such an orienting wisdom and largely turns it on its head, claiming instead that such results are not necessarily secure and that it is vanity to think that people can secure their lives through wisdom. Ecclesiastes would say, furthermore, that it is wisdom, not pessimism, to remember that people benefit from knowing their limitations. While wisdom does exceed folly, neither wise nor foolish persons will be long remembered (Eccl 2:13–16). The book of Job depicts profound debates over the Two-Way Doctrine of predictable acts and consequences. Was Job's suffering the result of his own folly? His friends,

4:30). The Egyptian and Israelite cultures had a shared sense of applicability. One can see this in modern times when comparing proverbs from different cultures. American folk wisdom will have some affinity with African and Asian proverbs, as each culture seeks success in steering through life's options and hurdles. While there are always elements unique to time and place, there can also be considerable overlap. One has only to compare the wisdom of a Chinese fortune cookie with that of *Poor Richard's Almanac*, a source of practical sayings from the American colonial period.

With a broad definition of wisdom such as "the art of steering," one could say that all books in the Bible would qualify as wisdom books! In defining a wisdom book, we must be guided by matters such as the literary properties of books, the dominant vocabulary and topics within them, and the traditions of readers who have come before us. The book of Proverbs, then, is a wisdom book for several reasons. It defines itself as a collection of "proverbs" (1:1), a form of expression central to the wisdom movement. It uses the Hebrew word for wisdom (*hokmah*) repeatedly, along with related vocabulary. The book is associated with the person of King Solomon, who was concerned with wisdom and knowledge of the world (1 Kgs 3:3–14; 4:29–34). He is credited with 3,000 proverbs and 1,005 songs, since "God gave to Solomon wisdom (*hokmah*), exceedingly great insight, and an expansive mind." Ecclesiastes, similarly, is associated with Solomon and uses the terminology and literary forms associated with the wisdom movement. As noted above, the attribution of the book of Job to the wisdom-books category is due primarily to its topic and vocabulary.

There are, of course, other materials in both Old and New Testaments that are formulated with the concerns of wisdom in mind. Some psalms, for example, can be characterized as wisdom literature on the basis of formal properties and content (Pss 37 and 72 are two examples). The account of Joseph in Genesis (Gen 37, 39–50), with his God-given insight, has wisdom overtones, as does the book of Daniel. Amos's prophetic use of rhetorical questions (Amos 3:3–8) could be another. Jesus's own use of sharp sayings and parables has enough in common with the concerns of wisdom that he can be characterized as a sage (wise person, teacher). Consider, for example, his proverbial saying that his disciples should not throw pearls before pigs (Matt 7:6) or his brief instruction that there are two kinds of gates for people, one broad and leading to destruction, and the other narrow leading to life (Matt 7:13–14). The letter of James also has some characteristics of wisdom in its collection of sayings.

Painting of Solomon welcoming the Queen of Sheba (not pictured here) adorning the Ethiopian chapel in the Church of the Holy Sepulchre, Jerusalem. By Alaqa Mezmur Za Dawit. *©Deror avi (Wikimedia Commons, CC-SA 3.0)*

How Did We Get Proverbs, Ecclesiastes, and Job?

Like the book of Psalms, the book of Proverbs is a collection of collections spanning a major portion of Israelite history from the united monarchy to the postexilic period. Whereas the Psalter is associated with David but also refers to other composers and compilers, Proverbs is associated with King Solomon, a dominant figure in Israel's historical narratives whose work as patron of a wisdom movement was supplemented by others as the centuries unfolded (see Table 30.2). There are references in the book to the officials of Hezekiah (Prov 25:1) and to an otherwise unknown King Lemuel (Prov 31:1). These references reinforce two things about the book of Proverbs. The first is the role of a monarch as a patron who uses the scribal resources of the court in collecting, copying, and disseminating such a large collection. Perhaps some of the material in Proverbs was used to educate people at the royal court. The second is recognition that wisdom is the product of an internationally shared search. Lemuel was not a king in either Israel or Judah. Indeed, he is otherwise unknown. Agur son of Jakeh, another figure in the chain of collecting proverbs (Prov 30:1), is also unknown and may have been a non-Israelite.

Modern readers sometimes encounter the book of Ecclesiastes through another name, that of Qoheleth, or as occasionally spelled, Koheleth. It is a Hebrew term from the book's first verse—since the Protestant Reformation, usually translated "Preacher" in English, although "Assembly Convener" would be more accurate. That same verse, the book's superscription, identifies Qoheleth as David's son and king in Jerusalem. This points to Solomon, the patron of wisdom. In reading the book, one encounters both first-person speech, such as "I Qoheleth have been king in Jerusalem" (Eccl 1:12), and editorial, third-person speech, such as "Qoheleth sought to find pleasing words, words that are right and true" (Eccl 12:10). Thus, one way to read the book is to see it as an edited version of a first-person account. The first two chapters lend weight to this conclusion, since Eccl 1:1–2 is an editorial introduction in the third person, but the remaining contents are first person. Chapters 3–12 continue the Solomonic memoir, even though the first-person speech occurs less often.

Given the Solomonic connection, readers are called upon to decide if the two "voices" of the book are in actuality two different persons or if the Solomonic autobiographical voice and the editorial voice are in reality the work of one person, regardless of the tone of each. The latter option means that the autobiographical voice is a literary device of the author/editor. Related to this question of reading strategy is that of the book's dating on the basis of internal evidence. The majority of scholars have concluded that the language of the book best fits the postexilic period; whether this was during the Persian or the early Greek period remains a matter of debate. This conclusion would mean that Solomon did not write the autobiographical sections; their form is a literary device employed by the author/editor of the

Table 30.2. The Patrons of Israelite Literature

Literary Type	Patron[a]	Later Recognition
Torah	Moses	The Pentateuch = "the Torah of Moses"
Prophecy	Moses	Num 11
	Elijah	Mal 4:5; Matt 11:14
Poetry	David	"Psalm of David" = "in David's honor"
Wisdom	Solomon	"Proverbs of Solomon" (Prov 25:1)

a. A *patron* is the originator of something (in this case, major types of biblical literature). Later authors or editors may write similar works in their honor, and a patron's work sets the standard against which those later efforts are judged.

book. Scholars have also discovered examples of fictional autobiographies of kings in Mesopotamia, discoveries that help readers put Ecclesiates' form and content together in an understandable way. A presenter using "Solomon's" voice is interpreting the life of Solomon for readers. More specifically, the Solomonic memoir depicts a pensive older person who has come to see that life's inequities do not have an easy or a rational explanation. Indeed, the theme of the memoir is "vanity of vanities, all is vanity!" The Hebrew word translated "vanity" is *hevel*, which refers to something ephemeral, fleeting, or of little substance. On occasion it means "breath." Readers will also want to compare this presentation of Solomon with that in 1 Kgs 3–11, where the patron king of wisdom began well but did not finish well.

The book of Job has several characteristics that make it unique in the OT and perhaps contribute to its origins and transmission. The central figure, for whom the book is named, is described as originating from the land of Uz, likely in Edom or associated with Edomites somewhere east of the Dead Sea and the Arabah valley (= fault line), continuing south from it (Jer 25:20; Lam 4:21). Job's friend Eliphaz is from Tema/Teman (2:11), a region associated with southern Palestine and Edom (Jer 25:23; Ezek 25:13; Amos 1:12; Obad 9). Teman is also the personal name of the son of Eliphaz, who is the son of Esau in Genesis (Gen 36:10–11); possibly his identity is related to the geographic name. It may be a coincidence that the only other person named Eliphaz in the OT is an Edomite from the ancestral period, or it may be an indication that Job was considered a patriarchal figure from the time of Jacob and broadly related to the ancestral circles described in Genesis. He is not a figure set in the Israelite or Judahite state, even though he worships the Lord, but in Ezekiel (Ezek 14:14) he is remembered as a righteous man from an earlier time. The Hebrew text of Job contains a number of rare words and grammatical peculiarities, making it difficult to date the composition of the book based on its linguistic attributes.

The setting of a story, of course, can be different from the time and place of written composition. A likely explanation is that certain forms of a Job story are old and traditional, perhaps older in origin than the land of Israel itself in Canaan; the final written form originated in the exilic or early postexilic period. The book has a prose introduction (Job 1:1–2:13) and conclusion (Job 42:7–17), but it consists mainly of poetic discourses and disputational dialogues. What led to its written form, at least the written form preserved in Israel's sacred Scriptures? Given the impact of the destruction of Jerusalem by the Babylonians and the exiling of a portion of Judah's inhabitants, it is understandable that a number of interpreters have proposed that an old story of Job was given new life in written form. A traditional story about suffering would certainly take on renewed interest in light of national distress and pain. And although we know next to nothing about performative reading in ancient Israel, it is interesting to compare the book to a Greek tragedy. Such an analogy brings out the primary literary characteristic of Job—namely, its discourses and dialogues. Neither ancient Israel nor its neighbors show evidence of plays in theaters like Classical Greece, so the analogy is not to theater as such but to the performative reading of texts. Moreover, it is particularly important to remember that the book begins with a narrative introduction in which God and Satan have an encounter that leads directly to tragic events in Job's life, an encounter unknown to Job, his family, and friends. This is similar to watching a classical tragedy unfold; the hearers/readers know something fundamental that the leading characters (except God) do not.

The suggested analogy between Job and a Greek tragedy is, of course, only a supposition, as is the proposal that the book reaches its final written form during the exile or early exilic period. After all, suffering is a perennial issue and did not first rise to the surface in Israel as a result of the exile. And the performance aspect of Job (a dramatic reading) does not depend on any cultural connection to classical playwrights. We have a story whose characters (except for God!) have no firm connections otherwise to the story line of Israel and whose readers are left to ponder how such an exquisite account, with its dramatic rhetorical exchanges, emerged as part of Israel's sacred Scriptures.

What Would the Wisdom Books Do for Israel?

The wisdom books preserve accumulated counsel for life in the world created by God. They contain the voices of parents and keen observers in grappling with life's choices and conundrums. These books also complement Israel's story line as preserved in the Primary History, even though they only refer to it obliquely. The figure of Solomon is an intersecting point between them, however. His appreciation for the resources inherent in the broad wisdom movement was instrumental in their eventual inclusion in Israel's national traditions. God had called Israel into a covenant relationship and provided sources of instruction for the people. The resources of the wisdom movement were seen as one component of that provision.

When read together, the wisdom books provided Israel with sustained attention to matters on which there was disagreement. Perhaps that is one of the gifts of the wisdom movement, enabling different voices to engage in interchange. The book of Proverbs primarily provides counsel that orients readers to navigate successfully in life. And while it recognizes mystery in God's dealings with the world and human community, much of its wisdom presupposes the Two-Way Doctrine at work. Both Job and Ecclesiastes deal directly with the disorienting experiences of life, whether the experience of suffering or the related matters of inequity, and provide reflections on grappling with them.

The wisdom books also assisted Israel in seeing itself as a member nation among the peoples of the world created by God. Israel took the best of the international wisdom movement as guidance for both mundane matters and perennial mysteries. This perspective would be important later on, in the aftermath of Alexander the Great's conquest of the ancient Near East and the subsequent flowering of Hellenism among its inhabitants. The Greeks put much emphasis on the value of their philosophical and ethical schools, and their influence was deep and long lasting. Israel could assimilate what was valuable from them on the basis of a cardinal tenet of the wisdom movement: namely, that all truth was ultimately God's truth and should be gratefully employed when acquired. At the same time, Israel's wisdom books also provided them with resources to evaluate and critique Hellenism's wisdom and to assist them in maintaining their identity in the larger world.

BIBLIOGRAPHY

Bartholomew, Craig G., and Ryan P. O'Dowd. *Old Testament Wisdom Literature: A Theological Introduction*. Downers Grove, IL: InterVarsity Press, 2011.

Crenshaw, James L. *Old Testament Wisdom: An Introduction*. Louisville: Westminster John Knox, 2010.

Dell, Katherine. *Get Wisdom, Get Insight: An Introduction to Israel's Wisdom Literature*. Macon, GA: Smyth & Helwys, 2000.

Murphy, Roland E. *The Tree of Life: An Exploration of Biblical Wisdom Literature*. Grand Rapids: Eerdmans, 2002.

Perdue, Leo G. *Wisdom Literature: A Theological History*. Louisville: Westminster John Knox, 2007.

Weeks, Stuart. *Introduction to the Study of Wisdom Literature*. New York: T&T Clark, 2010.

31 THE BOOK OF JOB

THE BOOK OF JOB BEARS the name of its heroic main character, Job, whose righteousness was deemed legendary (Job 1:3; Ezek 14:14, 20). It raises universal questions about human suffering and integrity through the media of narrative and dialogues. As such, its wide appeal ranks it among the Bible's most-read books.

Structurally, the book has a prose introduction and conclusion (I, IX below), but most of its content comprises the cycles of poetic speeches between them. The book can be outlined as follows:

I. Job's Tragedy and the Wager between God and the Satan 1:1–2:13
II. Job Laments the Day of His Birth — 3:1–26
III. Job and His Three Friends in Dialogue — 4:1–27:23
    A. Eliphaz Speaks — 4:1–5:27
    B. Job Replies — 6:1–7:21
    C. Bildad Speaks — 8:1–22
    D. Job Replies — 9:1–10:22
    E. Zophar Speaks — 11:1–20
    F. Job Replies — 12:1–14:22
    G. Eliphaz Again — 15:1–35
    H. Job Again — 16:1–17:16
    I. Bildad Again — 18:1–21

The prose introduction sets the stage for the drama that ensues, narrating the tragedy that strikes the family of Job and then Job's own health and reputation. Job's integrity is the subject of an exchange between God and an angelic adversary, when the latter claims that Job's piety is only the result of divine blessing, implying that Job would give up his piety in the absence of that blessing. Three companions comfort Job but also insist that his own sinfulness has brought the devastation upon him and his family and that he should acknowledge that God has justly sent it. The back and forth of their exchanges constitutes about 40 percent of the book. Job's responses have some parallels with psalms of lament, as he maintains his innocence. His friends speak like opponents in a debate in making their case that he deserves the judgment that God has placed on him. Interpreters differ on the role of ch. 28 in the book. Some understand it to be a continuation of Job's speech that begins in 26:1; others see it as the narrator's presentation of the mysterious relationship between wisdom and divine activity. An interloper named Elihu offers a critique of both Job and his friends after their rounds of interchange. His comments are followed by two speeches by God from a whirlwind, Job's humbled response to the intricacies of the created order, and a final reckoning for both Job and his friends.

The Story

Job 1–2: The Narrative Introduction

As noted previously, Uz is east of Canaan proper, perhaps in the region of Edom. The Sabeans (Job 1:15) are an early Arabian tribe, and the marauding Chaldeans (1:17) are probably a people in the region who spoke Aramaic. They play no continuing role in the account. It is the exchange between Satan and God that sets the tragic circumstances of Job's family in motion. The term *satan* is actually not a name but a common noun meaning "adversary" or "challenger" (see the sidebar on p. 218). Note that the figure in Job 1 is part of the angelic host. His role in the story is indeed that of a challenger—something like a prosecuting attorney—who argues a case. In this instance, Satan questions God's own assessment of Job as "blameless and upright, fearing God and refraining from evil" (1:8), implying that Job's rectitude is made easy by the blessings that he has received and that his piety will evaporate with hardship and suffering. Moreover, his charge may also imply that God's blessing of Job is self-serving, giving God something to boast about! The adversary, like the Sabeans and Chaldeans, plays no continuing role in the book, and the conclusion to the book makes it clear that God is responsible for Job's circumstances.

Readers of the exchange between God and the adversary know that Job's sufferings are not the result of his sinfulness. None of the other characters in the account, however, know of the exchange. In Job's case, it is crucial to the story that his response to suffering be his free choice and not influenced by what the adversary claims about him—namely, that the removal of his blessings will result in Job's blaming God and cursing him. There is a sense in which God is betting on Job, that he will continue to fear God in spite of the loss of his family and health. In the case of the friends, their response to Job is conditioned by their worldview in general (see below), not on specific knowledge of God's action with respect to Job. And that may be one contribution of the story to the life of faith. There could be many occasions when a judgment about a person or persons is based on incomplete knowledge of their circumstances. Job's story, therefore, does not seem designed to answer the problem of evil in the abstract, what philosophers call theodicy, but to explain how a person responds to suffering and God's role in it, when no explanation/accounting is forthcoming. More specifically, the story represents how Job attempts to maintain his integrity and his fear of God without an answer to his dilemma. And his example may be one more contribution of the story to the life of faith.

Some interpreters see the figure of Job as a symbolic representation of the human condition in facing the mystery of suffering, albeit in the context of ancient Near Eastern culture. Others see Job as something of a special or extreme case: he is an extraordinarily righteous person who suffers a grievous, exceptional amount of suffering. If his relationship with God can remain intact, given these circumstances, then there is hope for others whose righteousness is less imposing and whose circumstances in life may be less threatened.

Finally, these opening prose chapters introduce readers to Job's three friends: Eliphaz, Bildad, and Zophar. Initially they will comfort him, but eventually each one will accuse him of bringing his suffering on himself and his family.

Job 3–31: Cycles of Speeches

Like Jeremiah (Jer 20:14-18), Job laments the circumstances of his birth (see Job 10:1-22). The prophet's attempt to follow God's leading resulted in fierce persecution. In Job's case, he can discern no reason why God should treat him so harshly, and thus he wonders early in his deliberations whether it were better that he had not been born.

Once his friends begin to speak, it becomes clear that their worldview is based irrevocably on the Two-Way Doctrine—namely, that act and consequence are so closely connected in human affairs that a wise person can examine circumstances and move back from them to discern their causes. The analogy is one of plants and originating seeds. As noted previously, the wisdom movement in the ANE was largely concerned to discern and then portray the relationship between act and consequence. Wisdom was, at least in part, the ability to discern the consequences of acts and to plan accordingly. In Job's case, his friends are motivated by their concern for him. They are saddened by his suffering and believe, based on a rigid application of the Two-Way Doctrine, that he should confess his sinfulness in hopes that God will remove his distress. Note, for example, Eliphaz's comments to Job in his first speech:

> Who that was innocent ever perished? Where were the upright cut
>   off?
> In my experience, those who plough iniquity and plant trouble reap
>   them. (Job 4:7-8)

Job Rebuked by His Friends, by William Blake. 1805.

Eliphaz compares Job to a farmer who plants evil and then reaps it accordingly. Thus Job could be neither innocent nor upright, given his distressing circumstances. The term translated "upright" (*yashar*) in 4:7 is the same term that God used earlier in commending Job to the adversary (1:8).

Nuance and detail characterize the give and take between Job and his friends in this section of the book. Job remains adamant that he did not bring his dreadful circumstances on himself and his family through impiety or hidden faults. Readers know this from the narrative introduction, while the friends work back from Job's dreadful circumstances to the assumed causes that he brought on himself. Once his exchanges with the friends is complete, he will offer a type of public oath that he has not failed his community and its expectations of a just public life (31:1-40). Job does not argue, however, that he is righteous or blameless in any abstract or comprehensive sense, nor does he dispute the cogency of the Two-Way Doctrine as a way to understand the world. He simply cannot see the connection between his prior acts and his current circumstances. Although he repeatedly says that he wants to make his case before God, who he believes is responsible for his circumstances, he also acknowledges that no one can win an argument with God (9:3, 14-15)—both beliefs being further evidence of his genuine piety. Like those who prayed the laments of the Psalter, Job brings his emotions and circumstances to the Lord. Indeed, he indicates that he would like to be put out of his misery by God (6:8-9), so vexing is his life! In one well-known claim, Job says that he knows his "redeemer" lives (19:25). Unfortunately, the context gives little clue to the identity of this redeemer. It is a reference to someone who can play the role of advocate and gain his eventual vindication. Such a person—often a kinsman—would be the opposite of an adversary (human or angelic), whose role it is to make charges. It could also be a reference to God, who Job may believe will eventually come around to seeing that his suffering is undeserved (see also the guardian-redeemer sidebar on p. 151).

From the side of Job's friends, there are variations in presentation but unity in the goal of convincing Job of the error of his ways. On the one hand, they point him to the retributive element in the Two-Way Doctrine. Suffering is the result of his transgressions. They have a rigid view of received wisdom and no place for mystery. Job's refusal to admit his failures moves them past their concern for his welfare, and they increase their efforts at convincing him of his culpability. They will seek to win an argument at the cost of losing a friend, whose obstinacy they cannot understand. Note the chilling claim of Zophar that God's toll on Job so far is less than he deserves (11:6) and that of Eliphaz, who charges that there is no end to Job's iniquities (22:5).

It seems that Job and the friends agree on some things. They acknowledge that God is rightfully the judge of the world and that God is not constrained by outside forces. Furthermore, both see Job's circumstances as the work of God's hand. The friends, however, have no questions for God, only assertions about Job and assumptions about what God has done.

Chapter 28 functions like a brief interlude, whether it is understood as a portion of Job's final response to his friends or as the narrator's provision of a poem. Wisdom is like the precious metals buried in the earth, which humankind works so hard to obtain. It is precious but often inaccessible.

Ultimately human wisdom must yield to the purposes and work of God, which God alone can interpret. Note the conclusion to the poem: "Fear of the Lord is wisdom" (28:28). Wisdom cannot be defined autonomously by human standards but only in relationship to the work of God in the world. This point anticipates God's rhetorical strategy in the whirlwind scenes (chs. 38–42).

Job 32–37: The Elihu Cycle

Interpreters often call chs. 32–37 the Elihu cycle, so named for the young speaker who offers observations on several matters related to the dialogues between Job and his friends. For one, Elihu objects to the approach of the friends. While they defend God, they still have no answer for Job. He objects also to Job, who he believes is first interested in asserting his own righteousness rather than that of God. The majority of his speech concerns the attributes and character of God. In the view of most interpreters, Elihu does not offer an answer to the dilemma of Job's circumstances. He does, however, extol God's character as righteous and majestic and regards human inquiries into God's work as ultimately futile, as though humankind could ever have the capacity to sit in judgment upon God. God's purposes exceed human capacity to understand them (37:5). This perspective does provide a framework in which to put Job's circumstances, although it runs counter to the modern Western tendency to question any assertions about God. Note also Elihu's related claim that human beings cannot always find God (37:23–24). In his view, this is not an excuse for human failure but a reason to fear God nevertheless and not to depend on self-righteousness. His perspectives lead directly to God's response from the whirlwind.

Job 38–42: God Speaks and Job Responds

This section has two speeches by God, each followed by a brief response by Job (40:3–5; 42:1–6). God, furthermore, instructs the three friends to see the error of their ways and to accept Job's intercessory prayer for them (42:7–9). Finally, a prose epilogue narrates the restoration of Job's health and family.

God's speeches come out of a whirlwind. As with Elihu's presentation, their subject matter is less about Job's suffering, although he is repeatedly addressed, and more about God's intricate governance of the world. Much of chs. 38–39 consists of questions to Job about God's relationship with the phenomenal world, which Job is unable to answer. The initial question, for example, asks Job where he was when God laid the foundations of the earth (38:4). The answer, of course, is that Job was not present and thus does not have the perspective to make judgments about the earth as God does. Interpreters have grappled with the purpose of these speeches, which essentially overwhelm Job with questions that he cannot answer. The goal may be to bring Job to recognize that he and his concerns are not the center of the vast, complex creation to which God is linked in multiple ways. It may be to further the observation of Elihu that some of God's ways are hidden to humankind, or relatedly, to show Job that he simply lacks the perspective with which to judge God's decisions. Job's first response (40:3–5) simply and briefly acknowledges his finiteness in the face of such vast evidence of God's supremacy.

The second speech out of the whirlwind continues the rhetorical tour of the phenomenal world and God's connections to it. Note God's initial demand that Job "gird up his loins"—that is, prepare to do battle—followed by the accusatory question that Job's actions seem intended to condemn God while justifying Job (40:7–8). Part of the rhetorical tour of the phenomenal world includes God's work with two powerful creatures, Behemoth and Leviathan. Interpreters differ somewhat on their identity, perhaps because their characteristics partake partly of poetic and mythological expressions. Behemoth may be the hippopotamus and Leviathan the Nile crocodile.

Job's brief response leaves much for readers to ponder (42:1–6). He confesses that he does not know enough to sit in judgment of God. He then adopts the posture of humility and repentance. Interpreters differ over the significance of Job's repentance. The word is capable of several related meanings. In its most basic sense, it means a change of action/perception on Job's part. Does his repentance mean that he is disavowing his long-standing demand that he be given an answer for the suffering he has endured? Is he expressing profound regret and/or confessing failure and seeking forgiveness? Or is his new perspective simply one of acceptance of his circumstances and his self-effacing way to express his fear of God, irrespective of an explanation?

And there is yet more to ponder in the concluding prose section. It seems ironic that God informs the friends, who wanted nothing more than to put Job in his place by defending God's judgments, that they have not spoken what is right about God. It will take Job's intercession, among other things, for God to accept them. Moreover, God affirms Job, who had searching questions for him, as speaking what is right! Nothing is said about God's earlier exchange with the adversary, which set the tragic circumstances in motion. It is frankly stated that God was responsible for the harmful things done to Job's family and health (42:11). Now God's blessing of Job entails twice what he earlier possessed, a tangible way to show that Job's restoration to God and human community is complete.

READING

Read Job 1–42 and formulate answers to the questions that follow:

1. Interpreters differ whether the satan described in ch. 1 should be identified with the malevolent being referenced in the NT or whether he is a figure playing an assigned role (adversary). How would you define his role in the book of Job, and how does the adversary relate to other references to a/the Satan in the Bible?

2. Job apparently is not an Israelite, although he certainly worships the Lord, the God of Israel. In what ways (if any) does his cultural or ethnic background make any difference to his role in the religious literature of Israel?

3. How would you describe the roles of Job's friends in the book? What did they get right and what did they get wrong in relating to Job?

4. It is stated above that most interpreters don't think that the book of Job answers the problem of evil in the world. Do you agree or disagree with this characterization of the book? How would you describe the purpose(s) of the book?

5. What do you think is meant by Job's repentance in 42:6?

6. In what way(s) do you think Job spoke what is right about God?

BIBLIOGRAPHY

Balentine, Samuel E. *Job*. Macon, GA: Smyth & Helwys, 2006.

Crenshaw, James L. *Reading Job: A Literary and Theological Commentary*. Macon, GA: Smyth & Helwys, 2011.

Goldingay, John E. *Job for Everyone*. Louisville: Westminster John Knox, 2013.

Hartley, John E. *The Book of Job*. NICOT. Grand Rapids: Eerdmans, 1988.

Longman, Tremper, III. *Job*. Grand Rapids: Baker Academic, 2012.

Newsom, Carol A. *The Book of Job: A Contest of Moral Imaginations*. New York: Oxford University Press, 2009.

O'Connor, Kathleen. *Job*. Collegeville, MN: Liturgical Press, 2012.

Wilson, Gerald H. *Job*. Grand Rapids: Baker Books, 2007.

32 THE BOOK OF PSALMS

Important Dates for Psalms
1010–970: reign of David
970–931: reign of Solomon and construction of Jerusalem temple
520–515: rebuilding of temple in Jerusalem
515–350: final collecting of songs and prayers into a book of Psalms

THE BOOK OF PSALMS IS a collection of smaller collections of prayers and hymns from various periods in Israel's history. It is the largest book in the Bible. Perhaps Proverbs provides a helpful analogy to Psalms, as it also is a collection of smaller collections gathered over centuries—though in its case the collection contains aphorisms and brief instructions related to wisdom. Both books were associated with the prominent kings (David = Psalms, Solomon = Proverbs) who were their patrons.

Interpreters have used several expressions to refer to the book of Psalms. The Hebrew title is *Tehillim*, a generic term for hymns. The English term *Psalms* is based on a related Greek term (*psalmoi*) used in early biblical manuscripts and then adopted by the Latin Vulgate. A related English term for the book, the *Psalter*, is also derived from a Greek word (*psalterion*), referring originally to a stringed instrument and by derivation to a performed composition.

Individual psalms could be sung and chanted in public worship; modern interpreters, therefore, have called the Psalter the "hymnbook of the (Second) Temple." The description is based, first, on internal evidence that a number of psalms were associated with the temple in Jerusalem (below) and, second, that the composing and collecting of psalms continued into the postexilic period (ca. 520–168 BCE). The comparison to modern hymnbooks, or a book of worship in more-liturgical traditions, is helpful not only to connect the psalms to settings in worship in ancient Israel but also as a reminder that the Psalter draws on previous collections and incorporates songs composed over a considerable period of time. Jews and Christians have sometimes used the shorthand term "David" for the book, since he is known as the "sweet psalmist of Israel" (see 2 Sam 23:1), and his name appears in the headings of approximately half of the biblical psalms. In the history of interpretation, David was often considered the author of all the psalms. Indeed, a notation in a Psalms manuscript among the Dead Sea Scrolls (11QPs^a) attributes over 4,000 compositions to him. Again, the analogy with the book of Proverbs holds: Solomon's name is associated with it as patron of a wisdom movement in Jerusalem, although materials in the book were derived from various sources.

How Did We Get the Book of Psalms?

The collection of collections was centuries in the making, and one can see evidence of the editing process in its final form. The book has, for example, 150 psalms arranged in 5 "books" or subsections. This is an editorial arrangement from the last centuries BCE, where the number 5 is clearly calculated to parallel the five books of the Torah. The parallel is made explicit in Midrash Tehillim, a Jewish, postbiblical commentary on the Psalter, which states in a comment on Ps 1:5 that "Moses gave five books to Israel, and David gave the five books of psalms to Israel." The number 150 may seem arbitrary, but it was recognized as fixed in Jewish circles. In the Septuagint version, there is actually a Ps 151, whose heading states in some manuscripts that it is "beyond the number"—in other words, that it is not part of the 150. This suggests that at a point in the collection process, 150 was accepted as the complete number, even though there were more compositions known and used in some circles. Moreover, although the Hebrew and Greek books of Psalms each have 150 numbered psalms, they are numbered differently through much of their respective collections. Two pairs of psalms in Hebrew and in English versions (Pss 9–10 and 114–15) are considered one psalm each in Greek versions. And two psalms in Hebrew and English versions (116 and 148) are each divided and become four psalms in Greek versions.

This modern sculpture of King David playing the harp is located outside the Old City of Jerusalem, near the traditional site of David's burial. *Photo by Patrick McInerney. Used with permission.*

Such compositions are known among Egyptians, Hittites, Assyrians, and Babylonians. No doubt individuals employed songs and prayers in their daily lives, but unless the author was a priest or monarch, it was less likely that his or her individual composition made it into a written collection. Thus, on the one hand, there are a number of parallels in form and content between the compositions of the Psalter and poetic compositions from the ANE. On the other hand, it is also the case that nothing comparable to the Psalter as a national collection, particularly with as many prayers of individuals, has survived from the ANE. Why is this case? Possibly, it is simply the result of the accidents of history. At any point archaeologists may find a Canaanite or Persian collection of hymns and prayers, composed over centuries of time and containing a large percentage of individual compositions. On the other hand, one of the motivating factors among Jews who preserved the Psalms was not simply to use them in temple and synagogue worship but also to study them for instruction in piety. This factor may have been crucial in preserving them over extended periods of time.

Psalms are composed as poetry, using reinforcing lines to compare, complete, and contrast a thought. They are replete with metaphor and imagery. Moreover, readers of the Psalter will recognize that many psalms have recurring formal features other than poetry and metaphor. Hermann Gunkel, a student of the Psalter in the early 20th century, made lasting contributions to its interpretation with his insight that some of the recurring features among the psalms are rooted in typical forms of speech (genre). This aspect of literary analysis is broadly known in English as form criticism. He was interested in the production and employment of the psalms in Israelite society, and he proposed that psalmists employed and sometimes adapted a handful of genres rooted in particular "life settings" in Israelite society, such as temple worship or the law court. Modern Western interpreters might think of such recognized cultural forms of expression as a newspaper editorial, an emergency announcement, a television commercial, or a mystery novel to recognize that form and content go together, even as each of these has its unique setting and intention. More unique to music, think of the formulaic elements in rap music, jazz, "the blues," and country and western ballads. While each of these has a certain amount of variation in presentation, it is the presentation formulas that informed listeners quickly recognize and that new listeners intuitively come to expect in defining a composition. Gunkel proposed hymns, laments (corporate and individual), and thanksgiving (individual and corporate) as the basic literary genres in the Psalter, as well as minor categories such as royal, Zion (= celebration of Jerusalem), and wisdom psalms, which are identified essentially by content or theme. Many interpreters have weighed in with refinements, but his basic insights linking form, content, and context stand the test of time and cultural investigation. In sum, the Psalter's contents gravitate between two poles: one of praise and thanksgiving, and the other of lamentation. It is also possible to scrutinize a psalm for its formal features unduly, as though each composition must fit a reconstructed form, and lose sight of an author's prerogative to vary and play while still accommodating an audience's expectations.

The Settings for Psalms of Praise and Lament

Sigmund Mowinckel, a Norwegian scholar and younger contemporary of Gunkel, has been the catalyst for another long-lasting discussion among interpreters of the Psalter. He took up Gunkel's interest in the "life-setting" of the various psalms, by which is meant the institutional place in Israelite society where such genres had their home. Mowinckel proposed a setting in the worship life of Israel for the vast majority of the psalms, associating them with particular festivals and feast days at the temple. He even reconstructed an extensive New Year celebration for the Israelite cult, although the biblical evidence for it is meager, and gave a prominent role in public worship to the king in Jerusalem. The setting of at least some psalms in public worship is obvious, as their vocabulary calls attention to the connection with the temple and its services. Consider, for example, the following citations:

> I shall recount your name to my kindred; among the congregation I
> shall praise you. (Ps 22:22)

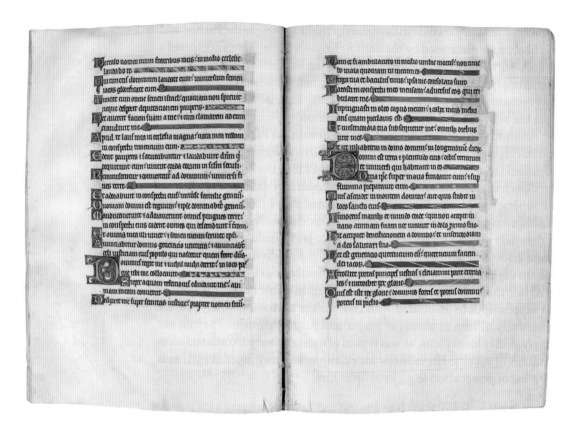

Interior pages of an illuminated (or color-highlighted) Psalter in Latin from Britain, now in the Metropolitan Museum of Art in New York City. Thirteenth century CE. The two oversized letters mark the beginnings of Psalms 23 and 24.

Just as there are five books in the canonical Torah of Moses, so the Psalter is structured as a Davidic Torah, providing liturgical and hymnic instruction for the faithful. In recent years interpreters have also asked the related question whether this arrangement also includes intentionality regarding the order of the individual psalms in some or all of the five books. Given the fact that smaller collections (e.g., the Psalms of Ascent, the Psalms of Korah) were included over time in the Psalter, most interpreters have not proposed a psalm-by-psalm rationale for the order of the completed collection. This, of course, does not mean that there was no attention to order in the Psalter's composition, only that such things as compositional size, chronological arrangement, authorship, or theme do not immediately present themselves as reasons for the final sequence of compositions in the Psalter. Gerald Wilson has proposed that the psalms at the seams of Books I–III are a structuring device that moves from attention to the Davidic king and the Lord's covenant with David to the loss of the king at the hands of the Babylonians, so that

Book IV reframes the question of kingship as that of the Lord's cosmic kingship. Nancy deClaissé-Walford suggests that the five books of the Psalter should be read against the background of Israel's history and its movement from promised land and temple to life in exile and dispersion, while affirming the faithfulness of God and hope for the future. If one takes the setting of the postexilic period as the point of departure for reading the Psalter, then she likely has a point. It is not clear, however, that the Psalter interprets this national narrative by arranging its contents psalm by psalm.

How Have People Used This Collection?

Psalms is a repository of hymns and prayers. It served as a resource for and a reminder of the worship life at the temple. It preserved the prayers of generations of Israelites as models. Those who recited a historical résumé such as Ps 105 learned and celebrated God's faithfulness in bringing the nation of Israel into being. Those who recited Asaph's plea for Jerusalem were trained in petitionary prayer.

Readers of the Psalter can discern at least two themes at its beginning and end that can shape the reading experience of the Psalter as a whole. Psalm 1 introduces readers to the two ways of relating to God and divine instruction. The way of the righteous and wise is that of "meditating" on the instruction of the Lord (Ps 1:2–3) while engaging in a manner of life known as the "way of the righteous" (1:6). As the introduction to the Psalter, Ps 1 is a guide to those who will read and meditate further on the Psalter's contents. The last five psalms (146–50) are all marked by praise of the Lord, who preserves his people and blesses creation. Indeed, these last five psalms begin and end with the exclamation "Praise the Lord!" (*halleluyah* in Hebrew). In a collection (Psalter) also marked by laments over difficult circumstances, particularly in Book I, this extended doxological conclusion is the final voice for those who meditate on the riches of the Psalter. It will move them to praise of the Lord.

Walter Brueggemann has suggested, based in part on the primary genres in the Psalter, that psalms function to orient, disorient, and reorient readers, both ancient and modern. This is a function of the form and content of psalms and not a claim about the structure of the Psalter as a whole. Hymns of praise, psalms about creation and divine rule, and those that promulgate the value of Torah orient a reader to the rule of the Lord over his world. Poignant laments and confessions of sinfulness give voice to pain, tragedy, and judgment received and reflect the power of disorienting experiences and the debilitation of suffering. Psalms of thanksgiving, whose voices frequently move from plight to deliverance or from threat to gratitude for security, can serve to reorient readers to the mysteries of divine help.

Although many of the psalms are rooted in the worship life of the Jerusalem temple, they have been used in various ways in the long history of their reception. They have been studied and recited in Jewish synagogues and Christian churches; they have been part of the formative worship life in Christian religious orders and monastic disciplines; and they have been the basis of or the inspiration for Christian hymnody. With respect to formal citations, the Psalter is the most commonly cited book in the NT. One may sense some of the spiritual impact of the Psalter in a treatise written by Athanasius, a 4th-century Christian bishop from Alexandria, Egypt. In a letter to a certain Marcellinus, Athanasius presents the Psalter as an epitome of the Scriptures because it brings to mind much that can be found elsewhere in the Christian Bible. It reminds readers/hearers of such matters as the great story line of Israel's birth as a nation (Pss 78, 105–6, 132, 136), of God's provision of king, temple, and capital city (Pss 2, 24, 46, 48, 100), of God's rule in justice and righteousness (Pss 97–99), and his instructions for faithful living (Pss 19, 119). Moreover, psalms function frequently like a mirror for the human soul, enabling readers to perceive their own emotions and to present them before God. Variations on these two claims by Athanasius are echoed down through the centuries. Martin Luther, for example, termed the Psalter a "little Bible," and John Calvin, while adopting Athanasius's metaphor of the mirror, also described it as an "anatomy of the human soul." The impact of the Psalter on Christian hymnody is immense, beginning with the NT era (Eph 5:19) and continuing to the present, as psalms have been adapted to music for singing in Christian worship.

The Presentation

Book I: Psalms 1–41

As noted previously, Ps 1 is an introduction to the Psalter as a whole. It defines two ways of life in God's world: one that is guided by divine instruction and blessed, and the other that is the way of the wicked and will perish. Reading and meditating on the Psalter will illumine the two ways set out by this initial psalm.

Psalm 2 also lacks a superscription, and it too may function as another entry point or orientation to reading the Psalter. Its theme is that God has installed his "anointed one" in Zion (2:6) and that the nations should take note that God intends to rule through him (see the sidebar on the Lord's anointed on p. 162).

Beginning with the third psalm, all the compositions have headings except Pss 10 and 33. Psalm 10, as noted above, is read together with Ps 9 in some versions. The majority of the psalms are individual laments.

Psalm 7 is a good example of an individual lament, exhibiting the basic characteristics that form analysis has discerned for this type of prayer. The psalmist invokes God with pleas for deliverance (7:1) and for judgment on enemies (7:6). Laments typically describe the circumstances that have occasioned the prayer, whether persecution by enemies or such matters as sin or sickness that also threaten the psalmist. In the case of Ps 7, as with the majority of laments, the circumstance is persecution without cause. The author describes the ferocity of pursuers who threaten to tear him apart and drag him away (7:2). There is an affirmation of innocence with regard to the specific circumstances that led to persecution (7:3–5). If the debilitating circumstances had been the psalmist's sin, then the lament would have a confession of wrongdoing instead of the claim of innocence. One finds a robust expression of confidence in God's power to judge evil and willingness to do so (7:6–16). Note the claim that the persecution and violence of the evildoers will return upon them (7:15–16). This illustrates the confession of Ps 1:6 that the way of the wicked will perish. The psalm concludes with a vow that the psalmist will praise the Lord for his righteousness (7:17), following a common statement that the one who has been delivered will offer public praise and worship as a fitting response.

One can take these typical elements of a lament and find them in Ps 22, perhaps the best-known lament in the Psalter due to the quotation of its startling first line in accounts of Jesus's crucifixion (Matt 27:46; Mark 15:34). It is not the only lament that is so directly expressive, indeed accusatory, in representing the suffering of an innocent person and the experience of abandonment (see Ps 13). The NT writers see in the suffering of the innocent/righteous a prefiguring of Jesus's suffering. We might see it also from the standpoint of Jesus's representative humanity. In his death he represents not only sinful humanity but also suffering humanity.

Psalm 15 is one of two psalms in Book I that likely served as an entrance liturgy to the temple. It begins with a question to God, "Who may reside on your holy hill?" That question is then partially answered in 15:2–5 by a priest or prophet or other temple official. Note the emphasis on a social and relational righteousness. A similar question occurs in Ps 24:3, the other psalm that orients a worshiper who enters the temple courtyard, with a briefer but similar answer in 24:4. The psalm concludes with a call to the gates and doors of the courtyards to recognize that the King of glory, the Lord mighty in battle is coming in (24:7-10). Such a call presupposes that something representing the Lord also made its entrance into the holy place. It may well have been the ark of the covenant, which represented God with the people when they went out to war (see Num 10:35-36; 1 Sam 4:1-9), perhaps returning from some public procession.

Book II: Psalms 42–72

The superscriptions to the psalms in this section show quite a bit of variety. They contain references to the Korahites, David, Asaph, and Solomon, along with other notations. The first psalm is a marvelous expression of desire for God's presence, and the last is a hymnic celebration of the privileges and responsibilities of the king in Jerusalem.

Perhaps the best-known penitential lament in the Psalter is Ps 51, with its notation in the heading that it is David's sorrowful response to

Table 32.2. Superscriptions: Psalms and David's Life	
Psalm 3	His Flight from Absalom (2 Sam 13)
Psalm 7	A Special Song[a]
Psalm 18	His Praises for Yahweh's Many Rescues (2 Sam 22)
Psalm 34	His Feigned Insanity among the Philistines (1 Sam 21)
Psalm 51	His Grief over Adultery with Bathsheba (2 Sam 12)
Psalm 52	His Betrayal to Saul by Doeg the Edomite (1 Sam 22)
Psalm 54	His Betrayal to Saul by the Ziphites (1 Sam 23 and 26)
Psalm 56	His Seizure by the Philistines at Gath (uncertain)
Psalm 57	His Hiding from Saul in a Cave (1 Sam 22 and 24)
Psalm 59	Surveillance of David's home by Saul's troops (uncertain)
Psalm 60	Communal Prayer for Help (2 Sam 8; 1 Chron 18)
Psalm 63	David's Prayer in the Wilderness (1 Sam 23?)
Psalm 142	David's Prayer from a Cave (1 Sam 22–24)

a. In Ps 7:1, "Cush, a Benjaminite" may designate either a tune or an occasion.

his affair with Bathsheba (2 Sam 11). One can hear and feel the different tone to the psalm when the matter is confession of sin rather than affirmation of innocence in the face of threat. Note also how the psalm concludes (Ps 51:18-19). The prayer for Zion's restoration and the desire for acceptable sacrifice at the altar both presuppose a time in Judah's history considerably later than that of David. The conclusion is a good illustration of how the songs and prayers of the Psalter underwent periodic updating, just as do songs of one generation that are passed on to other generations in various cultures.

Jerusalem/Zion is the focus of two hymns in this section (Pss 46, 48). These hymns are good illustrations of the conviction that God had chosen the city as the seat of Davidic rule and the hill for his temple, where he was spiritually present (cf. 2 Sam 5-7; Ps 2:6; 78:68-72; 132:11-17). It is "the city of God" (46:4; 48:1), the habitation of "the great King" (48:2), who is the Lord. One of the frequent themes of the Psalter is that the Lord is the refuge of his people (46:1, 11; cf. 57:1; 61:4). The marvels of Jerusalem, its walls, towers, and temple, were visual reinforcements of God's sure protection (48:3, 12-14). The metaphors of Jerusalem/Zion as Daughter or Mother are found in the Psalter (Ps 9:14; 147:12-13) and are part of the rich imagery associated with her identity elsewhere in the OT.

Jerusalem is God's chosen city, and David's family is God's choice for king. Testimony to these convictions pervades the Psalter, and indeed, the OT. As mentioned above, Ps 72 is a hymn that celebrates the provisions that God has made for his people through the rule of his "son" (Ps 2:7; cf. Isa 9:1-7). It is an expansive vision in more than one way. The king is to exercise a protective and restorative rule for God's people based on justice and righteousness (72:2-4, 12-14). He is also to have preeminence and rule among nations (72:8-11; cf. Ps 2). The hymn apparently interprets the promises of blessings to the nations in Genesis (Gen 12:3; 22:17-18) as centered in the rule of God's king (Ps 72:17). In time this expectation would take on an eschatological interpretation, when there was no longer a Davidic king on the throne in Jerusalem. Finally, one can see editorial shaping at work in the conclusion to the psalm, a benediction, which also concludes the collection in Book II. At some point in transmission, what is now Ps 72 was the conclusion to a collection of psalms associated with David. The notation that "the prayers of David son of Jesse are ended" (Ps 72:20) is evidence for that. In the final shaping of the Psalter, there are other "Davidic" psalms to come.

Book III: Psalms 73–89

Book III consists mostly of psalms associated with Asaph and Korah. These are names known from 1–2 Chronicles and accounts of the worship life at the temple. As a postexilic composition, Chronicles likely reflects not only older data about the time of the First Temple's design and so forth but also traditions associated with work and worship at the Second Temple, which was constructed after the return of the Babylonian exiles to Jerusalem. Asaph and his sons formed a guild of Levitical singers (1 Chr 25:1–4; 2 Chr 5:12), while Korah was also a Levite and provided musical support (1 Chr 6:22, 37).

Psalm 73 reflects on the seeming prosperity of the wicked and emphasizes the personal encounter with God that comes in worship. Psalm 89 praises the Lord and rehearses the Lord's choice of David as king over Israel, only to conclude with lament and wonder regarding the taunts and charges against the Davidic king (89:38–51). Between these two psalms are laments (individual and corporate), a thanksgiving (Ps 75), and some prayers regarding Jerusalem (Pss 84, 87).

Psalm 78 presents Israel's history in poetic résumé, beginning with the sojourn of the people in Egypt and concluding with the establishment of Jerusalem and the Davidic dynasty as institutions through which the Lord would rule his people. One should compare this song with Pss 105, 106, and 136, each of which takes a different tack in representing God's work in and through Israel. They show the selectivity of reference used to accomplish a particular purpose. In the case of Ps 78, it is to show God's faithful continuance with Israel in the face of disobedience and ingratitude (cf. Ps 106), whereas Pss 105 and 136 reiterate God's saving acts, to which the people should respond with praise and thanksgiving.

Psalm 80 also employs historical résumé in its plea for God to restore Israel's national fortunes. God is addressed as Israel's "shepherd," a metaphor that is also used in the affirming prayer of Ps 23 that the Lord is the psalmist's shepherd.

Table 32.3. Named Collections of Psalms

"of David"	Pss 3–9, 11–32, et al.
"of the Korahites"	Pss 42, 44–49, 84–85, 87–88
"of Solomon"	Pss 72, 127
"of Asaph"	Pss 50, 73–82
"of Ethan the Ezrahite"[a]	Ps 89
"of Heman the Ezrahite"[a]	Ps 88
"of Moses"	Ps 90
"Songs of Ascent"[b]	Pss 120–34

a. The Ezrahites may have been a group of priestly musicians related to the Korahites (1 Chron 15:17).

b. Pss 122 and 127 may have formerly belonged, respectively, to the David (122) and Solomon (127) collections.

Psalm 88 is an individual lament over threatening circumstances, whether the speaker is a nameless individual or represents the voice of a threatened Davidic king. The psalm is marked by a consistent presentation of harsh circumstances without any expressed hope for deliverance. It and the somber conclusion to Ps 89 leave readers with questions regarding the fate of the nation and its king. The last word of the section, however, is a doxology (89:52).

Book IV: Psalms 90–106

The bookend psalms in Book IV offer reflections on Israel's history as lessons for readers. The superscription to Ps 90 refers to Moses, the man of God. At Mount Sinai, Moses asks God to turn from his wrath against the Israelites in judging them for the sin of constructing the golden calf (Exod 32:12). Similarly, the psalmist prays that God will turn from judgment and have compassion on his servants. Psalm 106 uses several examples from Israel's history to remind the people of past failures.

This section of the Psalter contains several beautiful hymns, including those that celebrate the Lord's cosmic kingship and rule (Pss 93, 95–99). Given the precarious status of the Davidic king in Ps 89, these compositions are an affirmation that God's rule is not at issue, even if the affairs of Judah (Israel) and its king remain under threat. Both the verb "to be/rule as king" and the noun "king/monarch" are used of God in these psalms.

Psalm 96 is a good example of a hymn dedicated to extolling the character of God. Israel, the heavens, the earth, and the sea are all enjoined to rejoice and to praise God. Hymns typically have elements that simply describe God in the third person as "he" or "the one" who is worthy of praise (96:3–6). God's kingship can be shouted and affirmed in the world and among nations (96:10). With the affirmation that the Lord is king typically comes praise regarding the characteristics of his reign. God will judge the world with righteousness and people with truth (96:13). According to Ps 97:2, righteousness and justice comprise the foundation of God's throne. Such affirmations have wide influence in the OT. On the one hand, the laments that seek redress for wrongs and inequities offer their

Table 32.4. Psalms for Occasions	
Psalm 30	temple dedication (perhaps Hanukkah)
Psalm 45	wedding
Psalm 92	Sabbath day
Psalm 100	thanksgiving
Psalm 102	individual, bitter affliction

pleas on the belief that God has integrity and rules accordingly. On the other hand, God's justice and righteousness are expectations of the rule of God's adopted son, the Davidic king (cf. Ps 72). And the prophets who advocate for justice and righteousness among the people are not simply seeking better social conditions but the implementing of God's standards for public life.

Psalm 103 is a composition that employs hymnic elements in a longer song of thanksgiving. It begins and ends with a refrain, a (self-)command to bless the Lord (103:1, 22; cf. Ps 8:1, 9; 117). Psalm 103:3–5 contains the language of praise in description of God's attributes. God is the "one who forgives iniquity," "heals diseases," "redeems from the pit," "crowns one with faithful support and mercy," and "satisfies one with good things." In addition to affirming God's just dealings (103:6–7), the psalm celebrates God's fatherhood and compassion (103:8–14).

Psalm 100 is a brief hymn set in the context of worship in the temple. The temple context is indicated by references to God's "gates" and "courts" in 100:4. Verse 4 also employs two Hebrew nouns for worship ("praise," *tehillah*; "thanksgiving," *todah*) that can refer elsewhere to a "song of praise" and a "song of thanksgiving." One might, therefore, translate the verse "Enter God's gates with a song of thanksgiving and his courts with a hymn of praise."

Book V: Psalms 107–50

This last section of the Psalter begins with thanksgiving and concludes with hymns of praise. And although the language of thanksgiving and praise predominates, there is still variety of expression in it. Psalm 109, for example, has some of the harshest language regarding enemies of any text in the OT, and Ps 130 is a poignant plea for forgiveness.

Psalm 116 is a classic example of a prayer of thanksgiving. It does not provide many details regarding the dire circumstances that the Lord resolved but concentrates instead on their effects, potential and otherwise. The general language is likely suited to fit more than one set of circumstances so that others may find use for the psalm. One can see, for example, similarities between Ps 116:3–4 and Jonah's prayer in the belly of the great fish (Jonah 2:2–7). Note also the latter part of the psalm (Ps 116:12–19), where the psalmist makes public testimony of God's goodness, including participation in temple worship. This is typically a part of thanksgiving psalms.

Psalm 119 is the longest composition in the Psalter. It is arranged as

Palace wall relief at Nineveh (ca. 700–692 BCE) showing an Assyrian escorting three prisoners from Judahite Lachish playing lyres. The scene recalls the later exile to Babylon where "on the poplars we hung our harps, for there our captors asked us for songs" (Ps 137:2–3 TNIV). *Photograph by Mike Peel (www. mikepeel.net) (Wikimedia Commons, CC-SA 4.0)*

an acrostic; that is, the psalm follows the pattern of the Hebrew alphabet of twenty-two letters. It has twenty-two stanzas (eight verses per stanza), with each stanza beginning with a successive letter of the Hebrew alphabet. This pattern is seen also in Pss 9–10 and four of the five chapters in the book of Lamentations. We might describe Ps 119 as an "A-to-Z" description of the joys and values of divine instruction, along with recognition on the part of the psalmist that he or she is in constant need of it.

This section also contains a subcollection of psalms known from their common heading as the Psalms of Ascent (Pss 120–34). Jews, particularly those who made pilgrimage to Jerusalem, recited them as they ascended the Temple Mount to worship.

Psalm 137 reflects the experience of exiles in Babylonia who lamented the destruction of Zion and who yearned for judgment on those who were involved. It is the one psalm in the Psalter whose contents reveal a specific historical event as the occasion for recitation.

Psalm 139 contains the voice of one awed at the presence of God and the experience of being intimately known by him. This is one of the most introspective of the Psalter's compositions. It concludes with a plea that God would deal with the wicked, along with a claim that the psalmist hated those who hate the Lord (139:19-24). Interpreters have long struggled with such sentiments.

The Psalter ends on a sustained note of praise. Each of the last five hymns begins and ends with the acclamation "Hallelujah!" It is a fitting conclusion to the collection and consistent with the "way of the righteous" portrayed at the Psalter's beginning, in Ps 1. "Let everything that has breath praise the Lord" (Ps 150:6).

READING

Read Pss 1–150 and answer the following discussion questions:

1. How do you understand the preserving activities of God in Ps 23:5? What might it mean in ancient Israel to have a table prepared before enemies or to be anointed with oil?

2. Read Ps 37. How is evil characterized in it? How does one oppose it, according to the psalm?

3. Compare the hymn "A Mighty Fortress" by Martin Luther with Ps 46, its inspiration. What are the major themes Luther draws from it as inspiration for his own setting?

4. Read Ps 44. What kind of psalm is it? To the extent that you can, identify the speakers in it. What kind of circumstances in Israel's history would produce such a prayer?

5. Read Pss 1 and 73. How does Ps 73 see the wicked differently from Ps 1?

6. How does Ps 89 tell the story of David and his family's rule in Judah?

7. How does Ps 84 interpret the temple as a place of worship?

8. How might one define justice and righteousness in light of Ps 97?

9. Read Pss 105 and 106. Are there perspectives in these psalms that are different from or complement the narratives in Genesis, Exodus, and Numbers?

10. Is there such a thing as "perfect hatred" (Ps 139:22), and if so, what might that be? What clues in the psalm assist in answering the question?

11. Psalm 137 is a psalm that takes up the question of remembering one's heritage. Why do you think the memory of Jerusalem is so important to the psalmist?

12. Read Ps 119. How would you characterize the descriptions of God's instructions in it and the motives for keeping God's commandments?

13. In reading through the Psalms, what terms would you use to characterize its contents and effect on readers?

14. Have you discovered a favorite psalm? If so, why?

BIBLIOGRAPHY

Brueggemann, Walter. *The Message of the Psalms: A Theological Commentary*. Minneapolis: Augsburg, 1984.

DeClaissé-Walford, Nancy. *Introduction to the Psalms: A Song of Ancient Israel*. St. Louis: Chalice, 2004.

DeClaissé-Walford, Nancy, Rolf A. Jacobson, and Beth LaNeel Tanner. *The Book of Psalms*. NICOT. Grand Rapids: Eerdmans, 2014.

Gillingham, Susan E., ed. *Jewish and Christian Approaches to the Psalms: Conflict and Convergence*. Oxford: Oxford University Press, 2013.

Gregg, Robert C. *Athanasius: The Life of Antony and the Letter to Marcellinus*. Mahwah, NJ: Paulist, 1980.

Gunkel, Hermann. *Introduction to the Psalms*. Atlanta: Mercer University Press, 1998. [German original, 1933]

Holladay, William L. *The Psalms through Three Thousand Years: Prayerbook of a Cloud of Witnesses*. Philadelphia: Fortress, 1993.

Jacobson, Rolf A., and Karl N. Jacobson. *Invitation to the Psalms: A Reader's Guide for Discovery and Engagement*. Grand Rapids: Baker Academic, 2013.

Janowski, Bernd. *Arguing with God: A Theological Anthropology of the Psalms*. Louisville: Westminster John Knox, 2013.

Mays, James L. *The Lord Reigns: A Theological Handbook to the Psalms*. Louisville: Westminster John Knox, 1994.

Mowinckel, Sigmund. *The Psalms in Israel's Worship*. 2 vols. Nashville: Abingdon, 1962. [German original, 6 vols., 1921–1924]

Wilson, Gerald H. *The Editing of the Hebrew Psalter*. Atlanta: Scholars Press, 1985.

33 THE BOOK OF PROVERBS

Important Dates for Proverbs
970–931: reign of Solomon
715–687/686: reign of Hezekiah
ca. 450: final collection/composition of Proverbs

A S BEFITS A HETEROGENEOUS COLLECTION of short discourses and brief sayings, there is no structured progression of thought in the book. Even the arrangement of chapters, which dates to medieval times, does not presume that proximity between passages assists with their meaning. Proverbs and didactic sayings typically stand independently as bearers of insight. It is the case, however, that the book evidences at least a few smaller collections that were included in it. The evidence appears in the form of superscriptions or "headings" to portions of the material:

> 1:1-9:18: "The proverbs of Solomon, son of David, king of Israel"
> 10:1-22:16: "The proverbs of Solomon"
> 22:17-24:22: "Sayings of the wise" (a heading preserved in the Septuagint)
> 24:23-34: "More sayings of the wise"
> 25:1-29:27: "More proverbs of Solomon copied by the men of Hezekiah, king of Judah"
> 30:1-33: "Sayings of Agur son of Jakeh"
> 31:1-31: "Sayings of King Lemuel; an oracle his mother taught him"

These headings provide several connections to the story of the wisdom movement in Israel. Solomon and Hezekiah were patrons of wisdom and provided the resources to preserve and to disseminate its traditions. It is possible that the materials gathered in Proverbs were also used at the royal court (Jerusalem) as part of a teaching role taken on by scribes and counselors associated with it. Whether there were formal schools in Jerusalem in the period of the monarchy is unknown.

There are two primary forms of expression in Proverbs: short discourses and didactic sayings. The former consist of several verses, while the latter are typically a single verse or a single sentence. Both employ poetic form in expression. For the most part individual texts seem to be collected in series without much attention to order. Occasionally, however, they appear to be organized on the basis of a common topic. Here are four examples of short discourses:

> 1:8-19: Parental advice regarding thieves and the destructive consequences of involvement with them
> 6:20-35: Parental warning to a son to avoid adultery and its grievous consequences
> 27:23-27: Counsel to care well for flocks and herds
> 31:10-31: An instructive celebration of a capable wife

A proverb or an aphorism is a short saying offering insight for life's choices. Proverbs come in several related forms. Here are some examples:

> *Contrastive or Antithetical.* The wise will take instruction, but fools will fail. (10:8)
> *Synonymous Reinforcement.* The path of righteousness leads to life; in taking it there is no death. (12:28)
> *Comparative.* Better is a little food with quiet than a feast with turmoil. (17:1)
> *Synthesis (of Sense and Motive).* Don't reject or tire of the Lord's discipline; it is like the love of a father for a son. (3:11-12)
> *Rhetorical Question.* Why should fools acquire wisdom when they have no sense to learn? (17:16)

The Presentation

The book of Proverbs has two main sections: (1) a series of short discourses (Prov 1-9); and (2) a series of wisdom collections (Prov 10-31). The small collections that comprise (2) include one that features classical, two-line proverbs (Prov 10:1-22:16), a second with mostly antithetical sayings (Prov 10-15), a third with mostly synonymous ones (Prov 22:17-24:22), a fourth initiated during King Hezekiah's reign (Prov 25-29), and pieces attributed to Agur son of Jakeh (Prov 30) and King Lemuel's mother (31:10-31).

Proverbs 1–9: A Series of Short Discourses

This first section of the book has more short discourses in it than do the subsequent sections. There are multiple references in this section of the book to parental counsel (1:8; 4:1; 6:20) in advising children, primarily males, to engage in certain behaviors and to avoid others (2:1; 3:1; 5:1; 6:1; 7:1). Much of this counsel follows the pattern of the Two-Way Doctrine. Readers/hearers are advised to engage in behavior that will lead to life, success, and health and to avoid those endeavors that lead to failure and ruin. Another prominent voice in this section is personified Wisdom. The Hebrew word for wisdom (*hokmah*) is grammatically feminine, and this leads to its personification as a wise woman who speaks authoritatively as a mother (8:32), a prophet (1:20-33), and one who has observed the work of God from the beginning in wisely creating the world (8:22-31).

As noted previously, a theme of the wisdom movement in Israel is provided in Prov 1:7: "The fear of the Lord is the beginning of wisdom." The search for meaning and success in life is not an autonomous human enterprise, even if a particular counsel seems secular and centered on human assessment and effort. Proper recognition of God's claim to the world and God's self-disclosure in it is crucial for readers and sages alike. A related theme appears in the personification of wisdom as an instructive agent. According to Prov 3:19-20, God's work in and through creation demonstrates his wisdom. In seeking out wisdom and understanding of the world and then responding appropriately to them, humans also encounter the world's creator. "She" (Wisdom) links the human community to the creator and sustainer of the material world. Put another way, experiences of life in the world can lead to experiences of God. Wisdom is a mediator to bring people to the right choices and right apprehension of matters in the world and

Relief plaque from Iran (5th–6th centuries CE), now in the Cincinnati Art Museum, showing the tree of life, a popular ancient artistic motif (note the confronted ibexes). In Proverbs it connotes the wonder and bounty of creation, as well as the well-being and success that wisdom promises (3:18; 11:30; 15:14). ©Daderot (Wikimedia Commons, CC 1.0)

thus to God, who wisely created them. Similar dynamics are depicted of Wisdom in the metaphor that she is a "tree of life" (3:18). This claim is part of her personification and likely draws on the paradise account in Gen 2–3. In the garden God provided a tree of nourishment to sustain the human life of those who served there, and in the larger world God also provides wisdom in order to sustain life.

One can compare Prov 1:8–19 to the command "you shall not steal" (Exod 20:15/Deut 5:19) in order to see the particular way in which wise counsel is formulated. The terse commandment in the Pentateuch is reported as direct speech from God and is formulated in absolute terms. There can be no doubt that theft and thieves fall under the condemnation of God's covenant righteousness, and thus Israel is enjoined not to steal. The short discourse in Prov 1:8–19 does not quote the Decalogue but presents the rejection of theft and thieves as sage counsel from parents. More particularly, the company of thieves is rejected on at least two grounds: first, thieves cannot be trusted as part of any shared community; second, since thieves poison human community, their efforts are ultimately self-destructive. Here one encounters wisdom's concern with act and consequence. The act of violating community standards by stealing is seen as inherently self-destructive: theft sows the seeds of failure in its core activity of breaking trust.

This section of Proverbs also has several discourses warning a young man to avoid the enticements of a "strange" woman, an adulteress, or a foolish woman (2:16–19; 5:1–23; 6:20–35; 7:1–27; 9:13–18). There are parallels in this material with the presentation against theft in 1:8–19. On the subject of adultery, it is also possible to cite an absolute command from the Decalogue: "You shall not commit adultery" (Exod 20:14/Deut 5:18). Marriage is an institution rooted in the creation account (Gen 2:18–25) and undergirded by divine sanction. Yet the strictures against the strange woman (NRSV, "loose woman") in Proverbs portray her wiles as destructive to life and health. Note, for example, the rhetorical question in 6:27: "Can one carry fire and not burn one's clothes?" By analogy, to get involved in adultery is to endanger one's well-being or indeed one's life. Note also the portrayal of the husband's anger regarding a wife's adultery in 6:34-35. His intent to take revenge on her paramour has no limits. Adultery is a game the adulterer can never win.

Some interpreters have seen an extended metaphor at work in the depiction of the "strange woman." While the overt topic is adultery, it is also possible to see in her depiction an analogy with false worship, that is, being led astray by the gods and goddesses of the larger Semitic world of which Israel was a part. It is indeed the case that some other biblical writers describe defection from the sole worship of the Lord as prostitution and adultery (example: Hosea), so that dynamic could be at work in the proverbial counsel as well.

Proverbs 10–31: A Series of Wisdom Collections

As noted above, there are several smaller collections of materials in Prov 10-31, each with a heading. Proverbs 10:1-22:16, the second collection of the book, is comprised primarily of classical, two-line proverbs. Chapters 10-15 are mostly antithetical sayings, while the majority of sayings in 16:1-22:16 are synonymous. The third collection, in 22:17-24:22, has many similarities to the Egyptian document known as the Wisdom of Amenemope. It is likely that the sages in Jerusalem knew the Egyptian document, and an adapted form of its wise sayings was included in the growing collection of wisdom materials preserved there. Proverbs 25:1 refers to Hezekiah's "men" (often translated as "officials") as preserving wisdom sayings. Hezekiah reigned from approximately 715 to 687 BCE. The work done at the court during his reign was apparently an important part of the transmission and editing process that continued until the postexilic period. The last two headings—those of Agur son of Jakeh (30:1) and of King Lemuel's mother (31:1)—refer to persons otherwise unknown. Lemuel's mother provides the often-quoted passage with which the book of Proverbs concludes: a poem of praise regarding a capable wife and her many activities (31:10-31).

The antithetical proverbs of 10:1-15:33 offer "points of light" for many situations in life. They provide example after example of the Two-Way Doctrine, whereby the wise and righteous preserve their life, whereas their counterparts, the foolish and the wicked, engage in self-destructive behavior. Here are a couple examples:

3. Some topics reappear in the proverbial collections. Which ones seem most frequent to you? Do you think that these concerns are as relevant today as they were to the ancient sages?

4. In what ways, if any, do you think there are connections between the approach to life in the wisdom movement and that practiced by modern science?

BIBLIOGRAPHY

Dell, Katherine J. *The Book of Proverbs in Social and Theological Context*. Cambridge: Cambridge University Press, 2006.

Fox, Michael V. *Proverbs 1–9*. AB 18A. New York: Doubleday, 2000.

———. *Proverbs 10–31*. AB 18B. New Haven: Yale University Press, 2009.

Heim, Knut M. *Poetic Imagination in Proverbs: Variant Repetitions and the Nature of Poetry*. Winona Lake, IN: Eisenbrauns, 2013.

Longman, Tremper, III. *Proverbs*. Grand Rapids: Baker Academic, 2006.

Waltke, Bruce K. *The Book of Proverbs: Chapters 1–15*. NICOT. Grand Rapids: Eerdmans, 2004.

———. *The Book of Proverbs: Chapters 16–31*. NICOT. Grand Rapids: Eerdmans, 2005.

34 THE BOOK OF ECCLESIASTES

Important Dates for Ecclesiastes

970–931: reign of Solomon in Jerusalem

600–500: possible reworking of traditions about Solomon

ca. 500–400: circulation of the book of Ecclesiastes

THE ENGLISH TITLE "ECCLESIASTES" IS the Latin transliteration of the book's title in the LXX (Gk. *Ekklēsiastēs*). As noted above, the Greek term translates the book's name in Hebrew (*Qoheleth* or *Koheleth*), a word thought to be the title of some official—for example, a "convener of an assembly," "teacher," or "preacher." An editorial, third-person narration (1:1–11; 12:8–14) frames the book's center: first-person reflections on life by "Solomon" (1:12–2:26) and primarily third-person further reflections (3:1–12:7). These characteristics give the book two distinct voices. We also noted that the book's postexilic Hebrew language casts doubt on the possibility that Solomon was its author (unless one assumes the later updating/rewriting of an original Solomonic work). In our view, the book is best understood against the background of examples of fictional royal autobiographies found in the ANE. If so, the two voices in Ecclesiastes in reality sound the single voice of the writer/editor. The result is a "Solomonic" interpretation of the king's life to instruct readers—a royal memoir with the thesis that life's unfairness has no easy or rational explanation ("All is vain!"). The Solomon of this book stands beside the Solomon of 1 Kgs 3–11, where the patron king of wisdom began his reign successfully, only to fail in the end.

The Presentation

Structurally, the book has four parts: (1) an editorial introduction (1:1-11); (2) "Solomon's" first-person reflections on life and wisdom (1:12-2:26); (3) primarily third-person reflections (3:1-12:7); and (4) an editorial conclusion (12:8-14). The book can be outlined as follows:

I. Introduction: Vanity and no advantage	1:1-11
II. Solomon's explorations for wisdom	1:12-2:26
III. A time for everything?	3:1-22
IV. Oppression under the sun	4:1-16
V. Observations on life, inequities, and other matters	5:1-11:10
VI. Remember God in your youth	12:1-7
VII. Conclusion: The preacher and a word about the future	12:8-14

Ecclesiastes 1–2: Introduction and Initial Explorations

The book does not contain a narrative base like that of Job, although as previously noted, it likely presupposes a narrative account about Solomon, using elements of a fictional royal autobiography or memoir. The lavish lifestyle noted in chs. 1-2 would fit that of the fabled court of Solomon's day.

The theme of the work appears in the introductory section. "Vanity [*hevel*] of vanities, all is vain" (1:2). The Hebrew term *hevel* indicates something is ephemeral, empty, or impermanent. The phrase forms a Hebrew superlative—"the vainest thing imaginable." And there is nothing new under the sun (1:9), even if things don't last!

Note the subjects the Preacher reflects on: pleasure and possessions, and then wisdom and folly. Pleasure is real but fleeting. One can indeed find joy in life, but it will not last. Life has much toil and many burdens. Wisdom is better than foolishness, just as light exceeds darkness, but the wise and fools end up sharing the same fate. These are all themes taken up multiple times in the book.

Ecclesiastes 3–12: Reflections on Life's Inequities

Ecclesiastes 3 opens with an oft-quoted proverb: "There is a season and a time for all matters under heaven" (3:1). It heads a poem on the varieties and rhythms of life (3:1–8). A question follows: "What gain is there for human workers in all this?" (3:9). The answer is a confessional reply about what God has done in making things appropriate for their times, just as the opening poem proclaims. God has also put a sense of eternity in the human heart. These are all things that God has done, yet human perception is not capable of grasping all of them (3:11). In other words, meaning and purpose, indeed appropriately timed events do happen, but humans may well not detect them. If they find joy along life's way, that is to be celebrated! If not, they shouldn't be surprised.

There are extended reflections and short discourses on the inequities of life that follow from these pensive formulations (see Table 34.1). Whereas Proverbs provides example after example of material that helps a reader cope with life's issues, this main section of Ecclesiastes points repeatedly to life's underside. Note, for example, the proverbial saying of 7:15, "There are righteous who perish in doing their righteousness; there are evildoers who live a long time in doing wickedness." The Two-Way Doctrine seems undone, at least as the only way to explain human fate. A similar statement appears in 9:11:

> The race is not to the swift; the battle is not for the strong; bread does not go to the wise; wealth does not go to the intelligent, nor fortune to the capable. Time and chance happen to them all.

Perhaps the Preacher intends that we should qualify the clauses with a "not necessarily." For example, a race does not go necessarily to the swift, but if one is involved in a race, it is better to be fit and swift of foot! This is ultimately not unlike the qualifications for proverbial wisdom and its time-honored Two-Way Doctrine. A short saying must be contextualized. It can be a pinprick of light in the right setting, but is misused if it is treated like a law of physics. Nevertheless, the tone of Ecclesiastes is different from the majority voice of Proverbs. The human condition can be opaque in meaning

Table 34.1. Speakers in Ecclesiastes

Text	Voice	Speaker
Introduction (1:1–11)	3rd Person	Editor
Reflections (1:12–2:26)	1st Person	Editor (as Solomon)
Reflections (3:1–12:7)	3rd Person	Editor
Conclusion (12:8–14)	3rd Person	Editor

and brutal in experience. Those who have a rational explanation for everything, whether it comes from voices of faith or skepticism, can overreach their explanatory power.

Modern philosophers use the term *epistemology* as a shorthand expression for the study of the nature and limits of human knowledge. Running through Ecclesiastes are aspects of epistemological skepticism but not necessarily a religious skepticism. This distinction is worthy of note, since interpreters sometimes describe the author of Ecclesiastes as a religious skeptic. Without qualifying the skepticism, this is a misleading description. On the one hand, the book affirms that God is active in the affairs of the world and human community. Religious activities are not rejected, as if they had no validity. On the other hand, the Preacher notes limits on what human beings can discern about God's work. Note, for example, how limits on human knowledge of God are expressed in what follows (Eccl 8:17):

> I have seen all the work of God, that no person can find out what
> is happening under the sun. No matter the effort expended in the
> search, no one can find it out. Even if the wise claim to know, they
> haven't discovered it.

Perhaps we should pay special attention to the last sentence and its reference to "the wise." It was the glory of the wisdom movement to pay careful attention to detail and to propose instructions for timely discernment and successful action—what we earlier called "the art of steering" in life. The Preacher, rather than denying that movement altogether, agrees with the philosophy that people should pay careful attention to their limitations. Truly wise people are cognizant of what they don't know!

Ecclesiastes does represent two other forms of skepticism. One is related to the worldview of Job's friends. They had no questions, only answers. The Preacher does not accept that the Two-Way Doctrine has universal explanatory power and gives voice to the inequities in life, which cannot be easily accounted for from a human vantage point. Interpreters differ on whether he represents the view that humankind must live with the mystery of inequities, given its limited point of view, or whether he sees capriciousness in God's dealings with human affairs and is simply resigned to it. The second skepticism concerns the merits of extended human effort. It is not the reflection of laziness but the observation that intense effort does not necessarily work to a person's advantage. Note in this regard the comments about brief prayers (Eccl 5:1–3) and the injunction to avoid being too righteous (7:16).

Interpreters also debate whether the Preacher is essentially an advocate of enjoying life while one can (a type of *carpe diem* philosophy), given its surprises and unpredictability, or whether he is essentially a somber observer of life's limits who nevertheless recognizes that human community can produce joy for a season. Readers can produce quotations from either perspective among his pointed sayings. The poem on old age represents a pensive and somber voice (12:1–8). It is vintage Ecclesiastes, taking resolute notice that there is a season and time for all things under the sun, including the difficulties that often come at the end of life. To adapt his own words, it is "vanity" to avoid the topic.

Vanitas Still Life, by Hendrick Andriessen. Ca. 1650.

As noted, the conclusion to the book is an editorial voice, whether it also comes from the author of the book as a whole or not. Note the comparison of wise sayings to a goad (= a stick to prod and guide animals)! Note also the observation that of the making of books there is no end. Perhaps this observation should be read with the strictures against those who think that they know what God is doing in the world (Eccl 8:17). One should not put too much stock in the received wisdom of books, for they, like human toil, can wear readers down.

The last two verses are summary in nature but leave plenty of room for the exercise of the imagination. The initial command to "fear God" is formulaic for the wisdom movement and may initially seem out of character with elements in the book. It is followed by the command to keep God's commandments, which is yet another formulaic counsel. The motive clause attached to these commands, however, continues a theme in the book, which is the mystery of what God is doing in the world. God will use the future to assess matters, even secret things. Even if matters seem opaque in the present, the future in God's hands will be different. Perhaps we can say that this kind of exercise of the imagination illustrates the wisdom movement in its maturity: mystery and divine action coexist, even if neither can be fully explained. Moreover, the confessional statement in

Eccl 12:13-14 may be a clue to the way to read Ecclesiastes' previous skepticism regarding human apprehension of God's work in the world. The fact that humankind cannot figure out God's plan does not mean that there is no future reckoning.

READING

Read Eccl 1-12 and formulate answers to the questions that follow:

1. When Ecclesiastes states that there is nothing new under the sun, what do you think that means? Is it primarily a statement about human activity and its consequences or something else? Do you think that statement is correct, and do you think it good news or bad news? Why?

2. Do you think that the author is primarily advocating finding joy where one can or providing a realistic assessment of human life, including its inequalities?

3. There are some brief comments above regarding the book and skepticism. How do you see the skeptical elements in the book? How do they relate (if at all) to your own beliefs?

4. How would you characterize the depiction of wisdom and its value in the book?

5. Do you find the tone and contents of Ecclesiastes to be different from those of Proverbs? How does the wisdom in Ecclesiastes compare with the wisdom in Job?

BIBLIOGRAPHY

Bartholomew, Craig G. *Ecclesiastes*. Grand Rapids: Baker Academic, 2009.
Boda, Mark J., Tremper Longman III, and Christian G. Rata. *The Words of the Wise Are like Goads: Engaging Qohelet in the 21st Century*. Winona Lake, IN: Eisenbrauns, 2013.
Brown, William P. *Ecclesiastes*. Louisville: Westminster John Knox, 2011.

Enns, Peter. *Ecclesiastes*. Grand Rapids: Eerdmans, 2011.

Fox, Michael V. *A Time to Tear Down and a Time to Build Up: A Rereading of Ecclesiastes*. Grand Rapids: Eerdmans, 1999.

Seow, Choon-Leong. *Ecclesiastes*. AB 18C. New York: Doubleday, 1997.

Sneed, Mark R. *The Politics of Pessimism in Ecclesiastes: A Social-Science Perspective*. Atlanta: Society of Biblical Literature, 2012.

35 THE BOOK OF LAMENTATIONS

Important Date for Lamentations

587: defeat of Judah, destruction of Jerusalem, and exile of thousands of Judahites to Babylon

THE BRIEF BOOK OF LAMENTATIONS is a collection of laments in response to the siege and subsequent destruction of Jerusalem in 587 BCE. In the Hebrew Bible it is a part of the third section, or Writings, while in the Christian OT the book is placed after Jeremiah. This association with Jeremiah goes back to the Greek translation of the OT, which adds a comment at the beginning (Lam 1:1 LXX) that Jeremiah wept and composed the book after Israel's captivity and the destruction of Jerusalem. The destruction of a city is a somber occasion in any culture; in the ANE city laments occasionally marked such events. A well-known example is the lamentation written after the destruction of Ur in southern Mesopotamia about 2000 BCE (see bibliography below). In that composition, both humans and gods express their horror over Ur's destruction. The biblical book of Lamentations stands in this literary tradition of city laments, expressing senses of tragedy, grief, and judgment over the city's fall.

Look What's Inside!

The book is an artful compilation. The poetry is exquisite, on occasion following a rhythm associated with funeral laments in ancient Israel, and

Tablet recording the Lamentation over the City of Ur, a Sumerian lament composed after the Elamites destroyed the city (ca. 2000 BCE). Now in the Louvre, Paris. In mourning Jerusalem's destruction, the Book of Lamentations invokes that ancient literary genre. ©*Dror Feitelson (Wikimedia Commons, CC-SA 4.0)*

He has abandoned his stable, his sheepfold (became) haunted, The wild ox has abandoned his stable, his sheepfold (became) haunted, The lord of all lands has abandoned it, his sheepfold (became) haunted, Enlil has abandoned the shrine of Nippur, his sheepfold (became) haunted, His consort, Ninlil, has abandoned it, her sheepfold (became) haunted. . . . On that day, I verily did not forsake my city, I verily did not neglect my Land; Truly I shed my tears before An, Truly I myself uttered supplication before Enlil: "May the city not be destroyed!" I said indeed to them, "May an end not be put to its people!" I said indeed to them. But An never changed that word, Enlil never soothed my heart with that "It is good, so be it!" . . . Verily they gave instructions that my city be utterly destroyed, Verily they gave instructions that Ur be utterly destroyed, Verily they decreed its destiny that its people be killed.

(COS 1.535–36)

using different speaking voices (poet, Jerusalem, Jerusalem's inhabitants, and an unidentified figure in ch. 3). To add to the complexity and overall effect, speakers quote enemies and observers as well. Jerusalem is personified and portrayed in various roles. She is "Daughter Zion" (Lam 1:6; 2:1, 4), a former princess, and now a widow (1:1). She represents the city's regal history as a place chosen by God but also the pain felt by Jerusalem's former inhabitants over the city's loss. There is also the related sense of representing the people of Judah. This cultural convention has a modern counterpart in the ways that a capital city is understood to represent both itself and the nation as a whole.

Each chapter of Lamentations is constructed on a recognized pattern (see Table 35.1). Chapters 1–4 are formulated as acrostics, using the sequence of twenty-two letters in the Hebrew alphabet as a mnemonic device. For chs. 1–2 and 4, there are twenty-two verses per chapter, and the initial word

the grief and despair of Jerusalem's demise by quoting the glee or celebration of the city's detractors (2:15-16). They sarcastically describe Zion as the "joy of the whole earth," using language from a Zion hymn (Ps 48:2) as a bitter parody. Zion accuses the Lord of killing her inhabitants and children without mercy (Lam 2:21-22), as if to say that the judgment on the city is too harsh. We might compare Zion's laments with Naomi's (Ruth 1:21-22) or Job's.

Lamentations 3

The voice in ch. 3 is that of individual travail. The unidentified speaker is a male whose voice and perspective are very much like those of the individual laments of the Psalter, though there is a segment (Lam 3:40-47) in the chapter where the speaker leads hearers together as a corporate voice. There is very little in the chapter to identify the speaker as other than someone affected by Jerusalem's demise. Some, of course, see this person as Jeremiah. Others see him as a kind of "everyman" who represents the community as a whole, similar in some ways to Jerusalem's personification. He alternates between the anguish of his situation, which is similar to the humiliation and suffering that Jerusalem has experienced, and confession that the Lord is good and attends to those who wait on him (Lam 3:22-26). Note the description of God as bear and lion (3:10-11). This is similar to the language used by Hosea (Hos 13:7-8).

Lamentations 4–5

Lamentations 4 rehearses again the pain associated with Judah and Jerusalem's fall, while ch. 5 builds on this sentiment with a communal plea to God to remember the plight of the survivors. One of the most poignant elements in the poetry of Lamentations is the description of children's suffering (2:12, 20; 4:2-4, 10). Siege and destruction are no respecters of persons, and the poet of Lamentations portrays in some detail the horrible conditions that prevailed during the siege of Jerusalem, which is so tersely described in Kings and Chronicles. The disaster that struck Jerusalem is compared with that of Sodom (Lam 4:6; cf. Gen 19:1-38), a historic example of fierce judgment. Mention is made of the Edomites as well (Lam 4:21-22). Like the prophecy of Obadiah, the poet here predicts judgment to come upon them.

The verb "remember" in Hebrew (Lam 5:1) has the sense of call to mind and thus to respond appropriately. The communal plea in the last chapter, therefore, has the function of setting the dire circumstances of the people before God in the hope that he will accept the lamenters and provide for them. Surprisingly, the book's conclusion leaves the matter of restoration open. That probably reflects the setting of the book's composition: Jerusalem still in ruins. Its later rebuilding would be a tangible sign that the Lord "remembered" his people.

We might also look at the matter of remembering and the function of memory from the standpoint of those who recited and prayed the book of Lamentations. The defiant voice of Ps 137 vows that, "if I forget you Jerusalem, may my right hand wither!" (Ps 137:5). Reciting Ps 137 or the book of Lamentations is one way to bring to mind the significance of Jerusalem's destruction, to assist corporate memory with important lessons from the past, and to present the needs of God's people before him. To paraphrase the philosopher George Santayana: Those who recite the past will not forget it.

READING

Read Lam 1–5 and respond to the following questions:

1. Cities are personified as female in the OT. How does the presentation of Jerusalem as a widow, forsaken princess, or virgin daughter influence your perception of the city and its role as representing a crushed people?

2. "Good and bad come from the Lord" (Lam 3:38). Comment on whether or not that is a quick summary of the book of Lamentations. If not, how would you want to qualify that statement after reading Lamentations?

3. According to Lam 4:13, some of Jerusalem's prophets and priests persecuted the righteous and were a reason for the city's demise. In what other places in the OT do you remember prophets and priests being accused of unrighteousness and leading the people astray?

4. What are your own personal reflections on the destruction of Jerusalem? What thoughts stay with you from your reading of Lamentations?

BIBLIOGRAPHY

Berlin, Adele. *Lamentations*. Louisville: Westminster John Knox, 2002.

Klein, Jacob. "Lamentation over the Destruction of Sumer and Ur." Pages 535–39 in *The Context of Scripture: Canonical Compositions from the Biblical World*. Edited by William H. Hallo and K. Lawson Younger. Leiden: Brill, 1997.

Linafelt, Todd. *Surviving Lamentations: Catastrophe, Lament, and Protest in the Afterlife of a Biblical Book*. Chicago: University of Chicago Press, 2000.

Longman, Tremper, III. *Jeremiah, Lamentations*. Peabody, MA: Hendrickson, 2008.

Parry, Robin A., and Heath A. Thomas, eds. *Great Is Thy Faithfulness? Reading Lamentations as Sacred Scripture*. Eugene, OR: Pickwick, 2011.

Renkema, Johan. *Lamentations*. Louvain: Peeters, 1998.

Thomas, Heath A. *Poetry and Theology in the Book of Lamentations: The Aesthetics of an Open Text*. Sheffield: Sheffield Phoenix, 2013.

Westermann, Claus. *Lamentations: Issues and Interpretation*. Edinburgh: T&T Clark, 1995.

36 THE BOOK OF THE SONG OF SONGS

Important Dates for Song of Songs

970–931: reign of Solomon

ca. 700–400: an anonymous writer compiles the book

THE BIBLE'S COMPILERS GAVE THIS book an apt name: the "Song of Songs" (*shir hashirim*), a Hebrew superlative form meaning "the best song ever" (compare "King of Kings," Dan 2:37). All the book's ancient versions refer to it by this original Hebrew name. In Jewish tradition, the book is read at Passover, which marks the beginning of the grain harvest and also commemorates the exodus from Egypt. It stands in the canon among "Solomon's Books" (i.e., with Proverbs and Ecclesiastes), undoubtedly because of the reference to him in the book's title and six other times (Song 1:5; 3:7, 9, 11; 8:11-12). But the picture of Solomon seems to us idealized rather than real—literarily, the paradigmatic wealthy king—and we observe that references to him are in the third person, which is an unusual style were he the book's author (but see Song 8:1). In our view, the opening verse ends with "in honor of Solomon" (compare "for Solomon," CEB), not "by Solomon," making the book an anonymous work of uncertain date with rich, rare language that reflects either Israelite folk poetry or a highly literate author. Theologically, like Esther, it makes no direct reference to God but shows its theology in the actions of the human actors and their compelling, enchanting statements of love. The Best Song Ever, indeed, offers a frank, explicit, unembarrassed, positive portrait of human sensuality. In part, that is why we like reading it: it calls us without embarrassment to accept our sensuality as no different from that of the book's lovers—and from that of God the Creator.

Look What's Inside!

The Best Song is unlike any other biblical book: in modern terms, The Best Song Ever is hot! That's why you rarely hear it read publicly in church! From start to finish its pages brim with wonderful, alluring, sensual, and at times erotic poetry that celebrates human sexual love (e.g., 7:7–9). The many examples of love poetry from both Mesopotamia and Egypt attest that the writing of love poetry was as common in the ancient world as it is today. Indeed, the parallels between ancient Near Eastern and biblical poetry make it likely that ANE exemplars significantly influenced both the style and contents of The Best Song Ever. The opening lines of Isaiah's "Song of the Vineyard" (Isa 5:1–2) strongly compares with Song 8:11, possible evidence that love poetry similarly played a role in Israel's larger cultural life (see Table 36.1).

Is The Best Song Ever a unified narrative or a drama with plot? Some scholars think so. We find the book to be full of "dramatic" moments but too loosely structured to support such a reading. As Dobbs-Allsop says (p. 351), what unites The Best Song is not an overall sequential narrative but "the heterogeneity of the love experience itself. The need, that is, for love to be taken one moment at a time, from day to day, and, quite literally, from

Table 36.1. Two Old Testament Love Poems		
Isaiah 5:1–2	**Literary Motifs**	**Song of Songs 8:11–12**
I will sing for the one I love a song about his vineyard: My loved one *had a vineyard* on a fertile hillside. He dug it up and cleared it of stones and planted it with the choicest vines. He built a watchtower in it and cut out a wine-press as well.	Introduction: A Vineyard	Solomon *had a vineyard* in Baal Hamon; he let out his vineyard to tenants.
Then he looked for a crop of good grapes,	Expectation	Each was to bring for its fruit a thousand shekels of silver.
but it yielded only bad fruit. (Isa 5:1–2 TNIV, italics ours)	Contrast	But my own vineyard is mine to give; the thousand shekels are for you, Solomon, and two hundred are for those who tend its fruit. (Song 8:11–12 TNIV, italics ours)

poem to poem." It serves up a repeating cycle of short speeches in poems by two young lovers—poems to explore various love themes (see structure below). Further, it walks readers through exotic places with exotic wildlife, foods, and fragrances—through an idyllic, Eden-like garden, but one where humans reside apparently free of serpents and forbidden trees. To read The Best Song Ever is to enjoy the sights, sounds, smells, and passions of love amid the lap of luxury, Oriental-style.

Song of Songs – Last, by Aharon April. 2005. ©*Aharon April (Wikimedia Commons, CC-SA 4.0)*

The Presentation

One striking, delightful aspect of The Best Song Ever is its use of enchanting metaphors. Sometimes the poet makes comparisons simply by juxtaposing words (e.g., "your eyes [are] doves" [1:15]) and at other times more explicitly as similes (e.g., "Like a lily among thorns is my darling among the young women" [2:2 TNIV]). Occasionally, the verb "to compare to, to be like" makes the comparative connection between a personal trait and something in nature (e.g., "I liken you, my darling, to a mare among Pharaoh's chariot horses" [1:9 TNIV]). The challenge, of course, is to unpack the metaphors—to decide what is it about "your eyes" that is so dove-like, or what about the woman's beauty conjures up images of Egyptian horses? The book's predominant rhetorical feature, however, is soliloquies in which the two primary speakers string together ornate metaphors from nature, extolling the other's physical beauty part by part (4:1-7; 5:10-16; 6:4-10; 7:1-9). These longer pieces compare to a unique genre of Arabic love poetry (Arab. *wasf*), so scholars commonly describe biblical examples by that Arabic term. Taken literally, the metaphors evoke amusing (if not grotesque) mental images of human physiques (see Tables 36.2 and 36.3), but poetically they convey the wondering pleasure each lover gains simply from gazing on the other.

Where in Israelite life did this collection of love poems originate? Some suggest that the collection of poems was read, in part or as a whole, as part of a marriage celebration, perhaps even royal (compare Ps 45). But there is apparently no wedding ceremony in The Best Song Ever; its focus falls on the wonder and sensuality of human love more generally rather

allegory to a literal reading of the book. As a result, some affirm that the book literally celebrates the marriage of Solomon to an Egyptian princess, a view first espoused by Theodore of Mopsuestia (4th cent. CE). Parallels in newly discovered Hellenistic and Greco-Roman literature also favor its reading as profane (even erotic) love poetry, the predominant way the Song is sung today.

How Should We Sing The Best Song Ever Today?

The above snapshot of interpretive history shows that every generation's interpretation of the Song of Songs is conditioned by its setting—by shifts in philosophical approaches, new archaeological discoveries, or cultural changes. Frankly, interpretive humility is called for, and a willingness to hold our views tentatively. So, for the moment, we offer the following suggestions on how to sing The Best Song Ever today:

1. Dive right in! Rather than trace its plot or expound its ideas, savor its mood, sights, sounds, and smells. Enjoy it as you would a stroll through the perfume section of Macy's or the aromas in a spice market. Let your imagination and senses run wild; revel in the feelings that arise; eavesdrop on the lovers' conversations and imagine yourself in similar circumstances.

2. Enjoy the thematic medley. Read the book not as a single drama but as a medley of songs that expound common themes that later melodies echo and on which they expand in their own way. Experience the cumulative effect of those recurrences.

3. Remember your loving Creator. In one sense, the picture of human sensuality that The Best Song Ever paints points us back to God. The sights, sounds, smells, tastes, and touches we experience in its pages all come as gifts from our loving Creator. They put on display God's beauty, passion, exuberance, and longing, because God is the source from which we ourselves receive them. The apostle John is right: "We love because he first loved us" (1 John 4:19 TNIV). Our capacity to give and receive love, whether to God or other creatures, ultimately comes from a generous God, and it's no accident that the marriage metaphor—Christ as the bridegroom and the church as his bride—describes God's relationship to God's people. Because God and humans share common traits, and because God the Creator is also our Redeemer through Christ, we can say that The Best Song Ever points beyond human love to a love greater than our own.

READING

Read Song 1–8 and formulate responses to the following questions:

1. What seems to be the basic story line that recurs throughout The Best Song Ever?

2. What does it feel like to read through the book? With what character do you most identify personally? Why?

3. Read Song 4:1–5 and 5:10–16. After listing the metaphors, suggest to what physical feature each corresponds and what the metaphors convey about that feature.

4. Read 8:6–7. List its main ideas and explain which of the book's main themes these verses summarize.

5. Read 8:13. Who is the speaker, and whom does that person address? Given what you've read in The Best Song Ever, how would you respond to the speaker's closing command?

6. Some Christians read The Best Song Ever as being about Christ and the church. Given your reading of the book, how do you respond to that view?

7. What do you think The Best Song Ever teaches you about God? How would you describe God's presence in and/or absence from the book's presentation?

BIBLIOGRAPHY

Assis, Eliyahu. *Flashes of Fire: A Literary Analysis of the Song of Songs*. LHBOTS 503. New York: T&T Clark, 2009.

Brenner, Athalya, and Carole R. Fontaine, eds. *The Song of Songs*. FCB. Sheffield: Sheffield Academic Press, 2000.

Davidson, Richard M. *Flame of Yahweh: Sexuality in the Old Testament*. Peabody, MA: Hendrickson, 2007.

Dobbs-Allsopp, F. W. "Song of Songs." *NIDB* 5:349–54.

Elliott, Mark W. "Ethics and Aesthetics in the Song of Songs." *TynBul* 45 (1994): 137–52.

Exum, J. Cheryl. *The Song of Songs*. OTL. Louisville: Westminster John Knox, 2005.

Fox, Michael V. *The Song of Songs and the Ancient Egyptian Love Songs*. Madison, WI: University of Wisconsin Press, 1985.

Hunt, Patrick. *Poetry in the Song of Songs: A Literary Analysis*. StBibLit 96. New York: Peter Lang, 2008.

Keel, Othmar. *The Song of Songs*. Translated by Frederick J. Gaiser. CC. Minneapolis: Fortress, 1994.

Longman, Tremper, III. *The Song of Songs*. NICOT. Grand Rapids: Eerdmans, 2001.

Murphy, Roland E. *The Song of Songs*. Hermeneia. Minneapolis: Fortress, 1990.

Norris, Richard A., Jr. *The Song of Songs: Interpreted by Early Christian and Medieval Commentators*. Grand Rapids: Eerdmans, 2003.

Schwab, George M. "Wasf." Pages 835–42 in *Dictionary of the Old Testament: Wisdom, Poetry, Writings*. Edited by Tremper Longman III and Peter Enns. Downers Grove, IL: InterVarsity Press, 2008.

Tanner, J. Paul. "The History of Interpretation of the Song of Songs." *Bibliotheca Sacra* 154 (1997): 23–46.

PART 6
Conclusion

37 THE CANON AND TEXT OF THE HEBREW BIBLE / CHRISTIAN OLD TESTAMENT

NOW THAT WE HAVE INTRODUCED the books in the Hebrew Bible/Old Testament (HB/OT), we examine their preservation process and thus their place in communities of faith that have treasured them over the centuries. In doing so we first define three important terms, Scripture, Bible, and Canon, and then take a look at ways in which communities of faith have transmitted and preserved these texts in different times and places.

Scripture, Bible, Canon

The term *scripture* bears connotations of an authoritative document, but the noun's basic meaning is "writing." A scripture is a writing accorded authoritative status by hearers and readers. Similarly, the word *Bible* is a rendering of the Greek word for "books," although it has come to mean a collection of inspired or authoritative books for a faith community. For centuries interpreters have used a third term, *canon*, as a shorthand reference to the authoritative or recognized collection of scriptures of a religion. The term goes back to a Semitic word for a straight reed that was used for making measurements. It has cognates in both Greek and Latin that were used by early Christians to refer to such things as the "*rule* of faith" or "*standard* of truth" in defining their faith. It came to be used for official lists of documents or even names/titles (e.g., church officials). In the 4th century CE, the term came to be used for the approved list of Scriptures for church use, and since then the term (biblical) *canon* is widely used as a synonym for the Bible.

The modern mind, therefore, typically equates the term *Scripture* with the terms *Bible* and *biblical canon*. This makes sense when one begins with current practices, but it is important to keep in mind that the faith communities of ancient Israel and the early church did not have modern formulations in mind in using such terms. There were scriptures (= authoritative documents) before there were authorized lists of them. In what follows, it is thus important to distinguish between these terms as an aid in a historical understanding of them. A canon of Scripture can refer to:

A. an authoritative list of documents/books or
B. a list of authoritative documents/books.

The distinction is subtle but significant, and in the long history of preserving the Scriptures one can see both senses of the term at work. What we call canon A refers to a list that has been examined and has reached formal agreement. A group or groups of people make conscious decisions that certain books already in use will be the recognized authoritative sources for the faithful. Some of these have also decreed what should not be (or no longer be) used. Authorized lists and church council decrees began in the 4th century CE. Three examples are: Athanasius, Bishop of Alexandria, wrote a circular letter on the canon of the Old and New Testaments (367 CE); a regional church council meeting at Carthage in North Africa (397 CE) made a list of the "canonical Scriptures" that should be read in the churches of its jurisdiction; and the Council of Trent (1546 CE) decreed that the Latin Vulgate and its books provided the recognized version of the Scriptures for the Roman Catholic faithful. These provided a formal definition of a canon of Scripture, even though there were differences among them.

Before the 4th century, there was what we can call a "canonical process" at work among Christian churches; indeed, there were multiple "implicit canons" in use among them. As noted, this was because there were authoritative writings in use before there were formal pronouncements about them. This is the point of Canon B. Christians in about the year 175 CE, for example, could point to a list of authoritative documents in use in their community, a list with some variation from community to community, because it was standard practice to use them. In the long history of Judaism, there is no surviving evidence of a council voting formally on the number and contents of their Scriptures—discussions and debates, of course, but no records of a formal vote! What we know about their process fits Canon B. Jews produced lists of authoritative documents in use by their community, even as they collected them in scrolls and eventually in a codex (a bound volume of leaves/pages sewn together). The list/collection may not have been formally ratified, or closed off, but it preserved what was accepted wisdom in their communities.

It is not easy to explain how the HB and the OT(s) reached their current canonical status. Part of the reason for the difficulty is the sheer length of time and complexity of detail involved in the process of producing authoritative collections for Jewish and Christian communities. It is also the case that we lack data on certain important decisions or processes behind current circumstances. Terms such as *tradition, providence,* and *who knows?* can conceal as much as they reveal by way of explanation, but they each play a role in describing the process. In what follows, we will first consider how texts were produced and transmitted over time. We will then look at the related process of collecting authoritative texts in Judaism and Christianity, with particular emphasis on lists and summary statements from both communities up to the 5th century CE. From that point, one can see how the canonical processes at work in Judaism and Christianity led directly to the standards and practices of modern times.

Texts, Transmission, and Translation of the Hebrew Bible / Old Testament

Since the invention of the printing press and now digital storage, standardized copies of the HB/OT are widely available. Western readers, in particular, can simply assume their availability in various formats and translations without giving the matter a second thought. Without centuries of prior efforts, however, certainly some and perhaps all of these books would not have survived antiquity. We know intuitively how elements from even a recent family history can disappear; how much more things from the remote past!

There are several factors to keep in mind in tracing the survival of copies of ancient documents into the modern period, all of which relate to the OT we read today. One is that documents on perishable materials such as papyrus and leather require periodic copying by human hand. There must be ongoing interest/demand for these documents for someone to undertake the time-consuming and thus expensive task of reproducing a text; hence the comment above about the prior preservation efforts of Jews and Christians. A text such as Genesis or Homer's *Iliad* was copied periodically and painstakingly over centuries.

A second factor in preserving a document is facility with its language by transmitters and readers. Some ancient texts originally written in an old and difficult language or writing system such as Egyptian hieroglyphics, Sumerian, or Akkadian did not continue to be copied as that language fell into disuse. This leads to a third and related factor, which is the translation of an ancient text into a language more commonly used.

If, for example, facility in Egyptian hieroglyphics fell by the wayside, as it eventually did in Egypt, and if there was less interest in preserving Egypt's older literary output, as happened with the rise of Christianity and then Islam, one can understand why some Egyptian texts were lost to posterity. In the case of the Hebrew Bible, the spread of Hellenism and the Greek language led Jews to translate its contents first into Greek (the LXX or Septuagint). With the rise of Christianity, Christians were the primary reason for the broad dissemination of Greek versions of the OT.

Like any composition, ancient documents can draw on still earlier written sources, and sometimes those source documents don't survive to modernity. It may be that already in antiquity a later document eclipsed the use of an older one, or it may be that the older sources fell prey to time and chance. A good illustration is the *Ecclesiastical History* written by Eusebius of Caesarea (ca. 260-339 CE) to account for the rise of the Christian Church in the first three centuries of its existence. Writing after Constantine's rise to power, he had access to a church library at Caesarea Maritima on the coast of Israel-Palestine that contained a number of ancient Christian sources, including early manuscripts of biblical texts. He made numerous references to them, including some quotations. Copies of some of those documents are extant today, and Eusebius's references can be checked. Sadly, the library was destroyed in antiquity. For some of Eusebius's references, therefore, all that remains of the ancient document is the small portion he quoted. Moreover, even when Eusebius was not quoting directly, he drew on both written and oral sources for his data.

The OT similarly cites a number of sources that are no longer extant. Numbers 21:14 quotes a poetic line from the "Book of the Wars of the Lord." Obviously this work preceded the book of Numbers. Since we don't have that document, all that we have to work with is the citation. This raises an interesting question, however, regarding other possible uses of that document in the OT, where it may have been used but not cited. Are there other elements in the Pentateuch, or say, Joshua and Judges, that came from it? Moreover, what would Jews and Christians do with a copy of it if an archaeologist found it? Joshua 10:12-13 cites a poetic account of the sun and moon standing still over the valley of Aijalon and attributes it to "The Book of Jasher." This ancient source too is no longer extant. In the narratives of the books of Kings,

there are references to sources that the writers drew upon that no longer exist (see, e.g., 1 Kgs 11:41; 2 Kgs 1:18). Think how exciting it would be if a version of one or more of these ancient sources suddenly appeared! These references are reminders that some of the books in the OT do not contain the earliest accounts of events but those that have stood the test of time.

We have the discoveries of archaeologists, anthropologists, and historians as well as serendipitous finds to thank for dramatic contributions to what we know about the literary output of the past, the OT included. Impressive cultural and written remains of civilizations such as the Philistines and Hittites, once only known from scattered references, have come to light as the result of patient scholarly work. The initial discovery of the Dead Sea Scrolls, for example, was accidental. The first group of them were found by chance by Arab shepherds in 1947, in a cave near the Dead Sea in Palestine of the British Mandate System. Their discovery set off a torrent of searchers in the area and resulted in discoveries in ten additional caves. Among the Dead Sea Scrolls were copies or fragments of every book in the Hebrew Bible except Esther, plus a number of unique Jewish documents that had not otherwise survived to modernity. These ancient texts and fragments have provided a whole new window on Jewish beliefs and practices. Given their dates (150 BCE–70 CE), these documents are important witnesses to what we might call the end of the OT period and the textual transmission of biblical texts at that time.

Excerpts from the Leningrad Codex, the oldest complete manuscript of the Hebrew Bible, dating to 1008 CE. Now in the National Library of Russia in St. Petersburg. Left: Folio 478 recto, one of the sixteen so-called "carpet pages" illuminating the manuscript. The Hebrew in the center reads, "The Torah of the Lord is perfect." Right: Folio 203 verso, a representative page from near the middle of the codex. This page includes the Hebrew text of 2 Kings 2:13–3:11. *Photographs by Bruce and Kenneth Zuckerman, West Semitic Research, in collaboration with the Ancient Biblical Manuscript Center. Courtesy Russian National Library (Saltykov-Shchedrin). Used with permission.*

Just as biblical writers cite sources that are no longer available for comparison's sake, so we have only later copies of OT books and no originals to consult. Until the printing press (15th century CE), texts were periodically copied by hand over centuries of time. So what texts do modern scholars consult? One widely employed study edition of the Hebrew Bible is *Biblia Hebraica Stuttgartensia*, published by the modern German Bible Society in Stuttgart. The Hebrew text that *BHS* uses comes from the Leningrad Codex, located in St. Petersburg, Russia, and dating to 1008 CE. The Scriptures in it are arranged in twenty-four books (see Table 37.1). That codex has a long transmission history behind it! It is not the oldest collection of the Hebrew documents but one that is heir to a long and careful preservation tradition among Jewish scholars known as the Masoretes (= those who handed on tradition). It includes vowel markings and other notations for public presentation. Scholars often refer to this textual tradition as the Masoretic Text (MT). Another that is closely related to it is the so-called Aleppo Codex, now located in the modern state of Israel. It dates from sometime early in the 10th century (ca. 925 CE). Though it was originally complete in twenty-four books, portions of it have been lost. There are Hebrew manuscripts for some of the OT books that are older, including texts from the Dead Sea scrolls noted above. Scholars consult

Table 37.1. Order of Books in the Leningrad Codex and Rabbinic Numbering

TORAH: 5	PROPHETS: 8			WRITINGS: 11
Genesis	Joshua			1–2 Chronicles
Exodus	Judges			Psalms
Leviticus	1–2 Samuel			Job
Numbers	1–2 Kings			Proverbs
Deuteronomy	Isaiah			Ruth
	Jeremiah			Song of Songs
	Ezekiel			Ecclesiastes
	Book of the Twelve:			Lamentations
	Hosea	Jonah	Zephaniah	Esther
	Joel	Micah	Haggai	Daniel
	Amos	Nahum	Zechariah	Ezra-Nehemiah
	Obadiah	Habakkuk	Malachi	

TOTAL: 24

these too as part of their research. One can, for example, compare the Dead Sea Scroll of Isaiah from the Cave 1 discovery with the MT to see how some ten centuries of transmission history played out. In this case, the consonantal text of Isaiah from approximately 100 BCE is very similar to the MT, although there are the inevitable copyist and spelling errors that come with reproducing texts by hand. In the case of other biblical books among the scrolls, such as Samuel and Jeremiah, there are fragments that preserve more variation with the later MT. Modern interpreters of the OT are fortunate in having more manuscript examples to compare than for most ancient documents, including something as central to Western history as *The Iliad*.

The HB/OT was not just copied repeatedly over time but was also translated into Greek, Latin, and Syriac, to name just three languages widely used for biblical texts from the early centuries of the Common Era. There are manuscripts in each of these languages that are also older than the MT. These manuscript traditions are another check for measuring the transmission process of the biblical texts over the centuries. The Old Greek translations, beginning about 250 BCE with the Pentateuch and continuing for centuries, produced the Septuagint and related versions. A legendary account of the translation of the Pentateuch in Alexandria, Egypt, during the reign of Ptolemy II, is contained in the Hellenistic Greek document, the Letter of Aristeas. It describes the work of seventy-two Jewish scholars in producing an agreed-upon translation, hence the name *Septuagint*, which means "seventy," and accounts for the widely used abbreviation, LXX. The term Septuagint is frequently used for the Old Greek translations of the OT and not just the Pentateuch. Jerome (died 420 CE) consulted both Hebrew and Greek manuscripts in his monumental Latin translation, now known as the Vulgate. The Syriac Bible, also known as the Peshitta version, was a production of an Eastern Christianity that reached China by the 7th century CE. Its OT texts were probably translations from the Greek versions, but a connection to some Hebrew texts or Aramaic paraphrases known as targums cannot be ruled out. Each of these languages represents a vibrant religious community that valued the OT and considered it authoritative in translated form. Judaism, of course, prized its collection of Scriptures in Hebrew, even as it produced the first translation of them into Greek. With the rise of Christianity and its adoption of the LXX as an authoritative version of the Scriptures, Rabbinic Judaism affirmed the Hebrew version as its authoritative collection.

Table 37.2. Hebrew Bible/Old Testament in Different Versions (Apocrypha in Italics)

Hebrew Bible	Greek Septuagint	Latin Vulgate	King James
	Genesis	Genesis	Genesis
THE LAW	Exodus	Exodus	Exodus
Genesis	Leviticus	Leviticus	Leviticus
Exodus	Numbers	Numbers	Numbers
Leviticus	Deuteronomy	Deuteronomy	Deuteronomy
Numbers	Joshua	Joshua	Joshua
Deuteronomy	Judges	Judges	Judges
	Ruth	Ruth	Ruth
THE PROPHETS	1-2 Samuel	1-2 Samuel	1-2 Samuel
Joshua	1-2 Kings	1-2 Kings	1-2 Kings
Judges	1-2 Chronicles	1-2 Chronicles	1-2 Chronicles
1 Samuel	[Prayer of Manasseh]	Prayer of Manasseh	Ezra
2 Samuel	1 Esdras	1 Esdras	Nehemiah
1 Kings	Ezra	2 Esdras	Esther
2 Kings	Nehemiah	Ezra	Job
Isaiah	Tobit	Nehemiah	Psalms
Jeremiah	Judith	Tobit	Proverbs
Ezekiel	Esther (+ additions)	Judith	Ecclesiastes
Hosea	1 Maccabees	Esther (+ additions)	Song of Songs
Joel	2 Maccabees	1 Maccabees	Isaiah
Amos	[3 Maccabees]	2 Maccabees	Jeremiah
Obadiah	[4 Maccabees]	Job	Lamentations
Jonah	Job	Psalms	Ezekiel
Micah	Psalms	Proverbs	Daniel
Nahum	[Psalm no. 151]	Ecclesiastes	Hosea
Habakkuk	[Odes]	Song of Songs	Joel
Zephaniah	Proverbs	Wisdom of Solomon	Amos
Haggai	Ecclesiastes	Ecclesiasticus	Obadiah
Zechariah	Song of Songs	Isaiah	Jonah
Malachi	Wisdom of Solomon	Jeremiah	Micah
	Ecclesiasticus	Lamentations	Nahum
THE WRITINGS	[Psalms of Solomon]	Baruch	Habakkuk
Psalms	Isaiah	Epistle of Jeremiah	Zephaniah
Job	Jeremiah	Ezekiel	Haggai
Proverbs	Lamentations	Daniel (+ additions)	Zechariah
Ruth	Baruch	Hosea	Malachi

Hebrew Bible	Greek Septuagint	Latin Vulgate	King James
Song of Songs	*Epistle of Jeremiah*	Joel	*1 Esdras*
Ecclesiastes	Ezekiel	Amos	*2 Esdras*
Lamentations	Daniel (+ *additions*)	Obadiah	*Tobit*
Esther	Hosea	Jonah	*Judith*
Daniel	Joel	Micah	*Additions to Esther*
Ezra	Amos	Nahum	*Wisdom of Solomon*
Nehemiah	Obadiah	Habakkuk	*Ecclesiasticus*
1 Chronicles	Jonah	Zephaniah	*Baruch*
2 Chronicles	Micah	Haggai	*Epistle of Jeremiah*
	Nahum	Zechariah	*Song of 3 Children*
	Habakkuk	Malachi	*Story of Susanna*
	Zephaniah		*Bel and the Dragon*
	Haggai		*Prayer of Manasseh*
	Zechariah		*1 Maccabees*
	Malachi		*2 Maccabees*

That the early church read the OT in various translations was both a cultural necessity for widespread dissemination and a theological commitment. Being able to read the text or at least hear it read in a current vernacular had high priority. And that commitment to translation continues to this day. Church bodies read biblical texts in officially approved versions and consider them completely adequate to bear the divine revelation they seek. Thus Ethiopian Christians appeal to Ethiopian versions of the Bible, Coptic Christians to Coptic translations, and Greek Orthodox Christians to the LXX. At one point in its history, a Roman Catholic Church council meeting at Trent (1545–63) declared the Vulgate the official version of the Scriptures for ecclesiastical usage, although now its scholars avail themselves of critical editions of the Hebrew, Greek, and Latin versions as the basis for study and debate. Protestant churches may or may not have a policy for validating modern translations or for appeal in dispute to the Hebrew or Greek versions, but the increasing number of modern versions is proof of the continuing appeal of timely translations. There are modern English translations of the OT based solely on the Masoretic Text or on a critical reconstruction of the Septuagint, but most modern translations follow Jerome's practice of carefully consulting various ancient texts before rendering in modern idiom.

22-23). Jeremiah dictated the complete scroll again, and that second copy probably found its way into the completed book of Jeremiah. An account of Isaiah's ministry during the reign of Hezekiah, Isa 36-39, has a close parallel in 2 Kgs 18-20. Likely two different compilers were drawing on commonly acknowledged material. In explaining the significance of the Babylonian destruction of Jerusalem, the Chronicler names Jeremiah and alludes to his prophecy of a seventy-year period of exile (2 Chr 36:21; cf. Jer 25:8-14). Daniel also references this prophecy of Jeremiah (Dan 9:1-2).

Jeremiah's own book recognizes the collective efforts of unnamed prophets who served the Lord through their efforts (Jer 7:25). The book of Ezra refers to the work of the prophets Haggai and Zechariah (5:1) in support of building the Second Temple, and Malachi (4:5-6) projects a future ministry for Elijah. Ezekiel names Job as a righteous man from the past (14:20). While this is not a reference to the book of Job, it is information to illustrate why Israel's growing collection of instructive texts could include one. The hymns and prayers in the Psalms refer to the "instruction" of the Lord (Pss 1, 19), material certainly related to the Pentateuch's contents as well as to the history of God's dealings with Israel (Pss 78, 105-6), again drawing on traditions now included in the Pentateuch and the Historical Books. The epilogue to Ecclesiastes urges the keeping of the Lord's "commandments" (Eccl 12:13) as true wisdom. Such "cross-references" indicate processes at work that in due time produced the HB of Judaism and the OT(s) of Christianity. Internal terminology recognizes a Torah (= Law) and a collection of Prophets as the basic building blocks of a growing collection of Scriptures.

The Wisdom of Ben Sira and the Collection of Israel's Scriptures

The Hellenistic Jewish work known as the Wisdom of Ben Sira (also known as Sirach or Ecclesiasticus) was translated from Hebrew into Greek in the year 132 BCE. The author's unnamed grandson was the translator, and it circulated widely among Jews and then Christians in antiquity. We don't have a date for the original composition, as we do for the translation, but it would have been sometime in the first half of the 2nd century BCE. The grandson added a prologue to his translation in which he refers to "the Law, the Prophets, and the other books of our ancestors." There are a couple of matters to note in this brief reference. First of all, he recognizes a collection of writings from Israel that he describes elsewhere in the prologue as Israel's "instruction and wisdom." Second, he offers a classification of these writings. From the comments of his grandfather (Sir 44–50), in which readers are invited to sing the praises of famous men in Israel, it is clear that "the Law" is the Pentateuch. The prophets also can be defined more specifically, but not completely. Ben Sira mentions Nathan, Elijah and Elisha, Isaiah, Jeremiah, Ezekiel, and the "Twelve Prophets" (i.e., the Minor Prophets, Hosea through Malachi). These last four references would each represent a separate scroll (or book).

There is no reference to Daniel in Ben Sira. Some Jews did not consider the book a part of the prophetic category, but a more likely reason is that the book of Daniel was written, at least in final form, about the time of Ben Sira himself and had not yet achieved a widespread circulation.

The third category is simply other books—that is, books that are not in the Law or Prophets but are a recognized part of Israel's "instruction and wisdom." From the references to David, Solomon, and temple worship, it is very likely that assembled texts such as Psalms and Proverbs are included. Indeed, these "other books" could include most if not all of the books eventually recognized as the Hebrew Bible. The grandson's description of Israel's "instruction and wisdom" is the earliest classification for the documents that we possess. Likely it is a classification that he inherited. The third category, if that is what we should call it, is ambiguous. The grandson does not

Table 37.3. Ben Sira's List of Godly Ancestors

Reference	Names	Hebrew Canon Section
Sirach 44–45	Enoch, Noah, Abraham, Isaac, Israel (Jacob), Moses, Aaron, Phinehas	Torah
Sirach 46–49:6	Joshua, Caleb, the judges, Samuel, Nathan, David, Solomon, (Rehoboam), (Jeroboam), Elijah, Elisha, Hezekiah, Isaiah, Josiah	Former Prophets
Sirach 49:7–10	(Isaiah appears in previous group [Sir 48:23–35]), Jeremiah, Ezekiel, Job (cf. Ezek 14:14, 20), Twelve Prophets	Latter Prophets
Sirach 49:11–16	Zerubbabel, Jeshua ben Jozadak, Nehemiah, Enoch*, Joseph**, Shem*, Seth*, Enosh*, Adam*	Writings, *1 Chr 1:1, 3, **1 Chr 2, 5, 7
Sirach 50	Simeon ben Jochanan	High Priest, Simeon I (ca. 300 BCE) or Simon II (ca. 200 BCE)

indicate further what he understands by the "others." Nevertheless, to this day the books of the Hebrew Bible are typically organized in the categories of Torah, Prophets, and Writings, essentially following this early classification, and Jews often refer to their Bible with a Hebrew-based acronym TaNaK. The *T* is for *Torah*, the *N* is for *Nevi'im* (= Prophets), and the *K* is for *Ketuvim* (= Writings).

Collecting Books in the Jerusalem Temple

The books of 1–2 Maccabees were written in the aftermath of the crisis brought upon Judaism by the Seleucid ruler Antiochus IV Epiphanes (175–164 BCE). He defiled the temple in Jerusalem and persecuted Jews. A revolt broke out against him and his forces, resulting in the restoration of the temple service and then increased autonomy for Jews in Palestine. Members of the priestly Hasmonean family, nicknamed the Maccabees, eventually became high priests at the temple and kings of the Jews (163–142 BCE). Two matters related to Israel's sacred texts are reported in 2 Macc 2:13–15. The first is that Nehemiah had earlier founded a library in Jerusalem and collected "books about the kings and prophets, the writings of David, and letters of kings about votive offerings." Second, in more recent times Judas (Maccabean leader of the revolt against Antiochus IV) had collected there "all the books that had been lost because of the war."

It was a widespread cultural practice in antiquity to preserve important documents in a holy place. This would have been the case also in Israel (Deut 31:9–14; 2 Kgs 22). If Nehemiah did establish a library in Jerusalem after the Babylonian exile, it would not have been the first. From the brief description, one cannot tell what "all the books" collected by the Maccabees mean. With regard to Israel's Scriptures, it would have included the Torah (cf. 1 Macc 2:48) and, one assumes, those mentioned in Nehemiah's list. It may well have assumed a list such as those noted next, but the phrase is ambiguous.

A Numbered List of the Scriptures among Jews: Three Examples

At the end of the first century (ca. 95 CE), the Jewish writer Josephus, seeking to explain and defend Judaism to Greco-Roman readers, states that the sacred Scriptures are contained in twenty-two books and that it is instinctive for all Jews to revere them (*Against Apion* 1.8). He describes them as follows: five by Moses, thirteen prophetic books from the death of Moses to the Persian king Artaxerxes, and four books of hymns and precepts. His comments assume that the collection of books is complete and recognized by all Jews. Such a presentation is too simple but is understandable, given that his primary audience is Gentile and that he wants to show them that his heritage has longer and more-exact records than those contained in the Classical Greek sources. His brief description certainly glosses over what he mentions elsewhere—namely, that there were differences of opinion and religious practices among Jewish groups such as the Sadducees, Pharisees, and Essenes. Most interpreters, for example, have concluded that the Sadducees recognized only the Pentateuch as authoritative. Unfortunately, we have no sources from the Sadducees that speak to a matter of this sort. The Samaritan community considered itself the authentic heir of Moses and held a version of only the Pentateuch as its authoritative text.

Josephus's arrangement of the Hebrew Scriptures in twenty-two books (i.e., scrolls) corresponds to the number of letters in the Hebrew alphabet. This is a tradition cited elsewhere among Jews and is likely something that Josephus was taught rather than that he invented. It is also a tradition known to early Christians. Would that Josephus had taken the time to name the twenty-two books individually! In any case, the five by Moses are collectively the Pentateuch. An educated guess is that the thirteen prophets are Joshua, Judges/Ruth, Samuel, Kings, Isaiah, Jeremiah/Lamentations, Ezekiel, Daniel, The Twelve, Ezra/Nehemiah, Chronicles, Job, and Esther. There are examples from other ancient lists and related discussions of placing Ruth with Judges, Lamentations with Jeremiah, and Ezra with Nehemiah.

The number of books in Josephus's prophetic category is higher than in some descriptions, such as the list provided in the Babylonian Talmud (below) or in the TaNaK arrangement of the books. For some interpreters, however, both Jewish and Christian, a prophetic inspiration was seen in all the Scriptures, and thus the category of a book was secondary to its broader prophetic quality. The final four could then be Psalms, Proverbs, Ecclesiastes, and the Song of Songs. This reconstruction of the twenty-two books assumes, however, that Josephus had in mind the books that comprise the received Hebrew Bible. One must also reckon with the possibility that one or more of those books are not, in fact, included in his twenty-two.

Another Jewish work, 4 Ezra, likely from the end of the first century

CE, refers to a list of books that Ezra reproduced by divine inspiration after the catastrophe of the Babylonian exile. Apparently the work was passed along and expanded in Christian circles. According to 4 Ezra 14:37-47, Ezra dictated ninety-four books to a group of scribes, over a forty-day period. The twenty-four books written first were to be made public, and the unworthy and worthy alike could read them. Seventy, however, were for the wise among Ezra's people. That the Jewish Scriptures comprised twenty-four books was yet another tradition cited by both Jews and Christians. It is not clear whether this number was a challenge to the twenty-two-book collection cited by Josephus and others or an alternative reckoning of them, simply using a different number of scrolls to classify the same sacred texts. Jerome, for example, who knew both Jewish traditions, accounted for the difference by noting that some rabbis numbered Ruth with Judges and Lamentations with Jeremiah, while others did not. Twenty-four is the number of books listed in the Babylonian Talmud and used in the TaNaK arrangement of Classical Judaism. Still, one can also show that there were discussions about books such as Ezekiel, Esther, Ecclesiastes, and the Song of Songs among Jews. The Mishnah (included in the Talmud) preserves these discussions. Some groups may have discouraged the use of one or more of these books, and this could account for the difference in number.

The reference to seventy additional books is unique to 4 Ezra, but it does reflect a broader phenomenon in Judaism and Christianity in which the number of "inspired" books in actual use in a given group can be larger than the reckoning of authoritative books with a longer footprint in tradition. This is an ancient and a modern phenomenon. On the one hand, a twenty-two- or twenty-four-book canon of Jewish texts is a tradition repeatedly cited in Jewish and Christian sources. On the other hand, as previously noted, Hellenistic Jews produced a number of other books widely read by Jews and then Christians as well. Some of these were (and still are) reckoned among the OT Scriptures of a Christian communion, while others had an influence for a time among Jews and Christians but do not any longer. The community of the Dead Sea Scrolls is another example of a Jewish group with a broad range of authoritative texts, however they sorted them.

The Babylonian Talmud preserves a baraita, a tradition received from earlier rabbis, that discusses the classification, order, and authorship of the sacred books (b. Baba Batra 14b-15a). That tradition could be as old as Josephus or 4 Ezra, but it is difficult to date. The Talmud is comprised of texts and traditions of various dates and was compiled about 500 CE. It has its own authority in Rabbinic Judaism to complement that of the HB and to interpret the latter's contents for Jewish beliefs. The Talmudic passage begins "our rabbis taught" and the list begins with the prophets. The prophetic books in order are Joshua, Judges, Samuel, Kings, Jeremiah, Ezekiel, Isaiah, and the Twelve Minor Prophets, a total of eight books. The category of writings has the following order: Ruth, Psalms, Job, Proverbs, Ecclesiastes, Song of Songs, Lamentations, Daniel, Esther, Ezra, and Chronicles. Counting the Pentateuch as five and assuming that Nehemiah is a part of Ezra (as was often the case), the number of books is twenty-four. The discussion in this baraita concerns the order of the books and their authors but contains nothing about decisions to include or exclude books from the collection of sacred texts. Their number and value are simply assumed, as is their language (Hebrew). These are the twenty-four books of the TaNaK used to this day in Judaism, although there was no one fixed order until the invention of the printing press. The rabbis, who passed along the twenty-four-book canon, followed the traditions of the Pharisees. In doing so, they passed along oral traditions that were also eventually written down in the Mishnah and Gemara to comprise the Talmud. These streams of tradition (TaNaK and Talmud) define Orthodox or Classical Judaism to this day.

The Dead Sea Scrolls (DSS) and Israel's Scriptures

The documents collectively known as the Dead Sea Scrolls are sometimes referred to as an ancient library. This seems appropriate. A prominent theory regarding them is that they belonged to a sect of Judaism known from other sources as Essenes, a group that sought to preserve their traditions of worship and holiness over against their contemporaries. For the purposes of discussion, it is not important whether the ancient community that owned and stored the scrolls was Essene in origin or not. The DSS community lived in the arid region next to the western edge of the Dead Sea, beginning at some point during the rule of the Maccabees (about 125 BCE). With the Jewish revolt against Roman occupation (66–73 CE), members of the community placed their prized texts in various caves and hoped to survive the advance of the Roman army that moved through their region in 70 CE and following. The ruins of an ancient settlement in proximity to the caves are usually associated with the pious Jews of the DSS community. They are located more specifically at Qumran, a place-name that is frequently used in reference to both the ancient texts and the community that owned them. The DSS have provided a wonderful window into the diversity and vitality of

Cave Four (in the center) – the fourth cave of eleven caves in which the Dead Sea Scrolls were discovered. Cave Four yielded more texts by far than any of the other ten. ©Lux Moundi (Wikimedia Commons, CC 2.0)

Judaism at the end of the OT period, including a number of unique writings. It is clear from various internal references that the DSS community differed from other Jews such as the Pharisees and Sadducees in their interpretation of the law, temple practices, and calendar reckoning. Describing the DSS community as sectarian requires careful consideration. There can be no doubt of their separatist outlook on life and eschatological orientation, but their "differences" with other Jews should be examined on a case-by-case basis.

As noted previously, there is textual evidence in the DSS for every book in the Hebrew Bible with the exception of Esther. Possibly this exception is due to coincidence or the vagaries of time. Since there were questions elsewhere among both Jews and Christians about Esther, it is more likely that the Qumran community did not read Esther. There is no evidence, for example, that they kept the Festival of Purim, whose origin is presented in the book of Esther. In any case, there is adequate evidence to show that the community of the scrolls used the books comprising the HB, with the probable exception of Esther, and assumed their sanctity and authority. From the surviving evidence, it is clear that the Pentateuch, prophetic books (Isaiah especially), and Psalms were especially valued. Put another way, in the use of these books, they were similar to fellow-Jews of the period. They would certainly agree with Ben Sira's grandson on the importance of the Law, Prophets, and other books of their ancestors.

What cannot be determined, and thus what interpreters continue to debate, is how the DSS community understood the authority of other texts they possessed and also clearly prized. Did they have a viewpoint similar to that of 4 Ezra, that there are recognized public books and then a larger collection for the wise, such as themselves? The community was also instructed by such texts as a Rule of the Community; a Temple Scroll with materials from the Pentateuch, along with unique first-person speech from God; a scroll of prayers; and books such as Jubilees and 1 Enoch, both known to be popular in certain other Jewish circles. Such valued documents did not preclude, for example, a distinction in the community's mind between Genesis and Jubilees (which treats material in Genesis), or between Exodus and the unique Temple Scroll, but we lack the evidence to say definitively what the distinction was. We might also ask a related question: did the community think that their authoritative writings were part of a fixed list—whether twenty-two, twenty-four, or ninety-four in number—or were the "list" and number more fluid and open ended?

As noted earlier, some biblical texts among the DSS show considerable textual variation in comparison with later rabbinic manuscripts. Moreover, some of their fragmentary texts reflect a style of composition that interpreters call "parabiblical" or "rewritten/reworked biblical texts." These texts use phrases and subsections of a biblical book but also reformulate and mix them in an eclectic, midrashic style. While such texts assume the importance of biblical materials, it is hard to know whether they themselves were considered scriptural as well. At least in terms of textual form and transmission, we cannot call the DSS biblical texts "fixed." That process was still underway at Qumran.

Israel's Scriptures in the New Testament

The NT writers were Jews by heritage, or perhaps one or more of them were Gentiles with significant exposure to Israel's Scriptures in Greek. Thus one can read the NT for data on Jewish matters of the period as well as for the emergence of Christian self-understanding in light of the conviction that Jesus was the Messiah of Israel. One of the striking impressions the NT makes on readers is its dependence on Israel's Scriptures. This can be seen first of all in the formal citations and second in allusions and the employment of scriptural vocabulary. Citations follow Hebrew and (more often) Greek versions. References may be paraphrased or two sources combined into one. The authority of Israel's Scriptures is assumed, even when their interpretation is under discussion. Note, for example, the beginning of Matthew's Gospel, where Jesus's genealogy is linked with Abraham and David and the subsequent kings of Israel and Judah (Matt 1:1-17), or Paul's discussion of Israel's purpose, which draws explicitly on various OT texts (Rom 9-11).

There is recognition in the NT that Israel's Scriptures exist in the form of "the Law and Prophets" (e.g., in Matt 5:17; 7:12). A reference to the "law of Moses, the prophets, and the Psalms" (Luke 24:44) possibly assumes a tripartite classification system of some kind for the authoritative texts. It is analogous to the classification of Ben Sira's grandson, but like his, the reference does not indicate whether a third category of Scripture is fixed or fluid in nature. The NT does not quote from every book in the OT. There is no formal citation, for example, from either Joshua or Ruth, but clearly these books are known and used. For example, the person of Ruth is named explicitly in Jesus's genealogy (Matt 1:5), and the accounts of Israel's conquest and division of the land of Canaan are noted as being instructive (Acts 13:16-25; Heb 11:30-31). We might think of these references as a type of allusion. The Revelation of John is full of allusions to the OT, often approaching a quotation, but it does not contain a single formal citation.

The NT writers also draw on other books that they find instructive, whether or not that means the documents have as widespread communal authority as Israel's Scriptures. Jude 14, for example, refers to a prophecy of Enoch (a figure in Gen 5:18-24) that comes from the book of 1 Enoch (1:9). First Enoch is a work that was read in the DSS community as well as certain other Jewish circles. It is part of the OT of the Ethiopian Church. Jude's reference could mean that he and his early community also valued 1 Enoch as a scripture. Minimally, it indicates the importance of the prophecy drawn from it for the community to whom Jude wrote. Although there are no formal citations in the NT from books now in the Apocrypha, it is abundantly clear that elements from them are known and valued.

Jesus's teaching about "laying up for yourselves treasure in heaven" (Matt 6:19) has a near parallel in Sir 29:11, where people are urged to "lay up your treasure according to the commandments of the Most High." Matthew's description of people as "sheep without a shepherd" (Matt 9:36) uses a phrase also employed in Judith 11:19. The writer to the Hebrews lists various afflictions of the righteous such as torture and being sawn in two (Heb 11:35-37). These references appear in the context of reminding readers of a written record of God's dealings with his people, beginning with Abel in Genesis. Those who are tortured but will receive a "better resurrection" (Heb 11:35) may refer to Jewish martyrs described in 2 Macc 6-7. According to a legend preserved in the Ascension of Isaiah, the prophet of that name was sawn in half by the wicked king Manasseh. The names of Pharaoh's magicians are not provided in the book of Exodus (7:11, 22) but were a part of later Jewish tradition. One finds them, for example, in the Damascus Document, a work discovered among the DSS, and in 2 Tim 3:8. None of these examples, with the possible exception of Jude 14, is a formal citation or is evidence that the texts in question are part of Israel's Scriptures (Canon B). They show how writers draw on recognized texts and traditions. Israel's Scriptures have pride of place and unquestioned authority in this broader category of recognized texts and traditions, but the NT cannot confirm (or deny) their limits to a twenty-two- or twenty-four-book collection.

The Earliest Christian List of Old Testament Books

In his *Ecclesiastical History*, Eusebius preserves the earliest documentation of a Christian discussion of books of the "old covenant" (*Hist. eccl.* 4.26.13-14). The phrase and its counterpart, "new covenant," have an interesting history. The OT itself contains references to various covenants that God made, including one mediated by Moses at Mount Sinai, which various writers accuse Israel of breaking. Jeremiah contains a prophecy that God will make a "new covenant" with Israel (Jer 31:31-34) in spite of the people's infidelity to the old one. Jesus, Paul, and the writer to the Hebrews all apply this term to the new reality that dawned in Christ's ministry and gave birth to the church comprised of believing Jews and Gentiles (Luke 22:20; 1 Cor 11:25; Heb 8:1-13). Paul, for example, speaks of Christians as "ministers of a new covenant" instituted by Christ whom he contrasts with Jews, who represent an "old covenant" from Sinai and do not grasp Christ's truth when Moses is read (2 Cor 3:4-18). It wasn't until later—sometime in the latter half of the 2nd century CE—when Christians came to associate a growing, complementary collection of Christian documents with the term "New Covenant" or "New Testament."

Eusebius preserves a portion of a letter known to him from the church's library in Caesarea but now lost in which Melito, the bishop of the church in Sardis (ca. 175 CE), responds to a certain Onesimus about scriptural matters. First, Melito notes that Onesimus had sought extracts from the "Law and Prophets." This implies that the Sardis region's access to written texts was limited. An interested Christian who could read apparently did not have access to all the texts of the Old Covenant that he wished to consult. Second, Melito reports that he had undertaken a journey to the east (perhaps Jerusalem and/or Caesarea) in order to ascertain more securely the number and order of the "books of the Old Covenant." This indicates that even for a bishop, these matters were a matter of ongoing interest and discussion. Melito's list is: five from Moses, Genesis, Exodus, Numbers, Leviticus, and Deuteronomy; Joshua, Judges, Ruth, four books of Kingdoms, two of Chronicles, Solomon's Proverbs and Wisdom, Ecclesiastes, Song of Songs, and Job; the prophets Isaiah, Jeremiah, The Twelve in one book, Daniel, Ezekiel and Ezra.

Melito makes an error in placing Numbers before Leviticus, which is probably a simple oversight. Since he does not provide a number for the collection as a whole, as is often done in such lists, the ambiguity of expression leads to different accountings of its contents. "Solomon's Proverbs and Wisdom" may be an expanded reference to the book of Proverbs, which some in the early church called "Wisdom," but it may also include a reference to the well-known Wisdom of Solomon. In the latter case, his phrase refers to two different books. Neither Lamentations nor Nehemiah is mentioned, but it is likely (not certain) that Lamentations is included with Jeremiah and Nehemiah with Ezra. Esther is missing and presumably not included.

Origen and the Hebrew Bible / Old Testament

Origen (ca. 185–254 CE) was a Christian teacher from Alexandria in Egypt and the greatest Christian scholar of his day regarding biblical texts. He also lived and worked for a time in Caesarea Maritima, where Eusebius later lived. These two cities had renowned libraries and strong Christian communities, giving him crucial access to copies of Israel's Scriptures and related early Christian writings.

Origen was a prolific author, responsible for literally thousands of works, including what was likely the longest book in antiquity, his *Hexapla*, or six-columned copy of the OT in various versions. In his comments on Ps 1, an excerpt of which is preserved by Eusebius (*Hist. eccl.* 6.25.1–2), he notes that there are twenty-two books in the "catalogue of the Old Testament" and lists twenty-one of them, giving both the Greek and Hebrew names. They are the Pentateuch (five), Joshua, Judges/Ruth, Samuel, Kings, Chronicles, Ezra/Nehemiah, Psalms, Proverbs, Ecclesiastes, Song of Songs, Isaiah, Jeremiah/Lamentations and Epistle of Jeremiah, Daniel, Ezekiel, Job and Esther (sixteen). The Book of the Twelve is an obvious oversight in the list and would complete the number twenty-two.

The connection of the Christian faith to Israel's Scriptures was a matter of primary importance to Origen; hence his exposure to Hebrew, his interaction with Jews, and his concern to provide a list of the books inherited from them. He interpreted texts according to multiple senses, including allegory. He also read from and commented on a wider set of authoritative documents, including the Wisdom of Ben Sira (Sirach in Greek), the Wisdom of Solomon, Tobit, Judith, and 1–2 Maccabees. *Authoritative* means recognition of their instructive value among many churches plus their public reading in the same (Canon B). Such books were frequently bound together with Israel's Scriptures in copies of the Septuagint and in the early Latin translations of the Septuagint.

Origen (ca. 185–254 CE). Illustration from the 16th-century *Vrais pourtraits et vies des hommes illustres*, by André Thévet.

In his list of OT books, Origen explicitly refers to the books of Maccabees with a Hebrew name but indicates that they are "outside" the Jewish canon. That would indeed have been the case for Jews of his day, at least according to the evidence noted above. But note also that Origen included the Epistle of Jeremiah in his list. Jews did not typically include the Epistle of Jeremiah in their twenty-two- or twenty-four-book collection, but it was often included with Jeremiah by Christians, along with another Greek text, Baruch. Does Origen simply know different Jewish practices in this regard, or does he name the Greek Epistle of Jeremiah because it was the practice of his community to include it along with Jeremiah? Perhaps the reason he mentions the books of Maccabees is that he knows the Hebrew name for 1 Maccabees, which was originally written in Hebrew. It provided another link to Israel's authoritative writings, even though it was still considered "outside" their canon. Second Maccabees was originally written in Greek.

The *Hexapla* was a massive work nearly thirty years in the making. Modern scholars estimate it to have been several thousand pages in length. Origen may have finished only one complete version, which was kept in the library in Caesarea, but certainly significant portions of it were copied and circulated among major churches. In any case, the master copy in Caesarea was completely destroyed in the 7th century CE along with the rest of the library. Only brief *Hexapla* fragments survive to this day. The first column was the Hebrew text inherited from Judaism, and the second was the Hebrew text transliterated into Greek letters. The third and fourth columns were the Greek versions of Aquila (a Jewish scholar of the 2nd century CE) and Symmachus, respectively, both of which had their supporters as translations superior to the LXX. The fifth was the LXX, the most widely circulated Greek version, and the sixth was the version of Theodotion. There are many fascinating questions that remain about the *Hexapla*. For our purposes we simply note that Origen's efforts demonstrate something of the great train of transmission of the Scriptures and that his marking out the differences in the versions shows a method to indicate better-attested readings. Jerome, who had the opportunity to consult the *Hexapla*, would later follow his lead in comparing texts.

The Institutional Church of the Fourth Century

With the rise of Constantine as the ruler of the eastern and western parts of the Roman Empire, the Christian church emerged as a recognized societal institution. By the end of the century, Christianity would be the official religion of the Empire. A first council of bishops, drawn from various parts of the Empire, held a historic meeting at Nicea in 325 CE. Of immense historical and theological significance, the council made no pronouncements about the Christian canon of Scripture. This is not say there was uniformity of thought and practice on the subject, only that there were no pressing matters about it. Constantine called the council together for other reasons. At its conclusion, he wrote to Eusebius, then the bishop of Caesarea, to have fifty copies of the "sacred scriptures" made so that new churches in Constantinople would have copies to read at public worship services. The letter is preserved in Eusebius's *Life of Constantine*. The emperor provided no list of the scriptures in mind, and we may doubt that he could provide a complete one on his own. We know from Eusebius's own writings that the extent of the Christian scriptures used in worship and teaching was a subject still under discussion. The concern was mostly for a handful of Christian writings and whether they should be included (or remain in, as the case may be) in the scriptures read in churches. There was still some diversity in the collections of OT scriptures, but he says relatively little about them.

Eusebius provided Constantine with the copies requested in the form of codices. These were increasingly popular for churches as a way to preserve copies of their authoritative texts in one or more bound volumes. A Christian codex of the 4th century would include the Septuagint, as a whole or in part, along with NT texts and even other valuable documents. The Septuagint portion of a codex included the Septuagintal Plus (which was not a fixed number; see below). This pattern continued into the next centuries and influenced the Latin and Syriac codices as well. We are fortunate to possess major portions of Christian codices from the late 4th and 5th centuries CE in Greek. Three are particularly important: Sinaiticus, Alexandrinus, and Vaticanus. Table 37.4 shows the books contained in the Septuagintal Plus of each of them.

The Alexandrinus Codex also preserves a letter from Athanasius, a bishop of Alexandria, on the value of studying the Psalms, plus some material from Eusebius about them. The inclusion of such texts shows that churches were keen to keep their valuable documents together for reading purposes, even if some of them were not recognized as part of an authorized list or used by all churches. The fact that no early codex has a uniform list of books also supports this conclusion.

Athanasius wrote a circular letter to fellow-bishops regarding the Church's *canon* of Old and New Testament Scriptures in 367 CE (see sidebar). He lists the books in each Testament and offers brief comments about the importance of Scripture for the Christian life. The OT has twenty-two books,

Table 37.4. Septuagintal Plus Lists Compared

Codex Sinaiticus	Codex Alexandrinus	Codex Vaticanus
Tobit	Tobit	Tobit
Judith	Judith	Judith
1 + 4 Maccabees	1–4 Maccabees	
Wisdom of Solomon	Wisdom of Solomon	Wisdom of Solomon
Sirach	Sirach	Sirach
	Epistle of Jeremiah	Epistle of Jeremiah
	Psalm 151	
	Baruch	Baruch

following Jewish precedence. His list is similar to that of Origen. Athanasius separates Ruth from Judges, does not include Esther, and places Lamentations, Baruch, and the Epistle of Jeremiah with Jeremiah. He also comments that there are books from the earlier fathers that are also read in the churches but are not part of the canon. He lists seven. Five are Jewish in origin and are not part of his OT: Wisdom of Solomon, Wisdom of Sirach, Esther, Judith, and Tobit. Two are Christian in origin and not part of his NT: the Didache and the Shepherd. His comments are further evidence for the conclusion that the early Christian codices collected valuable documents for a community, particularly those rooted in the prior practice of reading in worship. His treatment of Esther is also important in that he acknowledges that the book is read in churches. Obviously some churches (and Jewish groups) considered it part of their scriptures while others did not.

Correspondence between Augustine, the great bishop of Hippo in North Africa (died 430 CE), and Jerome, the great biblical scholar of his day (died 420 CE), set the basic options for Church practices regarding the OT that continue to this day. Augustine was an influential teacher whose native tongue was Latin, although he had facility in Greek. His practice, and that of many Western churches, was to read their scriptures in Latin. There were a number of Latin translations of the Septuagint that emerged in the 2nd and 3rd centuries CE. Their variations in quality led Pope Damasus, the bishop of Rome, to ask Jerome in the year 382 to work on a better Latin translation. Thus began a project that would occupy much of Jerome's time until 405 CE.

In his work, Jerome consulted not only the Septuagint and other Greek versions but also the Hebrew text of Israel's Scriptures. Jewish scholars had tutored him in Hebrew on several occasions, and he consulted with them on matters related to biblical interpretation. As a translator, Jerome compared Hebrew and Greek texts, noting differences and choosing what he felt was the better reading. In doing so, he was not above following the Hebrew texts available to him and thus changing some established readings of both Greek and previous Latin translations. He also made a distinction between the books included in the Hebrew Bible, following the twenty-four-book enumeration used in Judaism, and those books of the Septuagintal Plus that were part of early Latin translations as well. Jerome assigned these books to a category called the *Apocrypha*. The noun can be translated "hidden," but that was not the sense in which Jerome used it. Some Christian teachers such as Athanasius referred negatively to apocryphal documents not only as noncanonical texts but also as spurious and harmful to the Christian faith. For Jerome, the Apocrypha was a category of books that could be read profitably in churches, but he suggested that they not be used for establishing Church dogma. Athanasius had a similar category for such books with a long tradition of being read in church but simply used different terminology ("instructive" or "edifying").

Augustine was worried that Jerome's translations of the OT texts would undermine the authority of the Septuagint, which he regarded as a translation inspired by God. He knew, of course, what every textual critic knows, that there are differences in manuscript traditions, but the Septuagint texts in all their variety had been the received tradition of the Church. He was content to believe that God had inspired both the Hebrew and Greek traditions and that readers could benefit from comparing translations. He also worried about Jerome's dependence on a narrower OT canon, although he well knew that some Christians had passed along and affirmed the same belief. Again, the issue for him was church practice inherited from the past. While one church may have had a slightly different list of authoritative scriptures than another, there had been no practice of limiting readings to the books held in common with Jews. Augustine's own list was the twenty-four inherited from Judaism, plus 1–2 Maccabees, Sirach, Wisdom of Solomon, Judith, and Tobit. For the books of Daniel, Jeremiah, and Esther, he included the additional material contained in the Septuagint Plus.

Conclusion

By the end of the 4th century, Church councils began making pronouncements on the canon of the Christian Scriptures. The Latin-speaking churches generally followed the list of Augustine regarding the OT. That would hold true even until the pronouncements of the Council of Trent

St. Jerome, by Caravaggio. 1606.

in 1546. Greek-speaking churches and councils recognized Jerome's proposal regarding the OT canon without formalizing it in liturgical practice or decree. On the one hand, Jerome was a respected scholar and churchman whose proposal was similar to that of Origen and Athanasius. On the other hand, liturgical practice was a holy tradition in the Church, older than any decree, and its patterns prevailed. The communion of Orthodox Churches today is comprised of churches of various cultural forms whose OT lists are not as tightly defined as their respective liturgies! We might summarize by saying that authoritative texts for both Jews and Christians preceded any formal decisions (Canon A) or recognized lists (Canon B). Lists and decrees followed older traditions before creating new ones. And with new traditions, inherited practices might well have continued.

The Vulgate translation eventually became the standard for Western churches for the next thousand years in spite of Augustine's initial hesitations. It was expanded after Jerome's death to include translations of most of the documents from the Septuagintal Plus and even others such as 4 Ezra in an appendix. This is in accord with the criterion noted previously that churches kept their valued texts together, whether or not they had all been accorded canonical status by a recognized list or council decree.

Jerome's two concerns regarding the OT—the limits of the canon and the value of the Hebrew text—surfaced as a result of the Renaissance and Reformation movements in Europe. With respect to the OT, Martin Luther argued for an adoption of Jerome's canon in matters of determining doctrine and an acknowledgment that the Hebrew textual tradition was important for translators and biblical interpretation alike. And the various churches of the Reformation movement followed his lead in both practice and decree. The Reformation also spawned numerous translations of the Scriptures, efforts that show no sign of abatement five centuries later. The matter of including the Apocrypha in a translation varied among the translations. The tradition of including its books was so strong that they were sometimes incorporated as an appendix in Protestant-sponsored translations, even if they were no longer read in worship services. That was Luther's solution, for example, when publishing a German Bible translation in 1534. It was not until the 19th century that this tradition of inclusion finally came to an end in Protestant translations. A new one, however, has developed quite recently in some English Protestant translations, in which the various books of the Apocrypha are collected in an appendix between the two Testaments.

READING

After reading this chapter, formulate responses to the following discussion questions:

1. If a copy of the Book of the Wars of the Lord (Num 21:14) or of the Book of Jasher (Josh 10:13) were discovered by researchers and deemed authentic, do you think there would be proposals to include it in the OT? Why or why not?

2. What is the most surprising thing to you about the formation of the OT canon?

3. How do you understand the role of tradition (customary practice inherited from the past) in the formation of the OT canon?

4. How important are the NT references to Israel's Scriptures for understanding the OT canon?

5. Do you have a favorite translation of the Bible? If so, do you know the principles on which the translation is based and how the translators consulted different manuscripts?

BIBLIOGRAPHY

Canon

Barton, John. *Holy Writings, Sacred Text.* Louisville: Westminster John Knox, 1997.
Beckwith, Roger T. *The Old Testament Canon of the New Testament Church.* Grand Rapids: Eerdmans, 1986.

Glossary

Apocalyptic Literature: Based on the Greek term "to reveal," this style of writing employs symbolic language, numerology, and encounters with angels and other supernatural figures.

Apocrypha: Based on the Greek word for "hidden," the term refers to a number of authoritative Jewish writings read by Jews and Christians. They are not included in the HB or the Protestant OT. Some or all of these writings are included in Roman Catholic and Orthodox Bibles.

Babylonian Exile (Exilic Period): From the first Babylonian forced migration of Judahites in 597 BCE to the initial return of some exiles to Judah and Jerusalem in 538 BCE.

Babylonian Period: The time of the (Neo-)Babylonian Empire and rule in the ancient Near Eastern and Mediterranean areas, 605–539 BCE. See Table 10.2 on p. 119 for a list of Neo-Babylonian kings.

Bronze Age: Early (approximately 3300–2000 BCE); Middle (approximately 2000–1500 BCE); Late (approximately 1500–1200 BCE)—so named because some tools and implements were constructed of bronze. During much of the Late Bronze Age, the rulers of Canaan's various cities were vassals of the Egyptian pharaoh.

Coastal Plain: The Israelite geographical region along the Mediterranean coast.

Cult: Formal, organized worship system.

Deuteronomistic History (DH): Deuteronomy, Joshua, Judges, 1–2 Samuel, and 1–2 Kings.

Divided Monarchy: From the division of the kingdom after Solomon's death until the destruction of Samaria and the political end of the separate (Northern) Kingdom of Israel in 721 BCE. See Table 15.2 on p. 187 for a list of rulers of the divided monarchy.

Documentary Hypothesis: A theory that the Torah or Pentateuch is comprised of several sources. These include the Yahwist (or J source), which prefers the use of the divine name Yahweh; the Elohist (or E source), which prefers the name Elohim for God; the Deuteronomist (or D source), which refers to the book of Deuteronomy and some related passages; and the Priestly (or P source) writer responsible for much of the cultic tradition.

Ephraim: A son of Joseph and the ancestor of a major tribe in central Israel (sometimes used to refer to the Northern Kingdom, of which it was the largest tribe [literarily, one part is being used to refer to the whole]).

First Temple Period: Approximately 960 BCE (building by Solomon) to the destruction by the Babylonians in 587/586 BCE.

Former Prophets: The first half of the Prophets section in the Jewish canon of Scripture; includes Joshua, Judges, 1–2 Samuel, and 1–2 Kings.

Hellenistic Period: The time from Alexander the Great's conquests in the ANE, Mediterranean, and portions of Asia (332–323 BCE) to the rule of his successors in the eastern Mediterranean (Seleucids) and Egypt (Ptolemies), which ended with the Roman occupation of the eastern Mediterranean in 63 BCE. See Table 16.4 on p. 210 for a list of Hellenistic Rulers.

Hill Country: A spine of hills running north and south through Israel.

Iron Age: Early (approximately 1200–950 BCE), usually known as Iron Age I; middle (approximately 950–600 BCE), usually known as Iron

Age II; late (600–350 BCE), occasionally known as Iron III or referred to by political terminology: Babylonian and Persian periods. A period when some tools and implements were constructed of iron.

Israel: Another name for Jacob. The tribal confederation of Jacob's descendants called themselves Israel, as did the people ruled by the united monarchy. During the period of the divided monarchy, the Northern tribes kept the name Israel.

Judah: One of the sons of Jacob and the ancestor of the tribe of Judah and also the name of the separate Kingdom of Judah.

Judahite: A member of the tribe or state of Judah. A later form of this name is translated "Jew" or "Jewish."

Latter Prophets: The second half of the Prophets section in the Jewish canon of Scripture; includes Isaiah, Jeremiah, Ezekiel, and the twelve smaller, or Minor Prophets.

LORD: A common term and format used to translate the personal name of God (Yhwh or Yahweh) in English.

Lowlands: An Israelite geographical region that runs north and south between the coastal plain and the hill country.

LXX: An abbreviation for the Septuagint, the primary Greek version of the OT (the word comes from Latin and means "seventy").

Negev: The semiarid area of Judah located south of the hill country.

Neo-Assyrian Period: From the first struggles between Israel under King Ahab and the Assyrian army (approximately 860 BCE) to the destruction of Nineveh in 612 BCE. See Table 10.1 on p. 119 for a list of Neo-Assyrian Kings.

Northern Kingdom: A modern term for the state of Israel during the time of the Divided Monarchy.

Pentateuch: A Greek-based term for the first five books of the OT/HB.

Persian Period: The time of the Persian Empire and rule in the ancient Near East and Mediterranean areas, 539–330 BCE. See Table 16.2 on p. 209 for a list of Persian kings.

Postexilic Historical Books (PostHB): The historical narratives set in the postexilic period, including Ezra, Nehemiah, and Esther. First and Second Chronicles was written during the postexilic period and covers various periods in Israel's history.

Postexilic Period: From the initial return of some exiles to Judah (538 BCE and following) to the rise of the Jewish state under the rule of the Hasmoneans (Maccabean dynasty) in 142 BCE (see Table 16.3 on p. 209 for an outline of the Hasmonean family). This period essentially coincides with the Persian and Hellenistic periods in the Eastern Mediterranean.

Preexilic Historical Books (PreHB): The historical narratives set in the preexilic period, including Joshua, Judges, Ruth, 1–2 Samuel, and 1–2 Kings. Some, if not all of these books reached their final form during the postexilic period.

Preexilic Period: Technically, the entire period of Israelite political history before the Babylonian exile, but practically speaking, the period of monarchy down to the Babylonian destruction of Jerusalem in 587/586 BCE.

Primary History: The Torah, Joshua, Judges, 1–2 Samuel, and 1–2 Kings.

Prophets: The second section of the Jewish canon of Scripture, comprising the Former and Latter Prophets.

Second Temple Period: From 515 BCE (temple rebuilt by Zerubbabel and Joshua the high priest) to the destruction of the temple by the Romans in 70 CE. Herod the Great initiated a remodeling in approximately 20 BCE, with work on the massive courtyards continuing until its destruction by the Romans in 70 CE.

Septuagint: A common name for the primary Greek translation of the Old Testament. The term means "seventy" in Greek and is a reference to the legendary account in the Letter of Aristeas that describes the translation of the Torah into Greek by seventy (or seventy-two) Jewish experts during the reign of Ptolemy II in Egypt (ca. 250 BCE).

Southern Kingdom: A modern term for the state of Judah during the divided monarchy.

Stele: an inscribed stone monument.

Suzerainty Treaty: A political treaty designed by a great king (a suzerain) for a vassal king and his people. Such treaties were instituted by Hittite (Late Bronze Age) and Assyrian (Iron Age) kings with certain subjects.

TaNaK: An acronym for the Jewish biblical canon, representing the Torah, Prophets (*Nebi'im* in Hebrew), and Writings (*Ketubim* in Hebrew).

Torah: The Hebrew word for "instruction." Another name for the Pentateuch, the first five books of the OT/HB.

United Monarchy: The rule of Saul, David, and Solomon; approximately 1050 BCE to 930 BCE. See Table 15.2 on p. 187 for a list of rulers of the united monarchy.

Vulgate: A Latin-based term for the Latin Bible, which was translated by Jerome (finished ca. 400 CE).

Writings: The third section of the Jewish canon of Scripture.

Yahweh: An approximate pronunciation of God's personal name, which is sometimes written with its four consonants as YHWH.

Yehud: The Aramaic name of the Persian province encompassing much of what had been the preexilic state of Judah.

Zion: Another name of Jerusalem. Mount Zion is a reference to the hill in the northern part of the city where the temple was located.

Hebrew Transliterations

Hebrew Letter	English Equivalent	Example
aleph	ʾ	*ʾadam* = "humankind"
bet	*b* or *v*	*bagad* = "to deceive" *tov* = "good" *kavod* = "glory"
gimel	*g*	*gadol* = "large, great"
dalat	*d*	*davar* = "word, thing"
he	*h*	*halak* = "to go"
vav	*w*	*we* = "and, but"
zayin	*z*	*zebakh* = "sacrifice"
khet	*h* or *kh*	*hokmah* = "wisdom" *mishpakhah* = "family"
tet	*t*	*tov* = "good"
yod	*y*	*yehudah* = "Judah"
kaph	*k*	*kavod* = "glory"
lamed	*l*	*lekhem* = "bread, food"
mem	*m*	*melek* = "king"
nun	*n*	*naviʾ* = "prophet"
samek	*s*	*sagar* = "to close"
ayin	ʿ	*ʿebed* = "servant"
pe	*p* or *f*	*paneh* = "face" *shofet* = "judge, ruler"
tsadeh	*ts*	*tsedeqah* = "righteousness"
qoph	*q*	*qadosh* = "holy"
resh	*r*	*rosh* = "head"
sin	*s*	*sameakh* = "joy"
shin	*sh*	*shanah* = "year"
tav	*t*	*todah* = "thanks"

Subject Index

Jesus, 37, 38, 42, 61, 80, 81, 87, 162, 168, 175
Job, 405-6, 408-16
Jobes, Karen, 243
Joel, 367-68
Jordan River, 84, 126
Joseph, 50, 57
Josephus, 163, 270, 484-85
Joshua, 122-23
Joshua (high priest). *See* Zerubbabel and Joshua
Josiah, 236
    reform, 91, 198-99, 224-25
Jotham's fable, 141
Judah/Judahite (or Southern Kingdom), 34, 57, 118, 139, 178, 196-200, 296

Kadesh Barnea, 84
king/kingship/kingdom, 72, 141, 146, 157, 159-60, 184-85, 332, 433-34
    royal gradebooks, 197, 222
    royal reformers, 196-99
    royal sources, 178
    of Yahweh, 180

Laban, 56
Lachish, 92 (photo), 292 (photo)
lamentation, 166, 306, 435, 454-59
land
    distribution, 85, 131, 133
    inheritance, 87
Leah, 55-56
Leningrad Codex, 475-76
leuitikon (Gk.), 76
Levites, 85, 133, 144, 145, 203, 204, 207, 213 (table), 214, 231, 232, 233, 236
love poetry. *See* Song of Songs

Maccabees, 484
Malachi, 391-93
Manasseh, 197-98, 224, 361
Marduk, 33
Masoretic Text, 476-77
Mazar, Eilat, 311
medinot (provinces), 243
melek (king), 159

Melito of Sardis, 491
memoirs, 230
Merenptah Stele, 67
messiah, 87, 162. *See also* anointed of the LORD
Micah, 356-59
Midian/Midianites, 140-41
Milgrom, Jacob, 79
minhah (grain offering), 77
Miriam, 267
Moab/Moabites, 14-15, 148, 149
monotheism, 63
Mordecai, 113, 239-43
Mosaic core, 32
Moses, 31, 64, 68, 84, 85-86, 87, 109, 267
Mount Sinai, 70-71, 84
Mowinckel, Sigmund, 302, 423
Meyers, Carol, 61

Nabonidus, 337
nagid (ruler), 159
Naomi, 149-54
narrative (or story), 36-37, 112
Nazirite (Heb. *nazir*), 143, 158
Nebuchadnezzar, 199, 200, 311, 330-31, 361
Nehemiah, 233-36, 484
new covenant, 310, 491
Nineveh, 92 (photo), 360, 371-72, 373 (plan)
Noah, 43
numbers in Numbers, 87

Obadiah, 379-81
obedience, 160
offerings, 77-78
'olah (burnt offering), 77
Omride dynasty, 13-16
Origen, 465, 492-94

paqad (pay attention to), 149
Passover, 66, 99, 126-27, 198, 203, 223, 232
Patriarchal History, 41, 49-57, 53 (table)
Paul, 36

peripety, 239

Persia, 239, 240, 241, 243, 270, 296, 332, 336, 339. *See also* Ahasuerus, Darius I, Artaxerxes I

Pharaoh, 57, 62, 63, 64, 67

Philistines, 143, 157, 163-64, 167

plains of Moab, 84

postexilic Historical Books (PostHB), 111, 117, 205, 208, 380

preexilic Historical Books (PreHB), 113-15

priest(s)/priesthood, 32, 76, 77, 79, 85, 115, 117, 118, 144-45, 157

Primary History, 31, 93, 156

Primeval History, 41-45

programmatic texts, 3, 54, 68, 77, 86, 168

promised land (Canaan), 34, 84, 87

Proverbs, 398-401, 439-45

Psalter, 418

Purim. *See* feasts

Rachel, 55-56

Rad, Gerhard von, 309

Rahab, 124, 126-29, 130

Rebekah, 55

Rehoboam, 184

remnant, 225, 380, 384

reqam (empty), 148

reversal of fortune (theme), 148, 154

Ruth, 149-54

Samaria, 13, 20,186, 195, 230, 232, 284, 305, 315, 317, 318, 344, 356

Samaritans, 100

Samson, 142-44

Samuel, 158-60, 163-64

Sanballat (Akk. *Sin-uballit*), 234, 235

Sarai/Sarah, 52, 54-55

Satan (Heb. *hassatan*), 217 (photo), 218, 410

Saul, 159-64, 166

Second Isaiah, 293-96

Sennacherib, 92 (photo)

Sennacherib's Prism, 198

Septuagint, 474, 477

the settlement, 87, 132 (map), 133-34

seventy years, 225, 308, 331, 334, 339, 482

shafat/shofet (rule, judge), 137

Shechem, 128, 134, 184

shelamim (well-being offering), 77

Shema, 96

Sheshbazzar, 231

Shiloh, 122, 130, 133, 157, 158

shir hashirim (Song of Songs), 461

shrine at Dan, 144

sin of Jeroboam, 186

slaves, 98

Solomon, 403-4, 465, 466
    kingdom, 181 (map)
    punishment, 183-84
    succession, 182
    wealth, 183

Son of Man, 317, 338

Song of Songs (or the Best Song Ever), 461-68

speeches, 87, 90, 114, 122, 124, 133, 149-50, 363, 408, 414-15, 442, 463

Spirit of Yahweh, 140, 142, 143, 162

sun standing still, 129-30

Susa, 233-34, 239

tabernacle, 68-69

Table of Nations, 7-8, 44

TaNaK, 484, 487

Tel Aviv, 315

Tel Dan Stele, 171 (photo)

temple
    of Solomon, 175, 180, 182-83
    postexilic temple, 229, 231, 232, 384

Ten Awesome Blows (or Plagues), 65-66

Ten Commandments (or Decalogue), 68, 69, 95-96

Theodore of Mopsuestia, 466

theophany, 64, 174, 180, 337

Third Isaiah, 296-98

Thompson, Randall, 174

threshing floor, 98, 99, 152, 173, 175, 217

Tobiah, 234-35

the Torah (or the Law), 27, 232, 233,
    235–36
    contents, 27–29
    definition, 29
    ending, 31, 32, 103, 109
    historicity, 37
    influence in the New Testament, 38
    message, 32–36
    origin, 31–32
Tower of Babel. *See* ziggurats
Transjordanian tribes, 87
Two-Way Doctrine, 399–400, 411–13,
    443–34, 450
Tyndale, William, 79

united kingdom, 167, 180–84

Vashti, 239
vassal treaties, 92
violence, 141, 172, 242, 365, 377, 429
Vulgate, 477, 498

Walsh, Jerome, 189

wasf (Arab.), 463
Wenham, Gordon, 79
wilderness period, 84
Williamson, H. G. M., 230–31
Wilson, Gerald, 426
Wisdom of Ben Sira, 482–84
witch of Endor, 163–64
Wood, Bryant, 129

Xerxes I. *See* Ahasuerus

Yahweh, 158
    name, 65
    as warrior, 66, 362, 376
Yehud, 21, 206 (map), 234, 383

Zechariah, 386–91
Zephaniah, 361–63
Zerubbabel and Joshua (high priest),
    229, 231–32, 383–85
ziggurats, 44–45
Zincirli Stele, 103 (photo)
Zion, 167, 232 (photo), 260, 275, 293

Scripture and Other Ancient Sources Index

1 Thessalonians

5:1-3	379

2 Timothy

3:8	491

Hebrews

6:13-20	58
8:1-13	491
8:8-13	310
9-10	82
10:28	32
11:7	47
11:8	54
11:8-12	54
11:24-28	61
11:24-29	73
11:30-31	490
11:31	126
11:32-34	142
11:35	491
11:35-37	491
13:11-12	82

James

2:25	126
5:17	189

1 Peter

2:5	74
2:9	74
2:24	80
3:18-22	47

2 Peter

2:5	47
2:9	47
2:15-16	88

1 John

4:19	466

Jude

9	340
14	490, 491

Revelation

1:6	74
2:14	88
4-5	338
5:9	378
5:9-10	338
7:9-10	378
20:1-6	325
20:7-10	324
21-22	277, 325
21:2	347

DEAD SEA SCROLLS

1QIsa^a (Great Isaiah Scroll) — 281

4Q242 (The Prayer of Nabonidus) — 337

11QPs^a — 419

BABYLONIAN TALMUD

b. Baba Batra

14b-15a	486

b. Makkot

23b-24a	365

APOCRYPHA/ DEUTERO- CANONICAL

Judith

11:19	491

Sirach (Wisdom of Ben Sira)

29:11	490
44-50	483
44-45	483
46-49:6	483
48:23-35	483
49:7-10	483
49:10	263
49:11-16	483
50	483

1 Maccabees

1:10-2:41	336
2:48	484

2 Maccabees

2:13-15	484
5:15-7:42	336
6-7	491

4 Ezra

14:37-47	486

1 Enoch

1:9	490